THE WOLF:
THE ECOLOGY AND BEHAVIOR
OF AN ENDANGERED SPECIES

"Of all of the native biological constituents of a northern wilderness scene, I should say that the wolves present the greatest test of human wisdom and good intentions."

Paul L. Errington, 1967, *Of Predation and Life*

THE WOLF:

THE ECOLOGY AND BEHAVIOR
OF AN ENDANGERED SPECIES

BY L. DAVID MECH

PUBLISHED FOR

THE AMERICAN MUSEUM OF NATURAL HISTORY

THE NATURAL HISTORY PRESS

GARDEN CITY, NEW YORK

The Natural History Press, publisher for the American Museum of Natural History, is a division of Doubleday & Company, Inc. Directed by a joint editorial board made up of members of the staff of both the Museum and Doubleday, the Natural History Press publishes books and periodicals in all branches of the life and earth sciences, including anthropology and astronomy. The Natural History Press has its editorial offices at Doubleday & Company, Inc., 277 Park Avenue, New York, New York 10017, and its business offices at 501 Franklin Avenue, Garden City, New York 11530.

The line illustrations for this book
were prepared by the Graphic Arts Division
of the American Museum of Natural History
ISBN: 0-385-08660-1
Library of Congress Catalog Card Number 73–100043

9 8

This book is dedicated to Adolph Murie,
who in the early 1940's became the first biologist
to conduct an intensive and objective ecological study
of the wolf.

CONTENTS

LIST OF TABLES

LIST OF ILLUSTRATIONS

FOREWORD

Throughout the continents of Eurasia and North America primitive man evolved in association with wolves. Wolves competed with him as a hunter and raided his flocks and herds. Through the cold of winter the wolf made music in the mysterious darkness and sometimes, in curiosity, sat just beyond the dwindling circle of firelight and watched, his night-conditioned eyes reflecting twin sparks of light as a brand flared.

Inevitably our folklore became rich in tales of this powerful, resourceful competitor. The pasturalist feared and hated the creature for the damage it did; the returning hunter embroidered his prowess with tales of dangers surmounted as the wolf pack crowded around in the darkness; children were coerced into behavior with wolf threats.

Somewhere in early history a young wolf was brought into the family circle of man and through the years became the source of the domestic dog and our most successful and useful experiment in domestication. Even from early times there were those who found the wolf not all bad, as the delightful legends of Romulus and Remus and Mowgli testify. Many people acquired their attitudes toward wolves as they acquired their religion, and it is no wonder that the animal is still a subject of strongly held views.

Europeans reached North America with attitudes already formed. The wilderness and its creatures pressed in upon their tiny settlements in constant threat, and all energies were devoted to destroying it and turning its inexhaustible resources to use. Over vast areas of the continent the wolf went down with the wilderness before the unprecedented effectiveness of our technological attack on the ecology of a continent. Today, however, there is a great tide of concern over the consequences of our assault on the wild lands and wild creatures of the continent, and more and more biologists are devoting their knowledge and energy to searching studies of the various threatened aspects of our land and its native biota.

The wolf has been the subject of detailed study by a number of ecologists on this continent, making use of all the research devices now available to them. Wolves have been sung to by recorded calls, they have carried radio transmitters that reported their whereabouts on demand, they have been observed by the hour on the ground and from the air. Their dens have been invaded and their young taken for captive rearing. Thus field and laboratory approaches have combined to give us an unparalleled understanding of many aspects of wolf behavior and ecology. It is safe to say that despite the wolf's increasing scarcity, its remoteness and elusiveness, we now know more about the animal than about any other of the large wild carnivores of the world. Much of our knowledge is very recent, is increasing rapidly, and has resulted from the work of a mere handful of keen, resourceful, and courageous students of wolf biology.

I am delighted that Dr. David Mech has undertaken to write this book. To him it has been almost an act of homage to an animal with which he has spent so much of his life. As the first graduate student on the Isle Royale wolf study with Dr. Durward Allen, he opened up what has become a classic in the penetrating study of the interaction of a large predator with its large prey. He has studied wolves intensively and continuously for as long as any biologist in this land. This is the first book to attempt a complete account of the biology of the wolf drawing upon the rich literature from the two continents. It is most difficult to study this creature without becoming involved with it. To a certain extent only a sensitive and perspective involvement leads to scientific insight into the behavior of large mammals. Dr. Mech has acknowledged this and has been meticulous in maintaining a scientific absence of bias in the presentation of his factual material and in the extraction of truths from them. He has attempted the very difficult task of presenting his account so as to be of genuine value to the student of animal biology without making it incomprehensible to the many with a genuine but less professional interest in the wolf, its ways, and its role. I think he has been most successful in his task.

Those who have themselves sought to expose the lives of large mammals through field research will join me in admiration of the personal component that gives this book an unusual vitality: What better introduction to a discussion of social order and communication than:

"One day I watched a long line of wolves heading along the frozen shore line of Isle Royale in Lake Superior. Suddenly they stopped and faced upwind toward a large moose. After a few seconds the wolves assembled closely, wagged their tails, and touched noses. Then they started upwind single file toward the moose.

"This incident and several like it show vividly the two factors that must exist for groups of animals to function efficiently: (1) a system of order, and (2) a system of communication." This chapter, along with those on reproduction, family life, and hunting behavior, are rich in data for the ethologist.

The wildlife biologist will find the chapters on prey selection and the effects of predation of special concern. In these he will learn, for instance, that for every hundred attempts to kill moose, made by the wolves on Isle Royale, only 7.8 kills resulted. That in almost all species of wild game there is now ample evidence that it is the less able prey individual that is removed by the wolves. That at prey densities greater than 25,000 pounds of prey per wolf there is no evidence of the wolf serving as a limiting influence on its prey, but where densities range from 7400 pounds to 24,000 pounds per wolf, definite control of the prey populations by the predators has resulted. This method of relating a versatile predator to its prey by weight rather than organisms is a novel and valuable innovation in this study.

I found assessment of evidence relating to attacks on man by wolves of interest largely because of the re-examination of the Eurasian literature. It has been known for years that there are no authentic records of wolves killing humans in North America. But somehow history has presented the Russian wolves to us as a particularly vicious breed. This also fails to survive critical examination.

Dr. Mech, like all others who have studied wolves intensively, emerges with a devotion to assuring their continuation indefinitely as a unique and fascinating creature, a valuable asset to the human environment, inseparably related to the wilderness. His dedication comes through on the last pages where, speaking of the "wolf haters," he says, "Their narrow and biased attitude must be outweighed by an attitude based on an understanding of the natural processes. . . . Their hate must be outdone by a love for the whole of nature, for the unspoiled wilderness, and for the wolf as a beautiful, interesting, and integral part of both."

His work, with its simple, direct, perspective presentation and clear analysis, should do much to elicit the interest and concern that the wolf and its wilderness merit. It will also stand as the plateau from which new and still more searching studies will proceed.

For all this I am sure that Lightning, could she but understand, would accept her captivity with grace.

IAN MCTAGGART COWAN
Dean of Graduate Studies and
Professor of Zoology
University of British Columbia

PREFACE

The wolf is a complex, controversial, and colorful creature. The mere sight of one standing placidly in drab surroundings would greatly excite most people. But a wolf rarely stands placidly. The animal is usually bounding through the underbrush, trotting across a frozen lake, or frisking playfully on an open ridge. When it does stand still, it keeps its ears erect, its eyes alert, and its nose sifting every scent. A slight move on an observer's part and the wolf is gone.

Nor are the wolf's surroundings drab. The arctic tundra, Canadian spruce swamps, rugged mountain ranges, and many other wild and scenic surroundings are the usual haunts of the animal.

Several other traits of wolves help to fire the imaginations of nature lovers and outdoorsmen the world over. Wolves generally travel in packs of up to twelve animals, and sometimes more. They leave large tracks and many of them, for they may be in one watershed on one day and in another on the next. Their rich and wild howling often shatters the silence of the wilderness night and at times can be heard as far as four miles away. The most spectacular trait of wolves, however, is the most controversial: like man himself, wolves must sacrifice other creatures in order that they themselves might survive.

Many people strongly dislike the wolf; others rush to its defense. But no one denies that the animal is strong, powerful, intelligent, keen, and dynamic. Friend and foe alike marvel at the wolf, and both show up to testify when its future is discussed in legislative halls. Many people would spend the public's money to help eradicate the species; others would finance its protection. Few are neither for the wolf nor against it. And that includes myself.

I must admit to a bias in favor of the wolf. Nevertheless, I have tried throughout this book to regard the animal objectively. It is my firm belief that such a view is not only much more enlightening than the usual unfounded and mythical view of the creature but also is much more interesting.

Thus this book will have to stand solely on the merits of the information it contains and the manner in which it is presented. The information is drawn both from my own experiences with wolves and from the numerous publications of well-qualified biologists throughout the world. Some of the information has been known for many decades, but most of it was collected only in the past ten years.

Because intensive field studies of the wolf are rather recent, most of the past works on this animal were historically or taxonomically oriented. The most significant of these is Young's and Goldman's *The Wolves of North America.*

The present work, however, concentrates more on the wolf's habits, behavior, relations with other animals, and effects on the living community of which it is part. Such an emphasis has been possible because of the revealing studies of such workers as Adolph Murie, Ian M. Cowan, Milton H. Stenlund, Rudolf Schenkel, Erkki Pulliainen, V. P. Makridin, Douglas H. Pimlott, Robert A. Rausch, George B. Rabb, and their students and associates.

The intensive and long-range wolf research program on Isle Royale, directed by Durward L. Allen of Purdue University, has been especially productive of information about the wolf. Besides referring often to my own aspect of that study, I also have cited liberally from the reported results of Phillip C. Shelton and Peter A. Jordan, who carried out subsequent phases of the project.

The information included in the following pages is as up-to-date as possible, many of the studies cited having been published only a short time. I have tried throughout the book to document my statements either directly or by referring to the particular studies in the bibliography that support them. The reader is encouraged to examine such publications both for his own satisfaction and for further information on the subject of his interest.

Where only slight information was available on certain important topics, I have taken the liberty to speculate somewhat. While this will do nothing to endear me to those people who disagree with my speculations, it will serve to stimulate further thinking on the subjects, and perhaps this will help point up some interesting directions that future wolf research might take. I trust that the speculative sections are labeled clearly enough so as not to mislead anyone into thinking that they contain as well-established information as the rest of the book does.

The manner in which the material is presented herein also needs explanation. Essentially, I have tried literary tightrope walking. The scientific community was in need of a comprehensive, up-to-date reference book on the wolf; this work is my attempt to fill that need. But as pointed out above, a large segment of the general public is also interested in the wolf. To make the book useful to this group, I have tried to limit or explain the use of specialized language and to include anecdotes and personal experiences throughout. My hope then is that most members of both groups will find the work satisfactory.

Of course, this book could not have materialized without the helpful influence and generous direct assistance of a number of people, and it is a pleasure to acknowledge their contributions.

Mr. Laurence P. Pringle, executive editor of *Nature and Science,* enthusiastically encouraged me to propose this project, and (Mrs.) Ruth McMullin and Mr. James K. Page, editors of Natural History Press, were most helpful, patient, and co-operative throughout the entire duration of the project.

The administration of Macalester College, through faculty members Dr. L. Daniel Frenzel, Jr., and Dr. Edwin J. Robinson, graciously made available to me an office in which to carry out this project. In addition, I was provided with a part-time position as research associate, which increased my experiences with wolves in Minnesota.

Also helpful to the preparation of this book were the authors of the research papers presented at the A.I.B.S. Symposium "The Ecology and Behavior of the Wolf," held in August 1966. The reports were published in the May 1967 issue of *American Zoologist,* but the authors all sent me prepublication copies of their manuscripts, allowing me to begin work on the book several months earlier. Dr. Douglas H. Pimlott, of the University of Toronto, and Dr. John P. Kelsall, of the Canadian Wildlife Service, also permitted me to include references to significant manuscripts that they had in press. Dr. Erkki Pulliainen, of the University of Helsinki, even composed a special manuscript for me on the status, distribution, and taxonomy of wolves in Eurasia.

Mr. John A. Fletcher, director of the Como Zoo in St. Paul, and his staff invited me to carry out various observations and experiments with the wolves in their zoo. Fletcher also permitted me to raise the two wolf pups Thunder and Lightning in my home, a venture that gave me a great deal of insight into the animals.

A group of men to whom I owe particular thanks for improving this book are the various authorities throughout the world who carefully and critically reviewed the rough drafts of certain chapters. Mr. Robert A. Rausch, of the Alaska Department of Fish and Game, read Chapter II; Dr. Rudolf Schenkel, of the University of Basel, Chapter III; Dr. George B. Rabb, Chicago Zoological Park, Chapter IV; Dr. Durward L. Allen, Purdue University, Chapters VIII and IX; and Dr. Robert L. Rausch, Arctic Health Research Laboratory, U. S. Public Health Service, Chapter XI. All these researchers made many helpful suggestions, and some even offered me the use of unpublished data. R. L. Rausch was particularly helpful in criticizing the tables in Chapter XI.

Dr. Douglas H. Pimlott, of the University of Toronto, deserves special mention. He critically read the rough draft of the entire manuscript and suggested several important corrections and additions that no doubt made the book more accurate and complete.

At the same time, I must of course accept full responsibility for any errors or omissions that still remain.

In the personal realm, I will have to admit that this book was not written without considerable stresses and strains. Thus I would like to thank my wife, Betty Ann Smith Mech, and our children Sharon, Steve, Nick, and Chris, not only for bearing up under these pressures but also for helping me to withstand them. Various personal friends also deserve substantial credit for similar reasons.

In addition, I would like to take this occasion to thank Mr. Irving J. Quinn and Mr. Frank R. Dann, leaders of Boy Scout Troop 49, Syracuse, New York. Long ago these men unknowingly helped guide me through a "swamp" more tangled and treacherous than I have ever encountered in the wilderness. Without them this book probably never would have been written.

And lastly, to Lightning—if it is permissible to address a wolf in print—the only thing I can say is, "I'm sorry."

L. DAVID MECH

THE WOLF:

THE ECOLOGY AND BEHAVIOR
OF AN ENDANGERED SPECIES

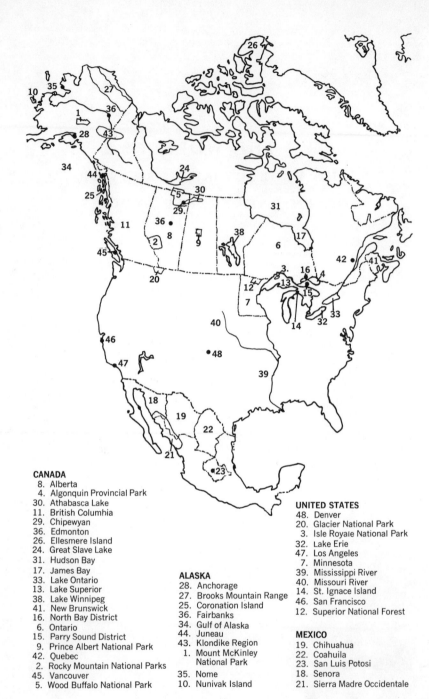

CANADA
8. Alberta
4. Algonquin Provincial Park
30. Athabasca Lake
11. British Columbia
29. Chipewyan
36. Edmonton
26. Ellesmere Island
24. Great Slave Lake
31. Hudson Bay
17. James Bay
33. Lake Ontario
13. Lake Superior
38. Lake Winnipeg
41. New Brunswick
16. North Bay District
6. Ontario
15. Parry Sound District
9. Prince Albert National Park
42. Quebec
2. Rocky Mountain National Parks
45. Vancouver
5. Wood Buffalo National Park

ALASKA
28. Anchorage
27. Brooks Mountain Range
25. Coronation Island
36. Fairbanks
34. Gulf of Alaska
44. Juneau
43. Klondike Region
1. Mount McKinley
   National Park
35. Nome
10. Nunivak Island

UNITED STATES
48. Denver
20. Glacier National Park
3. Isle Royale National Park
32. Lake Erie
47. Los Angeles
7. Minnesota
39. Mississippi River
40. Missouri River
14. St. Ignace Island
46. San Francisco
12. Superior National Forest

MEXICO
19. Chihuahua
22. Coahuila
23. San Luis Potosi
18. Senora
21. Sierra Madre Occidentale

CHAPTER I / THE WOLF ITSELF

The closest I have ever been to a free-ranging wild wolf is fifteen feet. That moment was one of the triumphs of my life, for I had arranged the meeting, and the scheme had worked even better than I had hoped. Bush pilot Don Murray and I had been following a pack of fifteen wolves by air in Isle Royale National Park, and they were heading along one of their regular winter routes. If they were to continue, they would file across the ice of a little cove, fifty feet from an old fishhouse along the shore a couple of miles ahead.

They did. And we were in the shed awaiting them. With the door cracked open just enough for a camera lens, we watched as each of the fifteen animals strolled onto the ice in front of us. It was a marvelous spectacle—a rare glimpse into wolf society. A tramp in a concert hall would not have seemed more out of place than we did. We excitedly clicked off pictures as the animals assembled in front of us. Then one individual wandered to within fifteen feet and stood broadside of us, calmly staring at the crack. I snapped the camera, and the wolf cocked its head. Its countenance was like that of a big friendly dog. It was easy to believe that I could have reached out and petted the beast.

That incident took place early during a three-year study that I was carrying out for Purdue University as a graduate student under Dr. Durward L. Allen. Although my standing face-to-face with a wild wolf had little scientific value, it certainly helped inspire me to learn all I could about the animal that had such a calm and gentle look yet earned its living by killing.

Of course, I had long before had enough biological training to know better than to apply moral judgments to natural processes. In fact, the objective study of predation and predators had fascinated me for years, and the wolf has always held a special appeal for me.

Thus I was elated when given the chance to begin studying wolves. The Isle Royale research occupied most of my time for the next three years, and when the data were in, it looked like the study had added some worth-while information to our knowledge of the wolf. The project certainly gave me a firsthand view of the creature and much of its life and habits.

During the next several years wolf studies were carried out in various other areas of the world. Many interesting and surprising facts were discovered about the biology and behavior of the animal, and a new picture began to emerge. Although biologists still have much to learn, enough information is now available to make it possible to take a close look at the life of the wolf.

A Preview

In this first chapter we will view the wolf itself, its personality and psychological tendencies, its physical traits and sensory abilities. We will then try to place the wolf in its biological context by tracing its evolution and its relationships to other, similar animals.

Once familiar with this basic information, we will examine wolf packs and populations, in Chapter II. The formation and maintenance of wolf packs, the sex and ages of pack members, and the seasonal history of packs will be discussed. In addition, the age and sex structure of entire wolf populations will be considered, along with survival and mortality rates, population stability, and relative densities.

In Chapter III, we will see how the social life of the wolf is organized. Leadership, the structure of wolf society, social behavior, communication within and among packs, and territorial spacing will all be discussed. We will find that wolf society is highly organized and complex, and that expression and communication in the wolf are also well developed.

In such a social animal as the wolf it would not be surprising to find that courtship, mating, and the raising of young are complicated undertakings, and in Chapter IV, we see that this is the case. Breeding; mate preferences; the effect of social status on mating; denning; the birth, growth, and development of pups; and the pack care of the pups will be considered in this chapter.

Chapter V deals with the wolf's wanderings. We will discover there that wolves are extensive travelers, especially in winter. They are most active at night during summer, but in winter they will travel day or night, and may cover thirty or forty miles per day. Reported ranges of individual packs vary from fifty to five thousand square miles.

In Chapter VI, the wolf's food habits are examined. From one end to the other the digestive tract of the wolf is superbly adapted to a diet of meat on a feast-or-famine basis. Thus, although wolves eat almost any kind of animal, they generally feed on large mammals such as deer, moose, elk, caribou, bison, muskoxen, and mountain sheep.

However, animals the size of most of the wolf's prey are especially hard to hunt and kill. Chapter VII discusses the fact that wolves must hunt far and wide and on the average make many attempts to capture prey for every animal they actually kill. A look at each phase of the hunt—locating the prey, the stalk, the encounter, the rush, and the chase—will show that the wolf's habits are well adapted to catching prey, but that the prey are well adapted to escaping. Numerous detailed descriptions of successful hunts of most of the wolf's prey will furnish us with details on the methods used in the actual capture.

When the abilities and habits of both predator and prey are so well matched, it is not surprising that most of the animals killed are the young, old, sick, and otherwise inferior individuals. That is the subject of Chapter VIII, in which the evidence for the selective effect of wolf predation is discussed.

The effects of such selection on the evolution, health, and vigor of the wolf's prey is one of the topics of Chapter IX. Other effects of wolf predation, such as the possible controlling influence on prey numbers, the increased productivity of herds preyed on by wolves, and the wolf's role in providing food for scavengers are also examined.

In Chapter X we will look at the wolf's relations with nonprey animals. Interactions between wolves and bears, wolverines, coyotes, foxes, ravens, lynx, and human beings are discussed, with descriptions of direct encounters given in many cases. Because the wolf's relations with human beings are most complex and important, several aspects of the relationship are covered: the possible predation upon man, the alleged adoption of infants by wolves, the adoption of wolves by humans, competition by the wolf for man's livestock and game animals, persecution of the wolf by man, and protection of the wolf by man.

Chapter XI reviews factors that are harmful to the wolf. We

will see that the wolf is subject to a number of detrimental influences including internal and external parasites, various diseases and disorders, injuries, malnutrition, social stress, and ruthless persecution of many types by man.

Because of the seriousness of human persecution of the wolf, the last chapter considers the future of the species. It will be concluded that the wolf's future will be short throughout most of the animal's remaining range. Thus a plea is made for more people to become aware of the ecology and behavior of the wolf in the hope that an increased understanding of the natural role of the species will result in a change in official government policies toward it.

Wolf Personality

Adolph Murie (1944: 30) who spent long periods observing wild wolves in Alaska, summed up his feelings about wolf personality in the following way: "The strongest impression remaining with me after watching the wolves on numerous occasions was their friendliness. The adults were friendly toward each other and were amiable towards the pups, at least as late as October. This innate good feeling has been strongly marked in the three captive wolves which I have known."

From all the available evidence, it appears that the personality of the wolf is related most directly to the animal's social nature. Probably the creature's strongest personality trait is its capacity for making emotional attachments to other individuals. Such attachments must form quickly and firmly, and in the wolf they begin to develop when the animals are only three weeks old. The pups become distressed when away from familiar individuals and objects, and relieved when back near them (Scott, 1967).

This ability to form emotional attachments to other individuals results in the formation of the pack as the basic unit of wolf society. When wolf pups are raised by human beings, this social tendency is especially noticeable. The animals usually become attached to the humans and dogs with which they have early or considerable contact. For instance, John Fentress, who studied the behavioral development of a wolf that he raised, noticed that the animal became extremely attached to certain farm dogs and to one in particular.

Lois Crisler and her husband reared a whole litter of wolves on the arctic tundra and gained intimate insight into their tendency to form emotional attachments. Much of Crisler's book, *Arctic Wild,* is devoted to the close relationships that developed between the Crislers and these wolves, which were allowed to roam freely in the Alaskan wilderness.

A second characteristic of wolf personality is the animal's basic aversion to fighting. Fentress' wolf avoided aggressive encounters with dogs, and Crisler described a tame wolf becoming "frantically upset" at witnessing its first dog fight. The wolf finally broke up the fight by pulling the aggressor off by the tail!

Further evidence of the basically docile nature of the wolf is found in several incidents of man's encounters with wolves in the wild. For example, Murie crawled into a wolf den and removed a pup, after the female had darted out of the den when he was twelve feet away. Both male and female did nothing but bark and howl in the distance until he left. Lois Crisler also reported that her husband once made off with a litter of pups, while the adult wolves just "bounded around crying."

An even more outstanding incident was related by D. F. Parmelee, of Kansas State Teachers College. On Ellesmere Island in northern Canada he and a companion came upon a male wolf and four pups. The men chased the wolves for a mile and captured two of the pups. Before returning to camp, the men shot several ptarmigans. When halfway back to their tent, in the pitch dark, with wolf pups cradled in their arms and ptarmigans hanging from their shouldered gun barrels, they heard something behind them. "Following close in my footsteps was the big she-wolf, her nose touching the ptarmigans as they swayed back and forth. Incredible as it surely is, we several times had to drive that wolf off with snowballs for fear that we would lose our specimens!" (Parmelee, 1964: 9). The female wolf remained just outside the tent all that night.

Additional records show that a wolf also readily submits to man when cornered. Canadian biologists George Kolenosky and Dave Johnston subdued adult wolves in steel traps merely by placing a forked stick over their necks and pinning them to the ground. Once pinned, the wolves offered little resistance.

The same was certainly true of a female wolf at least nine months old that I once handled in the same way (Mech and Frenzel, 1969). The animal had been captured around the chest by a snare set to close down tight enough to hold but not hurt her.

After I forced the wolf's neck down with a forked stick, my associates and I ear-tagged her, fastened a radio-collar around her neck, and examined her teeth. In the process we had to re-move the forked stick and hold the wolf by the scruff of the neck. She was just as docile as if anesthetized. In fact, when I eventually released my hold on her, and my companions stepped back to photograph her escape, nothing happened. The wolf just lay there apparently unconscious. A student who was especially interested in photographing the animal in motion stayed with her while the rest of us left. After he sat in the snow and cold for an hour and a half, he saw the wolf suddenly raise her head. Then in an instant she dashed off. The student never even got a picture!

These well-documented reports lend credence to a tale related to me by Minnesota conservation officer Robert Jacobsen. Accord-ing to Jacobsen, a northern Minnesota wolf trapper used to tell of his regular procedure of clamping his hands around the muzzle of a trapped wolf and giving the animal's head a quick jerk back-ward, thus breaking its neck.

Although this is difficult to believe, there is an even more fan-tastic report by J. J. Audubon and J. Bachman, whose reporting is usually highly respected. These naturalists accompanied an In-diana farmer in checking his "wolf pit"—a large hole in the ground baited to catch wolves. They discovered three large wolves in the pit, and the farmer descended into the midst of the animals. "We were not a little surprised at the cowardice of the wolves. The woodman stretched out their hind legs, in succession, and with a stroke of the knife cut the principal tendon above the joint, ex-hibiting as little fear as if he had been marking lambs" (Audubon and Bachman, 1967: 194). These probably were *not* coyotes, as some people might suspect, because two of them were black, a color rare in coyotes but not uncommon in wolves.

That a cornered or wounded wolf is not necessarily aggressive can also be vouched for by conservation officer-pilot Robert Hodge, of Minnesota, who has shot hundreds of wolves from an aircraft. Once when he had only broken an animal's front legs, he approached the wolf on foot to finish it off. Instead of finding a snarling and threatening man-killer, he encountered a meek and docile creature, which wagged its tail in the friendly, submissive gesture of a whipped dog.

Apparently in many circumstances the wolf realizes that man

is an overwhelming adversary, and does not even attempt to defend itself. It seems significant in this respect that the wolf pups that Parmelee captured turned friendly and docile as soon as they were grasped by the neck.

Under certain circumstances, however, the wolf will defend itself and its pups from other animals, and there have been claims that it will attack man even when unprovoked. There certainly are situations in which wolves do demonstrate aggressive behavior, primarily (1) when harassing prey, (2) when meeting strange wolves, and (3) when protecting the den or pups from other predators. All these subjects will be treated at length in later chapters.

However, in view of the above records, we can conclude that generally the wolf possesses the kind of personality that in humans would be labeled "agreeable." Its constitution seems to be much like that of its domesticated descendant, the dog. Many a house dog has been friendly and docile and completely tame and yet at night has killed the neighbor's cat or sheep; in many areas, pet dogs even turn to killing deer. In wolves, a nonviolent nature usually would be very advantageous, considering that these animals spend most of their time in the company of other wolves. A pack would function very inefficiently if its members were constantly at each other's throats.

This does not mean that all wolves possess exactly the same personalities. The personality described above was that of the wolf as a species. However, within that framework individual wolves can differ greatly, as people who have reared them can attest.

Lois Crisler characterized each of her wolves differently. She described Arctic, a male, as lordly, timid, and luxury-loving; Alatna, a female, was fearless, gay, playful, and inventive; Killik, another female, was hearty, affectionate, unjealous, and undemanding; Barrow, a male, was aggressive; and the female Tundra was sober, gentle, and withdrawn.

Doug Pimlott of Ontario, who also raised a litter of pups, devoted an entire chapter of a book to "Wolves as Individuals." He described some of his pet wolves as follows: "Dagwood and Blondie were big blondes, complete extroverts and complete people-lovers. Lupe (after Lupus) was friendly too, but she knew that there were basic differences between wolves and people. She would not be bossed around too much and was always quick to let you know if you over-stepped the bounds of propriety. Puppet was the mischief-maker and the tease of the litter" (Rutter and Pimlott, 1968: 145).

Intelligence

With the present state of knowledge in animal psychology it would be useless to try to compare the general intelligence of the wolf with that of other species. There are even serious difficulties in defining intelligence. However, certain scattered reports do give some indication of the wolf's ability to remember, to associate events, and to learn.

Stanley Young, a co-author of the book *The Wolves of North America,* cited reports that during the heyday of the bison hunters, wolves learned to head toward the sound of gunshots. They would then wait around while the hunters skinned out their bison, and would begin to eat the abandoned carcasses just as soon as the hunters left.

In northern Minnesota, where wolves were persecuted extensively by aerial hunters, they soon learned to avoid open areas whenever they heard aircraft. On the other hand, biologists using aircraft to study wolves have been able to condition them in the opposite way. By following the animals without harassing them, the biologists found that wolves learned to remain in the open and behave normally even during low passes by the aircraft (Burkholder, 1959; Mech, 1966a).

It also appears that wolves learn to prey upon the more easily obtainable species in their area. Where both deer and moose are available, wolves tend to take a much higher proportion of deer (Chapter VI). However, on Isle Royale, where the only large prey are moose, wolves have learned to kill these animals efficiently.

The wolf's memory is also good. St. George Mivart reported that a tame wolf recognized its master after an eighteen-month separation from him, and later after a three-year separation. More recently, Jerome Woolpy and Benson Ginsburg, of the University of Chicago, showed that, once they had trained an adult captive wolf to become friendly to humans, it would remain friendly for at least eighteen to twenty-two months without any further handling.

At least some credence must be given to the many trappers' tales of individual wolves that learned to avoid even the most ingenious traps set especially for them. In nothern Minnesota trappers who are able to consistently take large numbers of wolves are still held in very high respect by their associates.

It appears, then, from the meager evidence available, that the wolf shows a high degree of adaptability to varying conditions. The animal seems to be able to learn readily and to retain what it has learned for long periods.

Wildness and Fear

Anyone who has spent much time in wolf country will verify that the wolf is one of the wildest and shyest of all the animals in the northern wilderness. Many an experienced woodsman has lived a lifetime without even glimpsing a wolf in its natural surroundings. I hiked approximately 1400 miles during four summers in Isle Royale National Park, which harbors one of the highest wolf densities known, and saw wolves on only three occasions during that time. In all cases, the animals ran off so quickly and silently that I was left wondering if I had really seen them.

This is not to say that wolves will not become somewhat accustomed to human beings. Being adaptable, they have at times become dependent on livestock for food, and during those times they have often ventured close to human habitations. In Alaska, wolves sometimes learn to visit human dumping grounds, and they become less shy of man in those areas (Murie, 1944). On the other hand, where they have not been exposed to people for generations, wolves may act quite tame when encountering them, as in the incident between Parmelee and the wolves on Ellesmere Island.

Nevertheless, in most wolf country, where the animals have had some exposure to human beings but not much, the scent of man causes a fearful and rapid avoidance. This is one of the main reasons that more people do not see wolves during their wilderness excursions.

Recent studies of tame and captive wolves have illuminated the subject of wildness in these creatures. It has been found that after wolf pups pass through a certain stage of growth they become resistant to forming friendly relations with other wolves (or with humans) that they have not already "befriended" (Chapter IV). As will be discussed in Chapter II, it is beneficial to a pup under natural conditions to form emotional bonds with other members of its pack but not to wolves of other packs. Thus as a pup grows increasingly older, it begins to shy away from unfamiliar individuals and becomes wilder.

Experiments at the University of Chicago have shown that the main factor preventing adults and older pups from "socializing" with unfamiliar wolves or humans is extreme fear. In the studies of Woolpy and Ginsburg, individual "unsocialized" wolves of various ages were suddenly exposed to persons sitting in their cages for ten to twenty minutes at a time. This procedure was repeated every few days for a period of several months, and the reactions of the animals were recorded. The human being did not try to force a friendship but only advanced in his relationship with the wolf as the creature acted ready. In this way, socialization, or the establishment of a friendly attitude by the wolf toward the human, eventually was accomplished. The animal had then lost its fear of people and was no longer wild.

After a wolf is three months old, the process of socialization becomes very difficult, and in adults it requires six or seven months of careful work. Four stages are recognized in the process. The first is the *escape stage,* characterized by the wolf showing extreme fear upon entry of the experimenter into the cage. The animal tries desperately to escape by digging at the concrete floor, pawing at the door, and jumping into the air. It then retreats into the corner farthest from the experimenter, crouches, cowers, pants, trembles, salivates, defecates, and urinates.

The wolf is forced to experience this fear over and over. While the human being just continues to sit harmlessly in the cage the animal gradually begins to overcome the fear. After about a month of this routine, the wolf learns to sit relaxed in the corner of the cage farthest from the experimenter and enters the *avoidance stage.* Early in this phase of the process, the wolf will revert to escape-and-fear behavior if the experimenter moves very much.

Several months later, however, the wolf will consistently allow the human to approach and eventually to start handling it. The wolf may even begin to approach the experimenter but will stop if stared at by him. Soon after this, the very critical *approach stage* begins. The wolf begins to investigate the experimenter by chewing his clothing, rolling in his scent, rubbing on him, etc. "Attempts to dominate the animal physically at this stage may either lead to a full blown attack or may provide a setback to an earlier stage of socialization that is then more difficult to overcome than the first time it was encountered" (Woolpy and Ginsburg, 1967: 360).

Considerable effort is then made to break the wolf of its investigatory biting without antagonizing the animal. If the wolf threatens and cannot be dissuaded from its threat, the experimenter must then either retreat slowly and casually or must depend on the intercession of a co-worker.

Eventually the *stage of socialization* is reached, and the wolf will wag its tail, approach without aggression, lick the experimenter, and greet him mouth-to-mouth with the usual wolf greeting (Chapter III).

In a variation of these experiments, an assortment of fear-reducing tranquilizers was administered to wolves during the process of socialization. The drugs reduced the time required to reach the final stage of socialization from several months to four days, presumably by overcoming the wolf's fear. However, the tranquilizers did not produce the permanent effect that long-term training did. It appears that conditioning actually rid the wolf of fear of the experimenter, but the drugs only blocked the fear temporarily.

Although months of care and effort are required to overcome an adult wolf's extreme fear of strangers, the results of the socialization process last for long periods, as mentioned above.

Of course, in the wild the first part of this process—escape—would be fulfilled, and the wolf would go on its way without showing the other symptoms of fear. Because the animal would never be forced through the socialization process, it would retain its fear—and its wildness—forever.

Physical Characteristics

The wolf is a large wild dog. It hunts, pursues, attacks, kills, and eats animals larger than itself, and many of its physical traits reflect these habits.

As a species, the wolf is the largest member of the dog family (Mivart, 1890), with adult males from most areas averaging 95 to 100 pounds and adult females, 80 to 85 pounds (Table 1). Although males rarely exceed 120 pounds, and females 100 pounds, a few individuals may weigh much more. The heaviest wolf on record remains the 175-pound male reported by Young from east-central Alaska. Another especially large animal, presumably a male, was taken in western Canada and weighed 172 pounds with a full stomach (Cowan, 1947).

TABLE 1. Weights of wolves (pounds)

Adults only[1]						
Location	*Number*	*Sex*	*Average*	*Minimum*	*Maximum*	*Authority*
Northwest Territories	18	M	98	90	116	Fuller and Novakowski, 1955
Northwest Territories	21	F	85	70	110	Fuller and Novakowski, 1955
Northwest Territories	80	M	97[3]	63[3]	133[3]	Kelsall, 1968
Northwest Territories	66	F	83[3]	50[3]	119[3]	Kelsall, 1968
Soviet Union	6	M	97	84	100	Makridin, 1962
Soviet Union	6	F	75	—	96	Makridin, 1962
Alaska	60	M	85[2]	60[2]	112[2]	R. A. Rausch, 1967b
Alaska	50	F	71[2]	54[2]	82[2]	R. A. Rausch, 1967b
Ontario	40	M	61	43	81	Pimlott *et al.*, 1969
Ontario	33	F	54	39	70	Pimlott *et al.*, 1969
Adults and partly grown pups						
Location	*Number*	*Sex*	*Average*	*Minimum*	*Maximum*	*Authority*
Alaska	6	M	90	64	112	Kelly, 1954
Alaska	9	F	67	50	80	Kelly, 1954
Alaska	24	M	90	72	114	Garceau, 1960, 61
Alaska	20	F	72	55	93	Garceau, 1960, 61
Minnesota	84	M	78	50	114	Stenlund, 1955
Minnesota	60	F	61	45	84	Stenlund, 1955
Yugoslavia	?	?	73	—	139	Knezevic and Knezevic, 1956
Soviet Union	23	M	88	—	108	Makridin, 1959
Soviet Union	23	F	74	—	90	Makridin, 1959
Finland	52	M	89	57	121	Pulliainen, 1965
Finland	33	F	70	53	99	Pulliainen, 1965

[1] Animals at least 1 year old.
[2] Skinned weights of animals over 1 year old. These are 10 to 15 pounds low, depending on size of animal. For weights of pups in their first winter from this area, see Table 14.
[3] Primarily animals over 1 year old, but includes about 10 per cent pups.

Wolves generally are just a bit shorter in length than people are tall. Males vary from 5.0 to 6.5 feet from nose to tail tip, and females from 4.5 to 6.0 feet. Of this length the tail accounts for 13 to 20 inches. Most wolves stand 26 to 32 inches tall, although a few are a full 3 feet high at the shoulders. These and many additional measurements can be found in the works of Fuller and Novakowski, Garceau, Makridin, Stenlund, and Young.

The entire dog family is more adapted to running than are any of the other families of meat eaters (Matthew, 1930), and the general build of the wolf is especially well suited to trotting (Young, 1944). The animal's chest is narrow and keel-like, and its fore limbs seem pressed into the chest, with elbows turned inward and paws turned outward (Young, 1944; Iljin, 1941). This allows both fore and hind legs on the same side to swing in the same line. In contrast, a dog generally does not place each hind foot in the track made by its front foot; rather the animal puts each hind foot beside its front foot track.

The build of the wolf's legs also aids the animal in its fast and far-ranging travels. Milton Hildebrand, who analyzed the body proportions of various members of the dog family, concluded that the wolf's legs are moderately long compared to the legs of other members of the group. This trait not only promotes speed but it also enables the wolf to overcome the hardships of the deep snow that covers most of the creature's range.

Like other members of the family, the wolf walks on its toes, rather than on the entire sole of its foot. There are four toes on each hind foot and five on the front, but one of the front toes does not touch the ground. Each toe has a large pad, calloused but soft, and a blunt, nonretracting claw. In addition, there is a large "heel" pad on each foot. This kind of foot possesses many of the advantages of the hoofs of such fleet-footed animals as deer and caribou, yet it also allows the wolf to walk agilely on rocks, logs, and other irregularities.

The actual speed of a running wolf is still debatable, for few chances occur for determining it. Young reported that a wolf was clocked at twenty-eight mph for two hundred yards and believed that wolves could not average over twenty-four mph for more than a mile or two. This agrees with information supplied to I. M. Cowan (1947) by people who have hunted wolves by automobile on large frozen lakes and who state that the animals seldom exceed twenty-five mph. However, Minnesota game wardens claimed to have chased a wolf across a frozen lake for four miles at thirty-five to forty mph (Stenlund, 1955). In addition, three Macalester College students in a truck recently paced a wolf running down a Minnesota road for a quarter mile at thirty-five to forty mph. I have seen wolves bound tremendously when pursuing moose and deer, and such bounds may measure sixteen feet in length (Dixon, 1934).

Wolves can maintain a chase for at least twenty minutes, although usually they do not make such a long pursuit at top speed. When a lengthy chase is ended, the wolves often rest for ten to fifteen minutes. Murie (1944: 29) described how exhausted a wolf can get after a night's hunt: "When he arrives at the den, he flops, relaxes completely, and may not even change his position for three to four hours. Often he may not even raise his head to look around for intruders."

Besides getting around remarkably well on land, the wolf also has little trouble with water. In Chapter VII, it will be shown that even in winter wolves will sometimes swim after prey that has sought refuge in water. In Minnesota, C. E. Johnson (1921) observed a wolf feeding on a floating moose carcass; the wolf was treading water while tearing at the moose.

The wolf feeds almost exclusively on flesh, bones, and other animal matter, so it is not surprising that several features of its head are adapted to catching and eating prey. The skull itself is large and long and tapers forward, averaging nine to eleven inches long and five to six inches wide. The volume of the brain case is 150 to 170 cm^3, which is at least 30 cm^3 greater than that of most dogs (Klatt, 1913). Massive jaws form the foundation to which the strong masseter, or chewing, muscles attach.

A total of forty-two teeth help the wolf in securing its food, the dental formula being: Incisors 3-3/3-3; Canines 1-1/1-1; Premolars 4-4/4-4; Molars 2-2/3-3. The largest teeth are the canines, or fangs, which may reach two and a quarter inches in total length, including the portion imbedded in the jaw. These are the tools that help the wolf hold onto its prey. Much of the cutting and chewing done in feeding is accomplished by the carnassials, or flesh teeth—the fourth upper premolar and the first lower molar. These specialized teeth are much like a pair of self-sharpening shears and function well in cutting tendons and tough flesh (Matthew, 1930). The massive molars help crush bones.

The power of a wolf's bite is incredible. I have watched wolves on the run leap at the rump of an adult moose and rip it open even though this meant tearing through four inches of finely packed hair and a thick hide. A wolf can, and does, hook its fangs into the rubbery nose of a moose. The creature can cling there despite the swinging head of the moose, which may even raise the wolf off the ground. According to Young (1944: 106), "A wolf can snap off the tail of a long yearling, a full-grown cow, or steer with the cleanness of cut as that of a scythe on maturing hay."

On the other hand, the wolf can also manage very precise maneuvers with its incisors, as Lois Crisler can testify (Crisler, 1958: 156). In the company of her tame wolf Lady, she was lying on the floor with her eyes closed. "Suddenly I felt fine pricks on my eyelids, like a row of needles. Lady was picking up the merest skin of my eyelid with her teeth, giving me grooming nibbles."

Sensory Abilities

Besides providing a base for rows of sharp teeth, the wolf's long skull also furnishes a large area for the animal's olfactory, or smelling, apparatus. Dogs, which are similar to wolves in this respect, have an olfactory area some fourteen times as large as that of human beings (Fuller and DuBuis, 1962). This probably accounts for the superior odor-detecting ability of the dog family. Researchers estimate that this ability is up to one hundred times more sensitive than that of man (Moulton *et al.,* 1960).

Little study has been done on the wolf's sense of smell, but certainly it is at least as sharp as that of most dogs, since the wolf depends on this sense for survival. Under most circumstances wolves can detect an animal when within three hundred yards downwind of it (Mech, 1966a). However, when the prey is downwind or crosswind of them, wolves may not sense it, or they may be unable to locate it even if they do get the scent. I once watched a moose feeding undetected for twenty minutes while one hundred yards downwind of a pack of fifteen wolves.

It is impressive to observe a wolf pack when the animals suddenly catch the scent of prey. In Isle Royale National Park, I often saw this from an aircraft while following a pack of fifteen wolves in winter. By knowing the wind direction and watching for moose that were upwind of the wolves' trail, I could predict just where the animals would catch the scent. When reaching that point, the wolves would suddenly stop and point stiffly upwind; then they would assemble, nose-to-nose, wag tails for ten to fifteen seconds, and veer straight upwind toward the moose. Once they did this when 1.5 miles downwind of a cow moose and twin calves, showing that under some conditions they can detect scent for that great a distance.

The wolf's hearing is also very sensitive. Joslin (1966) discovered that captive wolves four miles from him replied to his own attempt at howling, which was "unquestionably weaker in intensity" than that of the wolves. From this we might surmise that wolves can hear other wolves howling at even greater distances.

According to J. L. Fuller and E. M. DuBuis, the dog's ability to hear sounds above 250 cycles per second becomes progressively greater than man's as the frequency increases. For sounds below that frequency, man and dog possess about the same hearing ability. Dogs can detect sounds up to 26,000 cycles per second (Andreev, 1925) and can tell the difference between pitches one tone apart on the musical scale. Presumably the hearing ability of the wolf corresponds to these. It has been shown recently that a wolf can tell the actual howling of a person from a tape recording of the same howling (Chapter III).

Wolves depend primarily on their senses of smell and hearing, but their vision also seems to be sharp at least in detecting movement.

Pelage

Pelt color varies more in the wolf than in almost any other species. The full range of shades has been reported, from white through cream-colored, buff, tawny, reddish, and gray to black. Apparently such variation occurs throughout the wolf's range, for it has been seen in wolves from most areas of North America, Europe, and the U.S.S.R. However, gray predominates, as one of the popular names for this species, "gray wolf," implies.

The occurrence of colors other than gray seems to increase in the higher latitudes. In southern Ontario and in Minnesota, most wolves are gray, although there are a few blacks. In Wood Buffalo National Park (northern Canada), thirty-four of fifty-nine wolves examined there were gray, twenty-one were black, two were brown, and two were almost white (Fuller and Novakowski, 1955). In southeastern Alaska, fifteen of eighteen wolves taken from Etolin Island were black, but all except thirty of 259 wolves killed north of the Brooks Range in Alaska were light-colored (Kelly, 1954). Pierre Jolicoeur (1959) found that the frequency of pale wolves in Canada's Northwest Territories increased in a northeastward direction.

Several of the color phases are often found within a single litter. Such a situation helped Murie identify each of seven individuals in a pack that he observed during his classic study of the wolves of Mount McKinley National Park. Two of these individuals were marked so unusually that Murie believed he could have distinguished them in a large group of strange wolves.

A litter of six pups born in 1967 to a gray male and a reddish-white female in Minnesota's St. Paul Zoo contained five male pups that were distinctly red, plus one gray female.

Even a wolf that generally appears gray really has a coat of many colors. White, black, gray, and brown hairs are intermingled, with darker fur usually predominating along the center of the back and tail. The wolf's underside, legs, ears, and muzzle often are tawny. Very old wolves tend to be grayer than younger ones (Goldman, 1944).

The wolf's color depends on the color of its outer, or guard, hairs. But as with most mammals, wolves also possess underfur, which is shorter and much finer than the stiff guard hairs. In most members of the dog family, the hairs arise in groups of many underhairs and one guard hair in each "follicle." The follicles themselves occur mostly in bundles of three, arranged roughly into irregular rows; a guard hair of the central group is usually coarser than those of adjacent groups (Hildebrand, 1952) (Fig. 1). Wolves from more northern latitudes possess much longer and denser fur than those from southern ranges.

FIGURE 1. Hair pattern and arrangement in members of the dog family. (*Hildebrand, 1952*)

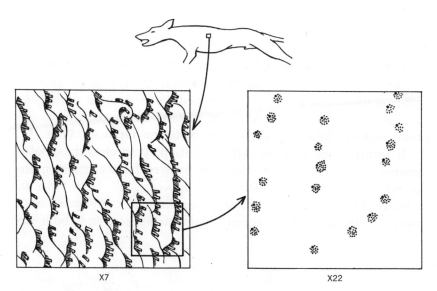

X7   X22

The rows of hair in members of the dog family are arranged in "tracts" that slope in different directions depending on their location (Hildebrand, 1952). On the top side of an animal they usually slope from the head toward the tail and from the center of the back toward the sides and extremities. The slope pattern of the underside is much more complicated (Fig. 2). Wolves, dogs, and coyotes have a special tract of long, erectile hairs, the mane, which extends along the center of the back from the neck to the back of the shoulders. When one of these animals is angry, its mane rises conspicuously.

Another special group of hairs in the wolf surrounds an area known as the tail (precaudal) gland. These hairs are especially stiff and are usually tipped with black, even in all-white animals. The tail gland itself is located on the top side of the tail, about three inches from its base. It occurs in most members of the dog family but is absent in the domestic dog (Hildebrand, 1952). The function of this gland is still unknown. According to an authority cited by M. Hildebrand, the gland is made up of modified sebaceous glands, and in the European red fox it produces a fatty yellow material. In the wolf, the gland is bluish black.

Authorities disagree about the molting, or shedding, of fur in the wolf. Goldman stated that wolves molt once a year, over a long period in summer. Meanwhile, new hairs replace those lost, and by autumn the entire new coat is present. It continues to grow, however, until winter, when it reaches its greatest length. On the other hand, Novikov (1956) contended that shedding occurs twice, first in mid-April and again during August to November.

Evolution

The wolf, whose scientific name is *Canis lupus,* had a long history of development and specialization from a more generalized carnivore (meat eater) that roamed the earth some 100 to 120 million years ago. W. D. Matthew (1930) has traced this evolution, and the following account is based on his work (Fig. 3).

It seems ironic that the wolf and its prey species, the hoofed mammals, or ungulates, probably all evolved from a common ancestor that lived a few hundred million years ago. Both types of animals became adapted to swift long-distance running on open plains, both developed relatively high intelligence, and, both de-

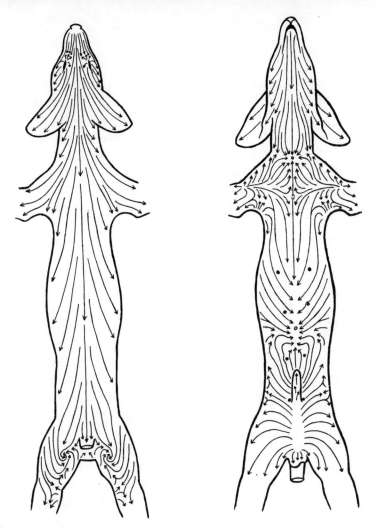

FIGURE 2. Hair slope patterns in members of the dog family. (*After Hildebrand, 1952*)

scended from forest-dwelling ancestors. Probably they evolved in long association with one another, since the wolf and its ancestors gradually developed better and better adaptations for killing and eating the hoofed animals; and at the same time the hoofed animals became better adapted to detecting, escaping, and defending themselves against wolves.

The primitive group of meat eaters, known as creodonts, originated in the northern hemisphere, and it is thought that the dog family itself developed in North America and gradually dispersed from there.

Approximately fifty-five million years ago, a mammal with partly specialized "flesh teeth," or carnassials, occurred. During the next ten million years a large number and variety of these creatures flourished, and one of them, known as *Miacis,* was more similar than others to members of the dog family of today. *Miacis* is a member of the family Miacidae, from which all the present families of meat eaters eventually arose: the dogs, cats, bears, weasels, raccoons, civets, and hyenas.

In the period thirty to forty million years ago, *Miacis* gave rise to two types of mammals that can be traced through two series of fossils to the dog and bear families. The predecessor to the dog family, *Cynodictis,* had the same number of teeth as the wolf. It was much smaller than a wolf, however, and its body was long and flexible like that of a weasel; its legs were of moderate length. In the next fifteen million years, the raccoon family branched from this group and developed separately.

Meanwhile, fifteen to thirty million years ago, a strong trend occurred toward the characteristics of present-day wolves, from *Cynodictis* through the animals *Cynodesmus* and *Tomarctus.* The creatures' legs became longer, the feet longer and more compact, the inner digit became vestigial on the hind foot and much reduced on the fore foot, the tail became shorter, and the entire proportions began approaching those of the wolves and the foxes.

From *Tomarctus* both the wolf and the fox arose and began developing separately some fifteen million years ago. Although the fox did not change much in size, the wolf grew larger and larger. A closely related type, the dire wolf (*Canis dirus*), also branched off, some of which were much larger than the present wolves; these are now extinct. By one or two million years ago, the wolf was much like it is today.

Classification and Genetics

The wolf (*Canis lupus*), also known as the gray wolf, the timber wolf, and the tundra wolf, is a member of the order of mammals known as the Carnivora, or meat eaters. As such, the species is related to the other families of Carnivora: the bears (Ursidae), cats (Felidae), weasels (Mustelidae), raccoons (Procyonidae), civets (Viverridae), and hyenas (Hyaenidae). The wolf's own family is the Canidae, or dog family.

As the name of the order implies, the characteristics common to all these families are primarily those related to food habits. Probably the most distinctive traits of animals in these families are their long, pointed canine teeth, or fangs, and their sharp shearing fourth upper premolars and first lower molars. Carnivores also possess a simple digestive system, to be discussed in Chapter VI, and their claws are usually sharp. In addition, their clavicles, which are known as collarbones in humans, are often comparatively small. Their brains are highly developed, and the animals are considered more intelligent than most other groups (Matthew, 1930).

FIGURE 3. Evolution of the wolf.
(*Modified from Matthew, 1930*)

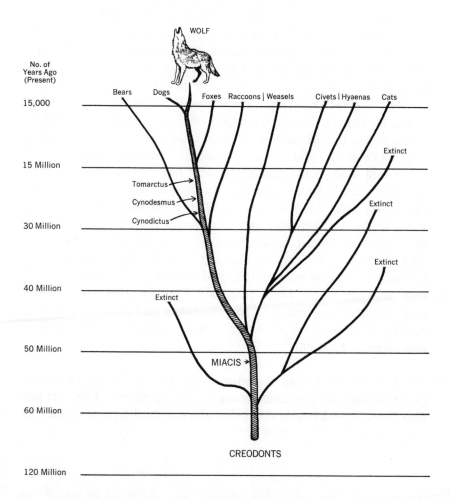

The forty-two teeth of each member of the Canidae distinguish this family from all other families of meat eaters except bears. There are three main differences between the dogs and the bears. Dogs walk on their toes, possess long tails, and have four toes on each hind foot, whereas bears walk on the soles of their feet, have a short tail, and have five toes on each hind foot.

Within the Canidae fifty-six extinct and fourteen living sub-groups, or genera, are now recognized (Walker, 1964). Of these genera, the genus *Canis* is the one to which the wolf belongs. The other living genera include the arctic foxes, red foxes, kit foxes, gray foxes, raccoon dogs, South American foxes, small-eared dogs, crab-eating foxes, maned wolves, bush dogs, dholes, African hunting dogs, and African big-eared foxes.

Besides including the wolf (*Canis lupus*), the genus *Canis* also contains the domestic dog (*C. familiaris*), the coyote (*C. latrans*), the golden jackal (*C. aureus*), the black-backed jackal (*C. mesomelas*), the side-striped jackal (*C. adustus*), and the dingo (*C. dingo*). The so-called red wolf, known as *Canis rufus,* has also been recognized as a separate species, but this has recently been questioned and will be discussed later. The wolf can be distinguished from most of these species solely by its large size.

There are two animals, however, with which the wolf is often confused. One of them is the coyote. A large coyote, or especially a coyote-dog hybrid such as reported from the northeastern United States (Pringle, 1960), may overlap in size with a small wolf. Compared with such animals, the wolf has a broader, more massive snout and a wider nose pad. In some cases, the only definite distinction must be based on skull measurements. Wolves have wider teeth, and their rostrum, or snout, is more massive, making the brain case appear small; the opposite is true for coyotes. Barbara Lawrence and W. H. Bossert (1967: 224), of Harvard University, recently analyzed these skull characters and concluded that "if width of the brain case, width across molars, and width between premolars anteriorly are also taken into account, the characteristic relatively small brain case of a typical wolf skull is immediately apparent."

The red wolf. Problems in distinguishing the wolf from the coyote occur because the two animals are so closely related. This fact has also caused considerable confusion about a third type of canid, the

FIGURE 4. Scientists know little about the Red Wolf of southeastern and south-central United States, and the animal is now seriously threatened with extinction. (*National Zoological Park, Washington, D.C.*)

"red wolf" (*Canis rufus*), of the southeastern and south-central United States, a form intermediate between wolf and coyote (Fig. 4). Three geographic races, or subspecies, of the red wolf have been recognized: the Florida red wolf (*Canis rufus floridanus*), the Mississippi Valley red wolf (*C. r. gregoryi*), and the Texas red wolf (*C. r. rufus*).

[NOTE: Changes in the scientific name of the red wolf have been especially confusing, and Doug Pimlott and Paul Joslin (1968) have reviewed the history of the changes. From 1944 to 1967, the red wolf was known as *Canis niger*, with the subspecies designated *C. n. niger*, *C. n. gregoryi*, and *C. n. rufus*.

However, recently R. M. Nowak (1967) showed that for technical reasons *Canis niger* was an invalid name and pointed out that the animal should be called *Canis rufus*, with the subspecies being *C. r. floridanus, C. r. gregoryi,* and *C. r. rufus* as originally named by E. A. Goldman (1937).]

According to Goldman, the Florida and Mississippi Valley varieties of red wolf are similar to the eastern gray wolf (*Canis lupus lycaon*) in size and general proportions, but they have shorter, more reddish fur. The Texas variety, however, ". . . is so small and in general characters agrees so closely with [the coyote] *C. latrans,* which it overlaps in geographic range, that some specimens are difficult to determine" (Goldman, 1944: 481).

During a study of the red-wolf problem, H. McCarley examined all the skulls of recently collected wolflike animals from Arkansas, Oklahoma, and Texas. The skulls were the same size as the skull of the large coyote of that area, *Canis latrans frustror,* and presumably were from that species. On the basis of his study of various forms of coyotes and red wolves, McCarley (1962: 234) thought that possibly ". . . the apparent extirpation of red wolves in these latter states was the result of (1) non-adaptability of red wolves to changing environmental conditions, including competition with coyote populations, and (2) probable hybridization between coyotes and red wolves, resulting in the blending of red wolf and coyote characters into a form known as *Canis niger rufus.*" This latter possibility would explain the gradation in various characters between the coyote and the red wolf.

But what about the similarity between *Canis rufus* and the eastern race of the wolf? That too has only recently been explained. The intensive study by Lawrence and Bossert appears to have furnished the answer. These biologists noticed four strange facts about the red wolf: (1) it occurred in a very small geographic area, (2) it was the only kind of wolf in the world that was not considered a race of *Canis lupus,* (3) in part of its range it overlapped in area with both the wolf and the coyote, and (4) in areas of overlap with either animal, it tended to resemble the species with which it overlapped, which is just the opposite of such situations with other animals. Usually two similar species *differ* the most where they overlap in range (Lawrence and Bossert, 1967).

Lawrence and Bossert used a computer and the statistical technique of linear discrimination. Thus they were able to make use of the multiple relationships of several measurements in skulls of the coyote, the eastern race of the wolf known as *Canis lupus lycaon,* and the red wolf. The technique provides a weighted sum of several characters that best separate two types of animals. With this method, they found that the red wolf of Florida and the Mississippi Valley appears to be not a separate species at all *but merely a race of the gray wolf.*

A limited number of specimens from the western part of the red wolf's range, and previously identified as red wolf, ". . . span the whole range of variation from coyote to wolf." The Harvard researchers believed that in this area there may have been hybridization of coyote and wolf.

However, since the publication of Lawrence and Bossert's results, J. L. Paradiso (1968), of the Smithsonian Institution, examined 279 *Canis* skulls taken from eastern Texas after 1960. They showed a wide range of variation between coyote and red wolf, as McCarley had found, and Paradiso suggested that they came from an interbreeding population of coyote×red-wolf hybrids. He further suggested that if this is the case it means that the red wolf and the coyote are the same species.

Pimlott and Joslin stated that this view of Paradiso and the view of Lawrence and Bossert are "diametrically opposed." However, this may not be strictly true; in fact, it seems that the two views can be reconciled. Lawrence and Bossert studied two eastern subspecies of red wolf, whereas Paradiso studied specimens from the range of the western subspecies. Thus it seems reasonable to suggest that when enough evidence is gathered the red wolf will be found to be properly known as *Canis lupus*× *Canis latrans*. In other words, the red wolf may be a fertile wolf-coyote cross, with eastern races of the hybrid population more strongly resembling the wolves that once occupied the forested Southeast and with whom they periodically bred; and with the western race of the hybrid population more strongly resembling the coyotes that still occupy the open area of Texas and with whom they still may breed.

The wolf and the domestic dog. The other species with which the wolf is often confused is the domestic dog. Indian dogs, huskies, malemutes, Laikas, and German shepherds are wolflike

FIGURE 5. The wolf has a distinct face that can help convey its mood to other members of its pack. (*Laurence P. Pringle*)

and are sometimes bred with wolves. The resulting wolf-dogs, or "demiwolves," are even harder to distinguish from wolves. In general, the wolf's tail hangs, but the dog's tail usually is held high and often is curly (Iljin, 1941). The wolf has a precaudal gland that is lacking in dogs (Hildebrand, 1952). The wolf's hind legs swing in the same line as its front legs, but the dog places its hind legs between the trail of its front legs (Iljin, 1941). Wolves breed only once a year; most dogs breed twice. The muzzle of most breeds of dogs is shorter than that of the wolf, with the collie's most similar to the wolf's (Dixon, 1916). In addition, the wolf has a distinct face resulting from wide tufts of hair that project down and outward from below its ears (Fig. 5).

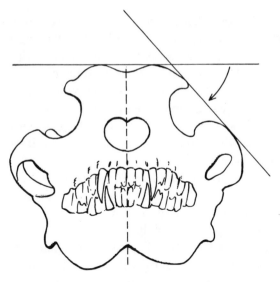

FIGURE 6. The orbital angle. In wolves
this angle measures 40° to 45°,
whereas in dogs it ranges from 53° to
60°. (*Modified from Iljin, 1941*)

The traits that best distinguish a wolf from a dog are skull characteristics. N. A. Iljin, who studied wolf-dog genetics, provided criteria from a review of the literature and from his own work. One of the best is based on the width of the orbital angle, which is the angle between a line drawn through the upper and lower edges of the eye socket and a line drawn across the top of the skull. In wolves this angle measures 40° to 45°, whereas in dogs it measures 53° to 60° (Fig. 6). "Only primitive dogs, e.g., the deer hound (52°), the German sheep dog (two specimens, 50°), Catack-dog and *Canis palustris* (the stone-age dog) (48°), are somewhat nearer to the wolf, though they still differ from the latter" (Iljin, 1941: 387).

A second difference is in the shape and size of the auditory or tympanic "bullae," two domelike protrusions on the base of the skull just behind the sockets for the lower jaw. Wolves and coyotes have large, convex, and almost spherical bullae, whereas those of dogs are smaller, compressed, and slightly crumpled. Lawrence and Bossert furnished further details on wolf-dog differences.

As already mentioned, wolves often breed with dogs. According to Young, such matings take place both with and without human prompting. American Indian dogs supposedly were crossed with wolves to such an extent that few purebred dogs existed in North America when Europeans arrived. Eskimos and other inhabitants of the far north have used quarter-breed, half-breed, and even pure wolves in their dog teams. The wolf-dog crosses show various dispositions, coat colors, and other characteristics, so no generalizations can be made about these traits.

To obtain information on wolf-dog genetics, Iljin crossed a wolf with a black mongrel sheep dog and carried out various crosses for four generations totaling 101 individuals. All offspring that were tested from all generations were fertile.

Iljin's summary of conclusions follows: "Typical Mendelian segregation has been demonstrated for many different characters, notably for hair colour and pattern, eye colour, ear form, size, and various skull characters. There is also evidence for segregation in certain physiological peculiarities such as season of rut and nervous disposition." Modifying influences due to environment may affect some of the skull characters, the form of the tail and the general appearance of the animal, though in all of these cases the differences are basically genetic. "Certain features such as the duration of pregnancy, the blind period in the young, the order of appearance of milk teeth and the moulting phenomena are identical in both wolves and dogs. All of these data taken together serve to emphasize the very close similarity in genetical constitution between the wolf and the dog, and suggest the *possibility* of the origin of the various races of *Canis familiaris* from a single wild species, viz. *C. lupus*" (Iljin, 1941: 410). In fact, the two species are regarded as so closely related that one authority (Bohlken, 1961) has proposed that the dog be considered only a form of the wolf and not a separate species.

As Iljin stated, the very close relationship between wolves and dogs suggests that dogs are direct descendants of wolves and not of any other species. Other authorities agree. G. S. Miller (1919) based his belief on the fact that skulls and teeth of various breeds of domestic dogs retain certain characteristics of those of wolves. Scott was most impressed by the strong similarities in the behavior patterns of wolves and dogs.

There is a popular belief that some breeds of dogs descended from the wolf but that other breeds were derived from the jackal. This notion resulted from Konrad Lorenz's popular book *Man Meets Dog* (1955), in which the idea was promoted. However, Scott (1967: 377) discussed the problem as follows: "Wolves are highly social animals, as are dogs, whereas jackals are like coyotes, ordinarily forming groups no larger than a mated pair. Dog vocalizations and wolf vocalizations are very similar and include nothing like the complex vocalization patterns of the jackal. . . . The latter evidence convinced Lorenz, and he has withdrawn his hypothesis of jackal ancestry."

According to Lawrence (1967), "man's best friend" probably was domesticated at least twelve thousand years ago in the Near East from a small subspecies of wolf, possibly the extinct *Canis lupus variabilis* or the living *Canis lupus pallipes*. By about 8400 B.C. the domestic dog had already made its way to North America and spread as far south as Idaho.

Through thousands of years of selectively breeding mutants that cropped up in his dog colonies, man has encouraged tremendous diversity in this species, and today there are some eight hundred true-breeding types throughout the world (Fuller and DuBuis, 1962). Because the curly or sickle-shaped tail occurs universally in domestic dogs, Scott believed that domestication took place only once.

Subspecies of wolves. The wolf originally inhabited most of the Northern Hemisphere, and any animal with such a wide distribution could be expected to vary considerably from area to area. So it is with the wolf. Some authors have even thought that there might be several species of wolves.

However, Mivart, Pocock, and Goldman all believed that local variations among wolves justified ranking different geographic races as only separate subspecies. They even regarded both the Old and New World wolves as the same species. This judgment has gone unchallenged for many years and is well accepted at present.

Goldman (1944: 401) considered the following characters important in distinguishing wolves of one area from those of another: "Gross average size; general color, whether light or dark, plain grayish overlaid with black, or mixed with varying shades from pinkish buff to tawny; general form and massiveness of the skull, including height of brain case, frontal profile, posterior extension of inion, length of rostrum, and size of auditory bullae; size and relative length and breadth of molariform teeth."

Many of these characters are evident only when a wolf is examined closely. However, there are two major groups of wolves that can easily be told apart, the "tundra wolves" and the "timber wolves."

J. P. Kelsall (1968), who studied both types of wolves in the Great Slave Lake area of Canada's Northwest Territories, described the most striking differences between these wolves. Timber wolves, which normally live in forested areas, tend to be gray to black, whereas tundra wolves generally are light in color, although some are black. Timber wolves tend to have pointed ears instead of the more rounded ears of their tundra counterparts. Finally, the fur of timber wolves is shorter and much less luxuriant than that of tundra wolves.

When a population of wolves from one area differs substantially from populations of other areas, it is assigned to a separate *subspecies*. However, researchers in the field of animal classification, or taxonomy, have traditionally disagreed on what constitutes a significant difference. Thus some taxonomists tend to become "splitters"—recognizing many subspecies; others become "lumpers"—lumping several subspecies to form one and thus recognizing fewer subspecies. Wolf taxonomists are no exception.

Because I have neither the ability nor the desire to jump into this particular arena, the subspecies included in Figs. 7 and 8 and discussed in Appendix A are adopted strictly from the most complete publications on the subject. They are provided for convenience and do not imply that I in any way approve or disapprove of them as taxonomic entities.

Approximately thirty-two subspecies of wolves are currently recognized throughout the world, the exact number depending upon the particular authorities accepted (Appendix A). In North America, E. R. Hall and K. R. Kelson (1959) recognize twenty-four subspecies (Fig. 7).

An additional eight subspecies of wolves are known for Eurasia (Fig. 8), based on a composite of information from Pocock, Ellerman and Morrison-Scott, and Novikov.

Wherever subspecies meet, their characters tend to blend as a result of interbreeding, or intergradation, as it is known. Thus,

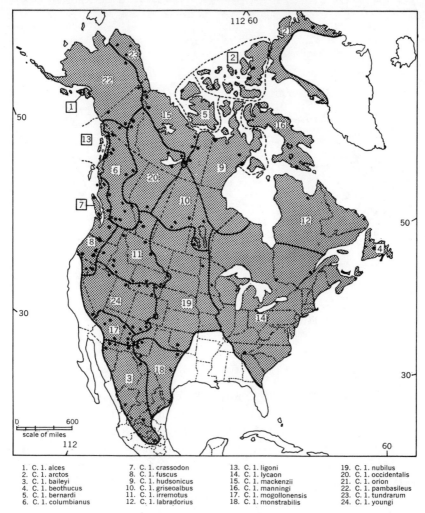

1. C. l. alces	7. C. l. crassodon	13. C. l. ligoni	19. C. l. nubilus
2. C. l. arctos	8. C. l. fuscus	14. C. l. lycaon	20. C. l. occidentalis
3. C. l. baileyi	9. C. l. hudsonicus	15. C. l. mackenzii	21. C. l. orion
4. C. l. beothucus	10. C. l. griseoalbus	16. C. l. manningi	22. C. l. pambasileus
5. C. l. bernardi	11. C. l. irremotus	17. C. l. mogollonensis	23. C. l. tundrarum
6. C. l. columbianus	12. C. l. labradorius	18. C. l. monstrabilis	24. C. l. youngi

FIGURE 7. Original distribution of subspecies of the wolf
(*Canis lupus*) in North America. (*Hall and Kelson,*
1959)

although Figs. 7 and 8 show well-defined boundaries for each
race, it must be understood that these are only arbitrary and that
there are no real boundaries unless they are geographic, e.g.,
islands. Kelsall emphasized this problem in his study of four
subspecies, whose arbitrary boundaries all meet on Great Slave
Lake in the Northwest Territories.

Distribution

The habitat of the wolf includes all Northern Hemisphere types
except tropical rain forests and arid deserts. Thus arctic tundra,

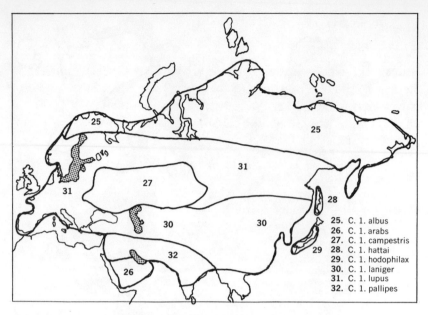

FIGURE 8. Original distribution of subspecies of the wolf
(*Canis lupus*) in Eurasia.

taiga, plains or steppes, savannahs, hardwood, softwood, and
mixed forest were all originally inhabited by the wolf.

The species at one time had an extensive range, occurring
throughout North America, Europe, Asia (including the Arabian
Peninsula), and Japan, with the exception of vast deserts and high
mountaintops in these regions. In North America, the wolf's range
extended southward to the southern end of the Mexican Plateau
below the twentieth parallel of north latitude (Goldman, 1944).
In Asia, the only area for which I find no information about
the wolf's presence is the Indochina Peninsula. Apparently the
species did not inhabit Africa (Mivart, 1890).

According to Goldman (1944: 389), "It seems doubtful
whether any other species of [wild] land mammal has exceeded
this geographic range, and this wolf may, therefore, be regarded
as the most highly developed living representative of an extraor-
dinarily successful mammalian family."

At present, the wolf's range is more restricted, particularly in
North America and Western Europe. Young traced its dwindling
range in North America, and two recent independent studies
(Cahalane, 1964; Aulerich, 1966) have outlined the present distribution of the species in North America (Fig. 9). Both show the
wolf present throughout Alaska and Canada, except for New

Brunswick, Nova Scotia, Prince Edward Island, Newfoundland, the more settled regions of Quebec and Ontario, and the southern halves of Manitoba and Saskatchewan. An estimated 17,000 to 28,000 or more wolves still inhabit Canada, and no more than 25,000 exist in Alaska.

The status of the wolf in the United States outside of Alaska

FIGURE 9. Present distribution and status of the wolf in North America. (*Modified from Cahalane, 1964*)

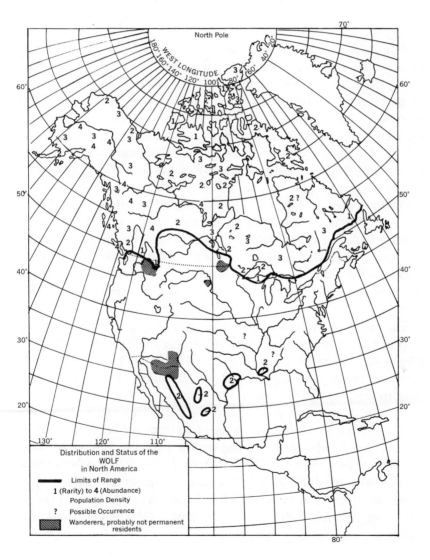

is much more precarious, however. The only substantial population left at present inhabits northern Minnesota. In and around the Superior National Forest a population estimated at from 350 to 700 animals (Cahalane, 1964), but possibly containing far less, lives in continual threat of a twenty-five to sixty dollar bounty and the invasions of the ubiquitous snowmobile. Another population exists in Isle Royale National Park in Lake Superior. A total of twenty-one to twenty-eight individuals live there under the protection of the National Park Service (Jordan *et al.*, 1967).

In all other areas of the country, excluding Alaska, the few wolves left no doubt will soon be gone. Perhaps some twelve to twenty wolves still remain on the northern Michigan mainland, but their numbers appear to be decreasing despite the repeal of the bounty and the institution of legal protection (Steuwer, 1968). The estimated fifty wolves that in 1955 were thought to remain in northern Wisconsin have since disappeared, even though legal protection was provided in 1957 (Keener, 1967). In northern Glacier National Park, a few wolves may be present (Martinka, 1967), but their numbers are thought to be static or decreasing (Cahalane, 1964). Recent records indicate that Yellowstone National Park may also harbor a few wolves (Cole, 1968).

On the basis of sight records and a wolf captured near Woodlake, California, in 1962, L. G. Ingles (1963) postulated that a small population of wolves might still inhabit the Sierra Nevadas. However, when the skull of the wolf specimen was examined in detail, the conclusion was reached that the animal was probably introduced from Korea or some other Asian country (McCullough, 1967).

The range of the red wolf once extended from eastern Texas to Georgia and Florida and northward through Oklahoma, Arkansas, Illinois, and parts of adjacent states (Goldman, 1944). By 1961, however, the animal was thought by McCarley (1962) to remain only in eastern and southern Louisiana.

Because McCarley's work was not generally known and because of the confusion about the identity of the red wolf, two later reports mistakenly gave the impression that the animal is more common than it really is. Vic Cahalane (1964), of the New York State Museum, stated that population estimates of the red wolf varied from 1800 to more than 5000; and R. J. Aulerich (1966) wrote that the red wolf occurred in Texas, Oklahoma, Louisiana. Arkansas, and possibly Missouri.

Nevertheless, later studies by Paradiso and by Pimlott and Joslin confirmed that the present range of the red wolf is extremely limited, and this conclusion resulted in the red wolf being declared an endangered species by the U. S. Department of the Interior.

Paradiso (1965) identified five animals trapped in southeastern Texas in 1964 as red wolves, and Pimlott and Joslin located fourteen red wolves there in 1965. The field work of the latter authors showed that small populations of red wolves exist in three isolated areas of Louisiana and in three counties in southeastern Texas. Nowak (1967) traced the decline of the red wolf in Louisiana, and Pimlott and Joslin summarized the present status and distribution of the animal.

In Mexico, the wolf is now restricted to three distinct areas: the Sierra Madre Occidental (about six hundred miles long), the mountains of western Coahuila and eastern Chihuahua, and the western portion of San Luis Potosí (Cahalane, 1964). The taking of wolves is now prohibited in all Mexican states except Sonora and Chihuahua, but the population is still declining and is in danger of extinction (Villa, 1968).

The present status and distribution of the wolf in Europe has been reported to me by Dr. Erkki Pulliainen, of the University of Helsinki. "In the east the range of the wolf covers almost all the suitable areas. In many parts of Eastern Europe wolves have been so numerous in the 1950's and 1960's that a great war against wolves has been started . . ." (Pulliainen, 1967a). According to Pulliainen, the increase is a result of the state's control of hunting in the Eastern bloc, which had been devoted primarily to the harvesting of furbearers and other economically important animals rather than to destroying wolves. The lack of intensive persecution of wolves plus the availability of large numbers of domestic animals allowed the wolves to multiply unchecked.

In Sweden, Norway, and Finland, approximately thirty wolves breed in the northern mountain area. Up to ten animals occur in the eastern frontier of Finland, some of which may wander to the southwestern part of the country. In Spain, Italy (including Sicily), Poland, and Czechoslovakia, wolves breed in the mountainous regions but sometimes travel into agricultural areas and even to cities such as Rome during severe winters. The wolves of Yugoslavia, Romania, Bulgaria, Albania, and Greece breed throughout the mountains, forests, and steppes, and serious efforts are being made to control them. Wandering wolves, probably from those countries, have recently been observed in Hungary, Austria, and East and West Germany. In the remainder of Europe, the wolf was exterminated in the 1800s.

Pulliainen (1967a) considered the wolf common in Asia. On the basis of his literature search, he stated the following: "The northern boundary of the wolf's range in Siberia approximately coincides with that of the reindeer, i.e., about 75° N. lat. In the south wolves are found in Syria, Israel, Irak, Persia, Arabia, Beluchistan, Afghanistan, India (not Ceylon), Tibet, Northern China, Mongolia, Manchuria, Korea and Japan [but see below]. This species occurs also in Kamchatka and the Isle of Sakhalin. In this vast area the wolf is not evenly distributed. In the Siberian taiga, for instance, there are large forest areas, where no wolves have ever been observed. The same concerns vast deserts and tops of mountains.

"In general it can be said that only small changes have taken place in the distribution of the wolf in Asia during the last century according to the literature available. Most of these changes have concerned numbers of wolves, not distributional boundaries."

According to Tsen Hwang Shaw (1962: 314), as translated for me by Dr. Ka Bun Chung of the University of Hong Kong, "In China [the] wolf is widely distributed in every province and district of China except Taiwan, Hainan [Island] of Kwongtung and the southern edge of Yuennan."

In Japan, however, the story is different. Although wolves did inhabit the islands of Hokkaido and Honshu, they were exterminated from Hokkaido in the late 1880s, and they have not been reported from Honshu since 1904 (Imaizumi and Hasegawa, 1967).

Ecological Niche

The role or "occupation" of a species in the living community of which it is part is referred to as the ecological niche of the species. The wolf's niche is that of *the* northern predator upon large mammals. Besides man and the wolf, the only other animals that regularly prey on large mammals in the Northern Hemisphere are the cats—mountain lions in North America, and tigers and leopards in Asia. Apparently these cats rarely reach the density and distribution that wolves may attain. It seems safe to state that by far most predation on large mammals in the Northern Hemisphere can be attributed to the wolf.

Adaptations for the role of the wolf as the major big-game predator in the Northern Hemisphere can be seen in all aspects of the animal's life. From the wolf's social nature and family life to its travels and methods of hunting, numerous specializations help make the creature superbly adapted to its role, and these will be examined in detail in the following chapters.

CHAPTER II / WOLF SOCIETY
—PACKS AND POPULATIONS

All animals that prey on large mammals either weigh about as much as their prey or they hunt in groups. For example, the lone hunters of big game, members of the cat family, range up to the 550 pounds of the tiger. On the other hand, African hunting dogs, weighing less than fifty pounds, run in packs of four to sixty and attack even such formidable prey as the lion (Walker *et al.,* 1964).

The wolf fits into the second category. It is a group hunter. In fact, the basic unit of wolf society is the pack—a group of individual wolves traveling, hunting, feeding, and resting together in a loose association, with bonds of attachment among all animals. As with the African hunting dog, group living in the wolf is associated with the tendency of wolves to prey primarily on animals much larger than themselves. Although a single wolf may be able to kill even adult moose and elk (Cowan, 1947), no doubt it is much safer, easier, and more reliable for several animals to do the job.

Hundreds of observations from several areas attest to the wolf's social nature (Table 2). In Alaska, 68% of 1500 sightings of wolves involved more than one animal. Of 112 observations in Minnesota, 58% were of two or more wolves. In Lapland and eastern Finland, the figures are 62% and 40% for 118 and 460 observations respectively.

When the actual number of wolves observed is considered, the percentages are even higher (Table 3). Of over 5000 wolves seen in Alaska, approximately 91% were in the company of at least one other wolf. In Minnesota, 85% of 318 wolves were observed in groups of two or more. Of 311 wolves seen in Lapland, and 984 in eastern Finland, 86% and 72% were in packs.

TABLE 2. Percentages of observations of wolves in groups of various sizes¹.

Number of Observations	1	2	3	4	5	6	7	8	9	10	11	12	13-21	Location	Authority
310	24	28	13	8	8	4	5	3	3	1	(1/310)	(1/103)	—	Alaska	Kelly, 1954
1268	34	14	12	6	8	8	5	3	3	2	(1/127)	(1/63)	2	Alaska	R. A. Rausch, 1967b
112	42	21	6	6	7	6	4	3	3			(1/112)	—	Minnesota	Stenlund, 1955
118	38	24	19	10	1		3			3	(1/118)	(1/118)	—	Lapland	Pulliainen, 1965
460	60	18	8	3	3	2	2	1	2	1	(1/230)	—	—	E. Finland	Pulliainen, 1965

¹ Because packs sometimes split into smaller groups, these figures are not entirely accurate. However, because splitting is usually only temporary, and the total number of observations included here is so large, the figures are believed to represent reasonably actual pack sizes.

TABLE 3. Percentages of wolves seen in groups of various sizes¹.

Number of Wolves	1	2	3	4	5	6	7	8	9	10	11	12	13-21	Location	Authority
1041	8	18	12	11	14	8	11	8	8	4	1	3	·	Alaska	Kelly, 1954
4823	9	8	9	7	11	12	9	7	7	6	2	5	9	Alaska	R. A. Rausch, 1967b
318	15	15	7	9	13	13	9	8	9		4	4	—	Minnesota	Stenlund, 1955
311	14	18	21	15	2		9			13	4	4	—	Lapland	Pulliainen, 1965
984	28	16	12	6	7	6	6	5	8	4	2	—	—	E. Finland	Pulliainen, 1965

¹ Because packs sometimes split into smaller groups, these figures are not entirely accurate. However, because splitting is usually only temporary, and the total number of observations included here is so large, the figures are believed to represent reasonably actual pack sizes.

Pack Size

The number of wolves in a pack varies greatly. Excluding reports based on track counts or hearsay, the highest reliably recorded number of wolves per pack is thirty-six, reported from south-central Alaska by Robert A. Rausch (1967a). Unusually large packs of twenty and twenty-one have also been observed in Alaska, and a group of fifteen to twenty-two (Fig. 10) was recorded from Isle Royale in Lake Superior (Jordan *et al.*, 1967). On Isle Royale, I followed this pack for several weeks during the winters of 1958–59 through 1960–61 when it contained fifteen to sixteen animals. It was spectacular indeed to see such a number of wolves crossing the snow-covered ridges of that island wilderness.

Because pack sizes vary so much, it is hard to say what the usual number of wolves in a pack might be. R. A. Rausch recorded 1357 sightings of packs of two or more wolves in Alaska over a six-year period. He also reported the percentage of wolves seen in packs of eight or more in several regions each year. The unweighted average of twenty-four such figures was 28%, which shows that most wolves were assembled into groups of seven or less. The same is true for wolf packs in other areas (Table 3). In addition to these figures, records from the U.S.S.R. (Makridin, 1962), British Columbia (Cowan, 1947), and Wood Buffalo National Park in Canada (Fuller and Novakowski, 1955) also bear this out.

Rausch believed that the average size of packs in an area is an index to the abundance of wolves. He reasoned that if a pack is made up of adult wolves and their pups or merely of individuals meeting by chance, a large pack would mean either a high production of pups or many chance meetings of individuals. Whichever is the case, this in turn would indicate a high population. Rausch's statistical analysis of pack-size differences and wolf densities in various areas in Alaska supports his idea.

Possible limits on pack size. Within any area, variations in pack sizes can be explained by differences in such factors as mortality and reproductive rates. However, the factors that regulate the limits within which pack sizes vary are not yet known. Why, for instance, do wolf packs generally contain two to eight members instead of sixty?

FIGURE 10. This large pack of wolves in Isle Royale National Park, (Lake Superior) is the largest pack that has been intensively studied. (*William W. Dunmire, National Park Service photo*)

There appear to be four factors that might affect pack size: (1) the smallest number of wolves required to locate and kill prey safely and efficiently, (2) the largest number that could feed effectively on prey (i.e., not all of a pack of sixty wolves could feed on a 150-pound deer), (3) the number of other pack members with which each wolf could form social bonds (the social-attachment factor), and (4) the amount of social competition that each member of a pack could accept (the social-competition factor).

The fact that wolves do live in packs and kill prey much larger than themselves suggests that the first factor is operating. No doubt during the evolution of packs the ancestors of wolves that hunted together tended to survive longer and thus to produce more young with social tendencies than did the nonsocial ones. However, it appears that this factor operated only very generally because packs vary so much in size, and because large packs may not operate as efficiently as possible.

Evidence for the latter point comes from Isle Royale. There I spent sixty-eight hours watching a pack of fifteen wolves hunting moose. Seldom was the whole pack in on the kill; usually only five or six animals actually made contact with the prey. More individuals than this may have been important in helping locate, chase, or harass the moose, but I doubt that they provided two or three times the advantage over a smaller pack. In fact, this pack split up at times, and both smaller groups hunted very well. During this period each wolf even ate more than during the other periods. In addition, there was a pack of two and a pack of three wolves that often killed moose on the same island.

The second factor that could affect pack size was suggested by Murie (1944: 45). He stated that "a pack might be so large that, after the strongest members had finished feeding on a kill, there would be little or nothing left for the rest. In such a situation, hungry ones would go off to hunt again, and the strong ones, already fed, would remain where they were. There thus might result a natural division of a band which was too large to function advantageously for all its members."

This factor certainly would limit pack size if others did not. However, it appears that other factors do operate, for most packs contain fewer members than could feed on a single prey animal. If the capacity of a wolf's stomach is fifteen to nineteen pounds (Chapter VI), each of ten wolves could fill its stomach from one 150-pound deer. An 800-pound moose would provide a full meal for forty wolves. But, as shown above, packs of more than seven wolves are the exception (Table 3).

It appears that the above two factors could act only as secondary controls. Actual pack size must be regulated by the two social factors. As will be discussed later, wolves possess a high potential for forming social bonds, so the social-attachment factor would tend to increase the number of wolves in a pack. It probably accounts for the large packs that contain more members than necessary for efficient hunting and killing.

On the other hand, the larger the pack, the greater the competition would be for food, mates, leadership, or dominance

(Chapter III). When such competition reached a certain level, it probably would tend to disrupt pack organization to the point where the pack could not function efficiently; some members would be forced to leave. Apparently it is this social-competition factor that limits pack membership to less than the number of wolves that could feed effectively on a prey animal.

Another indication that pack size is regulated by social rather than food factors is the constancy of pack size (Table 3). There appears to be no substantial difference in the sizes of packs between areas where white-tailed deer are the primary prey (Minnesota) and areas where much larger animals such as moose are the main food source (Alaska).

Pack splitting. Although a pack usually operates as a unit, sometimes members do split off temporarily, or the entire pack may break into smaller groups. B. L. Burkholder (1959) followed a pack of ten Alaskan wolves that sometimes split into groups of nine and one and at other times into seven and three. Murie also observed packs breaking up into various combinations while hunting. Probably the best documentation of pack splitting is from the Isle Royale studies. P. A. Jordan *et al.* presented eight years' data on a pack numbering from fourteen to twenty-one animals over the years. This group split into such combinations as ten and five; thirteen and three; seven, seven, and one; and several others. Once the pack broke into four subgroups.

I made the first three years of observations in the Isle Royale studies and often watched the pack of fifteen to sixteen wolves split into smaller packs (Mech, 1966a). During 1959 and 1960 these divisions lasted only a few hours or days. However, in 1961, the group was split on thirteen of the twenty-five days that I saw it, usually into five and ten or seven and eight. When the pack divided, both groups used the same routes and ranges that they did when together. Jordan found the pack divided for at least eight consecutive days in 1965.

Although most wolves belong to packs, from 8 to 28% of the wolves observed in various studies were single animals (Table 3). Probably many of these were individuals temporarily straying from packs, but no doubt certain of them were truly "lone wolves." Just why some individuals do not associate with other wolves is not known, but there are a few ideas on the subject. Young (1944:

105) believed the following: "The lone wolf in the wild is generally an old male, but sometimes an old female that has lost its mate. When this occurs, old males or females seldom mate again or participate in group hunting forays. Such wolves hunt singly and stay much by themselves. Occasionally an individual becomes a lone wolf because great wear of its teeth prevent it from joining in teamwork with other wolves in obtaining food." However, no evidence is offered for these claims.

Another idea about the origin of lone wolves is offered by Jordan *et al*. Ever since the beginning of the Isle Royale studies, single wolves have been seen following the island's main pack. These are assumed to be old or socially subordinate individuals formerly belonging to the pack but now accepted very little. Such an animal remains about one hundred yards behind the pack and rests separately from the group. It cowers upon approaching the pack and is sometimes chased and attacked by some members of the group. Probably it feeds on kills only after the main pack has gorged and gone off to an open ridge or frozen lake to rest. It could then eat a full meal without harassment.

Eventually such an animal might fall far enough behind the pack to become one of the lone wolves often seen following a day or two behind the pack. During this stage, the loner would find little more than well-chewed bones and hide on which to survive. Since a scavenger like this is usually ten or fifteen miles from the main pack, it can truly be considered a lone wolf.

Pack Composition and Formation

The wolf pack as a social group has interested many people, and studies of both captive and wild packs have produced information about these groups. Captivity studies have emphasized social behavior, which will be discussed in Chapter III. Field studies have involved observing packs at dens, following packs by aircraft, and determining the age, sex, and reproductive condition of pack members. Nevertheless, no one has yet been able to observe identifiable individuals of free-ranging packs over a period of several years. Thus little is known about the origin of various pack members or of the formation of new packs.

Much of our present knowledge of wolf-pack behavior seems conflicting. For example, generally packs have been thought to contain a breeding pair of wolves and their pups; yet many packs include several adult wolves in breeding condition. Packs have been seen chasing and threatening alien wolves; yet at least one case is known where two females raised their young together. Even more baffling are observations where one group of wolves meets another group and the first accepts one member of the second group but chases another member.

However, there is at least one concept of the composition and formation of wolf packs that does fit all the information and contradicts none of it. Before this theory can be presented, certain basic facts about wolves and packs must be outlined:

1. Populations of wolves consist of packs occupying adjacent and sometimes overlapping regions of the range.

2. Most packs contain less than eight members (Table 2).

3. Wolves bear an average of six young per litter (Chapter IV).

4. Wolves become sexually mature at twenty-two months (Chapter IV).

5. Temporary associations of two or more packs sometimes occur, forming very large groups, although this is rare (Murie, 1944).

6. Several instances are known of packs chasing nonmembers.

7. In some cases, a pack has accepted one member of a different group and rejected another member (Shelton, 1966; Jordan *et al.,* 1967).

8. Strong bonds are needed to hold a pack together; if there were no bonds, each wolf would go its separate way.

9. Most packs include a pair of breeding adults, pups, and extra adults that may also breed.

Most of the above facts either have been discussed or will be in later sections. However, the last two, concerning social bonding and age and sex composition of the pack, require more detail before a theory of pack formation can be developed.

Social bonding. The existence of social bonds within a wolf pack is evident from the fact that the members remain together in a pack. The strength, permanence, and nature of the bonds were touched upon in the first chapter and will be described in more detail below. Very briefly, the wolf's bonds to other members of its pack seem to be about the same as a dog's bond to its master.

Indeed, it is this very trait of the wolf that has remained in the dog and made that animal "man's best friend." In the wolf, as in the dog, this bond seems to approach what might be called in man an "affectional tie."

The formation of strong bonds between animals probably would require both a psychological tendency for attachment within each individual and a long period of contact between individuals. I know of only three types of common relationships between wolves in which both these conditions are met: (1) the courtship and mating of a mature male and female, (2) the raising of a litter of young by adults, and (3) the growing and developing of the young in the company of their littermates.

A fourth type of situation might also meet these requirements, but more wolf psychology must be known before this could be established. This would be a case where all pack members with which an animal maintains social bonds are killed. Such conditions might create a need for a new attachment, and if two wolves with similar needs were to meet, regardless of age or sex, they might partly restore their previous psychosocial state by becoming emotionally attached to each other.

Some details about the nature of the attachment process have been uncovered recently by the work of Woolpy and Ginsburg. The experiments of these biologists in socializing wolves were described in Chapter I. Although this work involved the building of positive social relations between wolves and men, the results probably would also apply to the formation of bonds between wolves. Just as an adult wolf and a human being must interact for a long period before the wolf becomes socialized to the human, so too must two strange wolves interact before they accept one another (Woolpy and Ginsburg, 1967). The main element in both types of relations is the overcoming of fear (Chapter I).

Woolpy and Ginsburg found that it is easy to establish friendly relations with wolf pups less than twelve weeks old. After that age, however, it becomes increasingly harder. A fully adult wolf requires six months of training, whereas pups less than eight weeks old make positive responses upon the first contact. On the other hand, young pups easily lose their positive feelings for others unless they are continually reinforced. Adults seem to retain these feelings, once fully acquired, without further reinforcement.

In the wolf's natural way of life, these behavioral changes can be seen as provisions for maintaining the pack. As will be discussed below, the pups are in constant contact with each other from birth, and with adult pack members from about their twentieth day of life. Thus social attachments can be made and strengthened among the pups and between the pups and all other members of the pack. Soon after the pups leave the den (eight to ten weeks of age) and chance meeting strange wolves, however, their ability to form social attachments begins to decrease. By the time the pups are traveling with the pack (about seven months of age), their ability to form new psychological ties, without the forced training of experimental conditions, is almost nil.

The one type of situation in which two strange adult wolves might form bonds is in mating. The psychological tendency to form a social attachment in this case would, of course, be the sexual desires of the mature animal. The prolonged period of social contact would be the period of courtship. In this respect, two peculiarities of wolf courtship and mating may be important.

The first peculiarity in the sex life of the wolf is the unusually long courtship. Lois Crisler (1958) claimed that wolves begin choosing mates when one year old, even though they do not actually breed until about twenty-two months of age. She described how a male yearling wolf of hers was courted by a female wild wolf; the wild wolf (of unknown age) eventually killed the tame wolf's fourteen-month-old female littermate. Evidently some degree of sexual rivalry and attraction is present in wolves of this young age.

Young found that vaginal blood may appear in the wolf forty-five days before the end of the animal's heat period, again an unusually long time. Scott (1950: 1017) commented on "the comparatively long period of heat in the female, usually including a week or more of preliminary behavior and approximately two weeks of receptivity," and Murie recorded a similar observation. It is easy to imagine that such a long period of contact between animals in such an intense physiological state could produce lasting social ties.

The second peculiarity in wolf breeding is the "copulatory tie." The male and female become physically fastened back-to-back during sexual intercourse for as much as a half hour and cannot break the tie (Chapter IV). The function of this tie has baffled animal behaviorists.

It is possible, however, that the copulatory tie helps fix the social bonding that begins with less intimate contact during courtship. As will be shown below, during each of the other two social-bonding situations, there is a long history of physical contact between the wolves forming the bonds. Perhaps several copulatory ties during the heat period would substitute for the more prolonged, less intense contact of the other bonding situations.

Whatever the psychological mechanism of bonding may be, it produces a strong tie, which lasts for a long period, perhaps even for the life of the pair. Murie observed two wolves that mated with each other two years in a row, even though other mature animals were available in the pack. In captive wolves, a high degree of preference by both males and females for the same mates each year has been shown (Chapter IV). Young recounted an episode in which a male wolf had been trapped and his mate had returned for sixteen nights to his capture point until she herself was trapped there.

The second type of common relationship between wolves in which the two conditions for forming social bonds are met occurs between pups and the adults that raise them. This relationship will be described in detail in Chapter IV. Here it is only necessary to stress that both physiological need and physical contact pervade the relationship. During the pups' first few weeks of life their hunger is satisfied only when they contact their mother's teats. Later the pups obtain predigested food by touching their mouths to the lips of adult wolves. This stimulates the adult to regurgitate a load of meat for them.

It is important to note that the pups are fed in this manner not only by their parents but also *by other adult members of the pack.* Contact with other adult wolves also occurs when the pups play. Murie (1944: 30) described such activity: "The two gray males often sniffed at the pups, which frequently crawled over all five wolves in their play." Communal care even includes "baby-sitting." On three occasions, Murie observed a "foster" mother staying with the pups while the actual mother joined the other wolves on their hunt. Thus it is clear that conditions exist for the formation of social bonds not only between the mother and the pups but between every member of the pack and the pups.

Scott (1967: 375) recognized this "socialization period" as very important in the development of wolf pups and stated that "the unique behavior in this period is associated with the formation of emotional attachments to places and individuals." He believed that the chief mechanism in bond formation is a two-step process. First, the pups become distressed when away from familiar individuals. Second, the cries of the distressed pups bring the adults, and the pups then connect the relieving of their discomfort with the presence of the adults.

The strength of the parent-pup bond can be seen in the behavior of the mother wolf that stayed close to Professor Parmelee, who had taken her pups, as related in Chapter I. Observations by Murie also show the strength of this bond. He removed a one-week-old pup from a den in Alaska on May 15, 1940, and began raising it, keeping the animal chained behind his cabin. "On August 11, at 7 o'clock in the evening, the wolf pup was heard whining softly. On looking out I saw the black female only a few yards from the pup. The following evening at 8 o'clock I heard the pup whining again and saw the black female with it. She traveled slowly and reluctantly up the slope, looking back repeatedly. The pup tried to follow and when it reached the end of the chain, kept jumping forward to be away" (Murie, 1944: 47).

The third type of wolf relationship that might establish strong social bonds occurs as pups develop in the company of their littermates. In this relationship, the long period of both social and physical contact begins at birth and continues for as long as littermates remain together. During the first three weeks, the pups stay in the den, where they are in almost constant contact with each other. According to Scott (1967: 375), their only movement at this time is a slow crawl, and "an isolated puppy will continue this crawl until he touches some warm object, which may be the mother's body or the bodies of littermates."

Members of the litter thus stay in close contact throughout this period. The psychological tendency to form bonds during this relationship results from the mere desire for physical contact and warmth that is apparent in the young of almost all mammals. As the pups grow older, physical contact continues during play and eventually occurs daily among all members of a pack as they feed and perform various rituals to be described later. No doubt such contact helps strengthen the bonds already formed among pack members.

The nature of the littermate bond can be seen in incidents described by Crisler and by George B. Rabb *et al.* One of Crisler's tame but free-ranging wolves, a male almost a year old, found a frozen ptarmigan and began eating it, while his littermate watched hungrily. "But presently, when he had eaten over half of the bird, he rose, carried the carcass and laid it a foot from Lady's nose. Then he waited beside it, in order to snap, once only, as she delicately took it" (Crisler, 1958: 192). The male wolf also presented his littermate with a squirrel one day when she was sick.

Such "filial bonds" or "bonds of allegiance" were also reported in a group of captive wolves at the Brookfield Zoo, in Illinois. Often when a male is tied in sexual intercourse, other males will attack him, but in the Brookfield Zoo certain males defend certain others from such attacks. For example, Male 3 always sided with Male 1, protecting him from attack while in tie. Likewise, Male 4 and Male 5 shielded Male 2 at such times (Rabb *et al.*, 1967).

If there are any common situations in which social bonds could develop other than the three discussed above and the possible fourth mentioned earlier, it is difficult to imagine what they would be. Indeed, formation of emotional attachments between unrelated adult wolves, except in sexual pairing, would seem to be prevented by the intolerance often shown strange wolves (Murie, 1944; Mech, 1966a) and by the strong bonds already existing among wolves within their own families or packs.

Sex and age composition of the pack. Wolf packs apparently are groups of related individuals. S. F. Olson (1938) asserted that a pack was a family group, and by long-term observation of identifiable animals in Alaska, Murie showed that pups did join their parents in becoming part of the pack.

Many packs include more than just a breeding pair and their latest pups, however, as the following reports show. (Since yearling wolves are about the same size as adults, they cannot be told apart from adults in the field. Thus some of the following reports of "adults" may actually involve yearlings.)

Of six packs examined in Wood Buffalo National Park, Canada, five contained at least one "adult" besides the breeding pair and its pups (Fuller and Novakowski, 1955). In one pack there were two mature males, two mature females, and one aged female, plus the pups. In Alaska, six of sixteen packs examined included extra "adults," one pack consisting of three pups, two adult males, one pregnant female, two previously pregnant females, and one maturing female (R. A. Rausch, 1967a). Murie observed five "adults" traveling with a breeding pair of wolves and their pups. Joslin (1967) studied a pack of pups and eight "adults" and a pack of six "adults" plus pups. On Isle Royale, I saw at least three sexually mature females in a pack of fifteen.

Little is known about the sex ratios within wolf packs. The only area in which several complete packs have been examined is Alaska (R. A. Rausch, 1967a). Generally it appears that in packs from that area the sex ratio is even, with the possible exception that in pups there may be an excess of males.

Unfortunately very little information is available on the sex ratio in wolf litters either before or shortly after birth. Five pups found in a den in northern Alaska included three females and two males (Crisler, 1958), as did a litter of five taken from northern Ontario (Rutter and Pimlott, 1968). In northeastern Minnesota a litter of pups taken in 1969 contained five males and a female. Of six pups born to a pair of wolves in the St. Paul Zoo in 1967, five were males. In 1968 this pair produced a litter of seven males, and in 1969, six males and one female.

A theory of pack formation. If the concepts of social bonding developed above are correct, there can be little doubt that almost all regular members of most packs are related. The only exception would be one of the mates of the original breeding pair, which could have come from another pack.

A theory of pack formation can now be presented that is consistent with present knowledge of pack composition and behavior, and that explains certain conflicting observations.

The most basic element in a wolf pack is the breeding pair. At least one mature male and female or their pups were present in all of the sixteen packs examined from Alaska and six packs from Wood Buffalo National Park. It seems probable, then, that a pack is formed by the mating of a male and female in late winter, and that it is enlarged by their first litter, containing about six pups. The pups do not even begin traveling with the adults until late fall (Chapter IV), so, to learn to hunt, they must stay with the adults at least through their first winter.

Because wolves do not mature until almost two years old, there would be no sexual conflicts during the next breeding season, when the original pair would mate again. Thus, this probably is not the time when the pups disperse. The packs examined in Alaska and Canada that included both pups and pregnant adults support this idea.

In some mammals, notably the deer family, the young are forced on their own by the threats of their dam when they are a year old and she is about to bear young again. The same pattern might also apply to wolves, and some of Murie's observations at the East Fork River Den would support this view. None of the pups from 1940 were seen at the den in May and June of 1941, although they were observed with the parents on March 17, 1941, and were seen within two miles of the den in mid-May. However, Murie ended his study in early August, and the 1940 young could have rejoined the pack after he left. (In 1940 two extra adult-sized animals had joined the breeding pair in late July.)

Since it was shown above that breeding pairs tolerate even two-year-old wolves, and are often found in their company, it does not seem likely that they become intolerant of their one-year-old offspring at this time. Perhaps some yearlings do wander off temporarily while the parents are caring for their newborn young. However, the most likely explanation of the extra adult-sized wolves at Murie's dens in 1940 and Joslin's (1966) Ontario dens is that these animals were yearlings and related offspring from previous years. If they were not, it would be difficult to explain how they suddenly formed bonds with the mated pair, in view of our present knowledge of wolf psychology.

The same reasoning also applies in explaining the extra adults observed in winter packs of wolves. They probably are primarily the twenty-two-month-old young. In other words, the newly formed pack, two years after the mating of the original pair, would include this pair, their latest pups, and their young of the first year. If both litters were of average size and there were no mortality, the pack could then include fourteen animals. Mortality in either litter could lower the membership to the usual pack size of seven or less. Better survival could account for the larger packs of ten to fifteen sometimes observed.

At this time, the mechanism would exist for the breakup of the group. The young of the first year would have matured and would be seeking mates. There could be rivalry for the original female or for the female littermates, or there could be a desire to seek out new companions from other packs. Whatever the case, old social bonds could be broken by strong rivalry, or by the establishment of intense sexual bonds with strange wolves, and the pack-formation circle would be completed. Young believed that the twenty-two-month-old young remained with the pack until this time and then left.

However, littermate matings as discussed in Chapter IV might be the rule in most packs, especially where wolves are heavily exploited. If so, the newly matured individuals would not need to mate with strange wolves, and the integrity of the pack could continue. In fact, this would be the most likely explanation for R. A. Rausch's 1967a report of four sexually mature females in one pack and two pregnant females in each of three packs.

The next stage at which the pack might break up is during the next denning period—three or four weeks before the birth of the original pair's third litter of pups. Each mated pair might separate from the pack, dig its own den, and raise its own young. This new emotional situation would create strong new bonds and might help break the old ones. It might not actually cause ill feelings between former packmates, but the need of the new pair to care for its own pups could lessen the contact between the pair and other pack members. With a decrease in contact could come a weakening of old bonds.

When the new pair went afield with its pups and met its former pack, no doubt the old bonds would be remembered, and the two packs might travel together temporarily. But the new pack would have established its own travel routes and hunting areas, and during a food shortage might again go its separate way.

Unless there were frequent contact between packs over a long period, strong bonds probably would not develop between the pups of the new pair and members of the old pack. If the new pair moved to another region, there might never be any contact between their pups and their former pack. In either case, when the pups matured they would be strangers, or at least not close allies, to members of their parents' former pack, and probably would be considered rivals. A chance meeting of the old pack and the new might then result in the acceptance by the old pack of their former associates but a rejection of the latter's sexually mature offspring. In one more generation, two packs could exist that had had the same ancestors and were closely related genetically but whose members were complete strangers to each other's pack. A meeting of these two groups could bring antagonism.

On the other hand, under some conditions the new pair might not have to move far to produce its own litter. In this case, there would be frequent contact between packs and perhaps even a merging into one large pack. This actually happened in Mount McKinley Park with Murie's East Fork River Pack. In that case, two adult females belonging to the same pack in 1940, and both caring for the young in 1940, denned separately for a few weeks in 1941, but one brought her litter to the other's den in late June. They stayed together at least until August 3.

If communal denning occurs very often, however, most of the young must die or the litters must separate before winter, for such double litters or large packs are rare. Probably communal denning is rare; in most cases the pairs probably separate before denning, each forming a new pack.

The above detailing of a theory of wolf pack formation uses a hypothetical pack under ideal conditions. In most wolf populations, there may be so much mortality in each litter that by maturity wolves may have few littermates left. This would explain why most packs in winter contain fewer than eight members, many of which are adults. If all six young survived very often, there would be many more packs of about fourteen, or many packs of six pups and two adults. Instead only about one in one hundred packs contains even as many as twelve members (Table 2), and the average number of pups in the sixteen Alaskan packs examined in winter was 1.5, with a maximum of four (R. A. Rausch, 1967a).

Nevertheless, the basic concepts presented above are meant to apply to real populations. These concepts do not contradict any information that I know of, and explain many previously puzzling observations. Basically, the theory is a development and extension of the idea proposed by Young that the wolf pack includes the mated pair and their immature young. Schenkel (1947) also considered Young's idea but seemed more inclined to accept Mivart's (1890) proposal that young wolves become independent during their first fall or winter. Such a view now seems untenable in face of the evidence presented above.

Of course, there could be other ways that new wolf packs could be formed, and one of these is discussed on p. 70.

Seasonal history of the pack. The largest packs of wolves are usually seen in winter, whereas summer observations often are of smaller groups and lone wolves. Because of this, it has been thought that pack formation begins in early winter (Schenkel, 1947; Pulliainen, 1965). This idea is true in a sense, but it should *not* be taken to mean that, in late fall, groups of unrelated or strange wolves suddenly gather for the first time. There are three main reasons for the larger packs seen in winter: (1) the conditions for observation are best during that season, (2) the pups are then afield with the rest of the pack, and (3) the pack wanders a great deal at that time, so its social center, where most of its members gather, is not the den, as it is in summer, but rather it is the traveling pack itself.

There have now been enough summer sightings of wolves to prove that large packs exist year round and that social ties bind wolves together during all seasons. Observations cited previously of several adult-sized wolves associated with dens during summer show this. Packs of pups and several adults have also been seen afield together throughout summer (Murie, 1944).

On Isle Royale, I found indications of five wolves together in May and August and six in July (Mech, 1966a), and Philip C. Shelton (1966) reported sightings of a pack of at least seven wolves and another group of fifteen or twenty in August. He also counted a minimum of eleven wolves together in mid-November as he hid for two hours within one hundred yards of the resting and playing animals. Jordan *et al.* reported a pack of fifteen wolves seen on Isle Royale in October, and they tabulated all the records of wolf packs observed on the island during the nonwinter months.

Summer sightings of lone wolves or groups smaller than the winter packs in the same area do not really mean that larger packs break up at this time. As discussed previously, even winter packs split frequently. In summer, wolves could temporarily wander away from the den in smaller groups without disrupting the pack because they could always find each other upon return to the den. If these smaller groups were seen, it would appear that a seasonal breakup of a larger pack had occurred, whereas the split might have been no more significant socially than those seen in winter. In this respect, Murie's (1944: 45) observations at a den are important: "Although the East Fork wolves often traveled together, at other times they traveled singly or in various combinations. Quite often a member went off alone for a time but rejoined the band daily, so far as I could tell."

The social bonding of wolves, then, and the unity of the pack remains the same year round. In fall, the pups leave the temporary resting areas of the summer (Chapter IV) and begin traveling with the pack. Other pack members that had split off temporarily for hunting expeditions probably would also tend to stay with the group when the summer headquarters were abandoned. Once winter begins, the traveling packs, including pups and possibly several adults, can be tracked and followed, so the impression may be gained that a great pack has suddenly formed.

If the above is true, one would expect a pack without pups to travel as widely in summer as in winter, since there would be no summer headquarters for the group. It is significant that on Isle Royale a pack of three wolves has been seen several times during summer throughout the same area used by presumably the same pack of three during several winters (Mech, 1966a).

Wolf Populations

In any extensive area of suitable wolf country there will be many packs of wolves making up the population. Just as individual wolves and packs have characteristics, so do populations, and a knowledge of these is of great importance in understanding the life of the wolf.

Sex ratios. Several authors have reported the sex ratios among wolves killed in various areas (Table 4). In seven of the sixteen reports, the ratios were within 3% of being even. However, it is interesting that, of the nine reports of ratios differing more than 3% from 50:50, seven are biased toward males. In the two others, the ratios were 41% males to 59% females, and 42% to 58%. The greatest bias is in the sample of eighteen wolves from Finland, where the ratio is 89% males to 11% females.

There is no ready explanation for the excess of males in certain areas. M. H. Stenlund (1955) found 64% males to 36% females in a sample of 156 wolves from Minnesota. He ruled out a bias in capture methods by considering the wolves shot from an aircraft separately from those captured in snares. Both samples showed the same percentage of extra males.

TABLE 4. Wolf sex ratios.

Location	Number	Per Cent Males	Per Cent Females	P[1]	Authority
Alaska	122	48	52	—	Kelly, 1954
Alaska (pups)	550	53	47	<.10	R. A. Rausch, 1967a
Alaska (adults)	712	50	50	—	R. A. Rausch, 1967a
Manitoba	162	59	41	<.02	Kelly, 1954
Saskatchewan and N. W. Territories	159	42	58	<.05	Kelly, 1954
N. W. Territories	57	50	50	—	Fuller and Novakowski, 1954
N. W. Territories	146	55	45	—	Kelsall, 1968
Minnesota	156	64	36	<.01	Stenlund, 1955
Lapland	25	64	36	—	Pulliainen, 1965
Finland[2]	47	72	28	<.01	Pulliainen, 1965
Finland[3]	49	47	53	—	Pulliainen, 1965
Finland[4]	18	89	11	<.01	Pulliainen, 1965
Soviet Union	39	50	50	—	Makridin, 1962
New Mexico	68	50	50	—	Ligon, 1917
British Columbia	25	60	40	—	Cowan, 1947
Soviet Union	133	41	59	<.05	Makridin, 1959

[1] Probability that the given sex ratio in the sample could have resulted from a small sample size alone, based on X^2 test. Only probabilities of .10 or less are given.
[2] The Savukoski-Kuhmo District.
[3] North Karelia.
[4] The remainder of Finland.

Disproportionate sex ratios could result merely from the birth of excess males, for, as seen on pp. 50–51, this sometimes occurs. Or the explanation may be that males are more hardy or aggressive and that in populations under such stress as a low food supply or a high density they survive better than females. Much more advanced methods of finding population densities, mortality rates, and causes of mortality will probably be necessary before the cause of this phenomenon can be learned.

Although the cause of the preponderance of males in certain areas is unknown, its effect can be estimated. For example, in the Minnesota figures there were twenty-eight extra males for every hundred wolves. Thus instead of fifty potentially breeding females per hundred animals, there would be only thirty-six, or 28% less than in areas where there is an even sex ratio. Therefore, it can be assumed that an excess of males is one factor helping to control certain wolf populations.

An especially interesting aspect of biased sex ratios was discovered in Finland when wolves began entering the country, from about 1954 to 1963. During the early years of the influx, almost all the wolves killed were males, but gradually the percentage of females increased until the sex ratio became even. The following was concluded (Pulliainen, 1965: 255): "From the present study it seems that in the wolf it is mainly the males that migrate, whilst in the breeding area and its vicinity the sex ratio is very near 1:1. In North Karelia it could be seen that as the breeding area of the species approached the frontier, the sex ratio came nearer the ratio 1:1." It is tempting to suggest that the immigrant males were excess animals that could not find mates in their native areas.

Age ratios, survival, and mortality rates. Some of the most important characteristics of a population are the survival and mortality rates of its members. These figures provide insight into the life of a species by giving clues about the type of mortality factors and the means of population control. Generally survival and mortality rates are derived from figures on the proportion of various age classes in a population.

To obtain such figures, one must be able to tell adult animals from pups, and with wolves this has been difficult. Wolf pups grow so quickly that in the field they look like adults by late fall, although recently there seems to have been some progress made on this problem (Jordan *et al.,* 1967).

Carcasses of wolf pups taken during winter have been separated from those of adults by two methods. The first involves the use of differences in weights and in the wear on the teeth. In Canada's Northwest Territories, W. A. Fuller and N. S. Novakowski (1955) found that male pups weighed less than eighty-five pounds, whereas adult males exceeded ninety; female pups usually weighed less than seventy pounds, and adult females more than seventy. In addition, the pups lacked wear on their molar teeth, retained the points on their incisors, and had relatively short, unworn canines. The teeth of the adults were just the opposite.

The second method is more objective. It involves an appraisal of the growing point of the wolf's lower leg—the junction of the long bone itself (diaphysis) and the cap (epiphysis) at the lower end of it. The long bone grows at this point, so a line of cartilage is present there until growth stops. According to R. A. Rausch, this occurs when the wolf is about twelve months old. After that time, the two sections of the bone are fused, and no line is apparent.

"The radius seems to be the best bone to work with, and the junction near its articulation with the foot remains open for the greatest period of time. The technique is simple, easy to use, and does not necessitate cleaning of the long bones" (R. A. Rausch, 1961).

Ages of wolves have now been studied in five regions, and they show an interesting contrast between populations under natural control and those exploited by man. In two areas of the Northwest Territories, studies began when most of the mortality was natural, but continued into periods when artificial control was being carried out. In Ontario's Algonquin Park, research was conducted under just the opposite conditions. In addition, an Alaskan and a Russian population were investigated while under moderate to heavy exploitation. Most of these studies were based on animals killed during winter in control programs. The pup-adult ratios derived from them are listed in Table 5.

TABLE 5. Pup-adult ratios[1] of wolves. (Numbers in parentheses indicate sample size.)

Location	Population history		Authority
	Natural Control	Exploited	
Algonquin Park			
(Ontario)	31:69 (106)[2]	35:65 (48)	Pimlott *et al.,* 1969
Wood Buffalo Park			Fuller, 1954; Fuller
(Northwest Territories)	20:80 (59)	55:45 (20)	and Novakowski, 1955
Great Slave Lake			
(Northwest Territories)	13:87 (136–381)[3]	73:27 (136)	Kelsall, 1968
Alaska	—	45:56 (4,150)	R. A. Rausch, 1967a
Soviet Union	—	50:50 (39)	Makridin, 1962

[1] Ratio of pups to all nonpups (including yearlings and adults).
[2] Ratio of pups-yearlings-true adults was 31:17:52.
[3] Size of sample was not provided, but it was between these extremes.

The most significant findings in the Northwest Territories were the differences in the percentage of pups between the period of natural control and the period of artificial control. In Wood Buffalo National Park, the pup percentage increased from 20%, when control was started during the winter of 1951–52, through 35% in 1952–53, to 55% in 1953–54.

Similar results were obtained in the Great Slave Lake area of the Northwest Territories. When extensive wolf control was begun in the winter of 1955–56, pups composed only 13% of the population. By 1957–58 they constituted 46%, and by 1960–61 they made up 73% of the population.

In the Ontario study, an additional age class was recognized. Wolves were classed as pups, yearlings (one to two years old), or adults. From 1957 to 1959 after a long period of wolf snaring by park rangers, the ratio of these ages in the catch was 35% pups-40% yearlings-25% adults (Pimlott *et al.*, 1969). Wolves were then protected in the park from 1959 to 1964, and in 1964 and 1965 the ratio had changed to 31%:17%:52%. In a sample of seventeen adult females, only 59% had borne young in their previous year, and the average litter size was 4.9 pups.

The most extensive of all the wolf population studies was R. A. Rausch's (1967a) Alaskan investigation. In most regions of this study, wolves had long been trapped and hunted from aircraft. Between 1959 and 1966, some 4150 animals taken by these means were examined for age. In addition, 593 females were classed as pups, yearlings (almost two years old), and adults. Studies were also made of the percentage of females breeding and the average litter sizes.

The results showed that pups composed from 37% to 48% of the total population each year, and averaged 44% for all seven years. A slight variation in age ratio was found between different sections of Alaska. For example, pups made up 38% to 65% of the population each year in the arctic region, and averaged 48% for a seven-year period, whereas they composed 39% to 60% per year, and averaged 43% for the interior region during the same period.

The 593 female carcasses were aged by the condition of the reproductive tracts, and it was found that there were 246 (42%) pups, 170 (29%) yearlings, 177 (30%) adults.

Of eighty-nine female adult and yearling wolves taken during or after the breeding season, 89% had bred. Litter sizes averaged 6.5 for adults, and 5.4 for yearlings.

From the results given above, much can be learned about wolf populations under both natural control and human exploitation. If the Ontario figures are any indication, it appears that under natural control as many as 40% of the adult females may fail to breed, and those that do breed bear fewer young. There is also a very low survival of pups from birth to the age of five to ten months. Survival rates for this period, calculated from figures in the literature, range from 6 to 43% (Table 6). From five to ten months to the age of seventeen to twenty-two months, the survival rate increases to 55%, and after this the annual rate of survival is about 80%. In other words, once a wolf survives its second winter, present indications are that each year it has an 80% chance of living for another year, assuming no human exploitation.

An analysis of the Ontario figures, the most detailed available for a population under natural control, is given in Table 7. This shows that the major natural controlling factors operate both in "dampening" reproduction (44% of the total mortality) and in lowering the survival of pups from birth to the age of about five months (32% of the total mortality). Together they account for 76% of the reduction in the potential population. The possible mechanisms involved in this control are discussed in Chapter XI.

Exploitation by humans, on the other hand, seems to stimulate both reproduction and survival of pups at least until their first

TABLE 6. Apparent survival rates[1] of wolves (in percent).

Age		Population History	
From	*To*	*Natural Control*	*Exploited*
Birth	5 to 10 mos.	6–13[2,3] 10–20[4,3] 43[6]	— 88[4,8] 28–56[3,6,8] 45–52[5,8]
5 to 10 mos.	17 to 22 mos.	55[6]	(100)[6] 69[5]
17 to 22 mos.	34 mos.[7]	78[6,7]	36[6,7] 50[5,7]

[1] Calculated from figures in the literature. Calculations in Appendix B.

[2] Great Slave Lake area of Northwest Territories (Kelsall, 1968).

[3] Lower rate assumes 100% of adult and twenty-two-month-old females breed and bear six pups each. Higher rate assumes 59% breed and bear five pups (see text).

[4] Wood Buffalo Park, Northwest Territories (Fuller, 1954; Fuller and Nova-kowski, 1955).

[5] Alaska (R. A. Rausch, 1967a).

[6] Algonquin Park, Ontario (Pimlott *et al.*, 1969).

[7] This is the average annual survival rate, which is assumed to be the same for all wolves over two years of age.

[8] Because exploitation does not take place until fall and winter, these rates represent natural survival of pups between the time of birth and the beginning of the period of exploitation (September to March). After this period these rates will decrease according to the degree of control. For example, in Alaska the survival rate of pups from the time of birth through their first year, after the animals are exploited, may be only half that indicated in the table for survival from birth to the age of five to ten months.

winter, when they are subjected to snaring, poisoning, or hunting. Figures calculated from the literature show natural survival rates of 20 to 88% for pups from birth to the period of exploitation (Table 6). From that time on, the survival rate depends on the degree of exploitation. The figures from Alaska suggest that, under the level of attempted control there, up to half of the surviving pups may be taken during the winter exploitation period, as well as half of the adults (Table 6). The more limited Ontario data imply that there may be almost 100% survival of wolves from the age of five to ten months to the age of seventeen to twenty-two months; from that age on, the annual survival rate is calculated to be 36%.

TABLE 7. Distribution by age class of the total mortality occurring in wolves under natural control[1] (no human exploitation).

Age Class	Number of Individuals	Per Cent Mortality to Next Age Class	Number Lost	Number Left	Distribution of Total Mortality by Age Class
Potential pups[2]	1,000[3]	44[4]	440	560	44
Pups born	560	57[5]	319	241	32
5 to 10 months[6]	241	45[7]	108	133	11
17 to 22 months[6]	133	(22)[8]	29	104	3
Over 22 months	104	100	104	—	(10)[9]

Total 100 Per Cent

[1] Based on Ontario figures showing an age ratio of 31% pups to 17% yearlings to 52% adults (Pimlott *et al.*, 1969).

[2] Assuming the maximum average reproductive potential for the species. Data from R. A. Rausch (1967a) show that under heavy exploitation about 90% of the females breed and bear an average of 5.4 pups per litter for two-year-olds and 6.5 pups per litter for mature adults. Assuming a 50:50 ratio of two-year-olds to adults gives an average litter size of six.

[3] Arbitrary starting population.

[4] This is the per cent difference between the number of pups that could be produced under the assumptions of Footnote 2 and the number that actually would be produced in the Ontario population under natural control, assuming that only about 60% of the females breed and bear an average of five pups per litter (Pimlott *et al.*, 1969).

[5] See Appendix B, p. 354.

[6] Age at which the sample was taken.

[7] See Appendix B, p. 354.

[8] This annual mortality rate probably remains constant each year after this age. See Appendix B, p. 354.

[9] This is the cumulative percentage of total mortality to all individuals over twenty-two months of age. It was obtained by taking the difference between 100% and the total percentage of mortality in the younger age classes.

The discrepancy between the Alaskan and the Ontario survival figures for wolves from five to ten months old to the age of seventeen to twenty-two months might be caused by the small sample size of the Ontario figures (forty-eight wolves). Or it might result from the differences in methods used to capture the wolves. In Alaska, many wolves are hunted from aircraft, a method that probably does not select for any particular age. In Ontario, however, the wolves were snared (Chapter XI). Possibly more adults would be taken by this method because they would tend to be at the head of the pack and thus would be first to tangle in snares.

Because not all the wolf studies have separated yearling wolves from the pups and adults, it is useful to examine the meanings of the ratios between the percentage of pups and the percentage of wolves older than pups (yearlings plus adults). These are called the pup-adult ratios.

In any relatively stable wolf population, the pup-adult ratio really measures the amount of mortality in that population between the time the ratio is taken and one year later. For example, if during December 30% of the wolves in a certain area are pups and the population is stable, this shows that from December to December 30% of the existing wolves die. Within the same year, that 30% is replaced by new pups. In increasing populations, the estimated mortality will be somewhat high; in those decreasing it will be too low. Nevertheless, this figure generally gives an adequate measure of reality.

Thus the pup-adult ratios from various areas are of considerable interest (Table 5). One can learn from them that in wolf populations under natural control the annual mortality (or "turnover") of animals at least five to ten months of age ranges from 13% to 31%. In populations subject to moderate or heavy exploitation, the annual turnover is about 50%, but it may vary from about 35% to 73%.

Wolf-kill figures from Alaska, where the pup-adult ratio is generally about 44%:56%, show a constant or increasing annual harvest (R. A. Rausch, 1967a). This means that despite the exploitation wolf numbers are maintaining themselves. However, in the Great Slave Lake area of the Northwest Territories, where the pup-adult ratio reached 73%:27%, the population was known to be declining. Thus it can be concluded that wolves can compensate (by increased reproduction and survival) for annual losses of 50% and possibly more to animals aged five to ten months or older. Further, in order to control wolf numbers, then, it appears that at least 50% of the animals of this age must be killed each year.

Population stability. From the above, it should be apparent that great increases can occur in wolf numbers. That such increases do take place under some conditions is evident from R. A. Rausch's studies of a special wolf-management unit in Alaska, Unit 13. From 1948 through 1954, a control program resulted in the death of over 200 wolves in this 20,000-square-mile area. By 1953, no more than twelve wolves were thought to be living in the area, and in 1955 the estimate was thirty-five (Atwell, 1963). Since 1957, wolves there have been protected from legal hunting, although considerable poaching has occurred.

In 1958 the wolf population in Unit 13 was estimated at 120 animals. No counts were made again until 1961 and 1962, when 100 to 125 and 145 to 160 were the estimates. The 1965 count showed 350 to 400 animals present, based on a complete census of half the area. These figures suggest that the average increase from 1955 to 1965 was about 20% per year. It is significant that this increase took place after the population had been reduced to just a few animals, and in spite of widespread poaching.

In populations that have not been reduced no such increases have been found. Apparently in most areas wolves are held in check despite their great potential to increase. The possible factors limiting wolf numbers will be discussed in Chapter XI. The important point here is that regulation of wolf numbers takes place whether or not human activities such as hunting or trapping cause the mortality.

The existence of natural control has been well demonstrated by figures from Isle Royale National Park, a 210-square-mile island in Lake Superior where wolves can be counted accurately every year. Wolves first reached Isle Royale about 1949, probably by crossing a fifteen-mile stretch of ice from Ontario (Mech, 1966a). Early estimates of wolf numbers there provided only minimum figures, but estimates since 1958 are accurate to within one or two animals.

During the eight years for which adequate figures have been available, the winter population has fluctuated between twenty and twenty-eight wolves (Table 8). This is a maximum variation of only 21% from the eight-year average of twenty-three animals. In five of the eight years, the population varied less than 9% from the eight-year mean. Because the island is a national park, the wolves are legally protected. Thus this remarkable population stability at a density of approximately one wolf per ten square miles must result from natural adjustment of the wolves to their limited food and space resources. (Emigration from the island is unlikely for several reasons [Mech, 1966a].)

Natural control has also been seen in a unique experiment carried out on an island in southeast Alaska. In the fall of 1960, two male and two female, nineteen-month-old wolves were placed on Coronation Island. This thirty-square-mile island also supports Sitka black-tailed deer, and numbers of harbor seals visit its shores. According to Harry R. Merriam (1964), who conducted the project, if all the mature wolves produced an average number of pups each year and they survived, ninety-one wolves could have been present by 1964. However, in that year he counted only seven to eleven yearlings and adults and two pups.

These examples of wolf populations that have stayed relatively stable despite a lack of human control both involved islands. However, natural regulation of wolf numbers has also been reported from a mainland area. During the intensive study in Algonquin Provincial Park, Ontario, Pimlott *et al.,* using aircraft found no substantial change in wolf numbers between 1959 and 1964, even though wolves were legally protected during most of that

TABLE 8. Size of Isle Royale wolf population.

Year	Minimum Number Present	Best Estimate	Authority
1952	2	—	Hakala, 1954
1953	4	—	Hakala, 1953
1956	14	—	Cole, 1956
1957	15	—	Cole, 1957
1959	19	20	Mech, 1966a; Jordan *et al.,* 1967
1960	19	22	Mech, 1966a; Jordan *et al.,* 1967
1961	20	22	Mech, 1966a; Jordan *et al.,* 1967
1962	22	23	Shelton, 1966
1963	20	20	Shelton, 1966
1964	25[1]	25[1]	Jordan *et al.,* 1967
1965	25	28	Jordan *et al.,* 1967
1966	21[2]	23[2]	Jordan *et al.,* 1967

[1] Plus one found dead.
[2] Plus two found dead.

period. It seems significant that this population also leveled off at a density of one wolf per ten square miles.

Densities. Reported wolf densities vary considerably from area to area. The highest density known is one wolf per three square miles on the thirty-square-mile Coronation Island, and the lowest density reported is one wolf per one hundred to two hundred square miles in Ontario (Table 9). Some of the variation could have been caused by differences in the methods of estimation, and some variation appears related to differences in size of the areas covered. In general, the smallest areas studied seemed to contain the highest densities, probably because of the better coverage possible on smaller areas. Two of the high density areas are islands from which emigration is unlikely, so the high wolf numbers there might be regarded as special cases.

However, even if only mainland areas were considered and if all census methods were standardized, there is no reason to believe that wolf densities would be found to be uniform from region to region. In most areas wolves usually depend on only one or two species of large mammals for their food (Chapter VI). Since numbers of prey animals may vary from one range to another and from time to time, wolf populations dependent on them could also be expected to vary greatly.

TABLE 9. Reported densities of wolf populations.

Location	Area (Square Miles)	Density (Square Miles per Wolf)	Authority
Northwest Territories	600,000	16	Clarke, 1940
Northwest Territories	480,000	60–120	Kelsall, 1957
Mount McKinley Park, Alaska	2,000	50	Murie, 1944
Western Canada	4,200	87–111 (10[1])	Cowan, 1947
Minnesota	4,100	17	Stenlund, 1955
Saskatchewan	—	40–83	Banfield, 1951
Isle Royale, Michigan	210	7–10	Mech, 1966a; Jordan *et al.*, 1967
Coronation Island, Alaska	30	3[2]	Merriam, 1964
Unit 13, Alaska	20,000	50[3]	R. A. Rausch, 1967a
Algonquin Park, Ontario	1,000	10	Pimlott *et al.*, 1969
Ontario	10,000	100–200	Pimlott *et al.*, 1969

[1] Range compressed in winter.
[2] Artificial situation; four wolves were stocked here.
[3] Increasing population perhaps not yet stabilized.

Pimlott (1967b) summarized and discussed much of the available data on wolf densities and concluded that one wolf per ten square miles is a high density and that "populations of a much lower density are common over very large areas."

CHAPTER III / SOCIAL ORDER, EXPRESSION, AND COMMUNICATION

One day I watched a long line of wolves heading along the frozen shoreline of Isle Royale, in Lake Superior. Suddenly they stopped and faced upwind toward a large moose. After a few seconds, the wolves assembled closely, wagged their tails, and touched noses. Then they started upwind single file toward the moose.

This incident vividly demonstrated the two factors that must exist for groups of animals to function efficiently: (1) a system of order, and (2) a system of communication that promotes that order. If schools of fish, flocks of birds, herds of caribou, families, tribes, and nations of men, or packs of wolves lacked order and communication, they could not survive. Indeed, it is doubtful that any animal could exist if these two traits were completely absent from its populations. In wolves both are highly developed.

Order in the Pack

Order in wolf packs results from a well-developed social system. This system establishes orderly relations among the members of each pack and provides the means by which activities of the entire pack—such as traveling, hunting, and resting—can be governed.

Social system. There are many ways that the social behavior of animals can be organized, but one of the best known social systems is based on the "peck order." First found in domestic chickens, this system involves a social "ladder" in which each member of a group occupies a certain rank or position. In competitive situations, the highest-ranking bird can peck every other member of the flock without retaliation. The second highest accepts pecking only by the highest member and in turn can peck all lower-ranking birds.

And so it goes right down the line. The peck order has also been found in many animals that show their dominance in ways other than pecking, so this system is now more generally known as a "dominance order."

The wolf's social system is based on such a dominance order, and was first studied in captive wolves by Rudolf Schenkel (1947), of the University of Basel. According to his research, there are two separate dominance orders within each pack, a male order and a female order. As in chickens, these are both lineal, i.e., if animal A is dominant to B, and B is dominant to C, then A is also dominant to C. There are few equals. The highest-ranking male is referred to as the "alpha male," and the top female is the "alpha female."

The original alpha animals in a pack would be the mated pair that produced the young of which the pack is composed. However, as will be discussed in Chapter IV, the alpha male may refrain from breeding at some point, and a lower-ranking male may mate with the alpha female. Nevertheless, the alpha male remains dominant and directs the activities of the entire pack.

Besides the alpha pair, there may be three other classes of wolves in well-established packs: (1) mature subordinate animals, (2) "outcasts" or "peripheral" wolves, which rank so low that they avoid the main pack members and stay near the fringes of the pack's social center, and (3) juveniles, which do not become part of the pack nucleus until their second year of age (Woolpy, 1968).

A wolf's social status may be established early in life. Pups begin "play fighting" with littermates when about three weeks old. In domestic dogs, and probably wolves too, this activity eventually results in the formation of an order of dominance among the littermates, the heaviest pups usually having the greatest advantage (Fuller and DuBuis, 1962). However, under certain conditions, social status can be determined in wolf pups as early as their thirtieth day of life after several days of serious fighting (Chapter IV).

Dominance orders cross sexual lines in immature animals and do not divide into male and female orders until sexual maturity. Even then, the alpha female may continue to dominate most of the males (Woolpy, 1968). Rabb *et al.* (1967) have evidence that female wolf pups when mature may assume a dominant attitude by imitating the actions of their mother toward other females.

As the mating season approaches, all interactions among pack members become more intense and frequent, including friendly contacts as well as conflicts and rivalries (Schenkel, 1947). At that time some status changes may take place, although the basic stability of the pack usually continues. Most conflicts, as severe as they may be, are solved through ritualistic threatening and fighting, and only occasionally does the fighting cause any injuries. In conflicts that do become serious, several animals often "gang up" on one of the wolves involved (Woolpy, 1968), a move that may force quick submission with a minimum of injury.

The older a pack is, the more stable its social structure probably becomes, for as more and more pups mature under a particular alpha male, the status of this male increases and becomes more secure (Woolpy, 1968). Presumably, then, when the alpha male dies, or grows too old or weak to keep his status, the resulting competition for the alpha position may disrupt the social stability of the pack. Since the new pack leader would have no history of "allegiance" from the other members, he may not be able to hold the whole pack together. This could cause the breakup of a large pack and may be important in the formation of new packs (also see Chapter II).

The dominance shown by the alpha animals and other high-ranking wolves can be described as a kind of forceful initiative. When a situation does not require initiative, dominance may not be shown; for example, when a pack is resting. However, when food, favored space, mates, strange wolves, or other stimuli are present, initiative can be seen in the actions of the dominant animals.

There are two aspects of dominance in a wolf pack, privilege and leadership (Schenkel, 1968). In competitive situations, dominance takes the form of privilege, the dominant animals showing the initiative and claiming whatever is desired. Most pack members do not even try to dispute such a claim, although two animals of close status may compete. When that happens, the higher-ranking animal strongly shows its dominance and discourages its competitor.

There do seem to be some exceptions to the dominance privileges, however. Upon the birth of young, a female normally subordinate to her mate may suddenly dominate him, as I observed in 1969 at the St. Paul Zoo. The bitch had just given birth to at least three pups in the corner of the cage when her mate of at least 3 years approached her. The female instantly charged him in a dominant posture, and the male ran off submissively in an attitude very rare for him.

Another important exception to the privilege "rules" of the dominance order involves individual ownership. At least in some cases, a subordinate wolf can prevent higher-ranking animals from taking food that it already possesses. There seems to be an "ownership zone" within about one foot of a wolf's mouth, and anything within that zone is beyond dispute.

Although I saw indications of this when raising wolves, an experiment that I conducted with a wolf pack in the St. Paul Zoo on January 18, 1968, showed it most dramatically. The pack included an adult male (A) who constantly asserted himself over all the other pack members; an adult female (B) who was mated to A; and two of their nine-month-old male pups. Both pups were subordinate to both adults, but one pup (C) was clearly dominant to the other (D).

The wolves were usually fed twice daily and always ate voraciously. For the experiment, food was withheld from them for seventy-two hours. After this period, a ten- to fifteen-pound piece of meat was placed into half of the wolves' cage from which they were temporarily barred. Then the small door between both halves of the cage was opened. Circumstances were such that Animal C was the first through the door and to the meat. He immediately grabbed the meat and dashed into the other half of the cage, with his packmates following excitedly.

For the next ten minutes, Animal C possessed the meat without dispute, although both A and B approached him several times and appeared intent on feeding. However, each time they came within a few feet of C, he threatened them severely, growling, fully baring his teeth, and even biting them about the head. These threats stopped the advances of the dominant wolves, and Animal C ate almost half the meat.

However, eventually Animal B caught C off guard at one point, rushed in, and snatched the meat. C instantly grabbed the other end, and this resulted in a free-for-all in which all four wolves participated. It appeared that once the ownership of the meat was no longer clear all wolves regardless of rank were inclined to compete for it. After only a few seconds of tugging, however, Animal C regained the meat. He then continued to feed relatively undisturbed.

After a few more minutes, I repeated the original procedure, placing two more ten-pound pieces of meat into half the cage. When the door was opened this time, Animal A rushed in, urinated on the meat, stood guard over it, and picked at it lightly. He ate very little, however, and soon stopped guarding it. The other wolves then began pulling the meat apart, hauling it around the cage, and feeding on it. Animal A again urinated on a piece, which the other wolves soon ate.

After Animal C had consumed about half of his original piece of meat, he began some very unusual behavior. He suddenly left his meat, started whining, and very submissively approached Animal A, defensively snapping at A's mouth. Animal A responded by severe growling, snapping, and biting, and C then rolled over in passive submission. However, he continued whining and snapping at the mouth of Animal A despite the severe response.

A few minutes later, Animal C in the presence of D approached B in the same manner. B immediately regurgitated, and both pups (C and D) instantly ate the two to three pounds of food (see Chapter IV). This occurred even though C had already eaten five to seven pounds of food and there was excess meat all around the cage.

Once more, C approached A as described above, and again A responded severely, but, as before, C actually appeared drawn to A anyway.

One possible explanation of these events is that, since C assumed dominance over the original piece of meat, he was later stimulated to "appease" the dominant animals by demonstrating his usual subordinate rank. The dominant wolves, A and B, then responded by strong reassertions of their positions. With A this meant showing his strong superiority; with the female B, it meant reasserting her more "patronizing" role as mother of the pups, which would explain the apparently symbolic regurgitation.

Whatever the correct interpretation of Animal C's behavior, it was clear that he was subordinate both before and after he had the meat. However, when he once possessed the meat, he became temporarily dominant to the others in relation to it. Not only was he aware of his dominance, but so were both A and B. Thus it appears that, regardless of rank, once a wolf actually possesses a piece of meat, it is his beyond dispute. Of course, further work is necessary to determine how generally this rule applies.

In most situations, the alpha animal would take any pieces of food available before there was a chance of dispute, as I have observed with this same pack, and as Rutter and Pimlott (1968) have reported. Presumably, in the wild, the alpha animal would have the privilege of taking over the choicest part of a large carcass, while the other wolves each pulled off separate pieces of less-desired meat for themselves.

Leadership. Besides privilege, the other aspect of dominance in wolves is leadership. This form of initiative probably is the more important of the two in the normal life of the pack, since co-operative ventures usually outnumber competitive ones. Obviously each wolf cannot make its own decision on which direction to travel, when to rest, and whether or no to chase prey. Some member of each pack must show initiative, and others must follow its lead.

Field observations confirm the existence of pack leaders. Murie's study of a pack of seven adults and five pups around a den in Alaska provided an excellent description of the leader of that pack. The animal was a male, the largest in the group, and he appeared to be "lord and master" of the pack. Murie (1944: 28) wrote: "The other wolves approached this one with some diffidence, usually cowering before him. He deigned to wag his tail only after the others had done so. He was also the dandy in appearance. When trotting off for a hunt his tail waved jauntily and there was a spring and sprightly spirit in his step."

During three winters of work on Isle Royale, I saw leadership in a pack of fifteen to sixteen wolves (Mech, 1966a). Unfortunately, unlike the wolves studied by Murie, most of the Isle Royale wolves lacked identifying markings, so I could not be sure that the wolf showing leadership was always the same individual. Leadership, in this case, is defined as the behavior of one wolf that obviously controls, governs, or directs the behavior of several others. This definition excludes situations where a pack may be filing along a regularly used trail; in such a case, it appears that any of several wolves may be at the head of the line.

Leadership was evident in the Isle Royale wolves when they were attacking moose, traveling overland, or waking from a long rest. When approaching moose, the wolves usually strung out in line behind the first wolf, which probably was the leader. As that animal began running, the others followed suit. During all aspects of the attack, the wolf at the head of the pack was the most aggressive. (Shelton [1966] also noticed this on Isle Royale, and I have seen the same situation in wolves attacking deer in Minnesota.) Sometimes the first wolf pursued or harassed a moose long after the others had given up. Once I saw the leader stop, lunge at the pack members behind, and force them to give up the chase (Mech, 1966a).

When the Isle Royale wolves traveled overland through deep snow, one wolf would break trail and still remain many yards ahead of the others, as though of superior strength and stamina. The whole pack rested when the first wolf did, and began to move again when this animal started.

After the wolves slept for long periods, leadership became evident in their waking activity. Usually one animal would arise, walk over to each of the others, and arouse them.

Although any highly motivated wolf can serve as a source of impulse to its packmates, it is the alpha male that is consistently the most highly motivated (Schenkel, 1968). The leader of the Mount McKinley pack that Murie studied was a male. In the Chicago Zoological Park, the pack leader has always been a male (Rabb et al., 1967), and such is also the·case in the St. Paul Zoo. On Isle Royale, the animal showing leadership in the main pack during 1959 through 1961 was usually a large animal, presumably a male. Jordan et al. (1967) believed they could identify a lighter-colored male as leader of this pack from 1964 through 1966. Although Pulliainen (1965) claimed that the leader of a wolf pack is usually a female, it appears that about the only time an alpha male can be dominated by a female is when she is caring for newborn young (Schönberner, 1965).

Although leadership usually involves directing pack activities, it also has a guarding function. It is the alpha male that takes the initiative in reacting to intrusions on the pack. One time in the St. Paul Zoo, when a spectator stuck his hand through the bars of the wolf cage and tried to pet a pup about six months old, the pack leader made one bound across the twelve-foot cage and grabbed the intruder's hand. In the Chicago Zoological Park, the alpha male patrols the edge of the pack's enclosure and escorts the keeper out of the pen (Ginsburg, 1965).

The guarding function of the leader has also been seen in the wild. Murie (1944) described an incident in which the leader of the pack he observed around a den, a black-mantled male, remained especially alert for about two hours one day and then suddenly led an attack on a strange wolf that approached. The leader also continued the attack after the rest of the pack returned to the den. On another occasion, this wolf and the father of the pack's pups were the most aggressive animals in attacking a grizzly bear that invaded the den area (Chapter X).

Wolf government. As stated above, any highly motivated wolf can affect the activity of its packmates, and in relaxed situations such as play, pack government seems to be a result of the impulses and motivation of various members (Schenkel, 1968). However, during the more important aspects of wolf life, such as traveling, hunting, feeding, and mating, the alpha male usually takes the initiative, with the rest of the pack following.

The exact way in which the alpha male guides and directs pack activities is not known. His leadership could be strictly autocratic, in which case all pack members would follow his example without protest. Or the leadership could be democratic, the alpha male taking his cue by noting the behavior of each pack member. For instance, under such a system, if the leader noticed that most members were acting tired, he might stop the pack activity and rest. A third possibility is that the leadership is some combination of both autocracy and democracy.

If wolf government is strictly autocratic, one would expect to see pack members always following the leader blindly. They would have no influence on him. If it is democratic, most of the pack members would be expected to contribute to some unknown decision-making process. Little independent initiative would be left to the leader.

Actual observations show that neither of the above extreme forms of government exists in wolf packs. Strict autocracy is ruled out by an observation that I made on Isle Royale (Mech, 1966a). The island's pack of sixteen wolves was headed across the ice of Lake Superior from Isle Royale toward the mainland, some twenty miles away. The wolves had gotten about one and one half miles from the northeast tip of the island when dissension among them became evident. Although most of the wolves appeared unwilling to continue, the leader seemed determined. Several times he returned to the hesitant pack and apparently tried to urge the members on. They continued for another half mile or so until they came to a section of rough and jagged ice. After testing this, the pack returned to Isle Royale. I had the distinct impression that it was the hesitancy of most of the pack members that stimulated the leader to turn back.

On the other hand, the leader often does seem to act independently without communicating with other pack members. One example was the pursuit of a moose on Isle Royale, mentioned above, during which the lead wolf stopped abruptly and prevented the rest of the pack from continuing the chase. In another case, described by Murie, most of the pack members he was watching near a den became restless, and at least one appeared anxious to leave for the nightly hunt, but none departed until the leader was ready several hours later.

Although many more observations must be made on wild wolf packs before enough insight can be gained into wolf government, present evidence points toward a combination of autocratic and democratic systems. The leader usually seems to act independently of his packmates, with them dependent on him for direction. However, he is influenced somewhat by the behavior of other pack members, probably mostly by their hesitancy to react to a situation in the same way that he does.

Interactions within the pack. Because wolf packs are highly organized, order is the rule. Wolves within each pack generally interact predictably, and the social structure of the group is maintained. Much of the behavior of each pack member is directed toward keeping or raising that animal's own status, which creates a "pressure" that tends to keep the society stable. Schenkel (1947: 87) wrote the following:

"Every mature wolf has an ever ready 'expansion power,' a tendency to widen, not a personal territory, but his own social behavior freedom, and to repress his 'Kumpans' of the same sex. Consequently, he maintains a constant watchful interest in all socially important happenings within the pack. In particular, status quarrels are never private affairs between two individuals; the whole society takes a more or less active part in them. Individual differences in social initiative and the power of adaption to momentary situations are very clearly evident. For the status of the individual wolf these are of the greatest importance."

Thus, although a wolf's social rank may be established early in life, it can change if circumstances change. Any drastic disturbance in living conditions might trigger a status rearrangement, but probably social changes, such as the loss or addition of a pack member, would have the greatest effect.

A good illustration of how status can change was reported by Rabb *et al.* They removed their alpha male (No. 1) of three years from their captive pack in the Chicago Zoological Park during the fourth breeding season. The second-highest-ranking male, or "beta male," then became dominant and kept the alpha position ever since (three breeding seasons) even though the original alpha male, No. 1, was returned to the pack. No. 1 became the lowest-ranking male out of five during the next breeding season, and next to the lowest in the following season.

To preserve its status, a wolf must constantly assert its position, and this activity may take several forms, according to Schenkel. If the pack society is relatively stable, the mere "enjoyment" of an animal's rank helps to uphold it. In other words, if pack composition remains constant, there will be few threats or challenges to each animal's status. The mere self-assurance of each wolf, then, will tend to preserve the social balance. But, if the society is greatly disturbed, strong challenges and conflicts may take place as forms of status demonstration. Actual battles, says Schenkel, are rare, and they usually occur only between contenders for the alpha position. Most of the time, status displays remain somewhere between the extremes of peaceful self-assertion and battle.

Under stable social conditions, high-ranking wolves have little need for their aggressive energy, which then builds up. Apparently to release this energy, the dominant wolves often pick on the lowest member of the pack by pouncing on and attacking it. Such behavior is called "energy-displacement" activity. Schenkel (1947: 89) wrote the following about the captive wolves he studied: "Often joint attacks by the large wolves were directed against one animal over a considerable period of time. This animal steadily lost the significance of environmental social partnership, was robbed of all social initiative and, in certain circumstances, with repeated attacks, became mortally wounded."

In the Chicago Zoological Park, a similar situation was seen.

"The most subordinate animal, a female, was essentially an outcast and was persecuted when she strayed from her allotted territory, or otherwise attracted attention, especially of the most dominant female" (Rabb *et al.,* 1962: 440).

In England's Whipsnade Park, whenever a low-ranking wolf is removed, another member of the pack at once assumes the low status (Rutter and Pimlott, 1968).

The phenomenon of energy displacement may explain something I saw on Isle Royale in February 1959 (Mech, 1966a). A very subordinate animal had been following closely behind a pack of fifteen wolves. When the pack rested, the subordinate wolf tried to mix with the group, but two members chased and attacked it. They fought the animal for only a few seconds and then rejoined the excited pack. Twice more, however, they charged the subordinate wolf as it again approached the pack. After the third attack, the wolf temporarily gave up trying to join the others.

Although such violent incidents sometime occur within wolf packs, harmony is the rule. An important contributing factor to this harmony is "submission"—behavior that can be understood as an appeal for friendliness. As defined by Schenkel (1967: 319), "submission is the effort of the inferior to attain friendly or harmonic social integration." It is characterized by a "combination of inferiority and a positive social tendency ("love") and does not contain any component of hostility or obtrusion" (Schenkel, 1967: 326). (NOTE: this concept of submission differs from that of Lorenz [1963]; see p. 92.) During social interactions, a subordinate wolf submits to the more dominant individuals, behavior that might be thought of as an "active lack of challenge." The dominant animal often responds with a display of tolerance, friendliness, and superiority, but this response does not automatically occur.

Schenkel recognized two types of submission, active and passive. The body posture displaying each is described on pp. 86–92. Active submission features friendliness and is fostered by a friendly and tolerant response from the dominant wolf. It frequently occurs as a group ceremony in which all pack members submit to the alpha male, and is often accompanied by group howling (Woolpy, 1968).

Passive submission is a demonstration of inferiority and helplessness. It is the response of a subordinate wolf to a dominant animal showing more superiority and self-assertion than friendliness and tolerance. A low-ranking individual displays passive submission especially when surrounded by several more dominant wolves (Fig. 11).

Submission, then, is a basic part of wolf social behavior, and each pack member except the alpha male and female must frequently exhibit it. Of course, the lowest-ranking animal must practice submission most often. Only the alpha male and female can assert their superiority to all other members of their sex. Since each wolf is aware of its position in the social order and behaves appropriately toward other pack members, general social harmony is maintained.

FIGURE 11. A subordinate wolf often shows "passive submission" by rolling onto its back when approached by wolves of higher rank. (*Patricia Caulfield*)

Expression and Communication in the Pack

The presence of order in a group of animals depends on the ability of members to communicate among themselves. Without communication, the behavior patterns that promote organization would be useless. Communication is defined here as the conveying of information from one individual to another. For example, when odor from a female wolf in heat passes to the nose of a male, information about the female's sexual state is transmitted, and communication has occurred.

Communication among higher animals involves vision, smell, and hearing, and this is the case with the wolf. No matter which sense is involved, the individual doing the communicating behaves, actively or passively, deliberately or nondeliberately, in a way that is meaningful to another individual. In the following sections, the social behavior patterns and the information they express will be described for each sense through which their meaning is recognized.

Postural communication. Most of the communication among members of a wolf pack involves vision. Certain outward patterns of behavior, such as postures and gestures, express the inner state of a wolf; other wolves upon viewing these behavior patterns may respond in characteristic ways, depending on their own feelings.

The patterns of expression in the wolf are many and varied, and through them the animal can display a wide range of feelings, including even slight degrees of feeling intensity (Schenkel, 1947). These patterns have arisen from those basic to the entire dog family, as Devra Kleiman (1967) of the Zoological Society of London has pointed out. According to her studies, social behavior has remained similar throughout the family. In group-living species such as the wolf, specializations in behavior and postures have evolved that serve to hold the pack together and to reduce the aggression among its members, but these changes have been ones of degree rather than kind.

Evidently the behavior of young wolves and some domestic dogs is very similar in certain situations. Pulliainen (1967b) found that twenty- to twenty-two-week-old wolf pups responded to German shepherds that were twenty-one weeks old, seventeen months old, and three years old just as though they were other wolves; the dogs also reacted to the wolf pups like they did to their own species. My female wolf pup when twenty to twenty-two weeks old submitted enthusiastically to dogs as she had to her dominant littermate or to people, but the dogs, including a German shepherd and an Irish wolfhound (both adult males), paid her no attention whatever.

A pattern of behavior involves the entire animal. Usually there is a rearrangement of the posture and position of most parts of the body, and there may also be whimpering, growling, or other sounds. Perhaps certain changes in body odor also occur, but little is known about this. To a human being the most obvious aspect of behavior is the visual. In 1950, Scott described the visible aspects of fifty common behavior patterns in dogs and discovered that most of these patterns had also been reported in wolves. All but one of those that had not been observed in wolves have since been witnessed by researchers at the Chicago Zoological Park (Ginsburg, 1965).

Different behavior patterns result from various combinations of the wolf's basic motor capacities which are similar to those of the dog. Scott (1950: 1015–16) described these motor capacities as follows: "The dog is capable of moving the neck and trunk in the limited way characteristic of most mammals. The legs are chiefly capable of flexion and extension in the sagittal plane, and the front legs are capable of a limited amount of adduction. . . . The ears may be held erect or depressed. The tail may be moved down or up and may be wagged from side to side. The facial muscles are capable of considerable movement during emotional expression, although not so much as in man."

Schenkel (1947; 1968) studied most of the wolf's social behavior patterns in detail, and the following discussion is based on his work. It deals mainly with behavior termed "agonistic," that is, having to do with social competition. Schenkel recognized three levels of expression in wolves, although he felt that it is impossible to define accurate limits to them. One level involves the peripheral structures of the body such as the face and scent organs. A second level involves "nondirected" behavioral changes, for example, erection of hair, changes in breathing rate, and reactions of the pupils. The third level of expression includes social behavior that is clearly directed toward another wolf, and that may involve reaction, social exploration, and social impression all at the same time. Examples are threat, bluff attack, and invitations to play. Although these levels are discussed separately, in expressing each psychological state in the wolf they actually react together.

The position of a wolf's peripheral parts usually indicates the animal's social rank. Thus there are two extremes in posture, expressing either a very dominant or superior status, or a very inferior or subordinate rank; and there are several intermediate positions displaying different degrees of social acceptability between these extremes.

The wolf's most important visual expression center is the head. "The interaction of the colouring of the face and function of the facial muscles and, also, the activity of eyes, ears and nose makes the snout, lips, eyes, forehead and ears the bearers of extremely important and variable expression phenomena" (Schenkel, 1947: 96).

In general, bared teeth, an open mouth, mouth corners pulled forward, a wrinkled and swollen forehead, and ears erect and pointed forward all indicate a full threat by a dominant wolf. Complete insecurity and subordination are expressed by a closed mouth with corners pulled far back, a smooth forehead with slitlike eyes, and ears drawn way back and held close to the head. The position of each part of the face expressing various degrees of dominance and subordinance can be seen in Fig. 12.

Figure 12. Facial expressions of the wolf: a and b, normal expressions of a high ranking animal; c and d, anxiety; e and f, threat, g and h, suspicion. (*From Schenkel, 1947*)

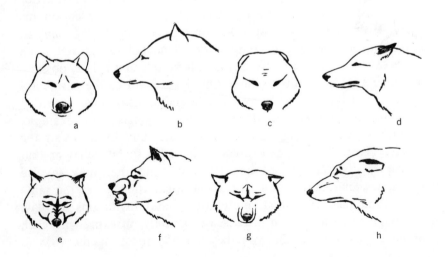

a   b   c   d

e   f   g   h

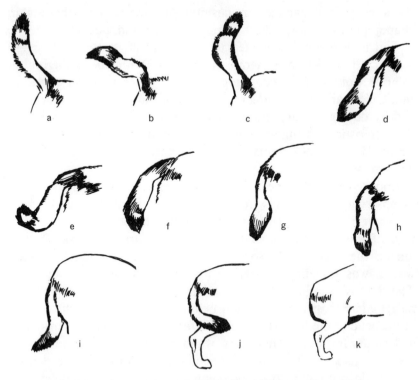

FIGURE 13. Expressive positions of the wolf's tail: (a) self confidence in social intercourse; (b) certain threat, (c) imposing attitude (with sideways brushing); (d) normal attitude (situation entirely without social pressure); (e) a not-entirely-certain threat; (f) normal attitude (similar to "d") particularly common during eating and observing; (g) depressed mood; (h) between threat and defense; (i) actively casting oneself down (with sideways brushing); (k) strong restraint. (*From Schenkel, 1947*)

The tail of a wolf is also a sensitive indicator of mood and status, and it has three properties that are significant in this respect: (1) position, (2) shape, and (3) movement. Differences in these properties occur during social interactions, either friendly or status-demonstrating. Under conditions without social tension, the tail hangs loosely from a raised base, either in a convex or concave curve.

Two extremes in tail position can be seen. A wolf threatening or showing dominance raises its tail above the plane of the back, sometimes perpendicularly. A submissive animal holds its tail very low, often tucked in between its legs or curved forward alongside its legs. Wolves of intermediate rank or individuals displaying dominance less forcefully carry their tails between these extremes.

As a wolf's tail changes in position, it usually also changes in shape. Fig. 13 shows these various shapes and positions.

Tail movements are related to various feelings. Loose, free tail wagging indicates a general friendliness, with the swinging in inferior wolves often extending to the entire rump and pulled-in tail. Quick, abrupt wagging of a tail tip or the whole tail sometimes occurs during an aggressive mood. A trembling vertical tail is characteristic of a high-ranking wolf meeting another wolf of high status. During mock fights, the attacker often beats its tail toward its opponent.

Knowledge of the meaning of tail positions is especially useful in observing wild wolves, for differences in positions can be seen for great distances, even from an aircraft. The best example I have seen of the significance of tail position occurred on Isle Royale during the breeding season (Mech, 1966a). A pack of fifteen wolves was traveling overland single file, led by the alpha pair. The male was primarily interested in mating with the female, so he remained half a body length behind her, which put the female at the head of the line. However, the female appeared inexperienced at leading, for she hesitated and wandered a great deal, and twice she backtracked. The rest of the pack often short-cut the lead pair, but would not cut in front of them. Rather, they took short cuts of about a hundred feet as the lead pair zigzagged, and then sat awaiting the pair. When the alpha animals came by, each wolf pulled its tail between its legs submissively. Meanwhile, the tails of the alpha pair stood vertically in the dominant position as these animals passed the subordinate wolves.

The position of the tail in relation to the anal area is also important. When held down, the tail covers the entire anal region, but when lifted it exposes the area. These two positions are important to the behavior patterns called "anal withdrawal" and "anal presentation." When two wolves approach each other, often one will check the other's anal area. The dominant wolf will present its anal region by lifting its tail and at the same time will check this area in the subordinate animal. The subordinate wolf, if of very low rank, will pull its tail in between its legs and withdraw the anal region (Fig. 14). This animal may also fail to show initiative in examining the anus of the dominant animal. However, if both wolves are high-ranking, each will check the other's anus and will present its own to the other animal.

FIGURE 14. Presentation and withdrawal of the anal parts. Dominant wolf in rear is presenting his anal area and is exerting control over the anal parts of the subordinate, who is withdrawing his anal region. (*From Schenkel, 1947*)

Female wolves rarely check the anal regions of other wolves, and throughout most of the year they withhold their own posteriors from examination. However, during the breeding season, a high-ranking female will present her anal region upon being checked by another wolf; usually only a subordinate female will withdraw her anal area during this season.

The above discussion concerned what Schenkel called the peripheral and nondirected levels of wolf behavior. Those levels include behavior that can be thought of as almost automatic and predictable. The directed aspect of wolf behavior, however, is much more complex. It features the wide variety of adaptable, quickly changing, "personal" behavior patterns that the wolf is capable of in social situations. These actions can change in direction, quality, and intensity, and it is this high degree of adaptability that makes Schenkel consider them so much "higher" than the more stereotyped behavior patterns of fishes, reptiles, and birds. In other words, the directed aspect of wolf behavior allows each personality and each degree of feeling in the wolf to be expressed.

Directed behavior patterns involve the entire body and consist of the co-ordinated activity of the face, head, back, tail, and anal area. In addition, the phenomenon of "social control" is superimposed on them. Social control is asserted by wolves of higher status merely by listening, smelling, or looking intently at animals of low rank, the looking control being seen most often. It is the privilege of dominant wolves to stare penetratingly at others. Low-ranking wolves immediately cringe at this, and restrict their own glances, although higher-ranking pack members may stare back in protest. Either freedom or restriction of sensory activity, then, is a part of each agonistic behavior pattern.

As mentioned previously, two extremes are apparent in agonistic behavior: (1) the threat or self-assertive pattern of dominant wolves, and (2) the defensive and submissive patterns of subordinate animals. Between these, several moderate patterns portray various degrees of either extreme. Since a wolf displays these patterns only to another individual, the personality and momentary feelings of both animals affect the display and its outcome. However, the dominant wolf has more effect and thus directs the behavior.

In a relatively stable group, or under peaceful conditions, a wolf of high rank might merely display its dominance rather than threaten. Probably the least intense and most frequent display of dominance is the "fixed stare" in which the high-ranking wolf stands with tail raised vertically and stares intently at a subordinate (Fig 15). If the dominant animal approaches the subordinate, the dominant may present its anal region ("anal presentation") and may exert "anal control" or checking of the subordinate, as described above.

A second behavior pattern of dominance is "standing across." The dominant animal stands stiffly across the forequarters of a lying individual. Schenkel observed that in captive wolves it only takes place between intimate animals and sometimes includes genital licking. I often saw this pattern of behavior in my hand-reared wolf pups after they were twenty-nine days old (see Chapter IV).

"Riding up" is also an attitude of dominance. In this position, the dominant wolf places its forelegs across the shoulders of a subordinate either from the side or from behind as in sexual intercourse. This animal may even symbolically bite the neck of the subordinate. In a variation on this pattern, the dominant wolf may ride up across the back of one individual while baring its teeth at another. Schenkel (1947: 108) claimed that "the riding-up action is not only the expression of superiority over the passive

FIGURE 15. A subordinate wolf usually shows "active submission" by holding its tail and head down when approaching a dominant animal. (*D. H. Pimlott*)

partner, but coincidentally it is the demonstration of social prerogatives over the whole society."

In a less stable pack, or when there is intense rivalry, high-ranking wolves may assert themselves more and threaten more in their displays. They may harass subordinates by crouching and threatening to spring, by baring their teeth, or by opening their mouths wide. The "bite-threat" posture may then be seen. In it the superior wolf bares its teeth, stares, raises its ears, and stretches out its legs. The animal's tail trembles, and its mane and rump hairs bristle. Continuous rumbling growls are emitted, and sometimes the tongue is rhythmically thrust between the teeth. The whole posture gives an appearance of "self-inflation" and "explosive readiness."

When confronting former rivals or the weakest individuals in the group, a dominant wolf may display the "surprise-attack

FIGURE 16. Dominant wolves sometimes display their rank by "ambushing" subordinate ones. (*D. H. Pimlott*)

threat." In this pattern, the superior wolf crouches in ambush as during a surprise attack (Fig. 16).

Either the bite-threat or the surprise-attack threat might lead to an actual attack, especially between alien animals. In such a case, if the outsider is cornered or cannot outrun the dominant wolf, it might be killed (see "Territoriality"). Obviously, conflicts *within* a pack rarely reach such an extreme, or the pack would eliminate itself.

Under the usual social stability, when displays by high-ranking wolves merely reaffirm their dominance, subordinate wolves assume protective patterns of either "active submission" or "passive submission" (Schenkel, 1967).

During active submission (Fig. 15) "the posture is slightly crouched, the tail is low, and the ears are directed backwards and lie close to the head . . . the inferior pushes the muzzle of the superior with his nose, licks it quickly with repeated strokes of the tongue, or seizes it tenderly without any pressure. In addition, he may perform pawing movements—lifting one forepaw and moving it in the direction of the superior, or, while making little steps, tapping the floor with his forepaws alternately. Often the tail is wagging sideways, and sometimes the whole hindquarters are also swinging sideways" (Schenkel, 1967). This behavior sometimes occurs as a "nose-push" by the submissive wolf when several feet away from the dominant animal.

At other times active submission becomes part of a "group ceremony," in which all pack members surround the leader (Fig. 17), nose-push, and lick his face or "tenderly" seize his muzzle. This group ceremony can take place spontaneously or as a greeting after wolves have separated and regrouped.

However, I have also seen the group ceremony performed when a wolf pack has scented prey, and under these circumstances it could be a food-begging ritual. As will be discussed in Chapter IV,

FIGURE 17. In a "group ceremony" pack members all press together and try to nuzzle the leader. This often happens when the wolves wake up or when the leader returns to the pack after temporarily straying off. (*Patricia Caulfield*)

wolf pups up to five months of age, or possibly more, will nip and lick at the mouths of adults, stimulating the adults to regurgitate food for them. Perhaps this ceremony also serves among adults to inform the pack leader that the members are hungry and thus to give him maximum motivation to lead the attack on the prey.

The main feature of active submission is friendliness and tolerance, and this is especially apparent in the "wolf greeting." Two members of a pack will greet each other after even a short separation, and this greeting is simply a form of active submission. The subordinate individual will excitedly nip, lick, and smell the mouth of the dominant wolf (Fig. 18).

Wolves socialized to humans will greet them the same way. Many were the mornings when my fifty-five-pound pet wolf, Lightning, aided and abetted by my early-rising wife, used to burst through my bedroom door, bound onto my bed, and awaken me with the full wolf greeting. Our children also were accustomed to this experience, for if at night we let Lightning into the house without closing their bedroom doors, the wolf invariably rushed to greet each one. Even in their sleep, however, the children automatically responded in their usual manner by instantly curling up into tight little balls like pill bugs.

Passive submission is more extreme than active submission. Its main characteristic is timidity and helplessness, which is usually displayed by a subordinate wolf under threat and self-assertion by a dominant wolf or by several higher-ranking animals (Fig. 11). "The inferior lies half on his side and half on his back exposing the ventral side of his chest and sometimes the abdomen. The latter occurs regularly as a reaction to olfactory investigation in the genital region. The ears are directed backwards and lie close to the head. The tail is more or less bent ventrally so that it passes between the thighs. The often enthusiastic and friendly activity of active submission is reduced. Sometimes the tail is wagging sideways with extremely reduced amplitude and the activity is replaced by a passive posture full of trust, devotion, and demonstrated helplessness" (Schenkel, 1967: 323).

Schenkel traced the development of both the active and passive submission patterns from food-begging and eliminative behavior in pups, and these will be described in Chapter IV.

Although the usual social response by subordinate wolves is

FIGURE 18. The typical greeting, in which a subordinate wolf thrusts its snout to the muzzle of a dominant one, is part of active submission, and resembles a food-begging ritual in pups. (*Patricia Caulfield*)

submission, they may have to resort to "defensive snapping" under stronger threat. This pattern includes a curved back, the tail curved downward, ears laid back, eyes uncertain, head held backward, and teeth bared and snapping. Both defense and threat elements are apparent.

Wolves of middle rank, or animals protesting, show a less defensive posture and more elements of threat such as growling and bristling of the back fur. Their "protest snapping" is directed close to their rival and is accompanied by sharp "battle barking."

Deeply subordinate animals, on the other hand, assume the defensive position in the extreme. They snap their jaws together loudly and repeatedly. However, such snapping is carried out thirty to forty feet from their opponent and is not directed precisely. Their posture gives the visual impression of "self-deflation," whereas the dominant, threatening animal appears "self-inflating."

Under continued and severe threat, such as would occur when

a dominant wolf meets an alien, the subordinate must flee or be badly wounded or killed (see "Territoriality"). However, if the alien cannot escape, "he shows symptoms of social stress such as diarrheic defecation, tail bent downwards between the hindlegs, and inhibited locomotion" (Schenkel, 1967: 321).

Much has been made about Konrad Lorenz's concept of what takes place when two aggressive, threatening wolves meet, as publicized in his popular book *King Solomon's Ring* (1952: 186): "Notice carefully the position of the two opponents; the older wolf has his muzzle close, very close against the neck of the younger, and the latter holds away his head, offering unprotected to his enemy the bend of his neck, the most vulnerable part of his whole body! Less than an inch from the tensed neck-muscles, where the jugular vein lies immediately beneath the skin, gleam the fangs of his antagonist from beneath the wickedly retracted lips."

Further (1952: 188), "Every second you expect violence and await with bated breath the moment when the winner's teeth will rip the jugular vein of the loser. But your fears are groundless, for it will not happen. In this particular situation, the victor will definitely not close on his less fortunate rival. You can see that he would like to, but he just cannot!" Supposedly the "offering of the neck" automatically blocks the superior wolf's impulse to deliver the death bite.

Recently Schenkel, who described the main forms of submissiveness in wolves, disputed this idea. He claimed that "it is always the *inferior* wolf who has his jaws near the neck of his opponent" (Schenkel, 1967: 320), and that Lorenz mistook the inferior wolf for the superior when he observed the conflict that led to his formation of the concept. As evidence of the misinterpretation, Schenkel republished a drawing of two dogs in such a conflict, originally presented by Fischel (1956). According to Schenkel, Fischel adopted Lorenz's concept, and in the drawing Fischel designated the wrong animal as submissive. (Lorenz has never illustrated the scene [Schenkel, 1967].) Scott (1967: 378) confirmed that "instead of the jugular vein, the dominant dog is most likely to be presented with a mouthful of snapping teeth."

Observations of wolf relations in the wild also tend to contradict Lorenz's idea. Murie watched a pack attack and wound a strange wolf; the animal's posture of passive submission did not block any biting. Indeed, only the creature's fleetness saved it. On Isle Royale,

I saw a similar occurrence (Mech, 1966a). A large pack charged a strange wolf; the wolf ran, stopped, and submitted. But the pack continued straight for the stranger, so it arose and fled. After an additional half-mile chase, the pack finally gave up.

In another instance, described earlier in this chapter, I did see two wolves from a large pack attack a lone wolf and then suddenly stop. This occurred three times as the wolf tried to follow the pack each time. Possibly the sudden stopping of the attacks could have resulted from the lone wolf "offering" its throat, but I could not see well enough to tell if this was the case. It seems more likely, however, that the attacks were not very serious to begin with, perhaps just "displacement of aggressive energy" directed at a pack outcast.

All the visual behavior patterns, postures, and gestures discussed above convey information about a wolf's disposition and social rank. They are recognized by the wolves to which they are displayed, and they then influence the behavior of these animals. This behavior in turn affects the wolf originating the displays. The process occurs almost continually among members of a pack, and it fosters the order that helps the pack function efficiently as a group.

Communication through odor. Communication through the sense of smell, or olfactory sense, is especially difficult to study, so less is known about it than about visual and auditory communication. Since man possesses such a poor sense of smell, he can only observe behavior involving an animal's nose and try to gather the meaning from that. Further complications arise from the fact that some behavior includes both visual and olfactory aspects. The following discussion is a summary of Schenkel's work on communication through odor.

Olfactory behavior patterns involve either the head and neck region or the anal-genital area. Smelling of the first region is a friendly act. Schenkel (1947: 91) wrote the following: "An attitude of peacefulness and lack of tension is a prerequisite to smelling the fur of the neck, the nose, the sides of the head and the mouth area," and "By snuffling the sides of the neck, the tip of the nose reaches the skin through the fur, so that the nose is completely lost in the hairs. The snuffler usually moves the head very slightly at the same time, whereby the tip of the nose moves searchingly in the fur of the partner." Any bone splinters, mud clots, or other foreign debris in the fur is investigated. This behavior occurs among friendly males, and just before the breeding season, between males and females—probably as part of the pairing preliminaries.

"Snuffling" of the lip area evidently tells a wolf whether or not another animal has eaten recently. This behavior is especially common in pups, and, as will be discussed in Chapter IV, it stimulates the adult to regurgitate food for its young. My hand-reared wolf pup used to snuffle me similarly when I played with her after just having eaten—although her efforts, of course, were in vain. The precise behavior is a very enthusiastic nipping and licking of the mouth area. In adults it becomes ritualized into a greeting ceremony as part of active submission (Schenkel, 1967).

The behavior patterns of anal presentation and anal withdrawal were discussed in a previous section because their major importance is thought to be visual. However, they also have an olfactory aspect. A dominant wolf "invades the social sphere" of a lower-ranking wolf by sniffing its anal area; at the same time, the dominant animal presents its own posterior for checking. Whether or not any information is obtained from the anal-genital odor of a wolf has not yet been learned.

There are five possible sources of odor in the anal area: (1) the genital glands, (2) traces of urine, (3) the precaudal gland, (4) the anal glands, and (5) feces. Schenkel thought the genitals and anus were more important in anal snuffling than was the precaudal gland during his observations. However, three of his figures (Figs. 4–6, Schenkel, 1947) show a dominant wolf sniffing the precaudal area of a subordinate, so evidently this gland is of some importance. Its function is still unknown, however, and so is the function of the anal glands. Genital sniffing appears to be important during courtship and mating and will be discussed in Chapter IV.

A special type of behavior with olfactory significance is the phenomenon known as "scent marking," in which a wolf leaves its body odor on a conspicuous object, and other wolves then investigate it. Little is known about the importance of scent marking to communication within a pack. Schenkel believed it to be important in pairing and in "legitimizing" the leader, and emphasized that it probably serves several different functions. A description and discussion of scent marking appears in the section on communication within wolf populations.

Vocal communcation. No doubt the type of communication for which the wolf is most famous is its howling. However, howling is only one kind of sound that the wolf delivers. Various authorities classify the types of wolf vocalization differently, but the system adopted by Joslin (1966) in his intensive study of the subject seems to be the most objective. He listed the following basic types of wolf vocal sounds: (1) the whimper, (2) the growl, (3) the bark, and (4) the howl. To these must also be added a fifth, the "social squeak," heard by Crisler and by Fentress.

The whimper, or whine, was described by Young (1944: 77), who wrote that it "is a high, though soft, and plaintive sound similar to the whine of a puppy dog, and is used mostly at or near the opening of the wolf den, particularly when the young whelps are out playing around." Further, "it seems to indicate solicitude for the offspring, and is made mostly by the adult female. As the pitch of this whine varies so much, it seems ventriloquial." According to G. Tembrock (1963), the frequency of the whine is about 760 cycles per second. Schenkel (1947) mentioned whimpering in connection with a dance step of an alpha female in heat, and with the insecurity of a subordinate wolf threatened by a dominant.

Lois Crisler (1958: 150) provided an intimate view of what probably was whimpering, although she called it "talking": "The wolf talking is deeply impressive because the wolf is so emotionally stirred. His eyes are brilliant with feeling. He seeks your eyes and utters a long, fervent string of mingled crying and wowing, hovering around one pitch."

Because whimpering is audible for only one hundred to two hundred yards (Joslin, 1966), humans have rarely heard it from wild wolves. However, Joslin detected it in Ontario on three occasions during a study in which he imitated wolf howling and kept track of wolves by listening to their replies. One time he and his assistant were sitting in a beached canoe on a lake shore after having exchanged howls with a nearby pack for most of the night. Local conditions were such that their scent probably was being drawn out onto the lake. Suddenly two wolves approached to within twelve feet of the men and paced to each end of the canoe, peering over the bushes toward them. One of the wolves whimpered about a dozen times and growled twice. After about twenty minutes both animals left.

On the second occasion when Joslin heard whimpering, he tried whining back. The wolf remained in the area for an hour and a half, sometimes coming to within one hundred feet of him. During that time, the wolf whimpered about four hundred times and howled one hundred times.

The third time that Joslin heard whimpering was when he sneaked to within one hundred yards of a litter of wolf pups to record their voices. He howled to the group, and a single pup replied and then rushed toward him, whining twice. Joslin suspected that the pup had mistaken his howling for that of one of the pack's adults and was coming to meet the adult.

From these observations, Joslin concluded that whimpering is a submissive or friendly greeting sound. The information cited above from other studies tends to support this view.

Growling, on the other hand, seems to convey just the opposite feeling—aggressiveness. This low, throaty sound has a frequency of about 380 to 450 cycles per second (Tembrock, 1963). It is made by a dominant, threatening wolf during the bite-threat posture, described in a previous section. Joslin heard growling twice during the first whimpering instance related above, when the two wolves approached to within twelve feet of him. On another occasion, discussed below, a wolf one hundred feet away alternately growled and barked at him for a half hour as he tried to approach a pack at night. It appears from this that growling is a threatening, unfriendly utterance (Joslin, 1966).

The third type of wolf sound is barking. The barking that I have heard was deep, guttural, and coarse, and Tembrock (1963) lists its frequency range as 320 to 904 cycles per second. Young claimed that barking is the call of the chase, whereas Tembrock believed it may indicate any kind of excitement. J. P. Scott thought that barking is basically an alarm call given when other animals infringe on a pack's territory (Joslin, 1966).

The only time I have heard wild wolves bark was when I had chased a pack of fifteen away from their freshly killed moose. As the animals retreated, several barked, and for the next two and one half hours they continued to bark and howl off and on in the distance while I examined the carcass (Mech, 1966a).

Joslin, who probably has had more experience with the sounds of wild wolves than has any other biologist, found that there are two kinds of barking. He believes that one serves as an alarm and the other as a threat or challenge to intruders. The alarm bark is short. Joslin has heard it on six occasions, and during four of these the barking was immediately followed by an abrupt ending of a howling session. This would seem to be evidence for its alarm function. The threatening or challenging bark will be discussed in the section on communication within the population.

The social squeak, a little-known sound, evidently is so soft that it has been heard only in pet wolves at close range. One of Lois Crisler's tame animals would make this mouselike squeak when it came upon the Crislers unexpectedly. A wolf raised by Fentress gave the social squeak when making contact with persons or dogs, and Fentress believed that this sound is of "considerable social importance." It perhaps should be regarded as a special kind of whine.

The most commonly heard wolf sound is howling. Subjectively, the howl has been described in many colorful ways, often depending on one's attitude. For instance, Shoemaker (1917–19: 29) quoted a trapper's description: "Take a dozen railroad whistles, braid them together and then let one strand after another drop off, the last peal so frightfully piercing as to go through your heart and soul . . ." In actuality, the howl might be more accurately described as a long, low, mournful moan.

Attempts to describe the howl objectively have been made only recently. J. B. Theberge and J. B. Falls (1967: 334), of the University of Toronto, applied spectographic and auditory analysis techniques to seven hundred howls of three adult male wolves and provided the following description: "[The howl is] a continuous sound from about half a second to 11 seconds in length. It consists of a fundamental frequency which may lie between 150 and 780 cycles per second, and up to 12 harmonically related overtones. Most of the time, the pitch remains constant or varies smoothly, and may change direction as many as four or five times. Total intensity does not greatly vary throughout." The authors added that this description applies to the three wolves they studied and is consistent with the howling of wild wolves they have heard but that it should not be taken as adequate for all wolf howling.

There is much variation in the howling of different wolves. In

FIGURE 19. When a wolf howls, it usually draws its lips forward and points its muzzle toward the sky; the howl can be heard for miles at times. (*L. David Mech*)

their analysis, Theberge and Falls recognized this variation in many separate qualities of the howl (Table 10). Although each animal they studied howled distinctively, there was even some variation within the howls of each one. Fentress also found this and claimed that with his hand-reared wolf he could tell howls after feeding from howls of loneliness.

Just before howling, a wolf often whines and wags his tail. Then the animal points its muzzle upward and forward and begins to howl (Fig. 19). Crisler (1958: 151) described in detail one of her tame female wolves howling: "Sometimes she ululated, drawing her tongue up and down in her mouth like a trombone slide. Sometimes on a long note she held the tip of her tongue curled against the roof of her mouth. She shaped her notes with her cheeks, retracting them for plangency, or holding the sound in with them for horn notes. She must have had pleasure and sensi-

tiveness about her song for if I entered [howled] on her note she
instantly shifted by a note or two; wolves avoid unison singing;
they like chords."

TABLE 10. Variation in howling characteristics of individual wolves[1].

Howling Characteristics	Wolf A	Wolf B	Wolf C
Type of beginning (first .5 sec.)	Smooth rise in pitch	Break upward in pitch	Break upward in pitch
Type of midsection			
A. Sudden drops in pitch?	No	0, 1, or 2	0, 1, or 2
B. Rise in pitch including highest note in howl?	Yes	No	No
C. Rises in pitch not including highest note?	No	No	0, 1, or 2
Type of ending (last .5 sec.)	Steady or no abrupt change	Slur rapidly down	Slur or steady
Average highest note	Middle A	C♯ high	D♯ high
Range of highest notes	14 semitones	5 semitones	8 semitones
Average lowest note	Middle C	—	F♯
Range of lowest notes	19 semitones	—	9 semitones
Average length of howls	3.5 secs.	4.7 secs.	6.4 secs.
Range of lengths	8 secs.	6 secs.	11 secs.
Number of harmonics	Up to 12	Up to 5	Up to 5

[1] Adapted from Theberge and Falls (1967).

During a howling session by a single wolf, which lasts an average of thirty-five seconds, the animal howls several times, according to Joslin. When a pack performs, one wolf begins, and after
its first or second howl others join in. Each animal starts more or
less by itself, beginning with a few long, low howls and working
up to a series of shorter, higher ones somewhat in chorus with
those of other pack members. Such a session lasts an average of
eighty-five seconds and is sometimes followed by a repeat performance, although this occurs less than half of the time.

After a pack of wolves once ends it howling sessions, there appears to be a period of fifteen to twenty minutes or more during
which the animals cannot or will not howl (Pimlott, 1960). This
information is based on studies in which wild wolves were made
to howl in response to recorded or artificial howling. Once a pack
replied to such a stimulus, they failed to respond again during this
"refractory" period. During Joslin's study, he usually howled about
every twenty minutes throughout the night once he had made contact with a pack. The wolves responded every forty minutes on the
average.

A wolf pack may howl at any time of day, according to Joslin.

Throughout his field work, from May through September, he heard just as much spontaneous howling during the day as he did at night. In addition, he got just as high a response rate, about 50%, to his artificial howling during the day as at night, although around dusk this increased to about 70%. Young stated that wolf howling usually occurs near dawn or dusk, and Murie described situations in which a pack often howled in early evening. I have heard wolves at this time but have noted their howls at most other times of day too.

Wolves probably howl throughout the year. I have heard them during every month that I have been in wolf country for any long period: February, March, May, June, July, August, October, and November. However, Joslin found a seasonal difference in the percentage of responses to his howling. In July and August, he obtained three times as high a response as in May and June. This difference was due to two factors. First, pack members, especially females with pups, seldom responded during early pup development. For example, adults replied three times as often during July as in May. This agrees in general with the reports of Schönberner (1965) and Rabb (*vide* Joslin, 1966), who observed that their captive adult wolves did not howl until the pups were nine and six weeks old, respectively. Joslin suggested that this lack of howling may help keep the den location a secret from other predators.

The second reason that the howling response rate increased later in the summer during Joslin's study was that the pups themselves then began to reply. The earliest that Joslin heard pups howling by themselves during three summers was July 26.

The effects of atmospheric conditions on wolf howling are not fully known. Joslin found no significant differences in response rate during variations in temperature, cloud cover, and phase of the moon. He did not have enough data to comment on the effect of rainfall. However, Joslin did find that wind affects howling. The response rate was almost ten times greater during calm periods than during windy weather, and was between these extremes with light to moderate winds.

All the functions of howling are not yet known. Once a wolf begins howling, other pack members often show a strong tendency to approach that animal and join the chorus (Fig. 20). Considerable tail wagging, excitement, and general friendliness usually accompany the howling. This is well documented by Murie for wild wolves and by Lois Crisler for tame but free-ranging wolves. Crisler (1958: 151) wrote: "Like a community sing, a howl is . . . a happy social occasion. Wolves love a howl. When it is started, they instantly seek contact with one another, troop together, fur to fur. Some wolves . . . will run from any distance, panting and bright-eyed, to join in, uttering, as they near, fervent little wows, jaws wide, hardly able to wait to sing."

These observations suggest that an emotional state related to the wolf's social sense is probably the stimulus for chorus howling as in the group ceremony described earlier. In this respect, it is significant that Theberge and Falls found that a high rate of spontaneous howling in one of their captive wolves was correlated with that animal's isolation from other wolves or people.

It does appear, however, that one of the main functions of howling is to aid in assembling the pack. Many authorities have described various circumstances in which one wolf began howling and immediately drew other pack members to it. The advantage of a method of assembling scattered pack members is obvious, and it

FIGURE 20. During "chorus howling" pack members all chime in together in what seems to be a highly exciting and emotional ritual that often precedes the nightly hunt. (*Patricia Caulfield*)

is easy to see how this function could have evolved from whatever social gratification howling may give.

Many people believe that howling is the call of the chase just as in certain breeds of hunting dogs. However, evidence for this is lacking. In fact, there are even some indications that wolves may be silent during the chase. On Isle Royale, where I used an aircraft to follow wolves, I once saw part of a pack of sixteen pursue a moose and hold it at bay while the rest of the wolves wandered around searching for it. If the first animals had been howling, the rest of the pack could have gone straight to the moose. In another instance, this pack chased and wounded one moose while a second moose lay undisturbed about a hundred yards away. It certainly seems that if the wolves had been howling, the second moose would have fled the area.

Probably much of the howling that people attribute to wolves hunting actually represents the assembly of pack members after a chase. Often wolves get separated during a hunt, and on such occasions one animal may climb a ridge, howl, and attract the other pack members to it (Murie, 1944; Mech, 1966a).

Another possible function of howling, advertisement of territory, will be discussed in the section on communication within the population and in Chapter XI.

Besides conveying the location of an individual wolf, howling may also identify that wolf. That is, each pack member may be able to recognize each other by its howl. Joslin made three observations in which wolves seemed to identify other wolves in this way. The amount of difference between the howls of individual wolves was described above (Table 10), and indicates that it is at least possible to tell one wolf from another by their howls.

Whether or not a wolf can distinguish between howls is still open to question. But Theberge and Falls have shown that wolves are capable of fine auditory discrimination. One of their captive wolves could tell the difference between a live (nonrecorded) simulated howl and a recording of the same howl. It replied to the former in thirty-nine of forty-three tests but to the latter only twice out of twenty-five trials. The only differences the experimenters could find in the recorded howling, upon spectographic examination, were: "a slight distortion of the fundamental, reversal of the relative strength of the first two harmonics, and a slightly lower total volume" (Theberge and Falls, 1967: 336).

There is some evidence that by howling wolves may even be able to supply information about their behavior. Theberge and Falls learned that there was a correlation between certain characteristics of a howl of one of their wolves and whether the animal was lying, walking slowly, or pacing. Correlations were found in both wolves studied, but the direction of the variations was different in each wolf. For example, one animal usually dropped in pitch while pacing, whereas the other increased its pitch during the same kind of activity. Thus communication based on these differences could occur only among associated wolves that had learned to relate each other's behavior to the changes in its howling.

Territoriality

Most of the insight into the organization of the wolf pack has come from research on captive wolves. Although social behavior within a group of wolves can be studied in captivity, the natural interactions of several packs are much more difficult to investigate. For instance, the way that packs space themselves in the wild can be seen only in areas of hundreds of square miles. Thus, information about order within wolf populations has come from natural observations and is less definite and more speculative than information on order within the pack.

The territory of an animal is defined as the area that the animal will defend against individuals of the same species. The defense of the area is the main difference between a territory and a "range" or "home range." On the basis of this definition, it would be difficult to determine directly just how territorial wolf packs are. One would have to observe a pack for long periods as it traveled over all the many miles of its range (Chapter V) and as it met other wolf packs. But the chance of one pack meeting another is slim, and such meetings have rarely been seen. The few instances of pack interactions reported are of large packs and single wolves or duos. It does seem significant, however, that in most cases intolerance was shown by the large pack.

The first documented case of intolerance between wild wolves was reported by Murie in Alaska. An alien wolf approached the five adults Murie was watching near Mount McKinley's East Fork Den in late May. The wolves ran to meet this animal and surrounded it. Then some began biting it. The animal rolled over on its back in passive submission. However, this did not deter the pack, and the wolf fled. The pack followed for about two hundred yards, knocking it down twice. The leader pressed the wolf even more and attacked it again. When the outsider finally escaped, its hip and the base of its tail were blood-soaked.

I have twice watched Isle Royale's large pack chase strange wolves (Mech, 1966a). In one case, the pack of sixteen pursued a lone wolf for a half mile, and even after the pack had given up, the wolf continued running at top speed for at least a quarter mile. In the second instance, the pack discovered two wolves feeding on one of its old kills. One animal headed into the woods, while the pack chased the other along the shore of the island for a half mile. This animal continued running for at least a mile after the pack had given up. Both chases made me think that if the sixteen wolves had caught one of the alien animals they would have killed it. Cowan (1947) reported a case related to him in which a large wolf had been killed by others, and another in which a single wolf had been wounded badly by a pack of four.

These instances of intolerance show that wolves are often unfriendly, if not completely hostile, to wolves outside of their own pack. This can also be seen in captive animals. When two unfamiliar adults are placed in the same cage, they fight continually for weeks before accepting each other (Woolpy and Ginsburg, 1967).

In a sense, aggression between unassociated wolves could also be regarded as defense of a range or territory, or at least it would have the same effect. On this basis, one could conclude that wolf packs are territorial to the extent that their territories include most of their hunting and traveling areas. If this is true, it would be expected that packs would become spaced throughout a range in such a way as to avoid or minimize meeting other packs.

Although the information about this subject conflicts somewhat, it appears that at least some territorial spacing does occur within most wolf populations. Both Murie and Stenlund reported that packs in their study areas used definite home ranges, although the ranges overlapped somewhat.

On Isle Royale, I learned that the largest wolf pack used the entire 210-square-mile island each winter for three winters but concentrated its activities in about one-half to two-thirds of the area (Mech, 1966a). Two smaller packs confined their movements

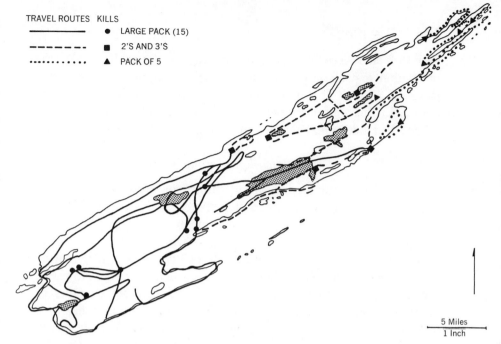

TRAVEL ROUTES KILLS

——————— ● LARGE PACK (15)

— — — — — · ■ 2'S AND 3'S

············· ▲ PACK OF 5

5 Miles
1 Inch

FIGURE 21. Apparent territoriality shown by wolf packs on Isle Royale in 1966. (*From Jordan et al., 1967*)

to the part of the island used least by the large pack. Observations during the following five winters supported these findings (Jordan *et al.*, 1967). Even a new pack of five wolves that was thought to have branched off the largest pack during the sixth year of the study occupied its own separate range (Fig. 21).

Most of the information on territories of the Isle Royale packs was gathered in winter, but the limited summer observations suggested that the packs were spaced about the same as in winter. In Ontario, where Joslin determined the summer ranges of packs by noting the locations of wolves when they responded to his howling, he found the ranges to be separate, with no overlap.

Even where overlap does occur between ranges of different packs, wolves could still be considered territorial. The concept of territoriality in mammals is not yet well understood. However, elsewhere I have presented limited evidence that mammals may maintain a certain minimum distance between themselves and others sharing the same range (Mech *et al.*, 1966). In other words, territories may be spatial-temporal rather than just spatial. In terms of such a widely ranging species as the wolf, this could mean that a pack might not use an area that another pack had traveled through less than a certain number of hours or days before. In this way each pack could lessen the chances of meeting others. For additional discussion of this subject, see Chapter XI.

Communication Among Packs

Just as there can be no order within the pack without communication among members, so too there can be no order within the wolf population without communication among packs. For example, there could be no territories—whether they are spatial or spatial-temporal—if each pack did not know where neighboring packs traveled and when they were in particular areas. However, the range of individual packs is often one hundred square miles or more (Chapter V), so obviously it is not merely the presence of a pack that discourages neighboring packs from using its territory. Some types of communication covering long ranges or lasting for long periods would be necessary to advertise a pack's use of an area. The only senses that would seem useful to the wolf for this function are the senses of smell and hearing.

Scent marking. The sense of smell could be very useful in maintaining a territory, and the puzzling phenomenon of scent marking could serve this function. Scent marking was defined by Devra Kleiman (1966: 167) as "urination, defaecation, or rubbing of certain areas of the body which is (1) oriented to specific novel objects, (2) elicited by familiar conspicuous landmarks and novel objects or odours, and (3) repeated frequently on the same object." In wolves, both urination and body rubbing meet these qualifications as methods of scent marking.

In scent marking by urination, male and female wolves assume different postures, according to Kleiman. The male uses three postures: (1) standing with one hind leg raised and crooked when squirting urine on a vertical object; and when urinating on the ground either (2) standing with all four legs slightly spread, or (3) standing with one hind leg lifted under the body. Females, which scent-mark much less (Scott and Fuller, 1965), either squat in their normal urination position or they squat and lift a hind leg under their body. Both sexes scratch the ground with fore and hind feet after marking, but this is much more common in males than in females. At times, the scratching disrupts the ground litter and soil for several feet. According to George Rabb, only the high-ranking males scent-mark in the Brookfield Zoo pack.

Kleiman believed that body rubbing is also a method of dispersing body scent onto the object rubbed. She (1966: 173) described body rubbing as follows: "When rubbing its body on an object on the ground, the animal will generally begin by bending its forelegs and thus dropping its forequarters. It will then rub the side of its neck and temple on the object or odour-bearing object several times in succession, sometimes alternating sides. This may be followed by the animal turning over completely on its back. When on its back the animal exhibits the wriggling and writhing pattern with which dog owners are so familiar.

"When rubbing its body against a vertical surface the animal successively presses the side of its temple, neck, and trunk against the surface. The tail is usually raised at the root."

Wolves will also rub in almost any strong odor, from that of rotten fish to that of expensive perfume, and this behavior occurs even in animals only three months old.

Objects that are marked by urine are called "scent posts" or "scent stations." They include rocks, stumps, logs, ice chunks, sticks, etc. On a wide-open expanse such as a frozen lake any conspicuous object may be a scent post. Sometimes several wolves in a pack will wait in line and urinate on the same object, and they may repeat this procedure each time they pass by. Thus large amounts of frozen urine accumulate on such a scent station over the winter. At other times, just one member of a pack squirts on an object as the pack passes. When a pack discovers the urine of a strange wolf, the members become greatly excited (Young, 1944).

Although there is still disagreement on the subject, some authors believe that scent-marking serves as territory advertisement (Schenkel, 1947). If each wolf can tell its own body scent from those of others, as dogs can (Scott and Fuller, 1965), then the animal would know whether or not it was encroaching on the range of another pack simply by smelling scent posts.

Even if territories are spatial-temporal, scent stations could still mark them because wolves probably can tell how old a scent is. Thus, perhaps when wolves smell a scent post marked only a day or so before by another pack, they might tend to avoid that route and seek another. A similar function for scent marking in tigers has already been proposed by Leyhausen and Wolff (1959). According to George Schaller (1967: 253), these authors "suggested that olfactory markings also help to prevent encounters, functioning somewhat like railway signals: 'Fresh mark=section closed, going on implies the danger of a hostile encounter. Less fresh mark=proceed with caution. Old mark=go ahead. The individual, before passing such a mark, regularly covers it with its own thus "closing the section."'"

Because more is known about domestic dogs than about wolves, and because information about dogs can give insight into wolf behavior, it is worth-while to look at scent marking in these domesticated "brothers" of the wolf. Dogs do not scent-mark consistently until they are eight or nine months old (Fuller and DuBuis, 1962), and under the influence of the male hormone (Martins and Valle, 1948). A dog released in an area without scent posts will mark many stations, but will not remark them until after another dog urinates on them (Von Uexküll and Sarris, 1931).

The normal scent-post checking routine in an area regularly inhabited by dogs was described by Fuller and DuBuis (1962: 428) as follows: "Ordinarily, male dogs who are allowed to roam in a village check the scent posts in their neighbourhoods at least once a day. The route covered usually encompasses several miles, and 2 or 3 hours may be spent carefully 'reading' each stop along the way. Small groups of dogs meet at various points on the route and continue together. Scent-post checking may be interrupted while individuals pursue other interests, but the average adult male does not return home until the usual course has been completed."

According to Schenkel (1968), scent marking in dogs contributes to territorial spacing, and he believes it has a similar function in wolves. Although more evidence is still needed, it seems reasonable to assume that scent marking does provide wolves with a certain amount of information about their neighbors and that this information probably has great significance in territorialism and population control. This will be discussed further in Chapter XI.

Vocal communication. Besides the sense of smell, the only other sense that might serve in communication between packs is hearing. In this respect, several findings by Ontario biologists are important.

Pimlott reported in 1960 that wolves often replied to recordings of howling broadcast near them. Since then, Joslin received replies in 13% of 476 trials, a high rate considering that during many trials there may have been no wolves within hearing distance. Under good conditions, Joslin often had a 50% success in receiving responses. Several other authors have also reported that wolves will reply to recorded howls, human imitations, and even fire sirens.

Since human beings can sometimes hear wolf howling up to four miles away and wolves can probably hear even better, Joslin concluded that howling could advertise a pack's presence over an area of fifty square miles. He has often heard wolves responding to the howling of adjacent packs. It certainly seems possible that howling could serve in the same way as singing does in male birds —advertisement and defense of a territory. Joslin claimed, however, that if it does it may just remind one pack of another's presence; wolves probably do not immediately seek out their neighbors howling in the distance and chase them. He believes this because he was never approached by wolves when he howled to them from a distance of two hundred yards or more.

When Joslin howled within two hundred yards of a pack, however, he often was approached by one or more animals. In such instances the wolves sometimes uttered their threatening or challenging bark. This differs from the alarm bark, described in an earlier section, in that the threatening bark is prolonged and has a definite pattern (Joslin, 1966).

Joslin (1966: 53) has heard the threatening bark twice, and he gave the following description of one of these occasions: "The incident happened to me on the night of June 13, while I was howling back and forth with the Fools Lake pack which was a few hundred yards away. From the direction of the pack I heard a single wolf come trotting noisily toward me through the underbrush. It came to within about a hundred feet and commenced to bark and growl. For a time it moved back and forth over a space of about 20 feet. As mentioned above, its barking had a definite pattern. It consisted of two, occasionally one, sharp barks followed by a more drawnout bark which ended in a series of softer, lower pitched bark. . . . It was repeated 37 times over a period of 27 minutes. Following each series of barks there was a pause of approximately 50 seconds. Frequent growling occurred during this pause. By the time the·wolf had stopped I had moved away about 150 yards through the forest."

It should be obvious from the above discussions that enough evidence is not yet available to allow definite judgments about the function of the two main means of communication within wolf populations. It does seem likely, however, that this communication is directly related to the order that exists within the population.

CHAPTER IV / REPRODUCTION
AND FAMILY LIFE

Like most other wolf activities, breeding and the raising of young involve the entire pack. As discussed in Chapter II, packs may contain several immature and mature animals of both sexes. Although not all these wolves bear pups, they do fondle them, help care for them, and feed them. The advantages of such group care of the young are obvious.

Courtship and Mating

The mating urge does not occur in wolves until they are about twenty-two months old. R. A. Rausch (1967a), of the Alaska Department of Fish and Game, examined the reproductive tracts of 246 female Alaskan wolves approximately ten months old during the mating season and found no sign of sexual maturity. Most of the twenty-two-month-old females (170) that he checked, however, were pregnant. Males are fertile when twenty-two months old (Rabb, 1968).

Courtship and mating in the wolf are intimately related to each animal's year-round ties with other members of its pack. As already mentioned, most matings might even take place between animals in the same family—i.e., between littermates or between parent and offspring. Thus, in one respect, courtship continues year round. Lois Crisler (1958) found strong affectional ties between her tame but free-ranging male and female littermates lasting until the animals were over a year old. At that time a "triangle" developed when a wild female wolf began courting the male and eventually killed the tame female. That was more than a half year before the actual mating season.

FIGURE 22. When mating, the male wolf mounts the female from behind. The pair then becomes coupled and cannot break apart for 15 to 30 minutes. (*Patricia Caulfield*)

Courtship behavior. Before female wolves actually come into heat, affectional behavior between the sexes consists mainly of head-to-head activity: mutual snuffling, head rubbing, snout bunting, or snout grabbing; this behavior continues into the actual mating period, but it is then supplemented in the male by snuffling and licking of the female's genitals (Schenkel, 1947).

George Rabb (1968), who studied courtship and mating in the wolves at the Chicago Zoological Society's Brookfield Zoo, described the courtship behavior of the male just prior to copulation as follows: "The male starts dancing around the female, lowering his front quarters like a playful dog, and wagging his tail. He may also nip the female's face, ears, and back, and mount her side, after which he tries to mount her from the rear."

Courtship also takes place on the part of the female. She may approach a male and place her forepaws, neck, or head across his shoulders. Or she may greet him in a submissive posture and then back up toward him, lifting her tail or turning it to the side, and displaying her genitals. Schenkel (1947: 93) described this procedure in detail: "With raised tail, the rutting alpha-bitch moves in a feathery dance step, while whimpering or 'singing' 'tenderly.' . . . Meanwhile she moves her genitals in slow, minute, pendulum-like movements in a vertical direction."

According to Rabb *et al.* (1967), males generally initiate three times the number of courtship actions that females do. However, this does not hold true for each individual male. For example, one of the males studied by these biologists received 81% of the total attention of four females during one mating season, yet he initiated only 9% of the total breeding attempts by five males during that period.

Although much courting takes place throughout the breeding season, only a small percentage of the courtship attempts end in copulation. Of 1296 courtship actions witnessed in the wolf pack at the Brookfield Zoo from 1963 to 1966, only thirty-one (2.4%) resulted in copulatory ties. During several days of observing a pack of fifteen wolves on Isle Royale during three breeding seasons, I saw copulation only four times (Mech, 1966a).

When a female decides to thwart a male's amorous attempts, she tucks her tail between her legs and may even sit on it. This may mean that she is not in full heat (estrus), as is often the case during similar behavior in domestic dogs (Fuller and DuBuis, 1962). However, there are other possible reasons for unsuccessful courtship, and they will be discussed later.

If the female is fully receptive and accepts the male's courtship, she stands firmly and turns her tail to the side, exposing her vulva. Or, between two individuals that prefer each other, this may occur without preliminaries.

The rest of the mating process (Fig. 22) continues as follows: "The male inserts his penis and thrusts forward and backward a few times. He then rocks sideways, alternately shifting his weight between his two hind legs. This probably helps push the bulbous base of his penis into the female's vagina, locking the sphincter and forming a tie. After the tie is made, he thrusts back and forth again and then ejaculates" (Rabb, 1968).

The copulatory tie mentioned above is peculiar to the dog family, but its function (if any) is unknown. In Chapter II, I suggested that it may be important in completing the psychological bond between two newly mated animals. The tie is caused by the swelling of the base of a male's penis, the *bulbus glandis,* and the constriction of the female's vaginal sphincter muscles around it (Fuller and DuBuis, 1962). When this process takes place, the male dismounts from the female by placing his front legs alongside her. While still tied, he lifts one hind leg over her back and turns his body away from hers. This puts the two animals tail to tail, and they lie quietly in that position, firmly attached by their genitals.

I first observed this phenomenon from the air, and directed my pilot to dive lower for a closer examination. As the aircraft bore down upon the coupled wolves, both animals stood and tried desperately to break apart and flee, but they could not. According to Rabb (1968), this tie may continue for as long as thirty-six minutes. I have seen it last fifteen minutes in the Isle Royale wolves. When a tie occurs, most members of the pack rush over to the pair excitedly and mill around the animals (Mech, 1966a).

In dogs, and presumably in wolves, ejaculation begins about the time of locking and continues throughout the duration of the tie. During the first thirty to fifty seconds, the semen is clear and contains few sperm; for the next thirty seconds, it is milky and thick and filled with sperm; after that it becomes clear and watery again and remains that way until the end of the tie (Harrop, 1955).

Mate preferences. It is commonly thought that wolves mate for life, although this idea would be difficult to prove. Information from the Brookfield Zoo pack demonstrates that wolves do show strong and long-lasting mate preferences, however (Table 11). Consequently, courtship usually is devoted to the preferred mate, and mating attempts by other wolves generally are spurned. Since not all mate preferences are mutual, this partly explains the low success rate of courtship activity.

Even though wolves usually show strong preferences, however, certain individuals will shift their sexual attentions, especially if their preferred mate is no longer available (Rabb *et al.,* 1967).

Dominance order in relation to mating. Dominance order, mate preference, and the number of successful courtships are closely interrelated. According to Schenkel (1947), the alpha pair, or top-ranking male and female, are the only members of a pack to mate. However, apparently he believed that most packs contain only a single mature pair, in which case, these animals would *have* to be the only ones to mate.

TABLE 11. Mate preferences[1] shown by members of a captive wolf pack[2].

Season	Male 1	Male 2	Male 3	Male 4	Male 5
1961	cF3[3]	aF1			
1962	cF3	aF1	—[4]		
1963	cF3	aF1	aF1	aF1	—[4]
1964		aF1	cF2	aF1	aF1
1965	dF3	cF2	cF2	aF4	aF4
1966	cF3	cF3	dF2	bF4	bF4

Season	Female 1	Female 2	Female 3	Female 4	Female 5
1961	aM1	—[5]	aM1		
1962	aM1	—[5]	aM1	—[4]	
1963	aM1	bM2	aM1	aM1	
1964	aM2	aM2	—[6]	—[6]	—[4]
1965		aM2	eM1	eM1	aM2
1966		aM2	dM1	dM1	aM2

[1] Based mainly on frequency of courtship activity.
[2] Chicago Zoological Park (Rabb *et al.*, 1967).
[3] Small letters before sex and individual animal numbers indicate dominance rank within sex.
[4] Animal was present but not mature.
[5] Data lacking.
[6] Animal present but no preference evident.

However, many packs include several mature wolves (Chapter II). Murie (1944) studied such a pack and concluded that the alpha male was not the father of the pups. In the Brookfield Zoo pack the alpha male was sexually one of the least active animals. During four seasons a particular alpha male was only once seen mating (Ginsburg, 1965). When this individual was removed from the pack, the second-ranking ("beta") male became dominant, and his sexual activity then decreased markedly (Rabb *et al.*, 1967).

Although the alpha male may not contribute to a pack's reproduction except when the pack is first established (Chapter III), the alpha female is very important. For five years, the original alpha female in the Brookfield Zoo kept her dominant position and each year produced the only litter born to the pack, even though the group also included at least two other mature females each year. In the two years after the alpha female died, however, the trend broke down. During the first year, the new alpha female bore the young, but the next year she was the only one of four females that did not produce a litter.

Several other patterns are apparent in the relationships among wolf pack members during the breeding season, based on the Brookfield Zoo data (Ginsburg, 1965; Rabb *et al.*, 1967), and these provide insight into such relations within wild packs: (1) dominance rivalries increase greatly just before the breeding season, especially among the females, and the dominance order is largely settled at that time, (2) the alpha male is often preferred by most of the females, (3) dominant males often disrupt courtship and mating attempts by subordinate males, (4) the alpha female tries to prevent other females from mating, (5) a dominant animal will often interfere with mating attempts by individuals of the opposite sex, (6) a subordinate male sometimes thwarts a superior's courtship of a mutually preferred female by moving between the two, and (7) the mate preferences seem to be related to the dominance order in the pack when the pups mature, with younger animals preferring older dominant wolves.

Regarding the last point, Jerome Woolpy (1968: 54) wrote about the same pack that "we have never observed an older wolf develop a first preference for a younger one, nor have we ever observed reciprocal preferences between wolves of different ages."

The net result of these complex interactions is a great deal of complicated courtship activity with few successful copulatory ties, as is evident from the following by Rabb *et al.* (1967: 306): "In subsequent seasons, only a single female mated successfully and gave birth. This bitch dominated the other two females by assaulting them physically or psychically whenever they solicited a male or were receptive to a male. The other females were confined by intimidation to small areas of the woods. . . . Consequently, only one of the others mated, and then only once, when the chief [alpha] bitch was herself in copulatory tie. The alpha bitch, female 1, preferred the alpha male, male 1, and actively courted and solicited him. . . . So did female 3. Male 1 reciprocated female 3's attentions, but rebuffed female 1. Female 1 thereupon accepted male 2. Male 1 punished male 2 while he was tied, as did female 1. However, the punishment was not severe or lasting. Male 1 discouraged many mounting attempts by male 2 simply by approaching the pair. Despite the increase of conflict in the mating season and restriction of lesser females' movements, the sociability of the group was maintained."

Reproductive Physiology

As early as a month and a half before the actual mating in wolves, blood may start seeping from the vagina of a sexually mature bitch (Young, 1944), a phenomenon peculiar to wolves, dogs, and coyotes (Scott and Fuller, 1965). In the Brookfield Zoo, however, vaginal blood usually begins flowing only one or two weeks before full estrus (Rabb, 1968). Murie reported that a captive wolf showed signs of heat for three weeks but did not accept a male dog until the third week, when she mated every day. Young stated that estrus continues for three to five days in wolves.

The breeding season of the wolf occurs from late January through April, depending on the latitude, with animals in the highest latitudes generally having the latest season (Table 12). Females coming into heat for the first time (twenty-two months of age) may breed a week or two later than fully adult females (R. A. Rausch, 1967a).

TABLE 12. Breeding seasons of wolves at various latitudes.

Location	Latitude	Breeding season	Authority
Illinois[1]	42°	Jan. 27–Feb. 19[2]	Rabb, 1968
Minnesota	45°	Feb. 24[3]	Fletcher, 1967
Ontario	47°	Mar. 4–Mar. 15[2]	Joslin, 1966; Pimlott, 1968
Isle Royale (Mich.)	47°	Feb. 21–27	Mech, 1966a
North Dakota	46°–49°	Jan.	Bailey, 1926
British Columbia	51°–53°	Mar., early Apr.	Cowan, 1947
Germany[1]	52°	Mar. 14[2]	Schönberner, 1965
N. Alberta	60°	Feb. 2–9[2]	Soper, 1942
N. Alberta	60°	Mar. 5–21	Fuller and Novakowski, 1955
Northwest Territories	60°–65°	late Mar.[2]	Kelsall, 1960
Alaska	63°	Mar. 9–15	Murie, 1944
Alaska	60°–70°	Mar. 15–Apr. 7	Kelly, 1954
Alaska	60°–70°	late Feb.–early Apr.	R. A. Rausch, 1967a
Finland	60°–70°	late Feb.–early Mar.	Pulliainen, 1965
N. Finland	70°	early Apr.	Pulliainen, 1965
N. Russia	71°	late Mar. thru Apr.	Makridin, 1962

[1] In captivity.
[2] Earliest and latest dates when copulatory ties were seen.
[3] Calculated from birth date, allowing sixty-three days of gestation.

Ovulation in the wolf probably occurs near the end of estrus, as it does in the dog (Whitney, 1947). The only intensive study of wolf reproductive physiology to date is that of R. A. Rausch on Alaskan wolves. He found that ovarian follicles measured six to nine mm. just before ovulation and that the average number of ova shed by full adults was 7.3. Of these an average of 6.5 actually im-

FIGURE 23. A wolf den is usually a deep hole in sandy ground with an entrance large enough for adults to enter readily. (*Robert J. R. Johnson*)

planted in the uterus. First-breeding females produced 5.6 ova and implanted 5.3 on the average.

Reported litter sizes of wolves from different areas vary somewhat, but in general the average litter contains from 4.0 to 6.5 young (Table 13). Although as few as three fetuses and as many as eleven have been found in female wolves, 88% of the sixty-nine litters whose precise sizes have been reported contained from four to seven pups.

The most exceptional data on wolf litter sizes come from Finland, where six litters averaged 2.8 pups and ranged from one to five. Evidently this is not the usual situation in Eurasia, for various authors on that continent have stated that five to six young are average (Pulliainen, 1967).

The gestation period for the wolf is reported as sixty-two to sixty-three days, with a three- or four-day variation (Brown, 1936; Woolpy, 1968).

TABLE 13. Average litter sizes reported for wolves.

Location	Number of litters	Average litter size	Range[1]	Information based on	Authority
Western Canada	4	5.0	4–7	pups	Cowan, 1947
Alberta	3	4.7	4–5	pups	Soper, 1942
Northwest Territories	5	4.0	3–6	pups	Kelsall, 1968
Ontario	17	4.9	3–7	placental scars and corpora albicantia	Pimlott et al., 1969
Minnesota	8	6.4	4–9	pups	Stenlund, 1955
Alaska	6	5.0	4–6	pups	Murie, 1944
Alaska	33	5.5	4–8	fetuses	Kelly, 1954
Alaska	175[2]	6.5	3–11	fetuses	R. A. Rausch, 1967a
Alaska	69[3]	5.3	?	fetuses	R. A. Rausch, 1967a
Finland	6	2.8	1–5	pups	Pulliainen, 1965

[1] Young (1944) stated that as many as fourteen pups may be found in a litter.
[2] From animals three years old or older.
[3] From animals two years old.

Denning

According to Young, pregnant wolves complete the digging of dens as early as three weeks before the birth of the pups. This is supported by Jordan *et al.* (1967), who found recent digging at a den on Isle Royale on March 13. Although these authors did not see wolves at the den, wolf tracks in the snow led from the den to a dead moose 1.2 miles away, upon which two wolves had fed for over two weeks. Since Isle Royale wolves mate during the fourth week of February (Mech, 1966a), this is evidence that den digging may begin four or five weeks before pups are born.

Several dens may be dug by the pregnant female and other pack members, and such dens may be close together or as far apart as ten miles (Young, 1944). Little is known about the travels of the female during this period, but Young claimed that she generally remains near one of the dens for three weeks before the young are born.

Most wolf dens that have been described are burrows in the ground, usually in sandy soil (Fig. 23). In tundra regions, dens are often dug into ridges of sand and gravel called "eskers." Wolves may originate the den, or they may enlarge holes of other animals, most often those of foxes. However, wolves have also been reported to den in abandoned beaver houses or dams, in the hollowed out bases of large trees, in hollow logs, in rock caves, or merely in shallow surface beds.

The following description of a typical wolf den is based on composite information from the literature. The entrance may measure fourteen to twenty-five inches in diameter, and it is usually oval in shape. The tunnel may be of the same size, but it is sometimes larger, and it generally extends six to fourteen feet into the earth. At the end of the tunnel is an enlarged chamber, where the newborn pups are kept; no bedding is used. Each den may have several entrances and passageways, and a large mound of soil from the excavation is usually present in front of the main entrance. Well-used trails radiate from the hole and sometimes extend for many rods away from the den.

Information about the interiors of wolf dens comes from people who either have dug out the den or who, like Murie, have crawled inside. Murie (1944: 22) stated the following about the East Fork Den in Mount McKinley Park, Alaska: "I wriggled into the burrow which was 16 inches high and 25 inches wide. Six feet from the entrance of the burrow there was a right angle turn. At the turn there was a hollow, rounded and worn, which obviously was a bed much used by an adult. . . . From the turn the burrow slanted slightly upward for 6 feet to the chamber in which the pups were huddled and squirming."

In selecting a site for a den, wolves usually prefer elevated areas near water. Of sixteen occupied dens described in the literature, at least ten were located on hillsides, ridges, or other rises. In addition, an occupied site in Minnesota, which I examined, was on the side of a sandy slope. One might gather from this that wolves prefer to survey their surroundings from the den. However, Joslin (1966) found that the visibility from six dens that he studied varied from five feet to two hundred feet and averaged only one hundred feet. Perhaps the main value of locating dens in higher ground is good drainage.

At least thirteen of the sixteen dens were situated near rivers, lakes, springs, or other water. In fact, five of the six dens studied by Joslin were within fifty feet of water and the sixth was within two hundred yards of a lake. The one I examined in Minnesota was within 125 yards of a lake. Probably a major factor in locating dens near water is the nursing female's great daily need for liquid.

The type and thickness of vegetation around wolf dens may vary considerably. Dens in Ontario were surrounded by spruce and balsam in one case, by sugar maple in another, and by beaked hazelnut in a third (Joslin, 1966). A wolf den studied by Stenlund in Minnesota was in a thick stand of balsam, and one I examined in that state was in an open stand of jack pines. A den in British Columbia was located in sparsely timbered country (Cowan, 1947). One den observed by Murie was twenty yards from timber, another was among cottonwoods and spruce, and a third was two miles above the nearest timber. In Manitoba a wolf den studied by Criddle was surrounded by various shrubs and trees. In the tundra region of the Northwest Territories, one den reported on by Kelsall in 1960 was located in stunted spruces, and another in thick willows.

It is interesting, however, that at a den in Algonquin Park the adult wolves showed a remarkable preference for the type of vegetation under which they bedded. Nine of the ten beds around this den were beneath black spruce or balsam, although the density of these conifers in the den area was only one-twelfth that of sugar maple (Joslin, 1966).

Adult wolves also prefer lying on high areas overlooking the den. All ten beds that Joslin studied were above the den. Criddle found several beds on a hilltop near the den he examined, and the adult wolves that Murie observed near the East Fork River in Alaska lay above the den on a slope. Such a habit would put the adults in the best possible position to detect intruders. Nevertheless, Murie (1944: 30) often sneaked up close to the East Fork Den before being discovered by the wolves: "Several times I was practically in the midst of the band before I was noticed. Once, after all the others had run off, one [wolf] which must have been sound asleep got up behind me and in following the others passed me at a distance of only about 30 yards. These wolves were scarcely molested during the course of the study, so they may have been less watchful than in places where they are hunted."

Generally, if undisturbed, a wolf pack will continue using the same den year after year. Murie observed the same wolf pack at the East Fork Den in 1940 and 1941. He and several other authors have also reported on other dens that had been used during at least two different years, probably—though not necessarily—by the same wolves. A den in Minnesota that was being used when I examined it in 1967 and in 1969 had also been occupied in 1955 according to Conservation Officer Robert Jacobsen, who directed me to it.

G. A. Novikov (1956) stated that wolves in the U.S.S.R. usually reuse the same dens each year, and Kozlov (1964) claimed that this was because permafrost made digging difficult on the tundra. On the other hand, Pulliainen (1965) indicated that in Finland and Lapland wolves dig new dens every year if possible.

It is difficult to draw conclusions about the effect of human disturbance on the reuse of wolf dens. None of five dens in Algonquin Park, Ontario, was reused the year after they were disturbed (Joslin, 1966). However, under certain conditions, human intrusion may have little effect, for the wolves in Mount McKinley Park's East Fork Den continued using it even after Murie invaded it and kidnaped a pup. No doubt such factors as degree of disturbance, history of the pack's encounters with humans, and availability of substitute dens all influence the relationship between disturbance and den reuse.

Wolves sometimes move their pups from one den to another before abandoning dens altogether, but to what extent these moves result from disturbance is unknown. Young reported that one pair of wolves and their litter used four dens in one season. Joslin concluded that one of the packs he was studying shifted its pups to a new den about 1.8 miles away when the pups were less than three weeks old. Banfield (1954) also recorded a wolf transferring her pups from one den to another. A female wolf in the Berlin Zoological Gardens moved her young from the birth den to one closer to water when they were nineteen days old, and to a third one even closer to water two days later, according to Dagmar Schönberner (1965). Murie found where one wolf shifted her pups into a new den with another female and her litter when the first pups were six to eight weeks old.

The age of wolf pups when the pack abandons the den is not yet known precisely. Young claimed that pups remain at the den until they are ten to twelve weeks old, and Pulliainen said twelve to fourteen weeks old, although neither author documented his statement. However, wolves that Murie watched kept their litter in a den for only eight weeks, and the two litters that he observed in the communal den abandoned it when eight to ten weeks old.

In Ontario, Joslin found that the pups he studied left their den after seven to ten weeks of life. In addition, the litter of captive pups studied by Schönberner used their dens very little after their eighth week of age. In view of the above, it appears that the usual time of den abandonment is when the pups are eight to ten weeks old.

Birth, Growth, and Development of Pups

As discussed above, a pregnant female begins remaining near the den about three weeks before her pups are to be born. About a day before birth of the young, the bitch confines herself to the den (Schönberner, 1965).

Although details of the birth of wolf pups are unavailable, the following description of the process in dogs, by Fuller and DuBuis (1962: 436), should give an approximate picture. Toward the end of the gestation period, the female spends much time resting and sleeping. Her retirement to the den, along with restlessness and frequent changes in position, marks the beginning of birth. When uterine contractions start, the female urinates often and strains about every ten minutes. Eventually she strains harder and harder, usually while sitting but sometimes while squatting in the urination position. Between contractions she pants freely and may examine and lick her vulva.

"During birth the puppies are presented at irregular intervals, occasionally within 5 to 10 minutes but more frequently spaced 20 to 60 minutes apart. When the first puppy is born, the female attends to it at once, breaking the amniotic sac and removing it by vigorous licking. With her jaws she then detaches the afterbirth if present; more often it is not passed until later. Within a few minutes the female chews through the umbilical cord 2 or 3 inches from the puppy's body and consumes it with all other waste. She attempts to clean her own hindquarters, but spends more time cleaning and drying the puppy and directing it to her side. When this has been accomplished, she curls herself protectively around the puppy and rests until the next birth begins." Whelping five pups requires about three hours.

Growth of pups. Newborn wolf pups are blind and deaf; they are darkly furred, and their ears are small, heads are rounded, and noses blunt or "pugged." Each weighs about one pound (Rutter and Pimlott, 1968).

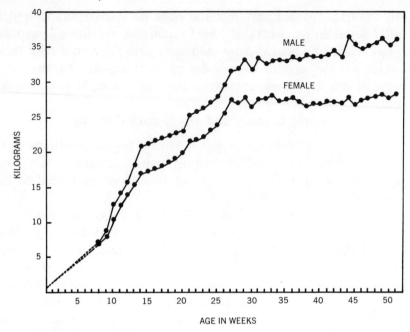

Figure 24. Comparative growth rates of male and female wolf pups. (*Pulliainen, 1965*)

The weights of wolf pups from birth to about one year of age (when they may reach adult size) increase at different rates depending on age. Pulliainen (1965) defined three periods of growth for captive pups: (1) the period of maximum growth, zero to fourteen weeks, in which the average increase is 2.6 pounds per week for females, and 3.3 pounds for males; (2) the period of rapid growth, fourteen to twenty-seven weeks—1.3 pounds per week for both males and females; and (3) the period of slow growth, twenty-seven to fifty-one weeks—.07-pound increase per week for females, and 0.4 pound for males (Fig. 24). These growth rates probably are maximum because of the abundance of food available to the captive animals.

Unfortunately, there are few records of the weights of wild wolf pups. Three littermates captured on July 24 in the Northwest Territories and estimated to be seven weeks old weighed the following: female, 15 pounds; female, 18.5 pounds; male 20.5 pounds (Kuyt, 1962). On the tenth and eighteenth of the following February, these wolves were recaptured, and they weighed sixty-six, seventy-six, and seventy-five pounds, respectively. It seems significant that the lightest pup remained lightest over the five-month period.

In Minnesota, Stenlund found that certain pups taken in September and early October, when about five to six months old, weighed as little as twenty-eight pounds, but that by November females were at least forty pounds, and males at least fifty.

The lightest of ten female pups taken in Alaska during November and December weighed approximately forty-seven pounds, and the lightest of fifteen males about fifty-six pounds (Table 14).

Measurements of young wolf pups from the wild are also difficult to obtain. Murie reported the following for a captive female pup born in Alaska about May 8: on May 15, her total length from tail tip to nose tip was 14⅝ inches; her tail was 3⅝ inches; hind foot, 2⅜ inches; and ear, 1 inch; her shoulder height was 14½ inches on July 12, 17½ inches on August 6, 19½ inches on September 5, and 24 inches on October 23. Kuyt gave the standard measurements of the three pups captured in the Northwest Territories at the age of about seven weeks.

Additional detailed weight and growth data on captive wolf pups are on file at the Alaska Game and Fish Commission (Garceau, 1960).

TABLE 14. Weights (pounds) of skinned wolf pups from Alaska[1].

Date taken[2]	Approximate age (months)	Male[3]			Female[3]		
		Number	Range	Average	Number	Range	Average
Nov.–Dec.	5.5– 7.5	15	46–76	62	10	37–56	50
Jan.–Feb.	7.5– 9.5	10	54–90	62	8	56–74	68
Mar.–Apr.	9.5–11.5	14	52–88	71	14	46–72	58

[1] R. A. Rausch, 1967b.
[2] 1965–66.
[3] Ten to twelve pounds should be added for approximation of live weights.

Physical and behavioral development. In analyzing the physical and behavioral development in dog pups, Scott and Fuller (1965) recognized four periods: (1) the neonatal period, from birth to the age of eye opening, (2) the transition period, from the age of eye opening to twenty days, (3) the period of socialization, from twenty to about seventy-seven days, and (4) the juvenile period, from twelve weeks to maturity. In general, it appears that wolf pups develop similarly (Scott, 1967). The following discussion is from Scott and Fuller except where otherwise indicated.

During the neonatal period, pups are blind and deaf and have little, if any, sense of smell; they have a poor ability to regulate their body temperature. They do possess a good sense of balance, of taste, and of touch—including perception of hot and cold, pain, and pressure—and they can whine and yelp. Their motor capacities are limited to a slow crawl, mainly with the front legs, and to sucking and licking.

Murie raised a female wolf taken from a den at an estimated age of less than one week. She was blind and could only crawl on her belly. She also whimpered a great deal and drank milk from an artificial nipple. When about eleven days old, she consumed 8½ ounces of milk per day, and four days later was drinking thirteen ounces per day.

Neonatal pups respond very little to outside stimuli. When cold, they seek warmth; when isolated or hungry, they whine ("et-epimiletic," or care-seeking behavior) and seek contact with another animal or a soft object ("contactual" and "investigatory" behavior). Upon contacting their mother's nipples, they begin sucking ("ingestive" behavior). Their ability to learn is very limited.

When pups during this period are rubbed on their underside with a warm wet object, usually their mother's tongue, they urinate and defecate ("eliminative" behavior), and the adult wolf licks up the waste matter. This behavior not only removes bodily wastes, but it is also thought to provide the psychological and postural beginnings of an important adult behavior pattern—passive submission (Schenkel, 1967). In this pattern, discussed in Chapter III, a submissive wolf assumes the same position as a pup submitting to its mother's stimulation to defecate and urinate: prostrate on back or side with a hind leg lifted exposing the genital and anal area (Fig. 11). The dominant wolf, during adult life, behaves the same as the mother stimulating her pup, investigating and licking the anal-genital area of the prostrate animal.

The next period of development, the transition period, begins when the pups' eyes open. In wolves, this may be from the eleventh to the fifteenth day. Wolf pups at the Moscow Zoopark opened their eyes on the eleventh to twelfth days (Iljin, 1941),

FIGURE 25. A wolf pup about three weeks old can already walk well and may romp and play around the den entrance. (*L. David Mech*)

and pups from two litters in Ontario had their eyes fully open at thirteen days of age (Rutter and Pimlott, 1968). In two zoo-born pups that I raised, the eyes were not wide open until the pups were fifteen days old, although they began opening on the twelfth day. Even when the eyes are fully open, pups see only very poorly and are not able to perceive forms until weeks later (Scott and Fuller, 1965).

During the transition period the abilities of the pups change rapidly, preparing the animals for a more adultlike life. Our pups began to stand, walk, growl, and chew during this period; one of them even showed the beginnings of an avoidance reaction by backing up. A few front teeth erupted on the fifteenth day of the pups' lives, and by their twenty-first day, both pups began to hear, marking the end of the transition period. At this stage, dog pups suddenly start to make associations between things and for the first time can be psychologically conditioned.

By this time our pups were each drinking about one pint of milk per day.

In the wild, three-week-old wolf pups (Fig. 25) begin appearing outside the den and romping and playing near the entrance (Young, 1944). Evidently they, like dog pups, can control their body temperatures much better at this age than during the neonatal period.

The period of socialization begins at this time, and it features both a rapid development of social behavior patterns and emotional attachments to places and individuals (Scott, 1967). "Playfighting"—the beginning of "agonistic" behavior—starts at this time, and, according to Fuller and DuBuis (1962), it eventually helps establish the dominance relations among the littermates (Chapter III).

It is possible, however, for a wolf pup's social status to be determined by serious fighting as early as the thirtieth day of life. I learned this dramatically while raising the two zoo-born pups. These animals were members of a litter of six born in the St. Paul (Minnesota) Zoo on April 27, 1967. On May 9, when twelve days old, the male, which we named Thunder, and the female, Lightning, were brought into our home. The male, who was the more aggressive, weighed 2½ pounds at that time, and the female 2⅜ pounds. We fed them separately from baby bottles, and after each feeding they chewed on clothing and rugs. This probably substituted for the extra non-nutritive sucking that they would have done on their mother's nipples (Fuller and DuBuis, 1962).

By May 21, a standard postfeeding ritual became apparent between the pups. It looked much like the "riding up" posture in adult wolves (Chapter III) and could be begun by either pup. One would place its forefeet and neck over the neck and back of the other from either the side or the back and try to press or ride the bottom one (Fig. 26). If done from the back, it was like the sexual mounting position of the male. As the top pup pressed, the bottom animal would growl, and then the top one would begin biting its neck or back. Loud, angry, and intense growling usually accompanied such biting, and the bitten animal would yelp loudly. It was difficult to break up the pair at this time, and when broken apart each pup would try to repeat the ritual.

Nevertheless, when placed together each night in a box, the pups slept peacefully. If allowed to choose their own resting sites, however, they usually selected separate ones.

On May 25, the pups fought a great deal. The female seemed to initiate most of the fights, even though the male was larger and usually ended up hurting her more. When I placed the pups in their box that night they fought intensely, each trying hard to bite and chew the other's back. I allowed them to continue their struggle for ten to fifteen minutes until it looked like they might seriously harm each other.

FIGURE 26. "Riding up" is a display of dominance seen even in young pups. (*L. David Mech*)

FIGURE 27. Wolf pups may settle their social status early in life. A. When 28 days old, a male and female pup raised by the author began fighting constantly, and had to be forcibly separated.

B. At the age of 30 days, when they were put together again, they immediately began pushing one another.

C. The contest then turned into a general wrestling match.

D. Each wolf kept trying hard to bite the other's back.

E. Eventually the female rolled over and began whining and the male suddenly raised his tail—a sign of dominance.

F. The female lay on her back in "passive submission" while the male kept his dominant posture.

G. While each pup held its position, the female mouthed the genitals of the male. The social order had been settled. During all future relations, each pup merely showed its status, and they never fought again. (*L. David Mech*)

When I separated the pups, each one's back was well chewed and was so soaked with saliva that the fur was matted. The female's back was more chewed than the male's, her skin was apparent for half its length, and a small amount of blood showed. After their separation, the pups lay still for several minutes panting, and it appeared that they might die from exhaustion. The male vomited several times, perhaps from the fur he had swallowed during the fight. I separated them for the night.

The next day, both wolves appeared uninjured, but they fought whenever they could get together. The female especially sought out her littermate and whined a great deal to get to him. When she did, she would immediately begin fighting again. We kept the pups apart throughout most of the day, the next night, and the next morning.

Then in the afternoon of May 27, we placed the pups together to photograph. They immediately growled and began fighting as usual (Figs. 27a–g). But this time there was a great difference. After just a few seconds, the female rolled over on her back, whined, snapped at the air, and assumed the position of passive submission (Chapter III). Immediately the male stopped his aggression and stood stiff-leggedly over her in the dominant "standing across" posture with tail held vertically. This behavior was repeated many times during the afternoon. In several cases the male turned around, and the female excitedly sucked his penis for about ten seconds. Sometimes he would then lick her genitals before leaving her.

When the pups rested that afternoon, they chose to lie within a few inches of each other. At first there was some growling and snapping but no contact. An hour later they were in a new site with their bodies touching. Some growling and short fights still occurred, but the pups remained next to each other. After another hour they were sleeping together peacefully. From then on, no serious fighting ever took place. Instead, each time the wolves got together, they performed the dominance-submission ritual.

Thus by the age of thirty days, the pups had determined their social status. The male remained dominant until his death from distemper at the age of fifteen weeks. Although he would submit to large dogs that entered the yard, he did assert his dominance through a fence to a German shepherd pup half again as large as him in the yard next door. At the same time, the female submitted to this dog. The dog gave no reaction to either display.

To learn whether or not serious fighting had occurred in the litter of pups from which ours were taken, I examined the backs of each pup in the zoo. There were no scars such as were evident on the backs of both our pups, so apparently no serious fighting had taken place among them, perhaps because the adults were present. Thus the way that social status was established between our pups is not necessarily the usual method. It does seem significant, however, that two hand-raised coyote pups studied by Carol Snow (1967) also fought seriously when about one month old until one animal eventually gained dominance. Perhaps this method of status determination is usual in the absence of adults.

Besides the development of social-behavior patterns during the period of socialization, the formation of emotional bonds is also very important at this stage in the life of the wolf. Dog pups can make these social ties to individuals when only three weeks old, and since human beings usually are included in their surroundings, the pups easily form attachments to them (Scott, 1967).

With wolf pups, the only individuals nearby are their littermates and the adult members of the pack, so the emotional attachments are formed among these animals, and the basis is laid for the formation or continuation of the pack (Chapter II). If a wolf pup is raised by a human being during this period, it will attach to the human instead of to packmates.

Lois Crisler provided an extremely interesting and detailed account of such human-wolf attachments. She and her husband raised a pair of wolf pups one year on the arctic tundra, and a litter of five pups a second year. The animals included the Crislers in their pack, and both wolves and humans roamed the tundra, howled, and displayed affection as members of the same pack.

The process of attachment between two animals involves (1) a mutual extension of friendliness, the reception of which seems to be a reward in itself (Scott and Fuller, 1965), and (2) the relieving of emotional distress by the rejoining of individuals whose isolation from each other causes the distress (Scott, 1967).

This process takes place during a period when members of a litter begin following one another, when three or four weeks old, and acting as a group, when about five weeks old ("allelomimetic," or imitative, behavior). Play-fighting and mounting and clasping patterns—the rudiments of sexual behavior—also become evident at this time. No doubt all these behavior patterns not only result from the attachment process, but also help reinforce it.

Reinforcement of emotional ties in wolf pups seems to be very important. Woolpy and Ginsburg (1967) found that captive wolves which as young pups had formed ties with human beings lost their attachments to people if kept from them for six months or more. Such a long absence of social interactions would not take place in a wild wolf pack, of course. Social contact between adult pack members and the pups occurs continually, and these no doubt provide the reinforcement necessary for the lasting emotional ties that hold the pack together.

The period of socialization is also marked by other important developments besides the formation of emotional bonds, however. In the very beginning of the period, the pups are forced to nurse while standing, to follow the female around near the den, and to become accustomed to eating semiliquid food regurgitated by the adults.

The feeding behavior of the pups after they have learned to eat this predigested food is of special importance. When an adult approaches the pups, they swarm around the animal and sniff, nip, and nuzzle its mouth (Fig. 28). The adult then disgorges its food, which the pups promptly swallow. But this begging behavior of the pups is thought to have much additional significance. Just as the neonatal posture of elimination appears to form the basis of the

FIGURE 28. When begging food, wolf pups mouth the muzzle of an adult, and the animal regurgitates food which they eat. (*D. H. Pimlott*)

passive-submission pattern in adults, so too begging behavior is thought to provide the postural and psychological basis for active submission (Fig. 15) (Schenkel, 1967). The similarity between this food-begging behavior and active submission is obvious.

Feeding on the semiliquid disgorgements of the adults leads to weaning, which is a more gradual, gentle process in wolves than in dogs (Ginsburg, 1965). Young claimed that weaning in wolves usually takes place when the pups are six to eight weeks old, but Schönberner's captive pups stopped nursing by their thirty-fifth day. Our pups began accepting solid food when twenty-three days old, although we did not completely discontinue bottle feeding until they were fifty days old. Their littermates in the zoo were still occasionally going through the motions of nursing when eleven weeks old, according to one of their keepers. No doubt there is a certain amount of psychological fulfillment in the nursing process even when milk is no longer available.

During the period of socialization (Fig. 29) wolf pups learn to run, climb, jump, and play in most of the adult patterns, although they lack stamina, strength, and speed. They explore a great deal and chew anything chewable. Further information about the physical development and general behavior of wolf pups in this stage is included in Table 15.

TABLE 15. Development of captive wolf pups during the period of socialization and the early juvenile period.

Age (days)	Event
27	Ears starting to raise[3].
28	Howling[1].
29	Ventured about six yards from den[2].
31	Ears standing at base but tips still flopped over[3].
32	Showed interest in bone[2].
34	Snapped excitedly at raw meat[3].
38	Began using area of 3600 square yards[2].
39	Eating meat; galloping behind adults[2].
40	Nibbling and eating leaves[2].
35–42	Showed fear and caution of strange objects[1,4].
42–70	Marked improvement of motor abilities[1].
46	Escaped from yard but returned when called[3].
52	Ran excitedly back and forth with adults just before feeding time[2].
56	Showed pelvic thrusts, pouncing, and interest in scent post[1].
57	Buried bone[3].
59	Fed independently of adults[2].
66	Adult hair apparent on face[3].
69	Chased pigeon[2]; geese[1].
70	Shook mop and growled menacingly[1].
73	Adult hair becoming apparent on body[3].
75	Tended to tear clothing and peel it when wrestling with people[3].
81	Hair on tail starting to stand out[3].
87	Rubbed neck in foul-smelling matter[3].

[1] Fentress, 1967.
[2] Schönberner, 1965.
[3] Author's observations.
[4] Woolpy and Ginsburg, 1967.

The development of two further aspects of wolf behavior during this period bears additional discussion, howling and predatory activity. A male pup raised by Fentress howled when twenty-eight days old. Our pups only whined at this age, however. Eventually the whines became prolonged until they could be recognized as howls when the pups were about fifty days old. The wolves howled only in response to fire sirens or imitations of them,

FIGURE 29. Wolf pups grow rapidly, and at the age of
two months have large feet and a large head. (*L. David
Mech*)

and began by whining and yipping much like coyotes. Pups in
Schönberner's captive pack did not howl until sixty-two days old.
The fact that the pup with least company howled at the earliest
age, and so on, tends to support the idea that there is a connection
between loneliness and howling (Chapter III).

The beginnings of predatory behavior are noticeable early during the period of socialization, and they continue to develop
throughout the period. When our pups were thirty-four days old,
the male snapped "viciously" at raw meat offered him; the female
was less aggressive in this respect. Chewing and determined tugging on soft objects was apparent in both animals even before this.
Fentress' wolf was seen pouncing—an activity especially useful in
catching mice—when it was about eight weeks old. By the tenth
week of life, a wolf pup will menacingly shake such woolly objects as mops and will even chase small animals (Table 15).

Wolf pups also take an interest in peeling and stripping things during this stage. Ours killed two ornamental trees in the yard by completely stripping the bark from them. When I would don old clothes and wrestle with the pups, they often ripped the clothes and then tried to peel them from me. The tugging and pulling involved in this act reminded me of the same activity that I had seen in wild wolves killing moose. Probably pups of this age in the wild would be presented by their parents with chunks of hide on which to practice this useful technique.

The above activities, and the tendency to nip at the hind legs of running animals, are the only ones I have seen in tame wolves that might be viewed as inborn patterns related to killing behavior. Under the usual conditions of captivity there are fewer chances for wolf pups to practice, develop, and integrate these patterns than there would be in the wild. Because several wolves have been raised that have not killed other animals, it appears that the wolf does not have an inborn tendency to kill. Rather, it is born with certain behavior patterns that *allow it to learn to kill.* When the wolf is reared under natural conditions, these patterns develop normally, and the animal does learn to kill. No doubt both imitation of the killing behavior of the adults and the association of killing with eating are important steps in the learning process.

However, it is also true that some wolves raised without exposure to wild adults have learned by themselves to kill. The wolf raised by Fentress killed a few chickens when it was thirteen weeks old, and four nineteen-month-old captive wolves released on an island learned to kill deer (Merriam, 1964). Evidently the various behavior patterns necessary for learning to kill are developed well enough in the wolf that it does not take much practice for them to become integrated into the entire killing procedure.

The fourth period of development that Scott and Fuller recognized is the juvenile period. It begins about the twelfth week and continues until the onset of sexual maturity, which occurs in wolves at about the age of twenty-two months, and it is characterized by gradual change and the maturing of motor capacities. Imitation also grows more and more apparent, and the pups begin behaving almost as a unit.

The wolf pup's ability to form emotional ties to new individuals decreases early in the juvenile period. By the time captive animals are three months old, it requires considerable effort to make them form new social attachments (Woolpy and Ginsburg, 1967). Fentress noticed that when his male was twenty weeks old the animal suddenly became very wary of new persons; he still greeted with enthusiasm the individuals he had met even weeks before, however. Our female also began acting the same way at this age. Whereas she had previously submitted to new persons and dogs, after her twentieth week of age she became very frightened of new people, especially of adult males.

Our wolf continued to submit to strange dogs brought into the yard after she was twenty weeks old, but she suddenly became very disturbed over those that entered the yards nearby. For the first time, the hairs on her mane and the entire length of her mid-back bristled, and her tail stood out horizontally. She tried very hard to get to the dogs as if to attack them.

It is easy to see how such a psychological change would benefit wolves in the wild. As pointed out earlier, during the first few months of life the pups would be surrounded only by their own pack members and thus would form emotional ties only to them. However, as they grow older and begin to move around more they might meet wolves from other packs. If the pups were to attach emotionally to these alien wolves, the unity of their own pack would break down, and so would the entire organization of wolf society.

Sometime much later during the juvenile period wolf pups begin to hunt. As will be discussed later, they spend several months in various temporary resting sites ("rendezvous sites") throughout the summer. During this time, the adults bring them food, or in the case of large carcasses they may move the pups to the food. The pups continue to use rendezvous sites at least through September. They may do some limited mouse hunting by themselves during this time (Murie, 1944), but probably do not yet join the adults in hunting big game.

The milk, or "puppy," teeth of wolves are replaced between the ages of sixteen and twenty-six weeks (Schönberner, 1965; Table 16), so the pups would not be physically able to kill large animals efficiently before that age.

Perhaps the pups do not become self-sufficient at hunting and killing until they are much older. In February 1968, I saw two instances in Minnesota in which a single wolf had killed a deer, eaten a small portion, and left (Mech and Frenzel, unpublished).

TABLE 16. Tooth development and replacement in a captive female wolf.

Age (days)	Event
15	Milk incisors present.
23	All incisors, canines, and at least one premolar present on both sides, top and bottom.
114	Middle four milk incisors, top and bottom, missing; outer incisors loose.
122[1]	Middle four adult incisors present, top and bottom; three of four outer milk incisors still present.
129[1]	All adult incisors present.
147	Adult upper canines ⅜″ long; lower milk canines still present; two adult premolars just erupted.
157	All adult premolars erupted and almost fully in; adult lower right canine ¼″ long; left lower canine pushing gum up; but both lower milk canines still present on outside of adult canines.
168	All milk canines gone and all adult canines about halfway in.

[1] Wolf was often mouthing and biting small pebbles at this time, presumably as an aid in teething.

In each case, the animal evidently brought the rest of its pack to the scene within twelve hours, for the next day only hair and blood remained of these carcasses. Tracks showed that packs of five or six wolves had fed on them.

In addition, a similar incident, observed on March 10, 1968, in the same area was reported to me. In this case, conservation officer Robert Hodge watched from his aircraft as a wolf killed a deer. Two and one half hours later (about 4:30 P.M.), the wolf was gone after having eaten part of the deer. About a mile away, Hodge saw a pack of seven wolves, with six lying side by side on their haunches; the seventh animal was sprawled out on its side as though engorged. By the next day, only a few bones remained of the carcass.

The most plausible interpretation of these events is that in each case an adult wolf had gone off to hunt by itself and had then brought the other pack members, including the pups, to its kill. This would merely be a continuation of the living habits of wolf families as known to occur in late summer and early autumn and outlined above. If this supposition is true, it would give further evidence that pups may not be very active hunters for at least their first ten months of age.

During the middle of the juvenile period, when the wolf pup is ten months old, physical growth and weight changes level off. The epiphyseal cartilage, or growing point of the long bone, closes at about one year of age, marking the end of skeletal growth (R. A. Rausch, 1967a). Physically the wolf pup looks much like an adult from the age of about six months on (Fig. 30), and at the age of ten to twelve months, it is very difficult to tell the two apart in the wild.

However, Jordan *et al.* (1967: 245), in collaboration with Ginsburg and Woolpy, of the University of Chicago, seem to have made some progress with this problem. They wrote the following: "More uniform dorso-ventral coloration, more fuzzy pelage, stubbier head, and shallower trunk are characters believed useful for classifying at least some pups. Walking or trotting gait

FIGURE 30. The six-month-old wolf pup already resembles an adult. (*L. David Mech*)

was more irregular, and the supposed pups were inclined to stumble on rough ice. We believe we could recognize certain immature postures on the basis of their similarity to those in domestic dog pups. The supposed wolf pups often attempted to elicit attention from adults or to engage them in play. When rebuffed, these animals retreated but did not display the sort of submissive postures shown by retreating adults."

Although general physical development ends after the first year, sexual and psychological changes continue until the wolf reaches maturity, toward the end of its second year. From then on, the only changes that might take place would be social (the possible increase in status that a maturing wolf may attain), or intellectual (the continued learning of when, where, and how to hunt). Undoubtedly learning continues throughout the life of the wolf.

The maximum life span of wolves in the wild has never been determined. Young summarized the records from captive wolves, and these reports show that a ten-year-old wolf is very old and that sixteen years is the maximum life span. Fuller and DuBuis estimated that old age in the larger breeds of dogs begins at about seven years of age.

Table 17 summarizes the significant points in the development of the wolf pups, and Table 16 traces tooth development and replacement.

Parental and Pack Care of the Young

During the first few days after giving birth, the bitch wolf remains with her litter almost constantly (Schönberner, 1965). Her behavior and that of her pups at this time probably are the same as that of domestic dogs and their pups. According to Fuller and DuBuis, the female dog lies stretched out on her side in the den with the pups resting on or beside her, in the same position in which she usually nurses them. If a pup strays away, it begins whining, and the dam picks it up and returns it to the nest (Scott and Fuller, 1965).

A mother wolf observed by Dagmar Schönberner in the Berlin Zoological Garden began to spend some time out of the den beginning on the fifth day of the pups' life. Fuller and DuBuis stated that two weeks after giving birth the female dog may remain away from her pups for two or three hours at a time.

TABLE 17. Summary of the developments in the growth and living habits of wolf pups.

Age	Significant Developments	Development Period[1]	Growth Period[2]	Approximate Weight (Pounds)
Birth		Neonatal ↓	Maximal growth	0.5–1.0
11–15 days	Eyes open	Transition ↓		3.5
20 days	Hearing begins	Period of Socialization		7.0
21 days	First emergence from den			
35 days	Weaning			13.0
8–10 weeks	Pups abandon den and live in temporary rendezvous sites			15.0–22.0
11 weeks		Juvenile		20.0–30.0
14 weeks			Rapid growth	25.0–45.0
16–26 weeks	Milk teeth replaced; winter pelage becomes apparent			28.0–70.0
27–32 weeks	Pups leave rendezvous sites and begin to travel with the pack (?)		Slow growth	30.0–80.0
1 year	Epiphyseal cartilage closes		End of bone growth	60.0–100.0
22 months	Sexual maturity	Adulthood		

[1] Scott and Fuller (1965); Scott (1967).
[2] Pulliainen (1965).

On the basis of his long observations at a wolf den in Alaska, Murie (1944: 29) gave the following description of the female's activity around the den: "The first few weeks the gray female spent much time in the den with the pups, both during the day and at night. When she was outside she usually lay only a few yards from the entrance, although she sometimes wandered off as far as half a mile to feed on cached meat. When the rest of the band was off on the night hunt, she remained at home. . . ."

As discussed in the previous section, the pups begin feeding on predigested food disgorged by the adults during their fourth week of age. The stimulus for the regurgitation seems to be the mere presence of the pups in some cases, or their begging behavior in others—licking, nuzzling, nipping, or pawing of the mouth or head of an adult (Fig. 28).

It is not known how long this behavior continues under natural conditions. However, experiments that I carried out with wolf pups in the St. Paul Zoo provide some information on the subject. On October 10, 1967, when the pups were about five and a half months old, the parents were separated from them and fed; the pups received no food. Adults and pups were than allowed to mingle. The pups immediately began whining and mouthing the muzzle of the female. After less than a minute, she regurgitated and the pups ate the food.

In a similar test with the same wolves on December 20, 1967, this behavior did not occur, at least during the first half hour after the feeding. However, during a different type of experiment with these wolves on January 18, 1968, the behavior was seen. Its total significance in that situation is unknown, but there was reason to believe that the behavior was at least partly symbolic.

No mature physiological or psychological state seems to be necessary for wolves to respond to the begging behavior of pups. Lois Crisler's tame year-old male and female wolves both regurgitated immediately upon seeing a litter of pups. Carol Snow (1967) reported that an unbred female coyote disgorged food to another female's pups as early as the dam herself did.

Crisler furnished details about this behavior that would be very difficult to obtain under the usual conditions. When the pair of wolves that she and her husband raised on the arctic tundra were a year old, the Crislers brought them a litter of five wolf pups (about five or six weeks old, judging from photos). The pair immediately took charge of feeding and caring for the entire litter.

The female usually stayed with the pups, and the male brought back food for all. However, both seemed to "enjoy" regurgitating food to the pups. The adults could control the amount of meat they disgorged, and sometimes would leave it in several piles. If the pups did not finish the entire load, the adults might eat it again. If the pups were full, the adults would cache their disgorgements. According to Crisler (1958: 237), "the wolves hated to give the pups stale meat but when they had choice fresh tidbits they could hardly wait to get to the pups and give up all they had; it gratified them to do that." These "tidbits" consisted of sinew, connective tissue, and strings of intestinal fat. If the adults were empty when the pups begged for food, they would promptly begin hunting, even in midday.

Adult pack members will travel long distances from the den for food. Crisler estimated that her male wolf once carried a load of caribou meat in his stomach for eighteen miles, since the nearest caribou were at least that far away. Dixon (1934) recorded a wolf carrying meat for over twelve miles to a den, and Murie stated that a usual hunting jaunt is ten or fifteen miles. In the Northwest Territories, wolves sometimes hunt as far as twenty miles from the den (Kelsall, 1957). Crisler's female wolf once brought the lower leg and hoof of a caribou home to the pups from a carcass a mile away.

On the tundra, wolves depend on migrating bands of caribou for food. Since these caribou herds may move hundreds of miles, no one knows what wolves that are restricted during the denning period would do for food in such a situation. It is thought that they may kill a large number of animals before denning so that the carcasses would be available to them and the pups throughout the denning period (Young, 1944). However, this idea arose merely as an explanation for the finding of several wolf kills in a small area in spring. It is strictly supposition and must be viewed cautiously. Pimlott (1967b) believed that tundra wolves might be able to live throughout summer on the small bands of caribou stragglers such as Murie found remaining behind the large migrating herds. Food buried during spring might be another possible source of supply to denning wolves (Chapter VI).

Probably all pack members help feed the female and the young. At least three wolves other than the dam carried food back to the East Fork Den in Mount McKinley Park (Murie, 1944). They took some of it directly to the den, but cached much of it one hundred to two hundred yards away, and some as far as a half mile away. On three nights, an adult female other than the dam stayed at the den with the pups, while the dam accompanied the rest of the pack on its hunting expedition. Both females and the sire of the litter were very attentive to the young and even visited them in the den. The two other pack members, both males, also showed interest in the pups.

Other evidence of communal or pack care of the young comes from studies of captive wolves. In the Brookfield Zoo, care of the young was a pack project. The males fed the young but were not allowed in the den. For several seasons an unmated female, which had been harassed by the pack, served as a "dry nurse" for the litter and even kept the males out of the den. After performing her "nursemaid" role, such an outcast usually regained status in the pack (Rabb *et al.,* 1962).

In the captive pack studied by Schönberner, both the sire of the litter and an unmated two-year-old female became intensely excited over the pups. A day after the young wolves were born, the male was licking and playing with one of them. Usually, however, he was discouraged by the extra female from handling the pups. Nevertheless, whenever he could, he guarded and fed them, and cleaned their anal regions. The unmated female also carried out all these functions and seemed more concerned about the young than was the dam. A similar situation was seen in captive coyotes. An unmated female coyote played more with a litter of pups and fed them at least as often, if not more often, than their dam (Snow, 1967).

In Schönberner's captive group, both females carried the young from den to den, but would not allow the male to do so. During the transfer the male would follow these animals, whine, and lick the pups. When transporting the young, the adults may hold them by the back of the neck, by the entire body, by the neck and back, or by the belly and a hind leg or hip (Young, 1944; Schönberner, 1965).

Communal care of the young also extends to defending them from forays by other predators, primarily bears, but this will be discussed in Chapter X.

Rendezvous Sites

In the section on denning, evidence was presented that wolf pups leave their den when eight to ten weeks old. Until recently, however, little was known about their living habits between that period and winter. Murie did make a few observations of the Mount McKinley wolves after they abandoned the East Fork Den, and he assumed that the pups were left at some "rendezvous" while the rest of the pack hunted. Young also recognized "loafing spots," or resting sites, where the pups remain for periods of several days while the adults hunt the surrounding countryside.

However, only recently have details about the postdenning habits of the wolf pups been obtained. A revealing study of the summer activities of wolf packs in Algonquin Provincial Park, Ontario, was conducted by Paul Joslin. Using Pimlott's technique of stimulating wild wolves to reply to artificial or recorded howling, he located dens and several activity areas used by wolf litters after abandoning the dens. He called these areas "rendezvous sites," after Murie's terminology.

Following is a description of these sites by Joslin (1967: 286): "Eleven rendezvous sites were examined. With one exception, all of the sites bordered a small bog which had a small amount of open water and had a maximum field of vision of 300 feet or less. . . . The one exception was the Sunny Lake site which was situated on a point between two lakes and commanded a view of over 1,200 feet, most of which was water.

"Rendezvous sites were characterized by a system of trails, beds, and activity areas. In the latter, large areas of vegetation, usually sedges and grasses, had been leveled, presumably as a result of playing by the pups or adults."

The trails usually bordered the bogs, although some also crossed them. Most of the beds were at the edges of the forest surrounding the bog, and there were usually at least four or five. The activity areas themselves were in the bogs, in the forest, or both. They were usually about thirty square feet in area, but one covered 1100 square feet (Fig. 31). The area of an entire rendezvous site was about .5 acre, as measured from an illustration by Joslin (1967).

Litters of wolf pups used these sites for an average of seventeen days each, with extremes of six to thirty days. By howling to the pups and obtaining responses, Joslin learned that, although the pups remained at the sites most of the time, some or all of the adults were often away, probably hunting. Some of the rendezvous sites seemed to have begun as locations where adults had killed large animals; rather than transport food from the kill to the pups, they took the pups to the kill. Movement of the pups from one site to another took place overnight, even when the distance between sites was as great as five miles (Joslin, 1966).

In another part of Ontario, Kolenosky and Johnston (1967) also examined rendezvous sites, which they discovered by radio-tracking wolves to them. All five of the sites that these biologists found were in semiopen areas next to swamps or beaver ponds but were well drained themselves. They measured .5 to one acre

FIGURE 31. Rendezvous sites were characterized by a system of trails, beds, and activity areas. In the latter, large areas of vegetation, usually sedges and grasses, had been leveled, presumably as a result of playing by the pups or adults. (*P. W. B. Joslin*)

in area and were characterized by the presence of trails, beds, and droppings, much like the rendezvous sites studied by Joslin.

Just as dens are used year after year if undisturbed, at least some rendezvous sites may also be reused. One of the wolf packs studied by Joslin in 1961 and 1963 occupied some of the same sites during both years.

Use of rendezvous sites continues throughout summer and at least until late September (Murie, 1944; Joslin, 1967). The actual distances between rendezvous sites and the area that the pack covers during this period will be discussed in the next chapter.

CHAPTER V / THE WOLF'S WANDERINGS

"The wolf is kept fed by his feet." This old Russian proverb, unlike many popular sayings, contains a great deal of truth. One of the wolf's strongest traits is the urge to travel. Anyone who has tried to track a pack of wolves, even with an aircraft, cannot help but be impressed with the long distances over which the animals wander. There are few other mammals that on a day-to-day basis roam so widely as the wolf.

The wolf's wanderings are of two main types: (1) those that center around a den or rendezvous site, from April through late fall, and (2) those that take place throughout the rest of the year, when all the wolves assume wayfaring ways. Although the total distance traveled each day may be about the same during both periods, summer travel is much less extensive because the adults must return to the pups each day.

Summer Movements and Activity

There is usually a day-night rhythm in the activity of wolves during the warm seasons. The animals begin traveling early in the evening and return to the den or rendezvous site sometime during the night or at least by late morning.

Murie's (1944) observations at Mount McKinley Park's East Fork Den during May and June are a case in point. Five of the eleven times that he watched the adults start off on the night hunt, they left between 4:00 and 5:45 P.M. The six other times they departed between 7:00 and 9:30 P.M. They usually returned by morning, although on one occasion, three wolves stayed away from the den for at least twenty-eight hours.

In northern Canada, a similar study at a wolf den from June 13 to July 26 showed that the adult wolves rested near the den in the afternoon, but that in late evening there was an increase in hunting activity; usually at least one of the adults was absent from the den area from midnight until morning (Banfield, 1954).

In southern Ontario, Joslin (1966) also found that in summer most wolf movements take place at night. Kolenosky and Johnston (1967), who tracked wolves by radio in Ontario, confirmed this but also learned that some wolves do travel during the day at certain times. According to the preliminary data of these biologists, most extreme weather conditions (except heavy rain) do not affect the movements of wolves.

Perhaps the main reason that wolves are active mostly at night during summer is that it is too hot during the day. The two wolf pups that I raised in Minnesota usually spent their summer days trying to keep cool. They dug beds into the soil and upon each reuse of a bed would skim off the top layer of dry earth. They always slept in cool shady areas and seldom stayed in sunlight for even a few minutes. When they were active during a hot day, they panted a great deal and quickly became overheated. It is easy to see why wolves in the wild would save their extensive travels until nightfall.

In Chapter IV it was shown that wolves on the tundra may travel twenty miles from the den to obtain food, a forty-mile round trip each day. Although this seems impressive to us, it is a routine matter for the wolf. At the usual trotting rate of about five mph a wolf could make its round trip in eight hours, and it probably is a rare wolf that puts in merely an eight-hour day.

Probably tundra wolves must travel much farther for food than wolves in forested areas because prey animals on the tundra are distributed very unevenly. For example, in certain areas there may be no caribou for hundreds of miles around, yet in another small area there will be thousands. South of the tundra, wolves depend on a greater variety of prey, which can be found throughout most of the range.

In southern Ontario, where the summer prey of the wolf consists primarily of beavers, deer fawns, and moose calves (Pimlott, 1967b), the daily summer movements of wolves appear to be much less extensive than on the tundra. A yearling female tracked by radio traveled up to 3.5 miles (straight-line distance) in a day but averaged only one mile per day (Kolenosky and Johnston, 1967). The greatest distance between the points at which she was found during each week varied between 2.5 and 8.5 miles during July and August and averaged 5.8 miles. The wolf meandered and zigzagged a great deal, so the total distance that she actually traveled during these periods must have been much more than the straight-line distances given above. In addition, there were many times when this animal could not be located, so she could have gone much farther at these times.

Another radio-tagged wolf, a lactating female, which was tracked almost continually for three days in July, traveled a total distance of about six miles per day (actual rather than straight-line distance), and generally this animal's movements were more restricted than those of the other female.

When carrying food to the den, the wolf is said to travel in almost a straight line for miles (Young, 1944). An experience I once had in Minnesota's Superior National Forest seems to bear this out. On May 8, 1967, at 6:45 P.M., having just stopped my truck on a narrow dirt road, I saw a silver-black wolf rounding a bend about two hundred yards away. It trotted briskly toward me with its head down, appearing intent on reaching a particular destination. When it was about 150 yards away from me, the wolf noticed the truck, crossed the narrow road, and headed into the woods. I saw then that the animal was carrying something in its mouth. I drove to the point where the wolf had disappeared, and I walked toward where I had first seen it. When I returned to the truck, I saw the wolf emerge from the woods about 150 yards behind the vehicle and continue on down the road, having deviated only to bypass the truck.

The main summer travel routes for the wolves studied in Ontario were along waterways (Joslin, 1966). Wolves in northern Minnesota use waterways during summer, too, but they also travel extensively on dirt roads and game trails. Game trails and fire lanes were favorite wolf routes in Wisconsin (Thompson, 1952). On Isle Royale, the wolves use foot trails, long ridges, game trails, and shorelines for summer travel. Old roads and cattle, sheep, and game trails were used considerably by wolves in the southwestern U.S. (Young, 1944).

Most of the travel on such routes is a part of the wolf's regular hunting activity, but there is also another kind of summer movement. This is the shifting of the pups from one rendezvous site to another after they have left the den at the age of eight to ten weeks. Joslin, who is most familiar with these moves, found that the straight-line distance between successive rendezvous sites varied from about 0.5 mile to 5.0 miles and averaged 1.9 miles. When the pups were younger, the moves were shorter and less frequent. Those in May, June, and July averaged one mile, whereas those during August and September averaged 2.3 miles. The pups usually stayed at a single rendezvous site for some twenty days in the earlier months, but in August and September they moved about every seven days.

Of course, lone wolves and small packs without reproducing members would not be restricted to den areas. These animals probably travel much more widely in summer than do packs with pups. On Isle Royale, a pack of three wolves was seen in a certain region of the island during the winters of 1957, 1959, 1960, and 1961 (Mech, 1966a). Summer observations of what was probably the same pack were made throughout most of the same area, indicating that this apparently nonreproducing pack might have traveled as far in summer as in winter. In British Columbia, Cowan (1947) once tracked two wolves for twenty-two miles down a trail during summer.

Winter Movements and Activity

As explained in the previous chapter, wolf pups abandon their rendezvous sites sometime in autumn or winter and join the adults on their hunting forays. At that time, pack members may be limited in their travels by the pups' need for frequent rests, but they would no longer need to return to any particular spot to care for the pups. Thus the pack would be able to wander freely over its range until the next denning season.

Periods of activity. Although a day-night cycle is apparent in the activities of wolves during the warm seasons, wolves are active at all times of day in winter. Several times during March and April, Burkholder (1959) saw a pack of wolves in Alaska traveling and attacking prey during the day. On Isle Royale, various observers including myself have regularly tracked wolves during February and March and watched them travel, hunt, kill, feed, mate, fight, and play throughout the day; tracks indicated that they also carried on most of these activities at night. Preliminary work in northern Minnesota has indicated that the same is true of wolves in that area.

During winter, wolves rest as the occasion demands. After unsuccessfully chasing prey, they may rest for ten or fifteen minutes before continuing their hunt. After traveling for five or ten miles over easy routes, or fewer miles over more difficult trails, the animals sometimes rest for as long as several hours. Probably they rest the longest just after feeding. At that time, they may sleep for hours, feed some more, and then rest again (Chapter VI).

After wolves first abandon the remains of a kill, they also rest a great deal, especially during the middle of the day. However, the next day, if they have not made another kill, they continue traveling, and they rest for shorter, more frequent periods.

Extreme weather may also influence the winter travels of wolves. Once when temperatures dropped to −30° F. at night and winds gusted to forty mph for two days, Ontario researchers made ground checks on four packs; in each case the wolves were discovered resting in dense cover (Pimlott *et al.*, 1969). When the winds subsided during the night following this period, however, wolf packs in at least seven parts of the study area began moving again, and they continued traveling throughout the next day.

Travel routes. During their extensive winter travel, wolves continue to use game trails, woods roads, and ridges, and sometimes they even resort to highways. In fáct, during one year fourteen wolves (and seven coyotes) that were turned in for bounty in Ontario had been killed by cars (DeVos, 1949). When soft snow accumulates to a depth of a couple of feet or more, it is easy to see why wolves choose runways where the travel is easier. In northern Minnesota, I once watched six wolves picking their way overland through two feet of very fluffy snow. The lead wolf would make a two-foot jump, bringing its hind feet up to its forefeet, rest a few seconds, and make another bound. Each time, the animal sank in about eighteen inches. The other members of the pack followed likewise in its tracks, single file. In the same snow, I was sinking in up to eighteen inches on snowshoes.

Stanwell-Fletcher (1942) wrote that in British Columbia he tracked a pair of wolves through six feet of fluffy snow for twenty-two miles. They plowed chest-deep through the snow and never lay down to rest for the entire distance. No doubt they rested often in their tracks much as those that I watched in Minnesota.

A detailed study of the wolf's ability to travel in snow has been made by the Russian scientist Nasimovich (1955). He found that wolves have a "weight-load-on-track" of eighty-nine to 114 grams per square centimeter. Thus, according to this work, a snow density of .33 to .35 can support a wolf, but in snow with a density of .21 a wolf will sink to its chest. To travel efficiently under such conditions, wolves must use game trails or other packed travelways. Nasimovich believed that wolves may starve and their numbers decrease if reindeer are so scarce or dispersed that the wolves must break their own trails while hunting.

Where waterways are plentiful, they often become the major winter routes for wolves, for travel is easier on windswept and hard-packed ice. In the Thunder Bay region of Lake Superior (Ontario), wolves travel along the frozen shores of the numerous points, bays, and islands (DeVos, 1950). In the "Canoe Country" of Minnesota, the animals pick their way from lake to lake, often using the same portages that in summer are jammed with enthusiastic canoeists. Frozen riverbeds, streams, and beaver ponds are also used considerably by the wolves in that area. The wolves of Isle Royale travel routinely along that island's entire two-hundred-mile shoreline. When they head inland, they usually follow an old trail, or a chain of lakes and streams.

Wolves also travel great distances across large expanses of ice far from shore (Fig. 32). On Isle Royale, a pack of fifteen would regularly cross the mouth of frozen Siskiwit Bay, which is five miles wide (Mech, 1966a). When wolves first arrived on the island from the mainland about 1949, they had to have crossed a span of fifteen to twenty miles of ice to do so. In Alaska, a wolf was killed on Nunivak Island, twenty-eight miles from the nearest other land (Kelly, 1954); presumably this animal crossed on the ice that sometimes jams the intervening expanse.

When traveling on ice, wolves may be cautious and sometimes even hesitant. On Isle Royale I once watched seven wolves crossing a small bay where most of the ice was bare. The wolves were reluctant to walk on it, and tried to remain on some snow-covered chunks of ice that were frozen together by the newer bare ice. When they reached the end of the ice chunks, the animals followed the opaque cracks that extended across the snow-free ice. One individual, although tempted, would not continue with the rest of the pack when they reached the bare ice. Instead it stayed on snow-covered ice and tried to find another route across the bay. When it again faced bare ice, it returned to where the pack had

FIGURE 32. During winter, wolves often travel on frozen lakes where snow is windblown and hard-packed and traveling is easier. (*L. David Mech*)

crossed. But upon reaching bare ice once more, the animal back-tracked and skirted all the bare ice, following the snow-covered shoreline around the bay until it caught up to the pack a half hour later.

Another time, the entire main pack of wolves appeared to be leaving Isle Royale for the Ontario mainland, a distance of about twenty miles at that point. The ice "bridge" was made up of smooth ice in some places and rough chunks frozen together in others. Whenever the wolves reached ice that was different from the stretch they were on, they hesitated. Most of the animals were reluctant to continue, but the leader seemed determined to go on. After about two miles of travel, however, the entire pack turned around and backtracked to the island.

Use of the major travel routes in a region is generally considered traditional, the habit being passed on from generation to generation. Young described a runway in southeastern Arizona that was being traveled by wolves in 1917 and was still being used in 1940. On Isle Royale, where wolf routes are known in detail, they have remained basically the same for each of the last ten years. This is especially true for places where the wolves cross points or peninsulas or cut cross-country to a chain of lakes. Interesting evidence for the traditional use of a wolf runway in Minnesota was given by Stenlund (1955). While setting a snare along a wolf trail, he found "the rusted remains of an old homemade wolf snare" attached to, and grown over by, the same tree to which he was about to fasten his.

The wolf's habit of using special trails when traveling through a certain area is most advantageous in winter. When a pack passes single file (the usual travel formation) over a trail, the trail becomes hard-packed, and even after several more inches of snow accumulate, the trail is still easier to travel on than a stretch of unbroken snow would be (Fig. 33). Regular use of such a trail keeps it packed all winter.

Wolf runways or travel routes, such as described above, have been followed and mapped in several areas. They usually form a closed circuit, but they also branch and connect with other wolf trails, so unless an identifiable pack is actually followed, it would be very difficult to define the route used by any particular pack. In large areas where wolves are common, probably the trails of each pack usually interconnect into a vast network.

Such a situation was found in Prince Albert National Park, Saskatchewan, by A. W. F. Banfield (1951). He defined five interconnecting circuits of runways that existed at least partly within the park. These travelways varied little from year to year and were used by several packs of wolves. Banfield believed that, generally, different groups of wolves used different circuits, with a certain amount of overlapping. These circuits varied in length from twenty-seven miles to eighty-seven or more miles. In general, the longer the circuit was, the greater the number of wolves that used it.

In Alberta, a pack of eight wolves also followed a circuitous route. Over a three-month period in winter the runway of these animals enclosed an area of about 540 square miles and was

FIGURE 33. When moving overland, wolves travel single file, allowing most pack members to save their strength. The result is a deep and narrow wolf trail. (*L. David Mech*)

roughly oblong (Rowan, 1950). The pack of ten studied by Burkholder in Alaska also used an oblong runway. Over a forty-five-day period, this pack traveled around an area one hundred miles long by about fifty wide, and at the end of the period the wolves were still using some new regions (Fig. 34).

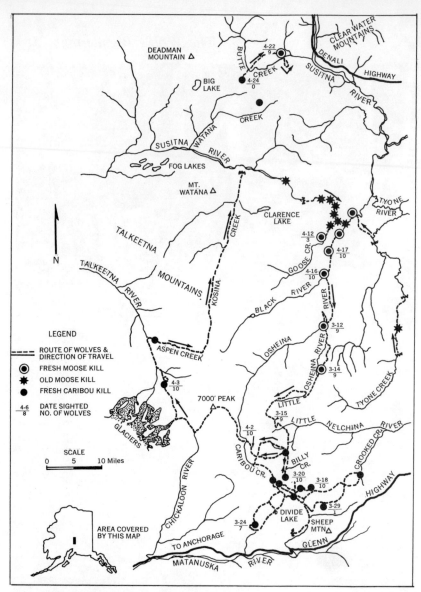

FIGURE 34. Movements of a pack of 10
wolves in Alaska. (*From Burkholder, 1959*)

Because wolf runways do form circuits, and the animals using
them usually return over the same runway several times each
winter, many old naturalists, trappers, and guides harbored mis-
conceptions about wolf travel. For instance, the notion has been
held that the wolf travelway deviates little from an actual circle
and that therefore wolves regularly return along any given stretch

at even intervals (usually every two weeks or every ten days) like clockwork. According to some of the older literature, wolves even travel their circuit only in a counterclockwise direction.

Actually, travel along a runway may be in either direction. Two-directional travel can come about when a pack suddenly turns around and retraces its trail or when it cuts across a larger runway loop and traces a figure eight or part of one. I have often seen wolves do this, as have others. Depending on the particular section of runway, wolves may return during any period from a few hours to several weeks after passing over it.

Speed and extent of travel. The usual gait of a wolf is a steady, tireless trot. W. O. Pruitt (1960) watched a trotting wolf travel one mile on the tundra in fifteen minutes, a rate of four mph. A pack of fifteen wolves that I observed on Isle Royale crossed a five-mile expanse of ice in one hour, and a lone wolf timed by Shelton (1966) traveled at a rate of 4.8 mph. Burkholder once saw a wolf pack in Alaska cover six miles in an hour during winter.

At the rate of five mph, wolves could travel 120 miles in a day. Of course, they could hardly be expected to continue for such a long period without rest unless "pushed" by hunters. It is interesting that Pulliainen (1965: 246) mentioned records kept by J. Magga from the tundra zone of Finland, where wolves are hunted hard, showing that "on hard snow wolves might travel as much as 200 km [124 miles] per day."

Most records of far-ranging travels in short periods are more moderate, but they still show the strong tendency and ability of wolves to travel. In Ontario, seven wolves moved forty miles in no more than twenty hours, and during that time they killed and ate one large and one small deer (Pimlott *et al.*, 1969). In Minnesota, a pack traveled thirty-five miles overnight on a chain of frozen lakes (Stenlund, 1955), and in Alaska a pack moved forty-five miles during no more than twenty-four hours (Burkholder, 1959). On Isle Royale, the fastest long-distance move I observed was also forty-five miles in twenty-four hours, mostly along well-established shoreline routes.

In contrast to these records, Pimlott *et al.* reported that a wolf pack in Ontario stayed near a concentration of deer for several days and killed and ate two of them during that time.

The above extremes show the variability in the wolf's winter travel routine. More significant than that, however, is the average distance traveled per day by the animals. Burkholder found that his Alaskan pack covered 233 miles during periods totaling fifteen days, an average of 15.5 miles per day including travel, hunting, feeding, and resting. Figures derived similarly by Pulliainen for forty-three days of tracking showed that wolves in the forest zone of Finland traveled 14.2 miles per day on the average.

On Isle Royale, I kept track of all the travels of a pack of sixteen wolves during thirty-one days from February 4 to March 7, 1960 (Mech, 1966a). They covered a total of 277 miles during that time, or an average of nine miles per day. On twenty-two of those days, however, the wolves were feeding on kills and were moving about only in localized areas. Thus they covered the 277 miles in only nine days, an average of thirty-one miles per day, or 1.3 mph, of travel, resting, and hunting.

In a separate assessment of wolf travel on Isle Royale, I found that the rate was 1.7 mph, based on one hundred hours of observations during eighteen instances throughout three winters. Considering both these figures, a more representative average rate for traveling, hunting, and resting appears to be about 1.5 mph.

Assuming the rate of 1.5 mph and an actual speed of five mph, we can then conclude that in winter about 30% of the time that a wolf spends getting from one kill to the next is devoted to travel itself. The remainder represents hunting and resting time along the way. This figure compares favorably with the 34% obtained by Kelsall (1957) for the percentage of time that tundra wolves spend traveling.

The urge to travel appears to be directly related to the wolf's need to locate vulnerable prey. When a pack has killed a large animal, the members travel little until the carcass is consumed. They may move up to five miles from a carcass to some preferred ridge or lake to lie in the sun after feeding heavily, but they then return to feed again. They usually do not abandon the carcass until they have completely consumed it, at least on Isle Royale and in northern Minnesota.

Many untrained observers coming upon partly eaten kills have gained the impression that wolves kill for sport and eat only a small part of each animal killed. However, it appears that in most of those cases the observers had found the kill while the wolves were off resting. Except during long periods of especially deep snow accumulations, all such kills that I have examined and then rechecked have been completely eaten within a few days. (See also Chapter VI.)

On Isle Royale, when the wolves left the remains of a kill, they tried to attack any prey they encountered. Once they dispatched one moose within three-quarters of a mile of their previous kill, but on another extreme occasion they traveled sixty-seven miles between kills. The average distance covered between kills was twenty-three miles, based on forty-four observations during five winters (Mech, 1966a; Shelton, 1966). This was in an area where the wolves' only prey was moose. In Alaska, where both moose and caribou were available, the figures were comparable. Based on six observations, the minimum travel distance between kills was six miles, the maximum was forty-five miles, and the average was twenty-four miles (Burkholder, 1959).

Strong evidence will be presented in Chapter VIII that generally only inferior prey or prey at a disadvantage is vulnerable to wolf predation. The conclusion seems unavoidable that extensive travel is necessary for wolves to locate the small numbers of these susceptible animals in the herds.

Migrations. On the tundra, where wolves depend mostly on caribou, it is often claimed that during winter the packs follow these herding animals on their migrations. In 1944, Young cited a few of these claims, and several others have been made since then. For instance, Banfield (1954: 45) wrote: "For the remainder of the year, autumn, winter, and early spring, most of the wolves follow the migrating herds of caribou. A few old or outcast individuals may lead a nomadic life all year. During the present investigation practically all the wolves observed from the air . . . were associated with herds of caribou."

Makridin (1962) stated that in the Yamal North of Russia, wolves wander with the herds of domestic reindeer beginning in autumn, and that no wolves are seen in winter except where there are caribou or reindeer. In Finland, Pulliainen (1965: 244) wrote that "to some extent wolves follow the seasonal movements of reindeer." Tener (1960) even believed that wolves stay with the moving caribou herds for ten months of the year on the Canadian tundra.

Concerning wolves in Alaska, Kelly stated explicitly that they accompany migrating caribou, and he gave specific examples. He also wrote (1954: 2): "Arctic wolves are extensive travelers. After making a kill they will often remain at the carcass until it is devoured. This time will depend on the number of wolves in the pack and the size of the animal killed. Then they may start traveling and cover 25 to 40 miles before making contact with the moving caribou herd. Wolves have often been trailed up to 35 miles before being sighted, and there is seldom any sign indicating they have stopped to rest."

Kelsall (1968) also provided convincing evidence that wolves follow caribou herds throughout much of the year: "The tracks of individual packs of tundra wolves, moving seasonally from tundra to forest or return, have been seen to travel in straight lines in forest for distances of nearly 100 miles. Sometimes they have been seen to follow caribou trails, and at other times to head for the nearest caribou herd with uncanny accuracy from directions not used by the caribou."

On the other hand, Soper (1942) claimed that in Canada's Wood Buffalo Park that wolves do not follow the caribou herds. It may be true that in a few areas of the tundra where enough food exists in winter wolves may remain year round. In most other arctic and subarctic areas, however, where the main source of food is migrating caribou, they would have to follow the caribou until the denning season forced them to become sedentary again.

Winter shifts. In regions with high mountains and very deep snow, such as the Rockies in North America and the Alps in Europe, wolves shift their activities to lower elevations during winter. Such shifts are probably caused by unsuitable traveling conditions and a lack of large prey during this season. In Jasper Park, Alberta, Cowan (1947) estimated that on their summer range wolves occur in a density of one individual per eighty-seven to 111 square miles. However, in winter, when these animals are restricted to valleys, their range is reduced to about ten miles per wolf. One pack was thought to move some sixty to seventy miles into the Athabaska River Valley in midwinter and remain there until April or May, when it would return to its summer range at a higher altitude.

During especially hard winters in Europe, wolves shift to the agricultural land at lower elevations and sometimes even venture into such cities as Rome (Pulliainen, 1967a).

Size of Home Range

The concept of "home range" is ambiguous and nonprecise, and researchers do not agree on the methods of calculating it. Usually, wolf authorities have used the term to mean the area of land either enclosed by the runways of a particular pack or available to use by the pack, given its usual travel habits. Such a concept when qualified by season of the year is useful in describing in a very general way the extent of the wolf's wanderings over long periods.

Evidence that tundra wolves range as far as twenty miles from the den during summer has already been discussed. If the den is in the center of a pack's range and the wolves forage that far in several directions, the area of the range would approach 1200 square miles. If the den is only on one edge of the range, the area would approximate 150 to 300 square miles. No doubt ranges vary considerably, but it is evident that on the tundra most of them must be relatively extensive.

Murie (1944: 42) wrote the following about the pack he studied in Alaska: "The East Fork wolves were known to move readily over a range at least 50 miles across. During the denning period their movements radiated from the den, and ordinarily the wolves traveled a dozen or more miles from it. But greater distances were readily traveled. In the spring of 1941, when a band of five or six thousand caribou calved some 20 miles away, the wolves traveled this distance nightly to prey on the calves."

Little is known about the summer ranges of wolves in forested regions, but the available information indicates that they are much smaller than on the tundra. Joslin tried to keep track of the movements of two wolf packs in southern Ontario during summer. By howling to the animals and noting where the replies came from, he learned that from May through September the range of one pack was at least eight square miles in 1961 and seven in 1963. The other pack ranged over an area of at least four square miles during one summer.

Probably the ranges of these packs were much larger than the figures indicate, for with the howling method wolves can be located only (1) when they reply, and (2) when they are within hearing distance of the investigator. Joslin believed, for instance, that the total summer range of one of the packs he studied may have been as large as twenty-five square miles.

Another study in southern Ontario, based on information gained by radio-tracking individual wolves, does show that summer home ranges may be larger than Joslin's work indicated. Kolenosky and Johnston reported that a preadult female that they located 336 times from July to December ranged over an area of at least nineteen square miles. An adult female located on seven occasions during July and August used a home range of at least twenty-seven square miles, and a preadult male traveled over an area of seventeen square miles or more from August to December, based on seven locations. On the other hand, 508 locations determined for an adult female with a litter indicated that she roamed an area of about seven square miles during July and August.

Like the howling technique, however, radio-tracking yields information only when an investigator decides to sample the movements of an animal and when the animal is within range of detection. For example, one of the animals mentioned above was located only during 64% of the attempts to find her. Her whereabouts during the other 36% of the times is unknown, but it could have been far from her known range. It is apparent that, although the above figures on the summer ranges of wolves are useful, they should be regarded as minimum.

The sizes of the winter ranges of wolves have been estimated in several different areas (Table 18). They vary from thirty-six square miles for a pack of two to 5000 square miles for a pack of ten. When standardized on a per-wolf basis, they range from ten square miles per wolf to five hundred. No doubt some of this variation comes from differences in methods of gathering data and some from differences in durations over which the figures were obtained. However, undoubtedly much of the variation is real. In areas with low densities of prey, wolves would have to travel much farther to locate vulnerable animals. Probably the number of wolves in an area also affects the home-range size.

The largest figure reported, 5000 square miles for a pack of ten wolves in Alaska, was based on a forty-five-day study (Fig. 34). At the end of that period, the wolves were still using new areas, so, had they been observed longer, their range would have

TABLE 18. Sizes of home ranges of wolf packs in winter.

Location	Pack Size	Home Range Size (Sq. Mi.)	Sq. Mi. Per Wolf[1]	Authority
Alaska	13	1,800[2]	138	Murie, 1944
Alaska	10	5,000	500	Burkholder, 1959
Northwest Territories	7	90	13	Banfield, 1954
Western Canada	4 or 5	50	10 or 12	Cowan, 1947
Alberta	8	540	68	Rowan, 1950
Minnesota	7	126	18	Stenlund, 1955
Minnesota	2	36	18	Stenlund, 1955
Minnesota	5	50	10	Stenlund, 1955
Minnesota	3 or 4	85	21 or 28	Stenlund, 1955
Isle Royale	2	105	52	Mech, 1966a
Isle Royale	3	105	35	Mech, 1966a
Isle Royale	15–21	210	10 to 14	Mech, 1966a; Jordan *et al.*, 1967
Wisconsin	3 or 4	150	37 or 50	Thompson, 1952
Michigan	4	260	65	Stebler, 1944
Finland	2	400	200	Pulliainen, 1965
Ontario	8	50	6	Pimlott *et al.*, 1969
Ontario	7	40	6	Pimlott *et al.*, 1969
Ontario	—[3]	120	—[3]	Pimlott *et al.*, 1969
Ontario	—[3]	60	—[3]	Pimlott *et al.*, 1969

[1] This is not necessarily a density figure because other wolves may also have occupied part of the ranges of these packs.
[2] Calculated area of a circle with a twenty-five-mile radius.
[3] Pack sizes varied from year to year.

proved even larger. This may also be true for several of the other figures.

The information on the sizes of winter ranges of wolf packs in Algonquin Park, Ontario, bears special discussion (Table 18). These data were collected during an intensive study using airplanes and helicopters from 1958 through 1964. The areas of winter ranges for four packs of from three to nine wolves each were estimated at forty, fifty, sixty, and 120 square miles each. Compared to the figures for home ranges of wolves in other mainland areas, these figures are quite low. This is especially true considering that home range figures on wolves from most areas are based on a few observations made during short periods, but that the Ontario information is based on data collected over long periods.

The difference in reported sizes of wolf ranges may be merely normal variation, as discussed above. However, it is also possible that the Ontario figures are substantially lower than the actual sizes of the home ranges. This is because the packs were identified by the number of wolves in them and by their location, a practice that can produce misleading results. The authors of the Ontario study recognized this and pointed out that their methods were not completely objective. But they added that they were reasonably confident in the accuracy of their interpretations.

It is obvious that identifying a wolf pack only on the basis of its location would be an invalid method of obtaining data on the range of the pack. Identifying a wolf pack by the number of animals in it can also be hazardous because (1) there may be several packs of the same size in the area, and (2) packs sometimes split temporarily (Chapter II). It is difficult to discover the true size of a pack unless one follows it almost continually for long periods.

These facts were impressed on me during field work on wolf movements in northern Minnesota in 1967. In some areas, packs of various sizes would be seen using the same travelways at different times. It was possible that these sightings all represented the same basic pack with various members missing at times. However, because of other information, such as the direction of travel of various sized packs and the timing of the visits, I began to suspect that these were really different packs using the same travelways.

This suspicion was confirmed when after a month of intensive aerial work in a certain area I suddenly spotted a pack containing three black wolves and another with a black wolf and a white one. Identifiable packs like these showed that in Minnesota some winter pack ranges definitely overlap, as Stenlund believed. Second, they suggested that at least certain packs travel so widely that they may show up in any given part of their ranges only occasionally. These limited observations made me realize how easily one could be misled when trying to study the movements and ranges of packs that are not identifiable.

This does not necessarily mean that the Ontario figures are incorrect. It merely indicates that there may be room for a certain amount of skepticism when considering them.

Long-Range Movements

Although most information on wolf movements has come from studies using aerial tracking in winter or radio-tracking in summer, some data have also been obtained by the marking-recapture method. In a few cases, especially long movements have been discovered by this technique.

A male pup tagged in Alberta in June 1949 was recaptured in November 1951, the shortest "reasonable" distance between the capture points being 162 miles (Banfield, 1953). Three pups captured in July in the Northwest Territories were retrapped the following February 185 miles away (Kuyt, 1962). In Ontario, a female pup (✳116) was snared in March 1963, eighty-five miles from its original capture point; a male pup (✳111) marked in the autumn of 1960 was killed twenty-five miles distant in November 1963; an adult male (✳181) trapped in October 1959 was recaptured in July 1961 twenty-eight miles from its original capture point; and another male (✳113), tagged in October 1960, was fifty miles away when recaptured in October 1967 (Pimlott *et al.,* 1969).

Whether these long-range movements represent dispersal, migration, home range shift, or just normal travel within the home range is still unknown. It certainly is possible that year-round home ranges of some wolf packs are much larger than previously thought. Obviously a long-term investigation of the movements of identifiable wolf packs will be necessary before this question can be answered. Such a study involving the radio-tracking of wolves from aircraft has just begun in Minnesota (Mech and Frenzel, 1969).

CHAPTER VI / FOOD HABITS

As anyone who is familiar with fairy tales knows, the wolf is a meat eater. Through millions of years of evolution and adaptation, the wolf has reached its present state of development with a digestive system and set of behavior patterns that make its carnivorous way of life most efficient. Just as deer and moose cannot live on meat, the wolf cannot survive on plants.

Digestive System

From one end to the other, the wolf's digestive system is adapted to processing animal matter—to catching, tearing, digesting, and eliminating it. At the forward end of this system the specializations of the front teeth for a meat-eating life are easily seen. Most plant-eating mammals possess chisel-like front teeth that are useful for cutting plant stems, or that can fasten around a clump of leaves, grasses, or twigs and break them loose. In contrast, the wolf's front teeth are sharp and pointed and adapted to puncturing, slashing, and clinging. Those most useful in this respect are the massive canine teeth, or fangs, but the incisors also serve as a powerful clamp in support of the canines. Several times I have watched wolves clinging to the rump of a fast-moving moose and being dragged about without loosening their holds. In one case, where a wolf had sunk its fangs deep into the rubbery nose of a moose, the moose lifted its head high and actually raised the wolf from the ground and swung it from side to side.

Behind the wolf's canine teeth are rows of pointed premolars and molars, useful for tearing and shearing once an animal has been killed. The fourth upper premolars and first lower molars, or flesh teeth, are especially well suited for this task because of their shearing action against one another. They are used for cutting tendons and small bones and for gnawing large bones. The massive rear molars aid in cracking and crushing bones. In plant eaters, these side and back teeth are very flat, serving to grind, mash, and chew the food. But the wolf does little chewing; its saliva probably does not even contain the digestive enzyme that occurs in so many other species, since it is absent in the dog (Whitney, 1949). Instead, the wolf's saliva is probably most useful as a lubricant, for the animal just rips large chunks of flesh and hide from its prey and bolts them down whole.

The size of the pieces of prey swallowed whole by a wolf is impressive. In Alaska, one wolf stomach contained the following parts of a caribou: an ear, tongue, lip, two kidneys, the liver, and the windpipe, plus hair and large chunks of meat (Kelly, 1954). Two whole caribou tongues were found in another wolf stomach during the same study.

Action by the wolf's tongue probably helps the animal substantially in bolting down such large items. This organ is long and supple and can be used to help lick meat off bones because it is covered with hundreds of horny projections called papillae. In addition, it no doubt aids the animals in licking up blood that flows onto the ground or snow. I have seen wolves eagerly feeding on such bloody snow as they waited around for a wounded prey animal to weaken. Since wolf scats sometimes contain much soil, I presume that the animals swallow this accidentally while licking blood from the ground during similar situations in summer.

One of the most important uses of the wolf's tongue is in drinking water. Water is necessary for digestion, and wolves require a great deal of it, especially after gorging. Adolph (1943) learned that dogs weighing about forty pounds consume more than a quart of water each day, so wolves probably would need about twice as much. Water, and any other liquid a wolf drinks, is lapped up by the tongue with a scooping motion.

After food or water passes down the wolf's throat, it enters the esophagus and accumulates in the stomach. The wolf's stomach is simple compared to that of many plant eaters. Some of these animals possess a four-part stomach in which tiny organisms break down the finely mashed plant matter and aid greatly in digesting it. But because the wolf's diet consists almost entirely of highly concentrated and easily digested fat and protein, the animal does not need such a complex stomach.

However, the wolf does require a stomach with a great capacity, because it cannot eat whenever it pleases. Whereas a plant eater can nibble vegetation any time, a wolf usually must find, chase, catch, and kill another animal before it can eat. Then when the creature has made a kill, it is faced with a feast and must devour as much as possible or lose it to other predators or scavengers.

A large stomach capacity helps solve this problem. According to Whitney (1949), a dog's stomach can hold a gallon of food. Although no volume figures are available for a wolf's stomach, no doubt its capacity is at least as great. Several authors have reported on the weights of wolf stomachs containing food, however. In Wood Buffalo Park, Canada, the stomachs of all wolves that died eating poisoned bait were weighed. Two stomachs were empty, but the average weight of the forty-seven that contained food was 5.3 pounds; the two heaviest each weighed eleven pounds (Fuller and Novakowski, 1955). Since the wolves had eaten poisoned baits, we can assume that they might have consumed more if they had not died.

The heaviest contents of thirty-three stomachs from wolves killed during a study in Russia weighed 13.2 pounds (Makridin, 1962). However, the contents consisted mostly of indigestible hair and bones. Thus the investigator thought that, including the meat that must already have been digested, the total amount eaten at one time may have been over twenty pounds.

The best records of wolf stomach capacity were furnished by Young. He raised ten wolves to the age of about three years, when they weighed an average of ninety pounds each. After not feeding them for two days, he then allowed them all the fresh horse meat, beef, and fat they could eat. When he sacrificed these animals immediately afterward, he found that their stomachs weighed an average of eighteen pounds each.

The heaviest stomach ever reported was from a male wolf in Colorado (Young, 1944). After capture from the wild, the animal was kept in a cage, but he would not eat for seven days. On the eighth day he gorged on fresh horse meat and fat and was then killed. He weighed 110 pounds and eight ounces in total; his stomach and contents weighed nineteen pounds, three ounces.

The stomach is a storage organ, allowing food to pass a little at a time into the intestine, as well as a digestive organ. Gastric juice containing hydrochloric acid and enzymes is secreted there, and a good start is made on the digestion of the protein in the meat.

Little digestion of fat takes place in the stomach, however (Whitney, 1949). Fat passes in almost its original form into the small intestine, along with the partly digested protein.

As food enters the small intestine, little by little, it is subjected to other digestive juices, secreted from the wall of the intestine itself and from the liver and pancreas, which empty into the upper end of the gut. Waves of muscle contractions sweep backward along most of the length of the digestive tract and move the food mass through the intestine, break the mass into smaller lumps, and bathe them in digestive juices.

One of the digestive agents most important to the wolf, the bile, comes from the liver, which in the wolf is a rather large organ. In twelve male wolves from the Yamal North of Russia, the liver averaged 2.6 pounds, with extreme weights of 1.6 to 4.2 pounds; in six females this organ ranged from 1.5 to 1.8 pounds, and averaged 1.6 (Makridin, 1962). The bile produced by the liver is stored in the saclike gall bladder attached to that organ. The gall bladder empties into the small intestine when food is released from the stomach. The bile lubricates the food mass and acts as a laxative. It also helps break the fat into tiny pieces and brings about the release of the digestive juices from the pancreas to further digest the fat.

The pancreas adds its juices to the bile, the intestinal fluid, and the food mass. In addition to helping to digest fat, these juices act on starch and they complete the digestion of proteins, breaking all these materials down into compounds that can be taken into the blood stream.

Digestion continues as the food passes down the entire length of the small intestine, which may be as long as eighteen feet in the wolf (Makridin, 1962). All during the time digestion is taking place, the products of digestion are being absorbed by the blood through millions of tiny "villae" projecting from the inside of the intestine. By the time the food mass reaches the end of the small intestine, all that is usually left is a wet glob of hair, thick chunks of hide, teeth, pieces of heavy bone, and other indigestible material.

When this mass continues into the large intestine, it is stored in the upper section until most of the water is removed and absorbed into the blood stream. The rest of the material becomes the feces or scats ("droppings"). If the wolf has eaten almost re meat, with little indigestible matter, its feces will be very dark and loose. They are sometimes passed almost as a stream of liquid, and I have often seen such streaks of loose feces staining the snow around freshly killed deer and moose.

Loose feces must represent the remains of many pounds of meat, for the digestive efficiency of raw meat is 95% (Whitney, 1949). Dogs fed exclusively on lean meat need to defecate only once a week (McCay, 1943).

According to Makridin (1959), digestion in the wolf takes place in a few hours. Thus wolves could feed several times during just one day, which would enable them to make quick use of a great volume of meat. This would explain how a few wolves can devour large carcasses in very short periods.

When much of a wolf's meal consists of hide, hair, and bones, after the pack has finished the flesh from a carcass, the indigestible material becomes specially arranged in the feces. Rarely does a bone project from the fecal mass. Instead the hair is wrapped around any sharp or hard object, thus protecting the intestine from puncture. Often the outside of a wolf dropping is all hair, while the entire inside is composed of bones.

Wolf and coyote scats are similar in appearance, so researchers studying wolf food habits in areas with both species must be able to separate them. The two types of scats overlap in size, but D. Q. Thompson (1952) found that coyote scats rarely exceed one inch in diameter, whereas most wolf scats range from one to one and one half inches wide. Thus if all scats less than an inch wide are discarded, there will be little chance of mistaking coyote scats for those of wolves.

Prey Species

It seems logical that the wolf would prey mainly on large animals, because of its size, its habit of traveling in packs, and its ability to consume and digest great quantities of food in short periods. Predators that feed consistently on small animals usually are much smaller, and they hunt alone.

Many studies of wolf food habits support this conclusion. In the seven most complete investigations of the contents of large numbers of wolf droppings, animals the size of beavers or larger composed from 59 to 96% of the food items (Table 19). In all but one of these studies, animals larger than beavers comprised from 59 to

88% of the items. The prey most represented were: white-tailed deer, mule deer, moose, caribou, elk, Dall sheep, bighorn sheep, and beaver.

Other studies have yielded similar results. In eight wolf stomachs and eight wolf scats from Michigan, deer and snowshoe hare were represented equally, and they made up the majority of the food items. Deer remains occurred in 80% of fifty-one wolf stomachs collected in winter from Minnesota (Stenlund, 1955). Remnants of bison were found in thirty-nine of ninety-five wolf stomachs and fifty-four of sixty-three scats from northern Alberta (Fuller, 1966). Caribou remains composed 66% of the items in sixty-two scats from the Northwest Territories (Banfield, 1954). Caribou was also found in 60% of seventy-five wolf stomachs from Manitoba, with moose occurring in 21% of the stomachs (Kelly, 1954).

The above figures are from areas where the wolf relies on wild prey almost entirely, so they should give an accurate idea of the wolf's natural food habits. Where man has substituted his domestic animals for the wild ones, wolves have made a similar substitution in their diets. This was true in North America before the wolf was exterminated from so much of its area. It is still the case in the U.S.S.R. (Makridin, 1962), Finland, and Eastern Europe (Pulliainen, 1965).

Domestic animals usually eaten by wolves include cattle, sheep, reindeer, horses, swine, dogs, and cats. These species have evolved under constant protection by man, and they are usually unable to protect themselves very well. Thus they fall easily to predators like the wolf, which evolved with the ability to catch and kill creatures that can defend themselves.

Because the wolf as a species ranges over a much wider area than any of its prey (originally most of the Northern Hemisphere), different populations of wolves must prey on different kinds of animals. In each region, only one or two species make up most of the wolf's diet (Table 19). For example, in much of the Great Lakes region of the United States and Canada, the white-tailed deer is the wolf's primary prey, with moose being a secondary prey species (except for Isle Royale, where moose is the only large prey available). On the arctic tundra, caribou is the main species taken. Elk make up the single greatest prey of wolves in certain areas of western Canada (Cowan, 1947).

Kelly's (1954) analysis of the contents of 131 wolf stomachs from various regions of Alaska markedly reflects the difference in the degree of dependence of the wolf on different species. In the arctic area, forty of sixty-five stomachs contained caribou, whereas thirteen contained moose. On the Alaskan Peninsula, caribou occurred in six of sixteen stomachs, and moose in seven. Moose remains were found in only one of forty-one stomachs from southeastern Alaska, but thirty stomachs contained deer, and twelve beaver.

If two or more species of large prey inhabit the same region, wolves apparently concentrate on the smallest or easiest to catch. For instance, where moose and deer coexist, wolves depend mostly on deer. Stenlund's studies in Minnesota, and Pimlott's in Ontario (Table 19) showed that. In addition, R. L. Peterson (1955) reported that even though moose were much more abundant than deer on St. Ignace Island, in Lake Michigan, deer remains occurred in 57% of seventy-six wolf scats collected there, whereas moose was found in 36%. In Mount McKinley Park, Alaska, where caribou, Dall sheep, and moose are available, Murie found very little predation on moose.

No doubt the best figures on wolf selection of certain prey species were presented by Cowan. He kept records of the numbers of each kind of big game seen throughout his three-year study in the Rocky Mountain National Parks of Canada. Further, he assumed that, with the possible exception of the bighorn sheep (which might be more easily seen), the proportion of each species observed would represent the proportion in the area. Then he compared those figures with the relative percentages of the kills found of each species and their relative occurrences in wolf scats (Table 20).

Cowan (1947: 164) concluded the following: "It will be noted that in several respects contribution to the annual diet is not strictly related to relative abundance. In comparison with the number of kills recorded, deer apparently contribute to the diet in greater proportion than they are represented in the population. For example, while only about one-third as many deer as elk were seen, deer kills were about half as numerous as elk kills.

"While elk, deer, and moose appear in the diet in fairly close relation to their relative abundance it is apparent that sheep and goat are in another category. They are apparently better equipped to escape the wolves than are the forest game species—

TABLE 19. Principal foods of wolves in five areas of North America.

Location	Number of Scats	Number of Items	Percentage of Occurrence									Authority
			White-tailed Deer	Mule Deer	Moose	Caribou	Elk	Dall Sheep	Bighorn Sheep	Beaver	Other	
Alaska	1,174	1,350	—	—	7	43	—	26	—	—	31	Murie, 1944
Western Canada	420	450	—	15	7	3	47	—	7	7	14	Cowan, 1947
Wisconsin	435	713[1]	59	—	—	—	—	—	—	—	41	Thompson, 1952
Isle Royale, Michigan	438	516	—	—	76	—	—	—	—	11	13	Mech, 1966a
Ontario[2]	1,435	—	80	—	8	—	—	—	—	7	5	Pimlott et al., 1969
Ontario[3]	206	—	27	—	—	—	—	—	—	59	14	Pimlott et al., 1969
Ontario[4]	226	—	42	—	17	—	—	—	—	37	4	Pimlott et al., 1969

[1] Calculated from data presented by Thompson.
[2] Algonquin Provincial Park.
[3] Pakesley area of Parry Sound Forest District.
[4] Marten River area of North Bay Forest District.

TABLE 20. Relative kill of various wolf prey in Alberta compared to their abundance[1].

Species	Number of Kills Found	Percentage of Total Kills	Percentage of Each Item in Scats Containing Large Mammals	Percentage of Each Species Observed	Number of Each Species Observed
Elk	64	54	59	33	1,721
Deer	27	23	18	11	595
Moose	14	12	9	4	156
Bighorn	10	9	9	42	2,251
Caribou	2	2	4	1	36
Goat	1	1	trace	9	458

[1] Modified from Cowan (1947).

or are hunted to less degree under the ecological conditions obtaining."

Not only do wolves concentrate on *species* of big game that are easiest to hunt and kill, but they also rely more on the *individuals* that are most easily caught. Thus during early summer they suddenly switch to newborn calves and fawns, which are helpless unless defended by an adult.

The results of the Isle Royale wolf-moose study showed this switch dramatically (Mech, 1966a). Throughout February and March, the wolves on that island killed primarily old adults and nine- to ten-month-old calves. However, once the new calf crop appeared in late May, little or no predation occurred on the twelve-month-old calves (then known as "yearlings"). These animals are only two or three months older, and not much larger, than those killed regularly a few months before, and they no longer are protected by the cow. Thus they would seem to be almost as easy for a wolf to kill as they were before, but evidently the wolves' concentration on calves saves them.

Most studies of the food habits of wolves in summer have been based on scat analyses. The studies that separated calf or fawn remains from adult remains usually showed a high percentage of calf or fawn in summer scats. Cowan found that remains of elk calves occurred about equally with those of adults in scats from western Canada, and that all the summer occurrences of moose were of calves. Almost half of the occurrences of deer in summer wolf droppings from Wisconsin were of fawns (Thompson, 1952). In Ontario, fawns made up 71% of the occurrences in the scats that contained deer hair, and calves 88% in the scats with moose hair (Pimlott *et al.*, 1969). On Isle Royale, 75% of the moose remains in summer scats were from calves (Mech, 1966a). About half of the caribou remains in wolf scats from Mount McKinley Park, Alaska, were those of calves (Murie, 1944).

Unfortunately, little is known about how the proportion of calf or fawn remains in scats relates to the proportion of calves or fawns actually killed. Young and adults of large animals differ much in size and weight. Thus an equal occurrence of calf or fawn remains and adult remains might mean that many more calves or fawns were killed than adults. For example, assume that moose calves at a certain age weigh one hundred pounds and that adult moose average eight hundred pounds at the same time. If half of the moose remains in scats at that time are those of calves, they could represent eight times as many calves as adults.

On the other hand, there also are factors that might affect the relationship in the opposite direction: (1) Calves are covered with a higher proportion of hair than are adults; (2) all hair is consumed from summer calf kills, whereas large chunks of hide are left at adult kills, at least in winter; (3) a wolf could eat much meat from an adult without getting hair, but this would be difficult with a calf; and (4) when an adult is killed in summer, probably the wolves travel little until it is finished, so most scats would be left nearby; however, wolves probably finish a calf quickly and then continue on, leaving a higher proportion of scats containing calf remains on trails, which is usually where they are collected.

Although none of the above possibilities have been demonstrated as a fact, if any one actually applies, it could seriously bias conclusions based on the proportions of fawns and calves found in scats. To date, Shelton (1966) has accepted these considerations, but Pimlott and his co-workers have rejected them. These latter authors have assumed that the proportions of items in scats actually approach the proportions of individuals of different ages in the kill. Nevertheless, before further conclusions based on this assumption are made, its validity should be tested. This could be done by trial feedings of captive wolves with equal weights of calves and adults.

The smallest animals preyed upon consistently by the wolf are deer fawns and beavers, although on Ellesmere Island in the Northwest Territories, arctic hares also form a large part of the wolf's diet at times. J. S. Tener (1954a) reported that 83% of seventy wolf scats collected in summer and winter contained remnants of arctic hares, whereas only 17% contained musk-ox remains.

Snowshoe hares, which are much smaller than arctic hares, have often been mentioned as a possible source of food for the wolf. However, most authorities have reported very low percentages of snowshoe hare remains in wolf scats. I have seen both a pack of fifteen or sixteen wolves and a single wolf each flush three snowshoe hares in one day while hunting and ignore them. However, perhaps in certain areas or during high hare populations these animals become more important to the wolf. In Michigan, Stebler found that snowshoe hares accounted for 29% of the food items in eight wolf stomachs and 38% in eight wolf scats. Nevertheless, this is the only report that snowshoe hares form more than a small part of the wolf's diet, so this animal cannot be considered of any major importance to the wolf.

Evidently in the long run it is more efficient for the wolf to concentrate on large species even though they usually are less plentiful and harder to kill. The large size of the wolf might prevent the animal from being an effective predator on small animals that can escape by dodging and dashing through small openings. Thus although wolves can catch hares under certain conditions, generally they probably would expend less energy per pound of meat obtained by hunting large animals.

That is not to say that the wolf does not eat smaller animals. Probably every kind of backboned animal that lives in the range of the wolf has been eaten by the wolf (Fig. 35). Remains of mice, mink, muskrats, squirrels, rabbits, and various birds, fish, lizards, and snakes are often found in wolf droppings. In addition, grasshoppers, earthworms, berries, and many other foods are eaten. In the Soviet Union, smaller miscellaneous items seem to play a larger role in the wolf's diet than in North America, although large animals still predominate (Novikov, 1956).

In the James Bay region of Canada, J. A. Hagar (1968) has found evidence of wolves feeding on substantial numbers of flightless ducks. From August 12 to 26, 1966, Hagar and companions noted abundant fresh signs of wolves, in the form of tracks, howling, and one direct observation, near their camp on Big Piskwanish Point. In the extensive marsh behind the beach they discovered "upwards of 40 duck kills," the details of which are provided in the following passage from a letter to me:

"Our attention was attracted to a network of beaten trails through the grass, and to places here and there where feathers and bits of bone were scattered about on the flattened vegetation over a diameter of 5–6 feet. We presently found that these trails and trampled spots conformed roughly to a pattern: virtually every pond-hole in the meadow was circled by a path some 10–12 feet back from the edge of the water, the beaten-down openings were strung along these circular trails, and the remaining trails for the most part ran from one pond to another. Closer examination of the openings showed that the feathers were those of ducks,

FIGURE 35. Although wolves usually feed on large mammals, they also occasionally take birds and other small fare. (*L. David Mech*)

many of them being the partly chewed ends of primary feathers still in sheath, and that some bits of bone could also be identified as coming from ducks, although in no case was any large bone left whole. . . . I felt reasonably sure that the wolves were trotting systematically around each pond, nosing out moulting ducks from the grass and when one was caught, lying down at once to eat it."

Wolves have also been known to put considerable effort into catching mice (Murie, 1944) and fish (Young, 1944). It is possible that such miscellaneous foods when abundant may at times help wolves over short periods when big game may be unavailable. Some biologists have even suggested that in certain areas of the tundra wolves must have to rely on small birds and mammals throughout the summer denning period. This is because the main herds of caribou migrate out of the ranges of many of the arctic wolf dens. Nevertheless, Murie found that wolves in Mount McKinley Park were able to survive on caribou stragglers that remained within range of the den. Pimlott (1967b: 271) suggested that "it is possible that such a situation exists in caribou range much more frequently than has been realized."

Whichever is the case, the fact remains that, when viewed in the total perspective of the wolf's food habits, predation on small animals is seen to play only a minor role in the life of the wolf.

One food item of special significance that is sometimes found in the stomachs or scats of wolves is wolf itself. Kelly reported wolf remains in six of 131 stomachs from Alaska and six of seventy-five from Manitoba. In Wood Buffalo National Park, Canada, two of forty-seven wolf stomachs contained remains of other wolves that had been poisoned (Fuller and Novakowski, 1955). In the Yamal North of Russia, Makridin has seen a wolf feeding on a wolf carcass.

R. A. Rausch (1967a: 258) wrote the following about cannibalism in wolves: "Once a wolf is injured or handicapped, fellow pack members may consume him. I have recorded six occasions where a wolf caught in a snare or trap was devoured, except for the skull and a few bits of hair and viscera, by remnants of the pack. Aerial hunters who leave unskinned wolf carcasses in the field have returned the following day and found the carcasses being devoured by the remaining members of the pack."

Because of the intense emotional bonds among members of a pack, it is hard to believe that wolves would turn on their pack-mates who were caught in traps. Perhaps in the above cases the trapped wolves had already died before the other wolves ate them. Or if they were still alive, the wolves that attacked them may actually have been from a rival pack. It is not readily apparent how the observers of the above incidents could have been certain that the wolves that did the eating belonged to the same pack as the trapped wolves. Probably in most cases of cannibalism in wolves, the animals are eaten as carrion.

Although wolves kill most of their food, they will also eat quantities of carrion. This habit was taken advantage of during wolf-poisoning campaigns in certain parts of Canada (Fuller and Novakowski, 1955). Chunks of meat from sixty to one hundred pounds were impregnated with strychnine and distributed throughout wolf range, and the wolves readily took the bait. Sometimes wolves even eat very putrid meat. On Isle Royale in late June wolves fed heavily on the carcass of a bull moose lying a few feet out in a lake. The animal's fully formed antlers without velvet showed that he had perished in autumn or early winter.

Even garbage is sometimes used for food by wolves, and the animals will venture to dumps to obtain it (Murie, 1944).

Food Requirements and Consumption

As stated in a previous section, a wolf can consume almost twenty pounds of prey at a feeding. This food is digested quickly, so the wolf probably eats several times a day when large amounts of food are available.

The Isle Royale pack of fifteen or sixteen several times consumed all edible parts of a moose calf with an estimated weight of three hundred pounds within twenty-four hours. On one occasion, they finished about half of a moose cow in less than two hours. They killed the moose at 2:40 P.M. on February 12, 1960, and immediately began to feed. By 4:10 P.M. only three wolves were feeding, and the carcass appeared at least half eaten. The cow was mature, but possibly it was smaller than average. Even if it weighed only six hundred pounds, the fifteen wolves ate about twenty pounds apiece in one and a half hours.

Other observers have reported similar feats. In a previous study on Isle Royale, J. E. Cole (1957) found two instances in which seven or eight wolves ate about three-quarters of an adult moose in two days, or about thirty-five pounds per wolf per day. In western Canada, four wolves consumed most of a mule deer doe in four hours; and in five days, a pack of three finished two mule deer and an elk calf (Cowan, 1947).

Ontario biologists once saw tracks indicating that a pack of seven wolves had traveled forty miles and killed and eaten about three-quarters of an adult buck deer plus everything but the stomach contents of a small deer, all in no more than twenty hours (Pimlott *et al.*, 1969). This is a consumption rate of about twenty-eight pounds per wolf in twenty hours or less, assuming the eaten parts of the buck weighed about 115 pounds and those of the other deer about eighty pounds.

Although the wolf can eat large amounts of food in a short time, such quantities are not always available, so the predator may have to go without eating for several days at a time. For this extended fasting, the wolf seems to be as well adapted as it is for feasting.

On Isle Royale, it appeared that the pack of fifteen or sixteen wolves once went at least ninety-five hours without eating anything except hair and bones that they might have gleaned from old kills (Mech, 1966a). Another time, half of this pack apparently ate nothing for five days except for a beaver and whatever scraps could have been found at old kills. Young reported on a wild male wolf that when kept in captivity would not eat for seven days; on the eighth day, he gorged. E. H. McCleery of Kane, Pennsylvania, who maintained a wolf "farm" as a tourist attraction for years, wrote me that he fed his animals every five days in winter and spring and every five to ten days in summer.

The longest a wild wolf is known to have gone without food is seventeen days. This record came from the Yamal-Nenets National Territory of the Soviet Union (Makridin, 1962). On February 13 eight members of a pack of nine wolves were killed, and the ninth member was wounded. This animal hid under some trees and was not found until March 3, when it was scared out of its hiding place by an aircraft. It ran as though healthy but was soon killed. It was very thin and still had frozen blood on its fur from its old wounds, but the wounds themselves had healed. Tracks showed that the wounded wolf had not left its bed, and thus could not have eaten, during the entire seventeen days.

Evidently the ability to fast for long periods has not been lost in the domestication of the dog from the wolf. According to Fuller and DuBuis (1962: 423): "Dogs have survived two months and more without eating, and deprivation for a week is readily sustained without serious effects. They are, however, less resistant to stress when body weight falls more than 15 per cent below normal."

In view of the above, it appears that the wolf probably could fast for two weeks or more while still traveling about searching for vulnerable prey, and that under certain conditions could go hungry for even much longer periods. Then when food is found again, the wolf, with its large stomach capacity, could replenish itself and thus would be ready for another long period of fasting. The value to a predator of such a system of feeding is obviously very great.

To get some idea about the amount of food the wolf requires, one must resort to figures on the requirements of dogs. It seems reasonable to assume that they will not differ too greatly from those of the wolf. According to figures by Jean Mayer (1953), very active dogs weighing about eighty pounds need some 2800 calories per day. To produce this much energy, approximately 3.7 pounds of meat such as lean round beef or veal leg would be necessary (Whitney, 1949). Probably the same weights of deer, moose, elk, and other wild creatures would contain similar amounts of calories.

These figures are about 25% higher than those for dogs with restricted activity. Relatively nonactive adult wolves (those in cages at zoos) have been kept for long periods on about 2.5 pounds of meat per day (Fletcher, 1967). Thus the "active" figure of 3.7 pounds per day would seem to allow for a great deal of activity on the part of an animal, and it probably can be regarded as an accurate minimum maintenance requirement for wolves in the wild.

Growing wolves need two or three times as much food per pound as do adults, for food is used by pups not only for heat and energy, but also for growth.

The extent to which cold increases the food requirements of wild animals is unknown. In much of the wolf's range, differences of 100° F. occur between summer and winter. At first consideration it would seem that any animal would lose much more body heat at −30° F. than 70° F. Whitney, however, believed that dogs kept in unheated kennels in winter would require only about the same increase in food consumption that has been found for pigs under similar conditions, i.e., 10%. The wolf's winter fur is a very efficient insulator, so perhaps the only significant heat loss by the animal during winter is that due to breathing the very cold air.

No matter what the difference is in the minimum food requirements of an active wolf during summer or winter, it is important to distinguish between this minimum requirement and the amount of food actually eaten. Probably most animals eat much more food than is really necessary, as do human beings and dogs. It has been found that wild bobcats in captivity also "overeat." Experimental cats maintained their weight on .048 to .061 pound of deer meat per pound of cat, but they actually ate twice these amounts when allowed all they wanted (Golley *et al.,* 1965).

The few figures available for wild free-ranging animals indicate that they also eat more than required. After thirty years of extensive mink-muskrat studies, P. L. Errington (1967: 24) wrote: "Ordinarily, on a straight diet of muskrats in spring, a big mink would probably be eating an adult-sized muskrat every other day. But a muskrat every other day far exceeds the minimum of flesh required for a subsistence diet. Very careful studies indicated that the minks of a central Iowa marsh were maintaining themselves in normal health for about half of one winter on as little food as the straight-diet equivalent of one muskrat per nine days."

The figure discussed above for maintaining very active dogs weighing eighty pounds was 3.7 pounds of meat per day, or .046 pound per pound of animal. The daily maintenance figures for caged wolves, which probably weigh about the same, was 2.5 pounds per animal, or about .031 pound per pound of wolf. However, Wright (1960) reported that wild African hunting dogs consumed .15 pound of prey per pound of body weight, about four times these amounts; African lions ate .11 to .13 pound per pound of body weight.

Consumption rates for wolves in the wild are comparable to these. They are based on estimated weights of prey animals and thus are subject to inaccuracies. Nevertheless, they should at least be correct approximations. For example, on Isle Royale, I estimated that members of the main pack of wolves each consumed an average of .18 pound of moose per pound of wolf per day in the winter of 1959, .13 in 1960, and .19 in 1961 (Mech, 1966a). Pimlott and his co-workers disagreed with my estimates of the weights of moose, so they adjusted these figures according to their own estimates. The resulting adjusted average consumption rate was .14 of a pound of moose per pound of wolf per day, or about ten pounds per wolf. Whichever rate is correct, it is two, three, or four times the maintenance figures discussed above. Less extensive information calculated from data by Cowan and Burkholder support this.

In assuming that the above figures are reasonably accurate, an explanation must be found for the fate of the extra calories consumed. There seem to be three possibilities: (1) wild wolves might spend much more energy than is now thought, (2) at least some of the extra calories are converted into fat, which would be of great advantage during times of food scarcity, and

(3) digestion may be less efficient at high rates of food intake.

Concerning the last point, some further information from Errington's (1967) mink-muskrat studies is pertinent. During one spring when muskrats were especially available, Errington found that a mink ate an average of two adult muskrats per day and that its droppings consisted of undigested meat.

Regardless of what happens to the extra calories that a wild animal may consume, apparent overeating would make it likely that the animal obtains a more adequate supply of vitamins and minerals, often found in very small amounts.

Because the prey of the wolf varies in size from the beaver to the bison, the rate of kill of these species varies according to the amount of food each provides. The smaller the prey, the more individuals must be killed to fulfill the wolf's food requirements. In Alaska, for example, a pack of ten wolves killed thirteen caribou and eight moose calves during a thirty-five-day period, or 1.7 prey animals per wolf per month (Burkholder, 1959). In Alberta, each of two packs of five or six animals took three elk in two weeks—one to 1.5 elk per wolf per month (Cowan, 1947). On Isle Royale, a large pack of wolves killed an average of .67 moose per wolf per month (Mech, 1966a).

The Isle Royale figures are the most extensive yet obtained on the average rate of kill by a wolf pack. The pack numbered fifteen or sixteen animals from 1959 through 1961, seventeen in 1962, and sixteen again in 1963, and killed at a very consistent rate throughout the five winters for which figures are available. During each of these years, the average rate of kill for the pack varied only from one moose per 3.0 days to one moose per 3.7 days (Mech, 1966a; Shelton, 1966). It is significant that the highest rate occurred when calves composed 67% of the animals killed, and the lowest rate was found when calves made up only 15% of the kills.

Feeding Routine and Use of Prey

Immediately after killing an animal, wolves begin feeding excitedly. They rip and tug at the carcass from all directions and bolt down great chunks of it. Once I saw thirteen wolves packed side-by-side so solidly around a freshly killed moose that there was no room for the two other members of the pack. The rump of a prey animal, which is the usual point of attack, is often the first part eaten, probably because the flesh is already exposed there. This is most apparent in kills made by lone wolves, for such cases are not complicated by the feeding of several animals.

I have examined both a moose and a deer shortly after a lone wolf had killed them. In the case of the moose, several pounds of the rump had been eaten, and then part of the intestines that had been exposed. The rest of the moose was intact. With the deer carcass, the wolf was still feeding when I approached. The animal had eaten a few pounds of meat from the rump and had then opened the belly from the side. It was peeling off long strings of fat from the intestinal membranes when interrupted. This may be highly preferred food in winter; in another situation I examined the contents of a wolf's stomach and found nothing but a large amount of such fat.

The next parts of a carcass to be eaten are the heart, lungs, liver, and all other viscera except the stomach contents. The flanks and one side of the rib cage are often devoured quickly, probably to allow entrance to the body cavity. In moose carcasses, the nose is usually eaten soon, but this may be because it is one of the points of attack. I have not seen the nose of any deer eaten unless most of the carcass was also gone.

Eventually the entire carcass may be consumed in the case of animals the size of caribou and small moose (Burkholder, 1959). More often, the skull, lower jaw, backbone, long bones, and a piece of hide are left, especially on larger prey such as adult moose (Fig. 36a and b). These bones are almost always gnawed clean of flesh. In nine-month-old moose calves on Isle Royale and most deer in Minnesota, the bones of each leg are separated and scattered. In adult moose and exceptionally large deer, these bones are usually left together, although each leg is widely separated from the others. In addition, half of the backbone is usually attached to the skull, and the other half to the pelvis. Chewing is apparent on the ends of the leg bones, and the edges of the pelvis, shoulder blades, and lower jaw.

At times the carcass of a deer may appear abandoned while a large piece of hide with the four lower leg bones attached still remains. However, such a carcass will be revisited sooner or later, either by the wolves that killed the animal or by others. It usually ends up as thoroughly eaten as described above.

FIGURE 36 A & B. After wolves feed on a large carcass, generally only bones and hair are left, as these remains of moose and deer show.

Although the wolf is often accused of eating just the "best" parts of its prey and therefore wasting the rest, most of the evidence does not bear out such a claim. On Isle Royale, all of the fifty moose carcasses that I examined were eventually eaten completely, except for one that I had interfered with during summer. Two-thirds of the thirty-one caribou and moose kills studied by Burkholder in Alaska were at least 75% utilized when examined. Of 477 deer carcasses inspected by Pimlott and co-workers in Ontario, 346, or 72%, were utilized 75% or more. During both studies, wolves may have returned after the examinations and cleaned up the carcasses.

Further evidence that wolves return to old kills comes from Banfield (1954: 49): "When caribou are abundant, wolves often kill in excess of their immediate needs. In the observation cited above, two calves were killed within about 25 yards of each other in one attack. One calf was consumed except for the intestinal viscera, lower limbs, hide, and vertebral column, but from the other carcass only the tongue and throat were removed. On August 27, the same wolf returned to the second kill and ate it."

An incident in Minnesota showed how an untrained observer could reach a mistaken conclusion that wolves were wasting the deer they were killing. About noon one day, I examined the carcass of a large buck that a wolf had killed only hours before in the middle of a wide, frozen bay. Only the rump and part of the viscera had been eaten, but the wolf was nowhere to be seen, so the carcass appeared abandoned. Nevertheless, when I returned about 5:00 P.M., the wolf was back feeding. Eventually this deer ended up a nondescript patch of hair and scattered bones like most other wolf kills. Only during long periods of unusually deep snow, when deer are especially vulnerable, have I seen where wolves have killed deer and abandoned them.

When wolves kill domestic animals, however, the situation may be different. Young cited many detailed accounts of such animals having been only partly eaten and then abandoned by wolves. In Finland, the same situation has recently been found. Pulliainen (1965: 239) wrote: "The wild animals killed by wolves were eaten almost entirely. Domestic animals, on the contrary, were generally only partly eaten. In North Karelia, for instance, in 1962, wolves ate the following domestic animals entirely: 31 sheep, 3 cows, 5 calves and one horse. The corresponding figures for domestic animals killed by wolves . . . were 149 sheep, 9 cows, 15 calves and three horses. It can be seen that 20–30 per cent of the domestic animals killed by wolves were eaten entirely. It is also to be noted that human activities often disturb wolves feeding on domestic animals. The small domestic animals like cats and dogs are generally eaten entirely."

In some cases, not all of the flesh from a carcass is consumed immediately. Some large chunks may be buried under the snow or in the ground (Murie, 1944; Cowan, 1947). This cached meat may be used when the pack visits the carcass again, but probably much of it is eaten by scavengers such as foxes and coyotes.

Little is known about caching and the conditions under which it takes place. I did not notice that behavior on Isle Royale, and I doubt that it occurred within the large pack of wolves on that island, at least during winter. My doubts arise because the pack usually remained at its kills until the members had thoroughly chewed and cleaned the bones. Presumably if they had cached meat nearby, they could have dug that up before resorting to the bones.

In the case of a deer kill in northern Minnesota I did suspect caching. The snow in the area was deep and unbroken except for the tracks where six wolves had chased the deer. The only remains of the kill, however, were a few hairs and a large spot of blood where the carcass had lain. From the air I had watched the wolves leaving the vicinity, and they did not seem to be carrying anything. Thus they either ate the hoofs, all the bones including the skull and lower jaw, and the entire hide, or they cached them. If the wolves did cache these parts, they must have hidden them under their own beds in the snow. I had followed all the trails leading from the area of the kill itself and had found no other broken snow except the trails and beds of the wolves.

Although I did not realize it at the time, it later occurred to me that this situation was very similar to one I had seen a few years before. At that time, I was searching for a snowshoe hare that was wearing a special radio-collar. My radio receiver indicated that the signal was coming from under a certain patch of snow. This was difficult to believe because there were no hare tracks nearby. The only tracks were those of a red fox, leading to and from a spot where the fox had bedded. The signal came from directly under the fox bed. When I dug there, I learned that several inches beneath its bed the fox had buried the head, shoulders, and radio-collar of the snowshoe hare that it had killed in a nearby swamp (Mech, 1967). On another occasion, I also found where a fox had buried a piece of prey beneath its bed in the snow, so this may be a common pattern.

Burying an item, as carried out by my wolf pups, involved digging with the front feet and placing the object by mouth into the shallow hole. Then by forward scraping with the top side of the nose, the animals would push soil back over the object. Packing the loose soil was done by bunting with the end of the nose. If one pup discovered the other burying something, the latter would dig up its cache and either begin chewing on it or find another hiding place. Before feeding on a piece of cached meat, a wolf will grasp it in its teeth and give it one quick shake, which removes all loose soil.

Caching would be advantageous in at least two situations. When only one or two wolves kill a large animal and cannot eat it all in a few days, burying various parts would save them from crows, ravens, vultures, and other scavengers that cannot smell. This would be true either in summer or winter. Secondly, in summer, when fly blowing would cause further loss of a kill within a few days, burying could help preserve the meat long enough for the wolves to use most of it.

A pack of several wolves would not need to cache meat from its kills because its members could clean up most of a carcass within a short period. Because a wolf's stomach can hold almost twenty pounds and digestion is rapid, wolves might feed several times a day. On Isle Royale, when the pack of fifteen or sixteen killed a moose, there was seldom a time during the first several hours when no wolf was feeding. In Alaska, a pack of ten fed on an old bull caribou for at least an hour after killing it (Burkholder, 1959). Since meat on a fresh carcass is readily available and wolves bolt their food down so quickly, all members of a pack should be able to fill themselves within an hour or so. Thus when wolves are seen at a carcass longer than that, they are probably animals that have returned for additional food.

After feeding intensively, wolves then seek a suitable spot in which to rest and sleep. If the sun is shining and the wind is light, they prefer open areas such as ridge tops or expanses of ice, and they will travel several miles to get to such places. There

FIGURE 37. On the second day after a moose is killed by the large pack of wolves on Isle Royale, usually only the skeleton remains, and individuals often wander back to chew the bones. (*Durward L. Allen*)

they sprawl out on their sides or bellies for several hours. During windy, snowy weather, they curl up in protected areas such as beneath evergreen trees, where they remain for long periods. They appear quite sluggish after having gorged, and tales have been told about early American hunters being able to stalk "meat drunk" wolves very easily (Young, 1944).

Resting after gorging appears to be a logical move. Traveling, hunting, killing, and feeding are all tiring, so rest is no doubt welcome. But in addition, rest also helps digestion and enables wolves to use their food efficiently. According to Whitney (1949: 26): "Digestion in the stomach and the passing of food into the duodenum are retarded by emotional excitement and by exercise." Inactivity would allow quick passage of the food and further engorgement.

On Isle Royale, the second general feeding on a fresh kill usually took place about six hours after the first. The wolves would arise from their beds and file back to the carcass for another extended feeding. Since much of the activity around a carcass occurred at night, the detailed history of the use of kills was not learned. However, I do know that usually within the first twenty-four hours, and probably within the first twelve, all the flesh of adult moose was consumed by the pack of fifteen or sixteen.

During the second day after a kill was made on Isle Royale, only the skeleton remained (Fig. 37). The wolves then spent their time dismembering the skeleton and gnawing the bones. At times, members of the pack wandered off and chewed the bones of an old kill. Gradually most of the animals became restless, and usually by the end of the second day they abandoned the carcass. At that time, they first performed a group ceremony (Chapter III). Then they would strike off again, single file, to begin a new trek in search of another vulnerable animal.

CHAPTER VII / HUNTING HABITS

Much has been written about the hunting behavior of wolves, and they have often been credited with the use of teamwork and complex strategy in their quest for food. However, most conclusions about the hunting habits of the wolf have been based on hearsay, old published descriptions by nonobjective observers, and interpretations of tracks in the snow. Actual observations of wolves hunting prey are scarce, and accurate published accounts of these incidents are even scarcer.

Obviously hearsay should only be accepted with skepticism by anyone interested in learning the truth about any matter. Old published reports by anyone not striving to separate the facts from his own interpretations of events are just as unacceptable. Some of these descriptions, as quoted by Young in *The Wolves of North America,* make fascinating, although fanciful, reading. If the facts within them could be sifted from the fancy, they would be very valuable to this chapter. But since they cannot, these accounts must be ignored in this treatment.

Even interpretations of tracks in the snow can be misleading, as the following example will illustrate. An observer in an aircraft might be tracking a pack of wolves in the snow when suddenly the single line of tracks splits. One set leaves the top of a ridge and heads diagonally into a valley. The other set continues farther along the ridge, merges with the tracks of a moose, and then veers into the valley. Where the two sets of wolf tracks meet, the remains of a kill are found. Obviously the wolf pack had suddenly sensed the moose, split up, attacked from two sides, and killed the animal. In so doing, the wolves appeared to show some simple strategy.

But is this interpretation of the tracks so obviously correct? Aren't there other possibilities? One other likely explanation is that long before coming to the moose a few members of the pack had stopped to rest and thus lingered for a half hour or so behind the others. By the time they began catching up, the first wolves had killed the moose. The lingerers, upon scenting the kill in the valley, might have split off from the trail of the first wolves and struck out directly to the kill. No doubt there are other possible explanations.

Because direct sightings of wolves attacking prey are so scarce, secondhand accounts and interpretations of tracks must be used. But utmost care should be taken in the process, and the interpretations must be viewed critically. In the following discussion, this practice will be used, and more reliance will be placed on direct sightings reported in the scientific literature.

The problems faced by a wolf pack in attacking different types of prey vary, so the hunting habits of the wolf will be discussed separately for each prey species. However, several broad principles that apply to the behavior of the wolf in hunting wild prey must be considered first.

General Hunting Behavior

The wolf's stimulus to leave the remains of a kill and begin traveling seems to result from a lack of edible parts remaining at the kill. As described in Chapter VI, the wolves on Isle Royale spent the last several hours at a kill in dismembering the skeleton and chewing the bones. Eventually they would become restless and then leave. Probably each wolf's digestive tract was almost empty at that time, and this helped trigger the departure.

When the primary prey of wolves are domestic animals, the wolves often leave before their kills are completely eaten (Pulliainen, 1965). This may be because hunting is so easy that the wolves take only whatever they consider the choicest parts of a carcass. When those parts are eaten, it may have the same psychological effect as the consumption of an entire carcass has on wolves killing wild prey.

In either case, after wolves abandon a kill, their immediate "goal" seems to be to make another. Any prey animal that they locate is subject to attack. In Alaska, a pack of ten wolves left the carcass of a nine-month-old moose calf at noon one day and by the next morning had killed and eaten another moose calf six miles away (Burkholder, 1959). As discussed in Chapter V, this was the minimum travel distance between kills in the area of that study. The maximum was forty-five miles, and the average twenty-four miles, based on six cases.

On Isle Royale, the same general pattern was apparent. The average travel distance between the consecutive kills made by a pack of fifteen or sixteen was twenty-three miles, based on forty-four instances over a five-year period. These wolves once showed interest in a moose only thirty-five minutes after abandoning their last kill. They had left at 4:30 P.M. and at 5:05 P.M. headed directly to a moose. The animal stood its ground as the wolves approached, and after a half minute they withdrew. (This is not uncommon, for many moose are too strong and healthy for the wolves to attempt killing.)

Another time, the same wolves killed a moose four to ten hours after having abandoned their last kill. In at least eight cases they successfully attacked moose within twenty-six hours after leaving their previous carcass. Almost all of the moose that fell prey to this pack while it was under study were killed within forty-eight hours after the wolves had left their last kill.

In discussing the hunger drive of the dog in the context of that animal's similarity to the wolf, the authors of *Genetics and the Social Behavior of the Dog,* J. P. Scott and J. L. Fuller (1965: 73) wrote the following: "The idea of a 'hunger drive' measured by the amount of hours since eating does not apply to the dog. The dog is, in a sense, always hungry, but he is not driven to eat. One of our investigators gave a dog an electric shock when it came near its food dish and then waited to see how long it would take before the dog came back to eat. The dog never came back. After waiting several days for the dog to eat, the experimenter stopped the experiments for fear of harming the animal." In terms of wolf hunting behavior, this suggests that as long as a wolf's stomach is empty the creature is ready to eat and therefore to kill; however, the animal is also prepared to wait until it finds prey that can be killed safely and without undue effort.

Because of this continued readiness, wolves are hunting whenever they are traveling. In fact, on Isle Royale I did not notice that the wolves had any special hunting grounds or behavior. The animals simply traveled over the island, and whenever they found a moose they tried to attack it. Wolves hunting deer in Minnesota seem to use the same approach, although my experiences in that area are more limited. Observations by Murie (1944) of wolves hunting Dall sheep and caribou in Mount McKinley Park and descriptions by Cowan (1947) of wolves hunting elk in the Canadian Rockies also seem to fit this pattern.

A few authors have mentioned certain hunting habits that suggest that wolves may recognize special hunting grounds and may hunt these areas in special ways. However, traced to their source, many of these reports turn out to be old tales of explorers, guides, and trappers whose main interest was not in seeking information about the wolf. Many such accounts even contradict each other.

After eliminating this type of "evidence," one is still faced with a few reports by biologists. For example, Cowan mentioned that wolves adopt a "line abreast" formation when hunting swamps, and Stenlund (1955: 30) wrote that "when a pack reaches an area to be hunted, it separates and drives through much like a party of human deer hunters."

The above reports, however, are not well documented. Stenlund's statement seems to be based on two observations, one of which appears to have been an interpretation of tracks in the snow; and Cowan described no specific incidents. Thus it appears that these men were offering their best opinions about the ways in which wolves hunt, based on the available evidence, which was quite limited. It certainly is possible that in some areas or situations the techniques described above are used, but there is not yet evidence to show that they are commonly employed.

Therefore, it appears at present that under most conditions wolves hunt merely by traveling widely over their range until they meet up with prey. In some regions, the animals may have to travel far through areas of game scarcity to get to "pockets" of prey. But since there would be little to sidetrack them along the way, they probably pass over these routes quickly and spend most of their time wandering, and therefore hunting, within the areas inhabited by prey.

Locating prey. When traveling through country containing prey, the wolves' first problem is to locate individual animals. They seem to use three main methods of solving this problem: direct scenting, chance encounter, and tracking.

Direct scenting probably is used most often. On Isle Royale,

I was able to watch from an aircraft as the pack of fifteen or sixteen wolves (or part of this pack) hunted moose on many occasions (Mech, 1966a). Of the fifty-one hunts in which I could tell whether the wolves trailed the moose or scented them, forty-two involved direct scenting. Lone wolves seen hunting moose on three occasions also located their prey by odor. Usually the wolves scented moose when within three hundred yards downwind of them, but once they detected a cow and twin calves about 1.5 miles away. Observations in Minnesota have shown that wolves may also locate deer directly by odor.

In scenting an animal, wolves must usually be directly downwind of it. This does not mean that they always travel upwind, although Shelton (1966) thought that they tended to do so. Whichever way they are traveling, when their route crosses the wind flowing from the direction of the prey, the lead animals suddenly stop. All pack members then stand alert with eyes, ears, and nose pointed toward the prey. If the wolves are in an open area, they may then carry out a group ceremony with the animals standing nose-to-nose and wagging their tails for a few seconds. If they are in deep snow, they usually just pile up behind the leader and point toward the prey. Then they veer abruptly from their route and head directly toward the prey.

A description of tracks seen by Burkholder (1959: 8) in Alaska suggests that at times wolves in that area also locate their prey by directly scenting it. Writing about a wolf pack detecting a moose on a bush-covered island in a frozen river, he related the following: "The wolves, moving upstream on the right bank, sensed the moose when they were even with the island, as evidenced by three trails 'fanning' out toward the moose at a distance of 30 yards. The moose was knocked down 5 yards from its bed." The wolves may have seen the moose first, instead of scenting it, but the type of cover on the island makes this seem unlikely.

No doubt careful, detailed observations throughout the range of the wolf would show that direct scenting is generally one of the most common methods of detecting prey.

A second method of locating prey involves chance encounter. I have no records of hunts on Isle Royale that I specifically ascribed to chance encounter. But there were twelve hunts in which neither direct scenting nor tracking was indicated. Such wording in my notes as "the seven wolves encountered three adult moose" or "seven wolves came within 20 feet of the nearest" suggests that at least in some of these instances the wolves located moose directly by chance.

The most chance encounters between wolves and their prey would take place where there are high densities of prey. Thus one would suspect that in areas inhabited by deer, which normally occur in high densities, chance encounter would be especially important. I have seen two hunts in Minnesota that show that wolves there do locate some deer this way (Mech, 1966b).

Chance encounter seems to be the main factor in the hunting activity of wolves that prey on Dall sheep. This is evident in several of the hunting incidents in Mount McKinley Park described by Murie. In one account, he wrote that "the sheep had fled to the highest points and were definitely cautious and concerned because of the presence of the wolves, which seemed to be coursing over the hills hoping to surprise a sheep at a disadvantage" (Murie, 1944: 103). However, because most of the descriptions are from tracks in the snow, it would be difficult to rule out direct scenting in all cases.

There is also evidence that at times wolves depend on chance to help them locate both elk and caribou. Cowan reported that in Banff Park, with eighteen inches of snow accumulated, wolves traveled the ridge tops until they spotted elk on the slopes below, and then rushed them. On the Canadian tundra, wolves are said to "patrol" an area, flushing caribou at close range (Banfield, 1954).

The third method used by wolves in locating their prey is tracking. On Isle Royale, members of the pack of fifteen or sixteen tracked their prey in nine of the fifty-one hunts in which the particular manner of locating the prey was apparent. I observed such a hunt on February 11, 1960 (Mech, 1966a: 175). The sixteen wolves left a swamp and struck out into an open burn; they appeared to be on a fresh moose track. When 250 yards crosswind of three adult moose (two lying, one standing), they stopped and scented the air (5:15 P.M.). The first animals lay on a ridge two hundred yards from the moose for a minute, while the rest caught up. Then they continued along the trail, noses to the ground. Two wolves remained downwind and about twenty-five feet ahead of the trackers. All three moose then were lying down, but when the first two tracking wolves got within twenty-five feet, they arose. Meanwhile, the rest of the wolves caught up.

It was evident on Isle Royale that the wolves followed only very fresh moose tracks. Most of the island was covered with older tracks, yet the wolves seldom followed any, old or new. On the few occasions when they did some tracking, they located the moose shortly after taking up the track. This would indicate that the tracks where first encountered probably were quite fresh.

Sometimes wolves can even scent moose tracks and/or droppings several yards away. One time on Isle Royale the pack followed fresh tracks in a valley from a ridge about twenty-five yards upwind, after the moose had left the area.

However, on other occasions the Isle Royale wolves ignored very fresh moose signs. Once I watched a moose cross in front of a wolf pack only one minute before the pack came to the point where the moose had crossed. When the wolves reached the moose track, one wolf followed it for about twenty-five yards and then gave up. The others ignored the tracks. This was not because the wolves were not interested in hunting, because both before and after this incident they chased moose.

The stalk. Unless wolves locate their prey by chance encounter, their manner of approaching the animal is usually the same each time. Direct scenting and tracking both allow sensing of the prey for long distances out of view of the wolves. As they close the gap between themselves and their prey, the wolves become excited but remain restrained. They quicken their paces, wag their tails, and peer ahead intently. Although they seem anxious to leap forward at full speed, they continue to hold themselves in check. This stage of the hunt is the stalk.

Wolves stalk several kinds of prey. In Mount McKinley Park, Murie watched a wolf stalk to within 150 yards of four Dall sheep before beginning its attack. Banfield (1954) found that stalking is one of two main methods used by wolves in approaching caribou on the tundra, and Lois Crisler (1956) described a hunt in which two wolves sneaked to within about one hundred feet of fourteen caribou. In Minnesota, I once watched a pack of eight wolves stalk to within one hundred feet of a deer, after having scented it about a quarter mile away (Mech and Frenzel, unpublished). On Isle Royale, I have seen wolves stalking moose many times. Stalking was used by lone wolves, a pack of three, and a pack of fifteen or sixteen.

In all cases when the restrained approach, or stalk, is used, the wolves sneak as close to the prey as they can without making it flee. At times, they can come very close, apparently because wolves move directly upwind (in the case of direct scenting of the prey) and approach slowly and alertly. I have often seen wolves get to within thirty feet of moose before the moose detected them, and once I saw wolves come right up to two moose in their beds.

The encounter. The stage of the hunt that immediately follows the stalk is the encounter. This is the point at which prey and predator confront each other. An individual prey animal can respond during this stage in three ways. It can approach the wolves, stand its ground, or flee. Seldom does a prey animal approach the wolves, but I have seen this happen once. On February 28, 1961, a moose on Isle Royale strode for about seventy yards to meet seven approaching wolves. When the moose came to within thirty yards of the animals, they turned and fled.

Many prey animals stand their ground when they sense approaching wolves. This is especially true of moose and will be discussed in detail in the section on moose. Elk (Cowan, 1947) and musk-oxen (Tener, 1954a) also show this behavior. When an animal has detected wolves but fails to flee, it faces the approaching predators. As soon as the wolves see that their quarry has sensed them but is not running, they stop their stalk. With moose, they may then proceed closer, but they do so quite cautiously.

In the case of the eight wolves seen stalking a deer in Minnesota, cited above, the deer detected the wolves when they were one hundred feet away, but did not flee. Although its body was turned away from them, the deer faced the wolves over its shoulder, and the wolves just stared back at the deer. For one or two minutes neither predators nor prey moved.

When larger prey such as moose stand their ground, they usually can fend off wolves, so standing is a form of defense with them. However, a small animal such as a deer or the calves of larger prey would be almost defenseless in trying to fight off a pack of wolves. I have seen four wolves kill a 250- to 300-pound moose calf once it was separated from its dam. A deer that stands its ground will do so merely as a stopgap effort; sooner or later it will have to run.

Nevertheless the importance of the above wolf-deer incident

is that, as soon as the deer and the wolves noticed each other, the wolves stopped advancing. The whole situation seemed tense, and it appeared that both the deer and the wolves were ready to bound away at any instant. But why didn't the wolves suddenly rush the deer? They certainly had little to fear from it. I believe that the reason they did not is that they needed the stimulus of a running animal. A nonmoving creature seems to inhibit the rush response. Either a stalk results if the quarry is *not* facing the wolves, or a hesitant approach results if the quarry is facing them.

Several pieces of evidence lead to those conclusions. On Isle Royale, any moose was safe from attack if it stood its ground against even a pack of fifteen or sixteen wolves, whereas moose that ran were almost always chased. (See section on moose for greater detail.) Also, it is common experience that many dogs will pursue animals or objects only when they move away. My own dog, a small terrierlike mongrel, when once faced with an Irish wolfhound weighing ten times as much as she, just stood staring at him. But as soon as the wolfhound ran off, my dog chased him. A similar instance was reported for a young (human-reared) wolf. This individual would run when approached by sheep, but would pursue the animals if they ran from him (Fentress, 1967).

Thus it is significant that in the above wolf-deer account the instant the deer finally bolted away, the predators sprang forward in pursuit with great bounds. On the arctic tundra, Crisler (1956: 340) witnessed a similar incident: "Once the caribou stopped and faced back, taking a look at her pursuer. The wolf immediately stopped also, and sat down. Our observation is that a wolf prefers not to be eyed when approaching its prey."

The rush. The flight of the prey during the encounter stage of the hunt almost always results in an immediate rush. Observations described or cited above of wolves stalking moose, Dall sheep, deer, and caribou all ended in the wolves making a sudden rush toward the prey. This behavior has been recorded for wolves in attacks on all species of large wild prey that anyone has observed wolves attacking.

The rush is the most critical stage of the hunt. If the wolves fail to get close to their quarry during this stage, the prey runs off at top speed, and the predators may never get close to it.

On the other hand, if the wolves quickly close the gap between them and their prey during the first few seconds of the rush, they may get a chance to attempt an attack. Or, if they do not come quite close enough to actually attack, they may at least gain enough ground to give them a good start during the chase.

The chase. This stage of the hunt is a continuation of the rush, in which the prey flees and the wolves follow. If the wolves catch up to their quarry, they may attack. If they fall behind, they give up quickly. Although the pursuit sometimes goes on for miles, it usually covers a shorter distance and lasts only a few minutes.

During chases that I have watched in which wolves actually caught up to a total of forty-one moose, the farthest the predators have ever followed any animal was three miles; in thirty-two of these cases, the wolves gave up in less than a half mile (Mech, 1966a). The longest distance that Lois Crisler saw wolves pursue caribou was five miles, and she was impressed with "how quickly the wolves had judged when a chase was useless."

Several other authorities have noted short pursuits by wolves. Dixon (1934) reported that he never saw tracks where wolves had chased their victims more than two hundred yards. Murie and Banfield each described cases of wolves chasing caribou for only short distances before giving up, and Murie also gave several accounts of wolves pursuing Dall sheep for a similar distance. I have watched packs of wolves chase nine deer in Minnesota, and the longest pursuit was no more than a half mile. The lengthiest chase that Cowan found signs of was one and a half miles, and Burkholder stated that "of the 22 fresh kills made, none showed evidence of a long chase."

The actual observations just cited contrast greatly with the following ideas about the wolf's hunting habits by Young (1944: 74): "[The wolf] can keep up its loping gait mile after mile, the whole night through if necessary; seldom is full speed resorted to except when the prey is to be pounced upon. The hunting technique of wolves is based on the exhaustion of their prey. Their greater endurance over that of most, if not all, of the big game animals, is one of their main assets in overcoming prey."

The above statements were not documented, so in view of the

contradictory evidence from direct observations, they must be discounted. In reality, the wolf's hunting technique is based on the sudden-rush tactic wherein stalking and a quick burst of speed, followed by a short chase, are the main factors in overcoming prey.

The behavior of animals upon the approach of wolves is well adapted to countering the sudden-rush type of attack. If prey sense wolves soon enough, they will hurry right out of the area. But if they can see the wolves, they may stand and watch until it is apparent that the wolves are after them. The moose on Isle Royale and the deer discussed above are examples, and both Murie and Banfield have described incidents in which caribou did not flee nearby wolves unless suddenly pursued. The result of this behavior is that the strength of the prey is saved until the encounter, when it is really needed.

Even when pursued, prey will stop soon after the wolves give up, and will turn and watch their back trail. I have often seen moose do this, and have also observed it in deer. In addition, this behavior is known for caribou and Dall sheep. It too has the effect of conserving energy; if wolves were to continue on the trail of the prey, the animal would again be able to make a quick dash away from them.

This energy-saving behavior seems to be so well developed in caribou that they have learned to tell a hunting wolf from a wolf not interested in hunting at a particular moment. At certain times wolves move among herds of caribou without alarming them, whereas on other occasions the predators greatly disturb the caribou.

Caribou may be able to distinguish a hunting wolf from a non-hunting wolf by its posture. W. O. Pruitt, Jr., noticed while watching caribou that they became greatly alarmed when he had his fur hood up over his head, but were not disturbed when it was down. He also noticed the similarity between the silhouette of a man standing with a fur hood up and that of a wolf approaching in the stalking posture, which shows the animal's furry mane. "Thus one may postulate that . . . one stimulus that releases alarm and flight in caribou is the outline of a wolf approaching directly, at a walk, with head somewhat lowered and pointing forward, his attention fixed on the potential prey" (Pruitt, 1965: 351).

Hamstringing

It is commonly thought that the wolf's usual method of killing is by hamstringing, or cutting the large Achilles' tendon that connects the hock (the heel in man) with the ham muscles. This notion has been fostered by the many historical accounts of wolves attacking both wild and domestic prey, drawn together by Young. Most of the passages quoted from the writings of explorers, trappers, guides, and other woodsmen specifically mention hamstringing as the usual killing technique of the wolf.

It is tempting to give some measure of belief to such reports when they are made by so many observers. However, these "records" are directly contradicted by the results of every modern study of the wolf's killing tactics. Either wolves have changed their ways, or the old reports were in error.

It does seem possible that when wolves depended a great deal on livestock for prey hamstringing might have been useful to disable an individual. Domestic animals have been protected by man for so long that they are not so quick and agile as wild species. Perhaps wolves could close in on them and slash their hamstrings without getting kicked by their hind hoofs.

With wild prey, however, hamstringing would be very dangerous. The hoofs of the wolf's prey are hard, heavy, and sharp and are wielded with great accuracy and agility. To hamstring an animal, a wolf would have to expose itself to the hind hoofs, which most wolves seem unwilling to do. Rather they avoid the hoofs and concentrate on the parts of the body farthest from them—the rump, flanks, shoulders, neck, and nose.

I have never seen hamstringing in witnessing wolf attacks on seven moose and examining several fresh kills of both moose and deer. In addition, Murie failed to mention hamstringing in relating his observations of wolves killing caribou and Dall sheep in Mount McKinley Park. Cowan reported from his extensive studies of wolves in western Canada that "no instance of hamstringing has yet been seen or reported to me." From Minnesota wolf-deer studies, Stenlund wrote: "No evidence of hamstringing of deer was found on freshly killed carcasses although the possibility does exist."

Further indications that hamstringing is rarely employed come from other authorities. Banfield, for instance, stated that "wolves are popularly supposed to hamstring their prey, but from reports by trappers and observations upon carcasses, it is concluded that this is seldom done." Burkholder reported that "I have never found evidence of an animal having been disabled by cutting of the Achilles tendons." Neither did Crisler mention hamstringing during her observations of wolves hunting caribou.

There is no escaping the conclusion that wolves seldom, if ever, hamstring their wild prey.

The Wolf Versus Various Prey

The above discussion of the general hunting habits of the wolf should give insight into the abilities of the animal as a predator on large mammals. However, as pointed out earlier, in different areas the wolf depends on greatly different kinds of prey. Some are herding animals, some are solitary. Some live in thick forests, others on the open tundra. Some depend on their speed for defense, while a few rely on their great size and strength.

Thus, as a species, the wolf must be very adaptable in locating, stalking, chasing, and attacking such a wide variety of prey. Nevertheless, in most cases, individual packs or populations of wolves need to learn only the tactics of catching the one or two types of prey that inhabit their particular region. No doubt wolves in each local area become very skilled at hunting the prey on which they specialize. But it is also possible that the same animals might be inept at hunting species they have never seen. It would be extremely interesting to take a pack that is accustomed to killing deer, for instance, and move it to an area where caribou or moose are the only prey available. Possibly such a pack would be at so great a disadvantage that it would fail to survive.

The specific way in which the wolf has applied its general hunting abilities to overcome the defenses of a wide variety of prey will be discussed below.

Moose. The moose is the wolf's largest antlered prey and one of its most dangerous (Fig. 38). Bulls weigh up to 1250 pounds, cows to 850 pounds, and calves from twenty-five to three hundred pounds, depending on age. Calves are defended by the cow throughout their first year. During their first two weeks of life they are left alone for various periods, but at this age they are thought to be odorless. In North America, moose range throughout most of Canada and Alaska, in parts of Minnesota, Michigan,

FIGURE 38. The moose is one of the largest prey of the wolf, and is the mainstay of the wolves of Isle Royale. (*L. David Mech*)

and Wisconsin, and in the northern Rocky Mountains. They also inhabit Norway and Sweden (where they are called "elk") and parts of Russia, Manchuria, and Mongolia.

Where wolves prey on moose, calves seem to make up a high percentage of the kills during both summer and winter. Nothing is known about the way that wolves locate moose in summer, but probably they use the same methods as in winter: direct scenting, chance encounter, and tracking. Once the predators have located a cow and calf, their attack must be directed at disabling the calf while avoiding the cow. If wolves should happen upon a calf unprotected by a cow, or if they can separate a calf from its dam, they can quickly dispatch the calf with no problem. Even during winter, when the calf may weigh three hundred pounds, it is almost helpless without the cow.

Two accounts of wolves attacking moose calves in summer have been recorded. The first incident took place in Alaska and was witnessed from a helicopter by G. Atwell. He first saw a two- or three-day-old calf lying in an area of muskeg and sparse alder cover, at 4:32 A.M. It was closely guarded by the cow but was prostrate as though having been harassed a great deal. According to Atwell's report (1964: 313): "The wolf approached the pair of moose, whereupon the cow, with head lowered, charged the wolf which then ran in an arc 60 to 75 feet from the calf. The cow suddenly halted at the extremity of the arc and the wolf once more attacked the calf. After 20 to 30 seconds the cow again rushed at the wolf which, upon evading the charge, returned to the calf. At 4:39 A.M., after 8 encounters such as described above (on one occasion the wolf picked up the calf by the middle of the back and carried it 20 feet), the cow relinquished its defense and the wolf began feeding on the calf."

The calf weighed thirty pounds. The wolf had pierced its brain just above the eyes. Two other punctures had been made in the skull below the eyes, and at least two more in the backbone. The left side of the rib cage was lacerated and the left lung punctured.

The second incident occurred in Isle Royale National Park on July 10, at 9:15 A.M. (Shelton, 1966). A park ranger in a boat saw a wolf biting at the neck of a moose calf standing on shore. When the wolf heard the boat motor, it temporarily gave up the attack. However, when the ranger returned forty-five minutes later, the wolf had already killed the calf and was feeding on the carcass. Again the wolf ran off and did not reappear for the rest of the day. Apparently the calf had been attacked after it had failed to follow its dam into the water and across a bay to the other shore.

After the wolf left the moose calf, a cow swam from across the bay and spent an hour searching along the shore. She then swam back across the bay, but at 9:00 P.M. she returned to the vicinity of the calf and stayed there all night. Twice during the night, an observer heard a great commotion on the shore, presumably the cow continuing to defend the calf carcass from the returning wolf. At sunrise the cow swam back across the bay, with a conspicuous wound on one flank.

No doubt many attempted attacks on calves are unsuccessful because the cow's defense of a calf is so vigorous. Murie wrote of a case in which a cow held off two attacking huskies the size of wolves and thereby saved her newborn calf. Other authors have related personal observations of the strong protective drive of the cow moose when she and her calf confront human beings (Peterson, 1955; Mech, 1966a).

Although wolves do kill numbers of moose calves during summer, they do not prey exclusively on them. I examined the fresh carcass of an adult cow killed in late August on Isle Royale. The original wound was high on the left hind leg. It was two and a half inches deep, four inches wide, and eight inches long. The only other exposed area was the pelvic region, where the wolves had been feeding. It is not known whether that area was the final point of attack or whether it was merely opened by feeding after the moose had died from the first wound.

Observations on the defense of adult moose against wolves during summer seem to be conflicting. R. L. Peterson (1955: 104) wrote in his book *North American Moose* that "moose regularly make for the nearest water when seeking protection from predators." Cowan reported the same type of defense for moose, elk, and deer in British Columbia, and on Isle Royale two parties related episodes to me in which wolves chased moose into water and then gave up. However, on two occasions Shelton watched a moose leave the pond in which it was feeding and run off into the bush as it detected a wolf traveling along the shore. These contrasting reports may show that the first defense of the moose in summer is to flee if possible, just as it is in winter (see below), and that the second defense is to seek the protection of water only when hard-pressed by pursuing wolves.

Much more is known about wolf-moose interactions in winter than during any other season. Most such information comes from Isle Royale, where moose are the only significant prey of the wolf. The wolves on that island are specialists in hunting moose, and the moose no doubt are specialists in defending themselves from wolves.

Information in this section, unless otherwise indicated, is taken from the U. S. National Park Service's publication "The Wolves of Isle Royale" (Mech, 1966a). It is based on my sixty-eight hours of direct aerial observation of a pack of fifteen or sixteen wolves, or part of this pack, hunting moose on Isle Royale during February and March of three winters. During the sixty-eight hours, sixty-six hunts involving 131 moose were witnessed. (Since moose often associate in groups, a single hunt usually included more than one moose.)

The method used to watch wolves hunt on Isle Royale involves flying about three hundred to five hundred feet above the wolves and somewhat ahead of them. In this way the observer can spot the next moose that the pack might encounter before either moose or wolves are aware of each other.

As already discussed, the wolves usually traveled over Isle Royale and along its shore and located moose by scent when they were directly downwind of them. After detecting the scent, the animals pointed alertly upwind, apparently checking it. Often they performed a group activity that involved much tail wagging and nose touching, possibly a begging ceremony centering around the leader (Chapters III and IV). Next the wolves headed off single file directly toward the moose. Wagging tails showed the wolves' excitement, but the gait of the animals was checked as they approached their prey.

Moose are large and powerful and can easily kill a wolf (Chapter IX). Nevertheless, on Isle Royale, if they detected approaching wolves soon enough, they tried to avoid an encounter. Of the 131 moose that I saw the wolves sense, eleven detected the wolves first and immediately left the area (Fig. 39). Each of the 120 others did not sense the wolves until the pack was stalking it or had already come upon it. Twenty-four of these 120 stood their ground and held the wolves off in each case. This defense tactic will be discussed later. The ninety-six others fled upon detecting the wolves; in many cases, moose in this category had sensed the wolves while still two hundred or three hundred yards away or more.

When any of the moose suddenly bolted away, the wolves immediately sprang forth in pursuit of it with great bounds. (From the air it was hard to tell whether the wolves had seen the moose bolt or whether they had merely heard them crashing through the brush; there seemed to have been cases of both.) Of the ninety-six moose that fled during the stalk, forty-three animals, during twenty separate hunts, gained such long head starts that the wolves never got close to them.

The speed of the wolf is reported to be from twenty-five to forty mph (Chapter I), and the speed of the moose thirty-five mph (Cottam and Williams, 1943), so the two animals are well matched in this respect. However, running conditions such as cover, topography, and snow depth may favor one over the other.

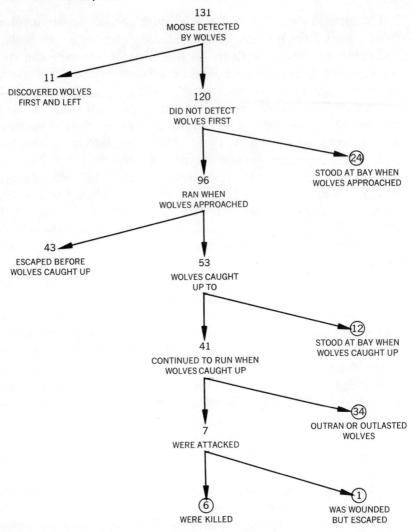

FIGURE 39. Results of interactions between all or part of a pack of 15–16 wolves and 131 moose in Isle Royale National Park. (Circled figures indicate those animals considered actually "tested" by the wolves).

It also appears that moose often do not run at top speed during a chase, whereas wolves do. In any case, on Isle Royale if a moose stayed more than a hundred yards or so ahead of the pursuing wolves for even ten or fifteen seconds, the wolves usually gave up the chase. On the other hand, on one occasion, the pack continued after a moose with a hundred-yard head start for a quarter mile before catching up to it.

Usually the wolves ran faster than the moose. If the moose did not have much of a head start, or if the wolves gained quickly during the first few seconds of the chase, the wolves usually caught up to the moose. Sometimes within two or three hundred yards they even overtook animals that had 150-yard leads. In such cases, the moose could have been hesitant about running, which would account for the lack of speed.

Although forty-three of the ninety-six moose that fled escaped without the wolves overtaking them, the predators did catch up with the others. Each of twelve of these animals stood at bay as the wolves closed in, but in forty-one cases the moose continued running. When a moose was pursued, it took long trotting strides that appeared effortless, but the leaps and bounds of the pursuing wolves seemed exhausting. However, both animals could continue running for twenty minutes.

When following moose, most members of the pack remained strung out in line behind the fleeing animal and traveled in its trail (Fig. 40). At times a few individuals cut off to one side or the other, if the moose curved, and this had the effect of short-cutting the moose. If the moose suddenly swerved toward the opposite direction, however, these wolves usually fell far behind or lost the pack.

When wolves catch up to a moose, most of the animals stay behind, but a few dash alongside it. Often the pack continues this way, sometimes for as far as two miles, without attacking. Then the animals suddenly give up and lie around resting, while the moose heads away. Such was the behavior of the Isle Royale wolves with thirty-four of the forty-one moose that they pursued closely (Fig. 39).

The reason that the wolves did not attack any of these thirty-four moose is unknown. It is not because they were not hungry, for as soon as they abandon a kill and begin traveling they begin hunting. In many of the cases, the wolves gave up chases and then succeeded in killing a moose a few hours later. Often during the unsuccessful pursuits, individual wolves tried to attack, but their quarry warded them off by kicking with its hind hoofs or striking at them with its front hoofs. If one of these moose had become exhausted or had been in ill-health or poor condition, it

FIGURE 40. When chasing moose, wolves make great leaps and bounds, while the moose takes trotterlike strides. Often most members of a pack remain strung out in the trail of the moose they are chasing, so only the lead wolves get close enough to begin the attack. (*L. David Mech*)

would not have been so able to defend itself. I certainly gained the impression while watching these chases that the wolves could have detected this and would have attacked any moose that faltered.

In other words, it appeared that such chases automatically set up testing situations in which the wolves had a chance to tell whether or not they could overcome their prey with a minimum of risk. Since these animals are well practiced at hunting moose, they can probably sense when an individual is not running quite so fast as usual or fighting quite so hard. Further evidence for this idea comes from the ages of the moose killed by the Isle Royale wolves. Rarely was a moose between one and six years of age taken, even though as a group this class makes up the greatest part of the moose herd (Chapter VIII).

Whatever it is about a moose being chased that might furnish the wolves with a clue to the creature's condition, it is not apparent to a biologist circling overhead in a small ski-plane. The wolves succeeded in making seven attacks while I watched (Fig. 39), but I could not see any difference between the animals attacked and the thirty-four that had also run but were not attacked. Three of the moose were calves and four were adults; one of the adults escaped after being wounded, so only three of them actually died right away. I saw the first part of the attack on two of these adults and on the one that was wounded. Each animal was attacked by the wolves within a hundred yards of where they encountered it or caught up with it.

In the first case, the moose had been browsing in the general vicinity of two others when ten members of the wolf pack approached. The wolves seemed to sense the moose when about three-eighths mile away, but did not appear to catch a direct scent until about 250 yards downwind of the moose. At this point the wolves suddenly charged straight toward the moose, which is the only time I saw them react this way while still so far from their prey. Two of the animals detected the wolves when just twenty-five yards away, and they began running. The wolves followed them only a short distance and then saw the third moose, which was closer. They immediately dashed the fifty feet to this animal and surrounded it. But the moose bolted away.

The wolves instantly gave chase (Fig. 40), and soon five or six animals lunged at their quarry's hind legs, back, and flanks. The moose continued on, dragging the clinging wolves until it fell. After only a few seconds it rose, then fell again. It rose again and fled toward a clump of trees, while the wolves continued their attacks. One wolf suddenly grabbed the moose by the nose, but the moose reached the stand of trees, and the wolves released their holds. Beneath the trees, the moose stood at bay, bleeding from the throat. Most of the pack lay down nearby, although a few wolves continued to harass the moose, without actually biting it. The moose appeared strong and aggressive, kicking at the wolves when they approached its rear end.

Darkness prevented further observations that day. The next morning the moose was still alive and in about the same spot.

The bleeding had stopped, but the moose walked stiffly. The wolves had abandoned the animal and had killed another, sixteen miles away. About two and one half weeks later, members of the pack were feeding on a kill within a quarter mile of where they had left the first moose, so perhaps they returned eventually and finished off the weakened animal.

The second adult that I saw attacked was a cow, eight to fifteen years old. She was standing on a ridge at 2:30 P.M. about two hundred yards upwind of the Isle Royale shore, along which the sixteen wolves were traveling. When the wolves scented the cow, they filed directly toward her. She ran hesitantly when the pack was a hundred yards away. The wolves charged up the ridge and caught up to the moose within another hundred yards. She stood at bay next to a bushy spruce, which she used for protection. As the wolves lunged, she charged and kicked at them with all four feet.

The moose continued her defense successfully for three minutes; then she bolted and fled toward the end of the ridge. The wolves attacked her rump and flanks as she ran, but they let up when she passed through some spruces. They pursued the cow for twenty-five yards to the edge of the ridge, and all plunged down the steep slope. When the mass reached the base of the ridge, the wolves were clinging to the cow's back and flanks, and one held her by the nose. The moose struggled for several minutes and even tried to rise, but the tugging wolves anchored her. Most of the animals worked on her rump and flanks, while two tore at her shoulders, and one continued holding her nose. After about ten minutes, the cow stopped struggling, and the wolves fed.

The third adult that I saw attacked was also an eight- to fifteen-year-old cow. The wolves detected this moose when about two hundred yards away, but she did not sense them until they were within twenty-five yards.

The animal fled, but the wolves caught up almost immediately. One grabbed her right hind leg just above the hoof. However, as the cow trotted through some spruces, she shook the wolf loose. She then ran in a semicircle toward a creek, and several times the wolves overtook her but failed to attack. Once when she ran through a snowdrift, the wolves lost ground, but they quickly caught up again.

As the moose started down a shallow valley, the wolves attacked her rump. She soon shook them, however, and proceeded to the frozen creek bed, where the wolves attacked again. One animal kept jumping at her nose and finally grabbed it; others fastened onto her rump and flanks. The cow fought hard and dragged the wolves about a hundred yards downstream. Three or four times, she lifted the "nose wolf" off the ground and swung it for several seconds before lowering her head. This wolf maintained its grip for over a minute. The moose continued fighting hard and finally shook the wolves and ran back upstream, with the whole pack following.

The cow started into the woods and the wolves lunged again. The moose kicked constantly and trampled two individuals into the snow. One of them crawled away but later seemed unhurt. The moose then stood next to a small balsam along the creek shore and continued to fight off the wolves, which soon gave up temporarily and lay on the ice. At 2:35 P.M. they went two hundred yards downstream and assembled. They returned to the animal three times but found her belligerent, although blood from her wounded rump covered several square yards of snow. Nevertheless, there appeared to be no mortal wound.

For most of the afternoon, the wolves rested nearby and kept the moose standing. Every time she lay down, a wolf would approach, and she would arise. Eventually fourteen of the wolves left and visited the remains of an old kill about a half mile away. Meanwhile, two remained curled up within twenty-five yards of the wounded moose, which was also lying. Just before dark the pack headed back toward the moose, but we had to leave because of darkness. No doubt the wolves killed the animal soon, for by the next morning they had eaten much of the carcass.

Because the wolves attacked each of these moose so soon after flushing them, this suggests that the predators quickly recognized that they were vulnerable.

With most calf moose killed by wolves, the condition of the animal probably has only minor importance, because wolves have little trouble killing a calf once it is separated from its dam. The condition of the cow, however, is undoubtedly important in these cases, for a healthy, aggressive cow can ward off the wolves most successfully.

Circumstances can also be important in determining whether or not wolves will manage to separate a cow from its calf. Often the Isle Royale wolves would chase a cow and calf for several hundred yards, and I once watched a three-mile pursuit. Throughout such a chase, the cow tries to stay right behind the calf, defending that animal's rump—the usual point of attack. But when the pursuit continues through different kinds of cover and over widely varying terrain, the chances increase for the cow and calf to become separated. This is especially true when several wolves are harassing both animals, and the cow is trying to ward them off. Nevertheless, in five of the eight cases that I saw of wolves chasing a cow and calf, the defense was successful.

One incident in which the cow's defense of her calf did not succeed involved a moose with twins. Of course, it is doubly difficult for a cow to defend two calves. In this case, the wolves successfully attacked one of the calves within a few hundred yards after catching up to the trio. Four or five animals tore at the rump and sides of the calf and pulled the animal down within fifty feet.

Another time, the wolves pursued a cow and calf for two to three hundred yards and then managed to separate them. Two wolves harassed the cow, while the rest of the pack chased the calf. Eventually a few wolves attacked the rump and flanks of the calf, and one grabbed it by the left hind leg. The cow caught up with the group and managed to stamp on one wolf, which arose instantly and appeared unhurt. The others released the calf and continued pursuing it for another hundred yards before attacking again. They finally pulled the animal down and tore at it, but it arose and the cow rushed in. Some of the wolves fled, but others chased the cow. Then the wolves assailed the calf once more. One grabbed it by the nose, and three or four tore at its neck and throat; others ripped at its rump. The calf's hindquarters went down, but the animal continued on, dragging its hind legs and the wolves that were attached to its body. It managed to stand once more, and the cow started to charge again, but one wolf chased her away.

The wolves made a final attack on the calf, and it was unable to arise. Then they lined up side-by-side around the carcass and began feeding.

In the third case, the wolves chased a cow and calf through a thick spruce swamp and the pair separated. The calf charged back out of the swamp, pursued closely by two wolves. Within two hundred yards the wolves began nipping at the hind legs of the moose. Then one wolf grabbed the animal by the throat and the other fastened to its rump. The moose stopped and trampled the front wolf, but this individual maintained its throat hold for about two minutes while the calf continued to pound it and drag it about.

Finally this wolf released its hold. But then it stood on its hind legs, placed its front paws on the calf's side, and began tearing at the animal's neck. The calf brushed this wolf off against a tree, but the wolf dove back under the moose and grabbed its throat again. This time the moose straddled the wolf and ran for about a minute, while the wolf ran with it, still attached to its throat. Meanwhile, the other wolf continued ripping at the calf's rump. Soon two more wolves caught up and joined the struggle.

One bit the calf around the head and finally grasped its nose. The other grabbed the right flank and then changed to the rump, where it clung for about a minute while the moose continued on. Thus, one wolf had the calf by the nose, one by the throat, and two by the rump. The animal soon stopped and was pulled down under a small clump of trees. In about three minutes, it ceased struggling (11:45 A.M.).

It is evident from the above accounts that the first point of attack on a moose is the animal's rump or ham area. Because this region is so far from both the front and hind hoofs of the moose and is out of view of the running animal, it is probably the safest place to attack. Although this area contains no vital organs, it is wide and meaty and affords several wolves a strong hold. A large amount of slashing and tearing of the rump muscles of a moose certainly hinders its running ability; and the weight of several wolves tugging at the area helps bring the moose down. When fallen, any prey would be much more defenseless.

It is possible that the mere sight of a fallen prey animal is a strong psychological stimulus for wolves to attack. Evidence for this idea comes from an observation that Fentress made about his tame five-month-old wolf and some horses. The pup became accustomed to the animals and usually paid them little attention. "If a horse rolled, however, the wolf became excited and had to be restrained" (Fentress, 1967: 346).

A second important point of attack is the nose of the moose. In five of the six incidents described above, one wolf hooked its teeth into the prey's nose; in the sixth case, trees partly blocked my view. The one attack seen by Shelton on Isle Royale also involved a wolf that grabbed a moose by the nose. The nose of a moose is large and rubbery. Although it contains no vital areas, a grasp on it seems to control the animal, much as a nose hold on a domestic bull gives a farmer control of that creature.

A wolf with a nose hold stands with its neck stretched and its body as far from the moose as possible, no doubt to avoid blows from the animal's most efficient weapons, its front hoofs. (The wolf's posture is much like that of a dog grasping a towel when playing tug-of-war with its master.) Once the nose hold is secured, the moose seems to concentrate on loosening it; thus the animal is distracted from the wolves that are attacking its rump.

Whether or not wolves use the nose hold on moose in areas other than Isle Royale is unknown. However attacks in the rump region of moose have been reported from Alaska (Burkholder, 1959) and Minnesota (Stenlund, 1955).

The way that moose are actually killed by wolves is unknown. Once an animal is down, wolves attack from every side. At this point the prey may go into shock, as has been suggested by Stenlund's reports of deer attacked by wolves. Or it might have heart failure, as was proposed for a certain caribou calf killed by wolves in northern Canada (Kelsall, 1957). Loss of blood from the many deep wounds inflicted before and immediately after the moose drops would cause death if nothing else did.

A pack of five or more wolves probably could kill a moose in much the same way as described above for the pack of fifteen or sixteen. Usually when this pack attacked moose, only part of the group actually made contact with the prey. Indeed, in 1961, when this pack was split much of the time, each subgroup succeeded in killing moose.

However, lone wolves, pairs, and smaller packs would have much more trouble with this species of prey. Supposedly even a single wolf can kill an adult moose (Young, 1944), and I have watched an individual try to attack three different adults without success. No doubt a lone wolf or even small packs would have to rely on only the very oldest and weakest moose, however. On Isle Royale, a pack of two and a pack of three wolves consistently killed moose, although they did so less often than the large pack did, since they required less food.

The usual technique of these smaller packs probably is to kill a moose in stages. Shelton observed a pair of wolves using this tactic, and I saw it applied by a lone wolf to a wounded animal

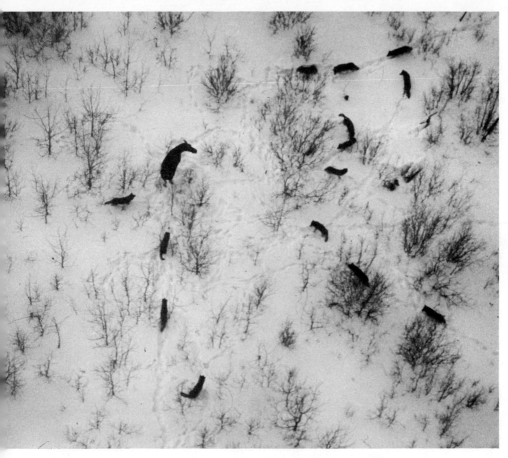

FIGURE 41. If a moose stands its ground upon attack, it is usually able to fend off the wolves. Here the moose stood for five minutes, and the wolves gave up and left. (*L. David Mech*)

that the large pack had left. In both cases, the moose had been wounded and temporarily abandoned. A few days later, it was harassed again and kept on its feet as much as possible. When such a moose can no longer arise, the wolves can rush in and kill it safely, as was done by the lone wolf just mentioned.

The moose is a very powerful and dangerous prey animal. Although many will run to avoid wolves or will flee when chased, others will even face the entire pack and defy the animals (Fig. 41). Of the 131 moose that I saw involved in hunts by the large pack of wolves on Isle Royale, twenty-four immediately stood their ground when confronted by the wolves (Fig. 39). Twelve others fled but then stopped, faced the wolves, and stood at bay until the pack gave up. Sometimes the wolves would abandon such a moose within thirty seconds, but other times they harried an animal for five minutes before leaving. In all thirty-six cases, they failed to attack.

It is easy to see why wolves do not attack a moose at bay. Such a creature can concentrate strictly on defense, whereas a running moose must watch where it is going and can use its front hoofs only against the wolves in front of it. A moose at bay is extremely belligerent and usually charges the closest wolves. Then it wheels around and lashes out with its forefeet at any animals that may have closed in toward its rump. Probably it requires much less energy to stand and fight off the wolves than it would take to flee, so if a moose has the "confidence" or disposition to stand and defy the wolves, it may be able to do so effectively for several hours. Possibly the wolves have even learned this; if after a few minutes' harassment they cannot force the moose to run, they waste no more time.

Just what makes certain moose stand their ground and others run is unknown. It *is* known that some of the moose that run are old, for these are the ones that are killed (Chapter VIII). It is also known that most of the moose in the Isle Royale herd are younger than those being killed. Therefore it is likely that a high percentage of the moose that stand their ground are younger animals. Probably these younger moose would be stronger and healthier, and perhaps even more dominant and aggressive toward other moose. If so, their tendency to intimidate most other moose might give them whatever "self-assurance" is necessary to stand off wolves.

Deer. The deer is the smallest important hoofed prey of the wolf (Fig. 42). Both white-tailed deer and mule deer are taken. Adult white-tailed bucks range from 150 pounds to over 400 pounds and average about 240, whereas does weigh 90 to 210 pounds; newborn fawns average three to four pounds. Mule deer weigh about one-fifth more than white-tails. Within the present range of the wolf, white-tailed deer are distributed generally throughout the northern United States and southern Canada, but mule deer live more in the western half of this range. No information is available on the interactions between wolves and mule deer, but some observations have been made of wolves hunting white-tails.

A casual look at the abilities of both deer and wolves might lead to the conclusion that wolves can kill almost any deer they come upon. However, this idea is easily countered by data from Ontario showing a strong selection of old deer in the wolf kill. This will be discussed in detail in the next chapter. Here it is only necessary to stress that such selection means that wolves in Ontario do not kill just any deer they come to; indeed, it shows that most of the deer encountered by wolves must escape.

Published firsthand accounts of wolves hunting and chasing deer are limited to a few observations from northern Minnesota and Ontario. The first series involved a pack of seven wolves that I followed by aircraft on an afternoon in January 1964 (Mech, 1966b). One wolf strayed away from this pack for a few minutes, and at that time the six others headed toward two deer lying

FIGURE 42. The deer is the smallest hoofed prey of the wolf; it probably depends on alertness and speed for its defense. (*L. David Mech*)

about a hundred yards away. There was no sign that either predator or prey was yet aware of the other. When the wolves came to within thirty yards of the deer, two other deer bounded by, pursued by the straying wolf. These alerted both the bedded deer and the wolf pack. Instantly the wolves gave chase, focusing on one deer. They got no closer than about fifty yards from the animal, however, and within one minute gave up.

An hour later, this pack advanced to within a hundred yards of two more deer, both bedded. The deer arose and fled before the wolves even sensed them. When the pack reached the beds, the wolves tracked the deer for less than a minute and then abandoned the track.

In an observation similar to these, cited in a previous section, a pack of eight wolves came to within a hundred feet of a standing deer, and then stopped as the deer detected them. After deer and wolves stared at one another for one or two minutes, the deer bolted and the wolves immediately sprang after it. Most of the pack got sidetracked when they flushed another deer, but the lead wolf continued after the first animal. However, the deer quickly outdistanced the wolf, and that animal gave up within 250 yards. We could not follow the other chase.

Within a few minutes, five members of the pack had reassembled on a small knoll and were resting. Then one wolf arose and started toward a third deer 150 yards away. I could not tell which animal bolted first, but suddenly both deer and wolf began running. The wolf lost ground quickly, however, and gave up the chase within about 125 yards.

All the above observations were made in brushy forests with a snow cover of at least fifteen inches. The snow seemed to hinder the wolves more than the deer. This is because a bounding deer comes far up out of the snow and back down into it at a much higher angle than does a wolf. The wolf, although it may travel as far in a single bound as a deer does, comes out of the snow and back into it at a very low angle and thus meets much more resistance. In Eurasia, Nasimovich (1955) considered that pursuit of prey by wolves becomes difficult or useless in snow depths of about sixteen inches or more.

Several secondhand observations of wolf-deer encounters and firsthand accounts based on tracks also support the conclusion that wolves have trouble catching deer in deep snow unless special circumstances work against the deer.

Rutter and Pimlott (1968), in their book *The World of the Wolf,* gave accounts of three kills of deer and one unsuccessful attempt, all based on interpretations of tracks in Algonquin Park, Ontario. The unsuccessful attempt was just one of several they have noted. In this case, the deer was sinking through two feet of lightly packed snow right to the ground at each jump, but the two wolves chasing it were sinking in only about four inches. Nevertheless, the deer was able to fend off one of the wolves that brought it to bay three times, and eventually it escaped both animals.

In one of the successful hunts described by these authors, a deer pursued by a single wolf that had chased it across a road ran in a circle of about two hundred yards in diameter. Upon completing the circle and starting to recross the road, the deer met three or four other members of the pack standing on the road and was killed there. Whether or not this was an intentional ambush, the incident did give that impression.

An ambush-like situation also developed in a second successful case in Ontario. This time a single wolf chased a deer in a semicircle of about two hundred yards in diameter, and when the deer jumped a windfall, it met two more wolves. It turned and scrambled up a rough slope, losing ground, and then plunged over a rock ledge, whereupon it was killed by the wolves.

The third kill described by Rutter and Pimlott showed how quickly a deer can be caught once it runs onto a frozen lake. Two wolves had been chasing or following two deer parallel to a lake for at least five hundred yards through snow three feet deep. One of the deer, the smaller, turned away from the lake and headed up a hill, while the other, a large ten-year-old buck, fled onto the lake (Pimlott *et al.,* 1969). There was much less snow there, and the wolves seemed to have made a desperate sprint as soon as they reached the ice, stopping the deer within 150 feet. The smaller deer continued on for about three hundred yards, stopped on a hill and apparently looked out over the ice, then walked away.

The difference between a wolf's ability to chase prey through snow and on a frozen lake was also evident in the kill of a female deer witnessed from the air by Minnesota conservation officer-pilot Robert Hodge. Hodge reported that at 3:00 P.M. on March 10, 1968, he saw a wolf following a deer through the woods southeast of the narrows in Jackfish Bay, Basswood Lake. The deer was moving at a fast walk about seventy-five yards ahead of the wolf, which was traveling at a steady trot.

When the deer reached the shore of the bay, she broke into a run, crossed the two hundred yards of ice, faced a large cliff, and started along the shore. Meanwhile, when the wolf reached the shore, it ran across directly toward the deer and thus gained on her. The deer then ran into the woods where the snow was soft and about eighteen inches deep. There she had no trouble out-distancing the wolf, and when about two hundred yards from the shore, she stood on a ridge and watched her back trail.

When the wolf approached the ridge, the deer started back down toward the shore, not on her back trail, where the wolf was, but on a path paralleling it. The wolf cut across below the ridge and joined the new trail, again gaining ground. However, the deer soon began outdistancing the wolf as she headed back toward the bay.

After reaching the shore, the deer cut directly across the ice to the opposite side. There she hesitated a moment in front of a cliff. The wolf meanwhile had emerged onto the ice, sped across the bay, and hit the doe from behind while she hesitated. The deer fell and never arose again. The wolf bit her behind the head while she was down, and within less than a minute she was dead. The wolf then lay there without feeding for at least the next fifteen minutes. By 4:30 P.M., however, the wolf had fed and left.

The same conservation officer that observed the above also witnessed a wolf attack on a deer several years earlier, and it was reported as follows (Stenlund, 1955: 32): "While flying over Little Indian Sioux River near the Chad Creek junction, Hodge and Nelson observed a large wolf trotting up the river on the ice. About 100 yards away stood a doe and fawn in a willow thicket. The fawn ran across the river and into the thicker lowlands on the other side. The wolf gave chase and passed within 50 feet of the doe which remained standing in the same spot. Within a hundred yards the wolf had caught up to the fawn and knocked it down. It grabbed the fawn near the right hip and shook it vigorously. The fawn got up on four feet and the wolf immediately knocked it down again. This time the fawn's hind feet were stretched out behind and the wolf grabbed at the front shoulder and neck. The plane now roared over the two struggling animals, and the wolf ran into the thicker woods and disappeared. The fawn remained on the ground a short while, then got up and walked across a small opening in the thicket. It left no blood trail and did not appear to be hurt. Hodge and Nelson flew over the area again a half-hour later. The fawn now lay under a balsam tree within 100 feet of the site of the skirmish."

In the above account, the wolf undoubtedly would have killed the deer if the aircraft had not broken up the pair.

The number of deer involved in these reports is small. Nevertheless, the observations do show that deer are not easily caught and that there is a very low success rate by wolves trying to do so. They also tend to discount the idea that, to escape wolves, deer must be able to outlast them. Rather it appears that the main defense of the deer is an ability to detect wolves at a distance and to make a very fast, short dash to safety before the wolves can rush in.

Most wolf-killed deer found during winter are located on frozen lakes, rivers, and beaver ponds. This could be because such kills are easiest to see from the air, but probably it is because these are the situations in which deer are most easily caught. On frozen waterways, snow depth is usually at a minimum because of wind action. Such conditions would be ideal for a running wolf and possibly for a running deer. However, there are not the great drifts and blowdowns that would tend to favor the deer over the wolf, and this may be why so many kills are found on waterways. Perhaps it is mainly the older deer or deer in poor condition that use frozen waterways when pursued because the going is easier for them.

During most of the year, flight to a waterway provides protection for several types of prey. According to Banfield (1954), caribou use this tactic and continue to resort to it during fall and winter, when they suddenly find themselves at a disadvantage. It appears from this that caribou cannot tell the difference between the protection afforded by open water and the advantage provided the wolf by frozen water. If this is also true for deer, it would explain why so many kills are found on the ice. It does not explain why most of these kills are of older individuals, however, unless it is only these animals that are hard-pressed enough by the wolves to resort to water as an escape.

It is true that deer, like other species of wolf prey, also run into water when closely pressed by wolves. A husband and wife ecology team, the Drs. Catherine and Robert R. Ream, reported a direct observation of such an occurrence to me. At 1:15 P.M. on August 31, 1967, they were canoeing on Nina Moose Lake in northern Minnesota when they saw a young buck standing on a large low rock about fifteen feet from shore. The deer disappeared for a few minutes in the vegetation along shore while the Reams pulled up to a nearby campsite.

Suddenly the couple heard splashing and saw the deer come bounding through the water, which was about two and a half feet deep there, back to the rock. About twenty feet behind was a wolf splashing after the deer. This time the deer did not stop on the rock but continued out into the lake swimming. The wolf suddenly detected the Reams and paused on the rock, cowered, and headed back to land. Three minutes later the wolf reappeared about twenty yards farther along the lake. It continued traveling the shore for another sixty yards and then disappeared inland, apparently having given up.

A deer dashing into water does not always discourage its pursuers, however, as the following incidents show. In Ontario, Joslin (1966) watched a deer that had sought refuge by swimming across a small lake. At least five adult wolves continued the pursuit, one even swimming out after the deer. Others ran around along the shore as if to intercept the deer when it emerged on the opposite side. Although Joslin was unable to see the deer after it reached shore, he did hear it bleat loudly and thought it had been killed.

A much longer and more dramatic hunt in which a deer entered water during winter to avoid wolves was witnessed from an aircraft by John A. Shannon (Pimlott *et al.*, 1969). On March 6, 1962, at 11:15 A.M., Shannon saw six wolves moving around the open water of the Opeongo River in southern Ontario about three hundred yards below a dam. The stretch of water was a hundred yards long by forty wide, and a deer was swimming to the south end of it. When two wolves ran around to that end, the deer swam back to the north end and stood on a sand bar in about two feet of water.

During the next hour and forty minutes, individual wolves swam out toward the deer on many occasions. In several of these cases, before a wolf did so, "the six animals came together as if in a huddle; a great deal of tail wagging occurred and they dispersed around the pool." When the wolf swam out, the deer would then move off the sand bar and swim to the deep part of the pool. The wolf would begin following the deer but would soon give up, climb out on the nearest part of the shore, and roll on the ice and snow. Most of the time it was then chased by one or two of the other wolves.

In a total of three hours and thirty-three minutes of observation during four periods throughout the day, one or more wolves entered the water on twenty-seven occasions. The average time spent in the river was forty-three seconds, with a range of five to 105 seconds. During three of these times two wolves were swimming at one time, and once three were in the water together.

The next day, the deer was still in the river at 9:00 A.M. At 11:09 it was standing in the water about three feet from shore, and the six wolves were resting about thirty feet away. By the time of the next check, 3:30 P.M., the deer had been killed about twenty feet up on shore and consumed; the wolves were gone. The deer had been a doe almost six years old. "It is likely that the six wolves had eaten or carried off between 15 and 25 lb (6.8–11 kg) each within a 3-hr period."

The usual points of attack on a deer are the rump, flanks, and abdomen. Even a single wolf, if it can once get close enough to a deer, will try to attack these areas. I have come upon both a buck and a doe shortly after they had been killed by a single wolf, in separate instances; in the case of the doe, the wolf was still feeding. In both deer, flesh had been exposed only in the hams and abdomens, and, judging from the tracks of the chase, neither wolf had had trouble killing its quarry. The doe lay within twenty feet of where she had first been attacked. The buck was killed within 175 feet of where the wolf had first knocked him down.

It is worth repeating that most deer probably are defenseless when wolves actually catch up to them; generally they depend for their safety on their ability to evade the wolves. Because of this, it is often claimed that when the snow crusts deer are especially easy prey for wolves. According to this notion, deer punch

FIGURE 43. In much of the far north, caribou or reindeer are the chief prey of the wolf. (*National Film Board of Canada*)

through the crust and flounder easily, while the wolves run merrily across the top. However, if conditions that would allow this ever occur at all, they must be rare indeed. Snow crusts that can hold a walking wolf are seen occasionally, but the instant a wolf begins bounding after prey, it breaks through most such crusts and flounders as much or more than its prey. Crusts hard enough to hold a bounding wolf will usually also support a deer.

Caribou. This prey animal is very similar to the domestic reindeer. Males usually weigh from two hundred to four hundred pounds, and females 125 to 250, but may grow much larger. Calves vary from twelve to one hundred pounds, depending on age. Caribou inhabit the taiga and tundra regions of the world, and they generally travel in herds of from a few hundred to several thousand (Fig.

FIGURE 44. When a wolf chases a herd of caribou, only the nearest animals show concern. (*A. W. F. Banfield, National Museum of Canada*)

43). Much of their time is spent migrating widely throughout their range.

Many caribou herds seem to have wolves with them for much of the year, so it is thought that the wolves actually follow the herds, as discussed in Chapter V. The presence of a wolf or wolves within a herd often causes little concern to animals more than about a hundred yards away.

The following excerpts from Banfield (1954: 49) illustrate this peculiar relationship between predator and prey especially well: "During the winter, caribou seem to become accustomed to the presence of wolves associated with the herd. On April 17, 1948, northwest of Eskimo Point, Keewatin District, a herd of 25 caribou was noted bedded down upon a ridge. As the aeroplane passed overhead, the caribou were watched as they jumped to their feet and raced away. Only then were two other animals seen about 150 yards behind the caribou band. As they arose and followed the caribou, it was discovered that they were wolves.

"Among the many herds of caribou migrating across Ghost Lake, Mackenzie District, on April 24, 1949, several wolves were observed trotting along the trails behind the caribou. In one case, a second band of caribou followed about 200 yards behind a wolf. On the same day, a herd of about 3,000 caribou in the shape of a doughnut was observed on a frozen lake. On closer inspection from the air, it was found that there was a single wolf in the centre of the ring. As the wolf ran in one direction the line of caribou fanned out in front. Those behind stood and watched." (Fig. 44.)

Thus in many cases, the "location" phase of the wolf hunt is unnecessary when the prey is caribou. Because the caribou is such a fast and tireless runner, however, the stalking stage probably is very important, and it has been observed both in the Canadian arctic and in Alaska.

According to Kelsall, author of *The Barren Ground Caribou,* wolves use three distinct methods of hunting caribou: (1) ambushing, (2) relay running, and (3) chasing large bands and then concentrating on any animals that stumble, fall behind, or in other ways become vulnerable.

Ambushing is used by both single wolves and by packs. When an individual wolf ambushes caribou, the wolf almost always hides where it can rush downhill at its prey. Packs using the ambush technique seem to show a sense of strategy. The following record by Kelsall (1968: 252) is probably the best documentation of the use of strategy by a wolf pack: "At Winter Lake, September 15, 1952, a pack of five wolves watched a small band of caribou move into a small clump of stunted spruce. Once the caribou were out of sight an adult wolf, presumably the 'killer' in the pack, moved just uphill from the spruce and secreted itself directly in the path in which the caribou were traveling. The other four circled the spruce, spread out along its downhill side, and commenced a stealthy 'drive' through it. The object was clearly to move the caribou toward the wolf waiting uphill. The hunt was foiled through one wolf, a pup of the year judging from its size, nearly stepping on a bull caribou, prematurely dashing after it, and putting all the prey to flight."

The use of relay running by wolves to capture caribou has not been proved, although it is often reported by nonbiologists. Kelsall believed that there is no reason to doubt the use of this technique, but it still seems best to view the tactic as only a possibility until it becomes well documented. According to reports, part of the pack chases a caribou, while the rest stay behind. If the chase leads the caribou back near the resting wolves, these animals take up the pursuit, and the others rest. This pattern is repeated until the caribou escapes or comes too close to a rested wolf and gets killed.

The third technique that Kelsall thought wolves used in hunting caribou involves the chasing of large herds until an advantage is gained over certain members.

Many direct observations have been made of wolves chasing caribou, and from them it can easily be seen that these predators have much difficulty catching most members of this species. Wolves pursue herd after herd of these animals, but unless they begin gaining on at least some individuals, they quickly give up. Crisler (1956: 342) wrote that "in every chase we have seen, it was apparent within a minute or two after the actual chase had begun whether a caribou would be caught or not."

It seems likely that this tactic of chasing large numbers of caribou would set up test situations such as those described for wolves preying on moose and deer. According to Kelsall (1968: 252), "Caribou, except for the incapacitated and very young, can normally outrun single wolves." Herd members in poor condition or with some disability, however, would be unable to keep up with the rest of the herd. As they fell behind, the wolves could easily detect this and could concentrate on these animals. Both Banfield and Kelsall, after their extensive caribou studies, concluded that this would be the usual result of such a technique, and both Murie and Crisler actually witnessed the expected outcome.

Murie's observations were made in Mount McKinley Park, Alaska. On one occasion Murie (1944: 167) was watching a wolf chasing several groups of caribou. The animal then focused its efforts on a band of about twenty-five cows and calves. "The wolf was stretched out, long and sinewy, doing his best. Then I noticed a calf dropping behind the fleeing band. The space between the band and the calf increased while that between the calf and the wolf decreased. The calf began to lose ground more rapidly.

The wolf seemed to increase his speed a notch and rapidly gained on the calf. When about 10 yards ahead of the wolf the calf began to veer from one side to the other to dodge him. Quickly the wolf closed in and at the moment of contact the calf went down. I could not be sure where the wolf seized it, but it appeared to be about at the shoulder. The chase had covered about 500 yards and the victim was about 50 yards behind the herd when overtaken."

A second observation involved a black male wolf and about 250 cows and calves. The wolf chased various groups within this herd and had them running in different directions. "It looked as though he were testing the groups, looking for an especially vulnerable calf" (Murie, 1944: 173). Finally four cows and a calf split off by themselves. The calf then strayed from the group and in trying to get back began losing ground. The wolf gained until about twenty yards behind the calf, but he could get no closer until the calf started zigzagging. Then the wolf advanced to within a few yards of the animal. After another two hundred yards or so, the wolf pulled the calf down and stood over it, apparently biting it. Suddenly the calf jumped up. It ran another seventy-five yards before it was pulled down again and killed.

Another time, the same wolf pursued a herd of about four hundred caribou, breaking them into groups of fifty or sixty. Then he started for a band of cows and calves. He chased them for about a half mile and kept gaining. Soon a calf dropped behind, which seemed to encourage the wolf. In less than a quarter mile, he closed in on the animal and killed it.

A lone calf was also the object of a successful attack that Murie watched. This animal jumped up when a wolf came to within 150 yards. The calf ran along a stream, which it crossed and recrossed several times. The wolf followed closely and gained easily, giving Murie the impression that this calf was much slower than most. About half a mile from where the caribou had started, it floundered in the stream, stumbled, and fell. The wolf caught up within a couple of bounds, pulled the calf across the stream, and killed it onshore.

Kelsall also described a hunt in which a wolf ran a caribou calf into a waterway and then killed it, but in that case the total chase covered no more than two hundred yards. The wolf had been lying in wait on a riverbank when a small band of caribou passed below. The wolf charged straight downhill toward them, singled out a two-month-old calf, and edged it into the river. There the wolf caught and killed the calf before it could reach deep water.

Wolves concentrate on capturing calves throughout summer, no doubt because they are weaker and less experienced. During their first day or two of life the calves are unable to run fast or far, but after a few days, they can almost keep up with the cows. According to Crisler, caribou calves are safest when alone, with their dam, or in small bands. In large herds pursued by wolves, the calves merely run as fast as the nearest caribou, and they become so confused by the commotion of the galloping herd that they do not know when a wolf is closing in on them. One day when thirty thousand caribou passed Crisler's observation point, two wolves killed four calves out of a herd numbering in the hundreds.

Although calves form a high percentage of the caribou killed in summer, during the rest of the year both calves and adults are taken. In a sample of fifty caribou from the Northwest Territories, assumed to have been killed by wolves, 74% were adults (Banfield, 1954). Even though this sample must be biased against very young calves killed in summer, it certainly shows that adult caribou are often taken. In Alaska, eight caribou killed by a pack of ten wolves in winter were adults (Burkholder, 1959).

With four of the Alaskan caribou, the tracks in the snow could be read well enough to give some idea about the circumstances of the kill. The first case involved a small caribou that met the wolves in a narrow canyon on an abrupt turn. It tried to climb the steep slope. Judging from where blood was found, the animal had gotten no farther than seventy feet up the slope when it was attacked.

In the second case, the wolves had been trailing a small band of caribou along a ridge. At the end of the ridge, three caribou headed left, while another veered to the right. One wolf took up the pursuit at this point and followed the single animal. Within 350 yards, the wolf had killed the caribou. The third case was similar to this in that a single wolf chased a caribou down a slope. After first being caught by the wolf, however, this caribou continued on for another two hundred yards before it was finally pulled down.

In the fourth case, an old bull caribou was attacked by the whole pack. The wolves chased the animal about two hundred yards and knocked him down about fifteen feet from where they had first attacked him. The evidence also showed that the bull had turned on his attackers before succumbing.

An additional record of successful wolf predation on a caribou was reported by Kelsall. In June 1957, a wolf was chasing a herd of 136 caribou on the rough ice of Mosquito Lake in northern Canada, when one in the middle of the group tripped and fell. The wolf then concentrated on this caribou until it caught the animal. The chase lasted seven minutes.

The above accounts include all the accurate, well-documented observations that I could find of incidents in which wolves killed caribou. In all these cases, involving both calves and adults, the animals were killed within relatively short distances, about three-quarters of a mile being the farthest a successful chase extended.

When attacking caribou, wolves seem to focus their actions on the front end of the animal, in contrast to their behavior with moose. This is evident in all the cases from which such information could be obtained, including the studies of Murie, Banfield, Kelsall, and Burkholder. According to Banfield (1954: 48), "The method that the wolf generally uses for killing a caribou is to race alongside of it and pull it down by grasping the flank, shoulder, or throat, with the jaws. Once the caribou is down, the wolf usually seizes it by the throat."

Burkholder listed the shoulder, neck, sides, and flanks as the points of attack on caribou. It is significant that the Alaskan wolf pack that attacked caribou in this way attacked moose in the rump, just as wolves do in other areas. In other words, at least with caribou and moose, the point of attack seems to depend primarily on the type of prey rather than on the behavior of individual wolf packs.

As can be seen from the above accounts, the main defense of the caribou is to outrun the wolves, which most do successfully. If wolves get too close during a chase and there is a body of water nearby, the caribou will plunge in to escape. Crisler once saw a bull making full use of this tactic. When suddenly pursued by two wolves, this animal headed into a lake and swam to the opposite shore. After the wolves raced to that shore, the caribou streamed back across the lake, only to meet the wolves again. This time the

FIGURE 45. Dall sheep are preyed upon by wolves in Mount McKinley National Park, Alaska. (*U. S. Department of the Interior, Fish and Wildlife Service*)

wolves surprised two other caribou and pursued them. In doing so, they startled the bull again, and he swam back across the lake a third time, this time to safety.

Mountain sheep. Both the bighorn sheep and the Dall sheep are preyed upon by wolves in North America, and no doubt similar animals are killed in Eurasia. Bighorn rams weigh up to 320 pounds, and the ewes to 175, whereas Dall rams average about 200 pounds, and the ewes slightly less. Bighorns are brownish gray above and creamy white below, but Dall sheep are almost pure white (Fig. 45). Both animals frequent steep and rugged mountainsides, the bighorns throughout much of the Rocky Mountains, and the Dall sheep in Alaska and the northern Canadian Rockies.

Little is known about wolf predation on bighorn sheep. In the Rocky Mountain National Parks of western Canada, wolves kill bighorns, but they seem to rely more on other large animals in the area (Cowan, 1947). Since the habits of this sheep are similar to those of the Dall sheep, probably most of what is known about wolf-Dall sheep relations also applies to the interactions of wolves and bighorns.

The subject of wolf-Dall sheep interactions will always bring to mind the name of Adolph Murie. Murie's classic study of the wolves and sheep of Mount McKinley Park in Alaska provided just about all the information known about the relations between these two species. The following details on this topic are taken from his 1944 publication *The Wolves of Mount McKinley*.

Wolves in quest of Dall sheep roam through the hills and encounter many bands of sheep by chance, although no doubt they are also aided at times by their sense of smell. Once the wolves have located sheep, they try to stalk as close as possible, giving them an advantage in the forthcoming chase. Sheep, like deer and caribou, depend for defense on their ability to detect and outrun wolves. However, unlike these other animals, the mountain sheep is especially well adapted to climbing very steep slopes with great speed and ease. Since the wolf does not have this ability, all a sheep has to do to escape wolves is to bound up the side of some rocky peak. On the other hand, if wolves can approach a sheep from above and prevent it from using this defense, they stand a good chance of catching the animal.

The difference between being above or below an approaching wolf is well illustrated by a wolf-sheep encounter that Murie described. On the basis of tracks in the snow, he found that a single wolf following a trail along a mountainside had come upon a band of five or six sheep. Those above the trail scrambled upward to safety. But the animal that had been feeding farthest down the slope, a lamb, was cut off from an upward escape. It fled along the mountainside, with the wolf following above it on the trail. The lamb then tried to head upward but upon reaching the trail veered downward again. The wolf then pursued the lamb directly. Gradually the chase led farther and farther down the slope, and the lamb was finally killed in a creek bottom. The chase had extended about a half mile.

Another time, Murie saw tracks in the snow showing that two

ewes and a lamb had been feeding in a low area when a pack of wolves had come along above them. The wolves evidently had noticed the sheep when some 150 yards above them but waited another seventy-five yards before rushing them. The sheep fled downward to a creek and then gradually up the creek toward some cliffs, with the wolves following closely behind. Just before reaching the slopes, however, the two ewes were killed; the lamb escaped up the cliffs. This chase also covered about a half mile.

Murie related similar incidents in which wolves killed sheep by chasing them downhill. In addition, he told of a case that showed how easily Dall sheep can be captured when caught off guard and unable to use their main means of escape (Murie, 1944: 109): "A ewe, lamb, and yearling were killed on the road at Mile 67 on September 20, 1939. The victims had been bedded down near a sharp corner. Four or five wolves had come around the corner, made a dash at the sheep and captured them before they had run more than a few yards."

As with wolves hunting other animals, those preying on Dall sheep fail much more often than they succeed. Most sheep try to keep an escape route open to them wherever they are. Even when feeding on flats rather than on a mountainside, they usually remain where they can quickly get to steep slopes. Any sheep is subject to wolf predation if it ventures far from a slope, if it frequents isolated bluffs, or if it is too weak to reach or climb a mountainside upon the approach of wolves. It is significant that 95% of the Dall sheep mortality that occurred in Murie's study area included only the very old individuals, the young, and the diseased (Chapter VIII).

Elk. Elk, or wapiti, average about seven hundred pounds for males and five hundred pounds for females (Fig. 46). Within the wolf's present range, they occur mainly in western Canada. The following information on wolf-elk relations is from work by I. M. Cowan (1947) in the Rocky Mountain National Parks of Canada.

Elk depend for protection from wolves on their alertness, speed, and in some cases, their size and strength, and they have been known to enter water as an escape. However, in certain cases, even a single wolf can kill an elk.

Evidently wolves hunt elk much as they do deer, by direct

scenting and chance encounter. Probably a stalk is also involved during the hunt, although no evidence of this has yet been reported. Wolves have been known to rush elk, however. Cowan has recorded certain details of a few successful hunts by wolves, apparently based on tracks in the snow. In one case, five wolves jumped a bull elk from its bed, drew blood within twenty yards, and killed the creature within the next hundred yards. In another incident, a small pack chased a yearling elk for a mile and a half before killing it. For the last quarter mile, blood showed on the snow. This was the farthest that Cowan noted a pursuit to extend.

Like moose, elk will sometimes stand their ground and successfully fend off wolves. Cowan (1947: 160) wrote the following: "Tracks revealed that a band of about seven wolves ran a cow elk

FIGURE 46. In some areas of western Canada, elk are important prey of the wolf. (*U. S. Department of the Interior, Fish and Wildlife Service*)

down the bank of the Athabaska River above the falls. At the falls, where the river plunges deep into a short canyon, the elk came to bay on a narrow promontory that gave her protection at her flanks and back. The wolves after a bit of skirmishing gave up the chase and went in search of other prey."

Because of the large size of the elk, the animal probably is almost as difficult for wolves to attack safely as is the moose, and no doubt most attacks on it are unsuccessful. In certain areas of western Canada, where prey that are easier to catch are available, wolves take fewer elk, although in summer, a high percentage of calves might be killed. On some elk ranges where there are no deer, there are certain wolf packs that seem to live almost entirely on elk.

In killing an elk, wolves tend to focus their attacks on the rear and side of the animal. According to Cowan, the flank where the leg joins the abdomen is the most usual point of attack, but the nose and throat may also be torn.

Bison. The bison, or buffalo, which is similar to the European wisent, is the largest and most formidable prey of the wolf (Fig. 47). Bulls vary in weight from eight hundred to two thousand pounds, and cows range from four hundred to a thousand pounds; calves at birth weigh thirty to forty pounds. Probably one solid blow from the hoof of an adult bison would be fatal to a wolf.

These herding animals once lived in great numbers throughout mid-American plains and mountains (Fig. 48). About the only herds remaining today within the present wolf range are in Wood Buffalo National Park, Alberta. These are really hybrids between the wood bison and the plains bison (Fuller, 1966).

Unfortunately, most of the bison and wolves were exterminated from their common range before any intensive study of wolf-bison relations was carried out. Except for the results of a single investigation, the only other discussions on the subject are those by guides, explorers, and old naturalists, widely quoted by Young. As noted earlier, it is almost impossible to sift out the facts from these narratives, so they are of little scientific value.

The one investigation that has yielded information about wolf-bison interactions was conducted by W. A. Fuller in Wood Buffalo National Park (Fuller, 1966). Analyses of both stomach and scat samples from wolves in the area showed that bison is the most important food of the wolf in the park. Carcasses or remains

FIGURE 47. The bison is one of the most formidable of the wolf's prey. (*U. S. Department of the Interior, Fish and Wildlife Service*)

of eight bison that had been attacked by wolves were also examined.

One of these bison was a five- or six-month-old calf that six wolves had followed or chased for eight miles. Evidently the animal did not go down without a great fight, for there was a trampled area twenty-five feet in diameter where it finally fell. It had been attacked in its right shoulder, flank, and thigh. Another calf, which had accompanied this one during the pursuit, was not attacked even though it stayed within thirty feet of the wolves.

On another occasion, a calf killed by at least two wolves was examined. "An autopsy disclosed fresh wounds on the fore and hind legs and two one-inch gashes in the abdominal wall. The paunch was bruised and the left lung hemorrhaged. There also were gangrenous wounds, several days old, in the large thigh muscles" (Fuller, 1966: 35). This case was similar to another, in which the calf had been wounded most recently in the right thigh but in addition had suffered old wounds on its front quarters.

This technique of first wounding an animal and then attacking it again sometime, perhaps even days later, may be used commonly with bison. During Fuller's study, there were indications that wolves had used this tactic not only on the two calves described above but also on an old cow. As already mentioned, it was sometimes utilized in attacking moose on Isle Royale.

The carcasses examined during the Canadian study were those of calves and old animals, plus one with severe tuberculosis, one with an infected bullet wound, and possibly one with a broken leg. There seems to be no doubt that most of the bison herd was safe from wolf attacks. Indeed, both Fuller and Soper (1941) saw packs of several wolves near or within herds of bison, whose members paid no attention to the predators. In one case, Fuller watched at least ten wolves approach to within twenty-five feet of four bison. Only one—a wounded animal—showed concern.

FIGURE 48. Large herds of bison were once the main sources of food for wolves on the prairies of the United States. (*U. S. Department of the Interior, Fish and Wildlife Service*)

Musk-ox. The musk-ox is another large and powerful herding animal. These shaggy beasts, which weigh from seven hundred to nine hundred pounds, live only in northern Greenland, certain arctic islands—notably Ellesmere, and on part of the arctic mainland of Canada. For protection, musk-oxen use their heavy hoofs and their strong recurved and pointed horns. In addition, they adopt a herd defense formation in which the adults surround the calves and face outward against intruders (Fig. 49).

J. S. Tener conducted a four-month study of the musk-ox on Ellesmere Island and gained some information on the relations between the wolf and this species. Regarding the defense formation, he found that, if a man approached the herd closer than about a hundred yards, the animals would break their line and flee. But when a dog or wolf advanced even to within less than fifty feet, they would still hold their defense posture.

The way that this protective formation works can be seen from the following excerpt from Tener (1954a: 18): "An observation of wolves attacking a herd of musk-oxen was recorded by the author on June 20, 1951. A herd of 14 musk-oxen that had been feeding undisturbed for several hours on the western slope of Black Top Ridge were seen to form a defensive group. Two wolves, one white and one grey were then noted lying down together 50 yards from the herd. Occasionally one of the wolves circled the herd and then returned to lie down. Eventually 10 of the musk-oxen lay down, while four remained standing facing the wolves. The calf in the herd kept close to the cows, grazing near the resting adults until the white wolf suddenly dashed around the four standing adults and toward the calf that was now outside the group of animals lying down. The calf immediately ran to the centre of the herd and all the musk-oxen rose to their feet. The one adult bull charged the wolf in an attempt to gore it but the wolf nimbly turned aside and trotted off to its mate. Both wolves left the vicinity about half an hour later, heading towards the eastern end of the fiord."

With prey using such an effective defense, about the only way wolves could kill an animal would be to seek out lone individuals or to catch a herd off guard. Tener found that old male musk-oxen, which could no longer compete for mates, tended to wander far from the herds, and he believed that these were the ones most likely to be killed by wolves. Of the remains of fourteen bulls

FIGURE 49. The defense formation of musk-oxen probably evolved as a protection against wolves. (*National Film Board of Canada*)

that he found dead from unknown causes, twelve were those of animals at least ten years old.

Evidently wolves do at least occasionally succeed in overcoming the herd defense also, for if they did not, it seems that they would hardly waste their time even trying. Tener did find two cases in which a cow and a yearling had been killed together, evidence of a defect in the defense system.

It may be significant that 83% of eighty-five wolf scats found on both the summer and winter ranges of the musk-ox contained arctic hare, and only 17% included musk-oxen. This is some indication that wolves in this range may depend on hares and capture musk-oxen only when an easy kill is available.

Beaver. As seen in Chapter VI, the beaver is an important secondary food source of the wolf in several areas. This species differs in many ways from all the above prey animals. It is a rodent rather than a hoofed mammal; its movements are greatly limited; it is relatively small, adults generally weighing thirty-five to fifty pounds, and it is semiaquatic. The animal is found throughout most of the wolf's range that is forested by broad-leaved trees.

Beavers usually live in houses of sticks and mud surrounded by a lake or pond that is either natural or caused by dams that the creatures build across waterways. In summer, beavers feed on aquatic plants, but they also venture onto shore a great deal for various herbs and the bark, twigs, and leaves of trees and shrubs. In winter, the beaver is locked beneath the ice and must feed on a submerged pile of branches stored there the previous fall.

Very little work has been done on the nature of the relations between the wolf and beaver. On Isle Royale, I found two places where beavers had come out through cracks in the ice in early March and had been killed by wolves, and in Minnesota I have seen where wolves tried to tear apart beaver houses in the spring. Whenever a pack passes a beaver pond, at least some members approach the house and investigate it. As streams begin to open and beavers wander onto land for fresh food, the animals would be easy prey to any wolves visiting their colony.

During early spring a wolf would only have to catch a beaver away from its crack or hole in the ice and the predator could readily kill it. In summer and fall, wolves probably would have to surprise the beaver farther from water because the animal would have the whole pond to escape to. To hunt beavers at this time of year, a wolf could merely follow stream banks until it found the fresh scent of a beaver that had gone onto land but had not returned. By following the trail, the wolf would catch the beaver away from water, its sole protection.

Arctic hare. The only place where arctic hares have been found to be important to the wolf is Ellesmere Island, in the Northwest Territories of Canada. These hares weigh several pounds and live in large groups. Tener (1954b) watched a wolf capture one of these animals. The wolf concentrated on one individual and chased it through a herd of about 125, which paid little attention to the pursuit. The hare broke from the herd and ascended a hill, and the wolf caught it just below the top. In running away, the hare hopped on its hind legs only.

Mouse. The only biologist who has described wolves hunting mice (voles) was Murie. In Mount McKinley Park, Alaska, he has seen both adult wolves and pups engaged in this activity, although most of his mouse-hunting observations were of pups. Murie watched an adult wolf make seventeen pounces in an hour one day, and he has seen pups hunting mice for as long as four hours at a time.

A wolf that is hunting mice will wander around a small area until it hears or possibly smells a mouse. It then pounces with force on the vegetation over the mouse, trapping the rodent beneath its large paws. The pounce may be preceded by several jumps to the mouse, but sometimes a wolf just turns aside from its travel and pounces on the mouse.

In the pouncing that my tame wolf did at the age of six months, she would keep her hind feet in position, lift her forequarters, and then drop them together with force upon the ground.

In the foregoing discussion, we have seen that, although the wolf will kill animals as small as a mouse, it is primarily a hunter of large mammals. Moose, deer, caribou, mountain sheep, elk, bison, and musk-oxen are the principal wild animals taken, and the available information shows that with certain variations the hunting techniques of the wolf are basically the same for most kinds of prey.

Wolves locate their prey either by encountering them through chance, by scenting them directly, or by following very fresh scent trails. In approaching unsuspecting prey, wolves move slowly and alertly, and often their stalking brings them much closer to their prey. During the encounter, when both wolves and prey suddenly sense that each is aware of the other, both may hesitate. Larger prey such as moose, musk-oxen, and bison may then stand and fight off the wolves. However, any animal that runs is instantly rushed, and a chase ensues. If the wolves are able to overtake their prey, they may attack its rump, flanks, or shoulders. They rarely, if ever, hamstring an animal.

Although detailed information on the behavior of wolves hunting some species of prey is available, much more research needs to be done on the wolf's relations with other species, especially elk and deer.

CHAPTER VIII / SELECTION
OF PREY

Chapter VII presented an apparent paradox: wolves are well adapted to hunting and killing large mammals, but these prey animals are well adapted to escaping wolf attack. The two opposing facts were reconciled, however, by evidence that wolves are often unsuccessful in catching their prey, and that generally they are able to kill only certain classes of individuals. The present chapter will examine these two subjects in detail.

Hunting Success Rate

The wolf cannot kill prey whenever so inclined. As seen in Chapter VI, even the animal's digestive tract is adapted for feast or famine, and several authorities have witnessed many unsuccessful attempts by both single wolves and packs to capture prey. Although it is difficult to make enough observations to compare the number of successful hunts with the number of failures, some progress had been made in this direction.

The Isle Royale studies have yielded figures on the hunting success rate of a pack of fifteen or sixteen wolves or subgroups of this pack. Of 131 moose that this pack detected while under observation, only six were killed (Fig. 39). However, fifty-four of the 131 moose escaped before the wolves ever encountered them, and thus in a sense were never "tested" by the wolves. In the cases of the remaining seventy-seven (those categories encircled in Fig. 39), the wolves actually caught up to the moose if they were running, or confronted them if they stood their ground.

Out of these seventy-seven that I considered to have been tested by the wolves, seven were attacked, and six of these killed; the wounded animal may or may not have died after abandonment. On the basis of the six known to have been killed, the hunting success rate, or "predation efficiency," was 7.8% (Mech, 1966a). In other words, the wolves killed an average of one out of thirteen moose that they tested. Since these figures were obtained, a follow-up investigation (Shelton, 1966) found that of ten moose that the same pack tested only one was killed, a predation efficiency of 10%.

No other study has yet resulted in figures allowing a comparison of hunting success for wolves preying on other species. I have begun such studies on deer in Minnesota (Mech, 1966b; Mech and Frenzel, unpubl.), but so far have seen only nine deer chased by wolves, all unsuccessfully. Packs of seven and eight wolves were involved in the hunts.

Nevertheless, other wolf studies have shown that there is a considerable number of failures by wolves hunting various prey. Murie gave several accounts of wolves chasing caribou unsuccessfully, and he wrote the following about wolves hunting Dall sheep (Murie, 1944: 109): "Many bands seem to be chased, given a trial, and if no advantage is gained or weak animals discovered, the wolves travel on to chase other bands until an advantage can be seized."

Lois Crisler (1956: 342) described several failures by wolves hunting caribou, and said that "most of the caribou we have seen wolves chasing were healthy enough to run away." Banfield (1954) also reported on a series of unsuccessful caribou hunts by wolves, although he never has witnessed a kill. Cowan (1947: 159) stated that "contrary to the opinion of many people the wolf is by no means always successful in capturing the object of its chase."

All these studies lead to the conclusion that wolves generally have a low hunting success rate, and that, to obtain enough food, they must hunt often and test many animals before finding one they can catch and kill. Further, this means that most of the individuals that wolves do capture must be disadvantaged in some way, for they would have escaped if they were not.

A prey animal could be disadvantaged in any of several ways. By accident it might be surprised by wolves in a situation where its escape route is cut off. It could be psychologically or behaviorally inferior, or have a poor sense of sight, hearing, or smell. Or, it could be newborn, inexperienced, malformed, sick, old, wounded, starving, or crippled. A Minnesota conservation officer who had just watched a wolf chase and kill a deer mentioned another possibility when he told me: "The deer was fat and in good condition, but it sure seemed stupid!"

Unfortunately, even if human beings observed many acts of predation, we probably could not recognize most of the circumstantial, behavioral, or physical conditions that might have made the prey vulnerable. About the only conditions that might be recognized are a few physical ones that are evident from the remains of kills.

Age, Sex, and Condition of Wolf Kills

Many people have long claimed that predators kill mainly the old, the sick, and the weak members of a prey population. This idea is based on reasoning using the following steps: (1) most animals possess strong escape and defense mechanisms and behavior that help protect them from predators, (2) predators must be able to overcome these defenses in enough individuals to meet their food requirements, (3) the escape and defense systems of old, sick, weak, and otherwise inferior individuals would be poorer than those of animals in good condition, and (4) therefore, the inferior individuals would be the ones most likely to fall victim to the attacks of predators.

Carried to its extreme, the logic of this reasoning becomes most clear. Few people would expect a blind and deaf rabbit, for instance, to avoid the talons of some hawk or owl for any long period. Neither would anyone hold much hope for a three-legged deer living along a well-used wolf route. However, what about a deer with arthritis of a foot? Or a rabbit with fleas? Would these seemingly minor conditions be serious enough to upset the defense and escape systems and thus make the animals with these conditions any more subject to predation? Even if they would be, are such animals the only ones that fall prey to predators?

These questions have been asked over and over again by countless researchers. But not very often are answers obtained. One of the main problems in gathering information about this subject is that victims of predators are rarely found intact. Usually a pile of hair and bones, or even less, is all that remains when a kill is discovered. If a great number of intact carcasses of animals killed by predators could be examined thoroughly and compared with a large number of carcasses from the prey population at large, many questions would be answered.

The problem would still be far from solved, however. Such conditions as abnormal behavior and poor senses—which might be more important than age or condition—could not be detected merely from carcasses of prey.

Fortunately, in the case of most large prey killed by wolves, at least some bones are usually left, and certain important information can be learned from them. In addition, a few relatively intact carcasses of various wolf prey have also been examined. The results show conclusively that, although wolves try to attack any prey they encounter, their killing tends to be concentrated on individuals of certain ages or physical condition, and sometimes of one sex or the other.

Age selection. Several studies have shown that wolves kill primarily animals less than one year old (calves and fawns—see Chapter VI) or those that have lived at least half the usual life span for the species in the wild.

The first investigation that indicated such differential predation was Murie's study of Dall sheep in Mount McKinley Park. Murie gathered the skulls of 829 sheep that had died in the area over a period of several years. He divided them into one class representing 608 animals that had perished before 1937 and another class of 221 that had died from about 1937 to 1941. Both groups showed essentially the same thing, but only the latter class will be considered here because "this recent material . . . is thought to present more accurate information of sheep mortality in the presence of wolves than does the old material" (Murie, 1944: 121).

Murie examined each skull to tell the age of the animal at death. His studies showed that at least 86% of the sheep died when less than two years old or more than eight (Table 21). (Perhaps the figure is even higher, because Murie probably missed many of the very young lambs that were completely devoured, leaving no remains.) Some of the skulls collected were from animals that had died of causes other than wolf predation, but wolves no doubt had killed many, if not most, of the animals.

The second detailed study showing that wolves kill primarily the young and the old involved only animals that wolves were seen killing, or that wolves were known to have fed on. Very few, if any, of these animals had died from anything but wolf predation. This study was the Isle Royale wolf-moose investigation. The results of the first five years of this project showed that, at least during the winter study periods, 94% of the moose killed by wolves were either calves or animals at least eight years old (Table 22).

TABLE 21. Age distribution of Dall sheep mortality in wolf-inhabited area of Mount McKinley Park[1].

Age (Years)	*Number* *Nondiseased*	*Diseased*		*Total*	*Percent*	
Lambs	8	—	—	8	4[2]	
Yearlings	22	7	(24%)	29	13	
2	2	1	(33%)	3	1	14% 2 to 8 years old
3	1	—	—	1	< 1	
4	—	2	(100%)	2	< 1	
5	1	4	(80%)	5	2	
6	3	3	(50%)	6	3	
7	—	8	(100%)	8	4	
8	3	3	(50%)	6	3	
9	20	12	(38%)	32	14	
10	21	4	(16%)	25	11	
11	26	6	(19%)	32	14	
12	30	2	(6%)	32	14	
13	—	—	—	—	—	
14	1	1	(50%)	2	< 1	
Misc.[3]	24	6	(20%)	30	13	
	162	59	(26%)	221		

[1] Modified from Murie (1944).
[2] This figure should be higher because the remains of many individuals in this age class are never found.
[3] Exact age unknown, but at least nine years old.

TABLE 22. Age distribution of moose killed by wolves on Isle Royale during winter[1].

Tooth-Wear Class[2]	*Approximate Age (Years)*[3]	*Number*	*Percent*
Calf	less than 1	22	28
I	1	—	—
II	2–3	—	—
III	3–4	—	—
IV	4–7	1	1
V	6–10	4	5
VI	8–15	17	21
VII[4]	10–17	7	9
VIII[4]	—	18	23
IX	—	5	6
IXa	20[2]	6	7
Total		80	

[1] Assembled from Mech (1966a) and Shelton (1966).
[2] Passmore *et al.*, 1955. (A tooth-wear class is a category into which all jaws with teeth having the same degree of wear are placed.)
[3] Sergeant and Pimlott, 1959.
[4] Four animals that Shelton placed in intermediate wear classes were assigned here to the younger wear class for simplification.

A sample of remains from ninety-nine other moose that had died on the island during all seasons and from all causes revealed that at least 82% of all moose mortality occurred in those same classes (Mech, 1966a; Shelton, 1966).

Both the Isle Royale figures and Murie's Dall sheep data require further explanation. In neither of these cases was the age structure of the entire prey population known. Therefore, it could be argued that the wolves killed only the young and the old animals because that is all there were in the population. If this were true, however, then both the Dall sheep and the moose herds would have died off within a few years because there would have been no inter-mediate-aged individuals left to replace those killed off. Of course, this has not been the case. In actuality, it has been calculated that from 65% (Shelton, 1966) to 80% (Mech, 1966a) of the non-calf members of the Isle Royale moose herd are from one to seven years old. No doubt a similarly large part of the Mount McKinley sheep herd contained animals of age groups that were seldom subject to wolf predation. In other words, both cases show beyond a doubt that the wolves were killing much higher proportions of young and old animals than occurred in the populations.

Figures from a study of deer killed by wolves during winter in Ontario demonstrate this even more clearly. In this investigation, the ages of 331 wolf-killed deer were compared with the ages of 275 deer killed from the same herd either by cars or by humans (and therefore assumed to be representative of the entire herd). The results (Table 23; Fig. 50) showed that, although deer aged

TABLE 23. Comparison of age distributions of wolf-killed deer and of general deer population in Algonquin Park, Ontario[1].

		Wolf-Killed Deer		General Population[2]	
Age (Years)		*Number*	*Percent*	*Percent*	*Number*
less than	1	56	17	20	54
	1+	19	5	28	77
	2+	10	3	17	47
	3+	24	7	14	39
	4+	32	10	8	22
	5+	39	12	6	16
	6+	50	15	2	7
	7+	29	9	3	8
	8+	72	22	2	5
	Total	331			275

[1] Modified from Pimlott *et al.* (1969). See also Fig. 50.
[2] Sample obtained from road-killed deer and animals sacrificed for research.

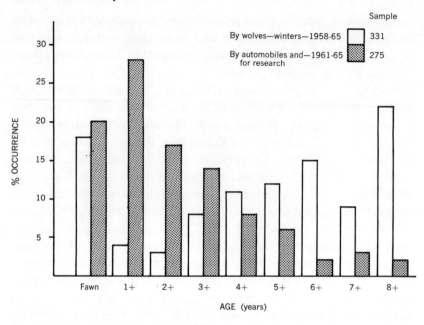

FIGURE 50. Age distributions of deer killed by wolves in Algonquin Park, Ontario, and deer killed by automobiles and for research in the same area. (*From Pimlott et al., 1969*)

one through three years composed 59% of the herd, only 15% of the deer that wolves killed were of these ages. Most (68%) of the wolf-killed deer were four to eight years old, whereas animals in this age class made up only 21% of the herd.

The results of the Ontario study contrast with the conclusion of a Minnesota wolf-deer investigation that "there is no indication that wolves tend to take old animals in preference to those in the prime of life" (Stenlund, 1955: 43). However, the Minnesota study involved only twenty-nine adult deer, which is a small sample, as the author pointed out. Even so, twenty (66%) of the twenty-nine wolf-killed adults were four years old or older, whereas only rarely would animals of these ages compose even 30% of a herd of adults. Thus this study also seemed to indicate differential predation on older deer. Similarly, an investigation still in progress in Minnesota appears to be yielding the same results. In a sample of ninety-three wolf-killed deer, 59% of the adults were four and a half years old or older, whereas only 20% of the adults in a sample of four hundred hunter-killed deer from the same area were in this age class (Mech and Frenzel, 1969).

Now that it has been shown by the Ontario study that, even with deer, the wolf's smallest primary prey, it is usually the young and old individuals that are killed, one would expect that this principle holds true for all of the larger prey of the wolf. Although detailed studies have not yet been attempted for all the wolf's prey, most of the evidence that is available does show that the young and old age classes of several other prey species bear the brunt of wolf predation, just as with moose, Dall sheep, and deer.

Banfield (1954: 50) stated of caribou in the Northwest Territories: "Of the kills which were classified by age, there were six adult bulls, nine adult cows, thirteen calves, seven yearlings, nine aged bulls, and six aged cows. Three of the aged animals showed lesions of actinomycosis. Those carcasses showing poor antler development and broken and greatly worn teeth were called aged. This small sample of 50 carcasses shows higher proportions of calves and aged bulls than one would expect in a random sample of the normal population. The data suggest that these classes receive the heaviest wolf pressure."

Other studies giving similar results include those on musk-oxen, bison, and bighorn sheep. For example, on Ellesmere Island fifteen of twenty-six musk-oxen found that had been fed upon by wolves, and probably had been killed by them, were at least ten years old; none were between two and one half and six years old (Tener, 1954a). Of ten bison known to have been killed or wounded by wolves in northern Alberta, three were calves and four were very old adults (Fuller, 1966). Cowan concluded that, with bighorn sheep in western Canada, generally the classes of "old or ailing" individuals were bearing most of the wolf predation.

In contrast to these studies, Burkholder (1959: 7) in Alaska stated that "all of the wolf kills [caribou] that I could check were in excellent condition and of the 'age of primeness,'" and Cowan judged that a high percentage of elk mortality (from wolves and other causes) in British Columbia occurred in "prime" individuals. However, in the Alaskan study Burkholder examined the remains of only five caribou that he could age precisely. Cowan did study the remains of sixty-six elk, twenty-nine of which he judged to be in the "prime years of life." Nevertheless, because the precise ages of these animals were not given, it is difficult to conclude much from the figures.

In view of the substantial results of the studies cited earlier, it seems reasonable to conclude that at least during winter wolves prey primarily on the youngest and oldest members of most, if not all, primary prey species. In summer, several scat studies have indicated that calves and fawns also compose a high percentage of the food items, as discussed in Chapter VI.

Selection by sex. One might think that with larger prey it would be easier for wolves to kill females because they often are smaller than males. On the other hand, even the large males must grow old someday and at some point in their lives become vulnerable. In addition, with musk-oxen, the bulls that cannot compete for a harem may lead a solitary life and thus be more subject to wolf predation. Therefore the question of prey selection on the basis of sex becomes of interest.

Unfortunately, the available information does not provide much insight into this subject. Murie's data on Dall sheep mortality, for instance, which show an even sex ratio, cannot be used because they apply to sheep killed by all causes. Even though the most important mortality factor probably was wolf predation, any selection by sex that the wolves might have made would have been obscured. Obviously if a herd has an even sex ratio, a large group of its members dying from many causes over a long period will also have an even sex ratio.

Another problem is that the sex ratio of kills alone does not necessarily give information about differential predation by sex. The sex ratio of the living herd must also be known so that it can be compared with that of the kill. In many cases it is reasonable to assume an even sex ratio in a population, but whenever possible this assumption should be checked.

The data on deer illustrate this problem. Pimlott *et al.* (1969) determined the sex of 257 deer killed by wolves in Ontario during one winter. There was a ratio of fifty-seven bucks killed to forty-three does, and this ratio was significantly different (95% confidence level) from an even sex ratio. However, this would not necessarily mean that wolves were preying more intensively on bucks—that is, taking a higher percentage of bucks than actually occurred in the herd. Indeed, if the sex ratio of the actual herd was fifty-seven bucks to forty-three does, no differential predation on bucks would be indicated. Unfortunately, no data on the sex ratio of the herd were available.

In Minnesota, Stenlund found an even ratio of bucks to does in eighty-two deer killed by wolves in winter. Because the sex ratio of the herd, as evidenced by hunting statistics, was also even, he concluded that "there is no indicated preference by the wolves for either sex." However, if Stenlund's sample of sixty-three *adult* deer is considered alone, the sex ratio is thirty-five bucks to twenty-eight does. Because of this, Klein and Olson (1960) thought that the sample actually indicated a selection by the wolf for bucks, especially when there were suggestions that the adult deer herd may have contained more does than bucks.

Because of these problems, both the Ontario and Minnesota studies must be considered inconclusive about the question of wolf selection of deer by sex.

A third difficulty in the study of the sex ratios in wolf kills may be a bias in the season when the kills are examined. On Isle Royale, I found that the ratio of moose killed by wolves during February and March of three winters was twenty-two cows to eleven bulls, and Shelton reported that the ratio for the following two winters was fifteen cows to eight bulls. Since the sex ratio of the Isle Royale moose herd appears to be even, we can conclude that wolf predation on Isle Royale results in a disproportionate number of cows being taken during February and March.

However, the above conclusion also means that either many bull moose are dying from causes other than wolf predation, or wolf predation concentrates on bulls during some period other than February and March. Evidently the latter alternative is true, for Shelton found an even sex ratio in the remains of thirty-seven moose that had been fed upon (and probably killed) by wolves during all seasons on the island.

The only other studies from which data are available on the sex ratio in a series of wolf kills are those of both Banfield and Kelsall on caribou and of Tener on musk-oxen. Banfield found an even sex ratio in thirty adult caribou thought to have been killed by wolves, but the ratio of sexes in the herd was unknown. In Kelsall's (1960) sample from caribou calving grounds, where cows predominate, there was a ratio of sixteen females to four males.

Tener reported that fourteen of twenty-one adult musk-oxen that he believed had been killed by wolves were males. This indicates a strong differential vulnerability of bulls because the musk-ox herd was found to contain only about 40% males. Tener believed that bulls were more vulnerable because they tend to become solitary when they fail to control harems. Thus they would not have the benefit of the defense formation of the herd.

In summary, it can be said that wolf predation may exert a certain amount of selection for one sex or the other in various species and in different seasons. In most cases the year-round mortality from wolves probably occurs evenly on both sexes.

Selection by physical condition. Although both the age and sex of the wolf's major prey can be learned from those parts of carcasses that often remain after wolves abandon their kills, only a few signs of poor condition or ill health can be detected. Most types of diseases, parasites, congenital disorders, and other physical maladies leave no evidence on the hair and bones. This is one of the major problems in trying to learn whether or not wolf predation culls out the "sick and weak."

A second problem that plagues students of this subject is lack of knowledge of the incidence of various diseases and physical disorders in the general population of a particular prey animal. Even if a high percentage of wolf kills showed sign of ticks, for instance, one still could not conclude that wolf predation was selecting out individuals with ticks. The situation may be that most members of the prey population are infested with ticks, in which case the predation would not be selecting such individuals.

Even if it were shown that wolves were killing a much higher percentage of animals with ticks than the percentage in the population, there is a further problem. It would be hazardous to conclude that the ticks helped "predispose" such individuals, or make them more vulnerable, to predation. The tick parasitism could be an innocuous condition associated with the actual predisposing factor, which might be old age, for instance.

The principles of logic and scientific objectivity must always be kept especially in mind when trying to gather new information on the subject of "culling" of prey species by predators. On the other hand, it would be foolish to lean so far in this direction as to reject the obvious. Take the hypothetical example of a two-year-old deer that had had one leg shot off and had then been killed by wolves. In this case, it would be reasonable to assume a connection between the crippling and the death of the deer, particularly if one found large numbers of such coincidences.

Some data on the physical condition of wolf prey are more strongly indicative of differential vulnerability on the basis of condition than are others, but for the sake of completeness all will be presented below.

In the Mount McKinley study of 221 Dall sheep remains, Murie kept track of the ages of sheep showing severe infections of diseases affecting the jawbones (Table 21). He stated the following about these conditions (Murie, 1944: 119): "Some animals affected by these bone changes would be unable to masticate the food well enough or fast enough. Others would have chronic infections in the mouth when the food kept the sores open and irritated. Still others would be ailing with the disease itself. All but six of the diseased sheep listed . . . are those showing severe cases of what has been referred to as actinomycosis."

Approximately 26% of the sheep remains found showed signs of this disease. In some cases a sheep was represented in the sample by only a skull or one side of a jaw. Since the disease may be evident on only one side, no doubt the incidence of this condition was higher than these figures show.

The significance of Murie's data, however, is not in the high percentage of sheep with this disease. Rather, it is in the different rates of infection for sheep that were killed at different ages. Of the remains from animals two to eight years old, 68% showed signs of actinomycosis, whereas only 20% of those that had died when over eight years old evidenced the disease.

Thus it appears that the older sheep were vulnerable to predation primarily because of conditions related to their age, but that the animals two to eight years old were vulnerable because of the disease. In Murie's (1944: 124) words: "From these figures it becomes apparent that disease is an important factor in the predation among sheep in the 2- to 8-year group. In the old-age group the effects of age in weakening the animal are, as we would expect, more important than the disease."

The Isle Royale project also contributed information on this subject. During the study, any evidence of disease, parasitism, or other abnormalities in moose killed by wolves was noted. Three main types of maladies were discovered: (1) diseases and disorders affecting the bones, (2) a general run-down condition as shown by fat-depleted bone marrow, and (3) heavy infections of hydatid-tapeworm cysts.

The most usual condition affecting the bones of wolf-killed moose was an infected swelling of the jaw, similar to the actinomycosis described for Dall sheep. Thirteen (21%) of sixty-one wolf-killed moose had moderate or severe infections of this type, known as "lumpy jaw" (Mech, 1966a; Shelton, 1966). The effect of such an infection in moose is unknown, but in view of its apparent role in predisposing Dall sheep to predation, one might suspect that it would affect moose similarly.

Other conditions affecting the bones of Isle Royale moose were found by Shelton. He noted a dislocated upper hind leg in one moose thought to have been killed by wolves, and a malformed jawbone in another in this category. In addition, he found that a moose that was attacked by two wolves had a deformed neck vertebra and an abscessed nose, neck, and head.

The second common disorder found in wolf-killed moose on Isle Royale undoubtedly is an indication of some serious condition in the moose. This is the depletion of fat in the bone marrow. Whenever a mammal fails to eat enough food to offset the amount of energy being used, that animal must begin burning its fat reserves. The last fat supply to be used is that in the bone marrow, and when this is exhausted the animal becomes extremely weak (Cheatum, 1949). Deer, moose, and similar species are generally considered doomed when such a state is reached. Fat-depleted bone marrow can result from the unavailability of food or from the inability of an animal to gather, eat, or use food efficiently. Unless there is a lack of good food (which does not seem to be the case on Isle Royale), this condition is a definite symptom of poor health.

On Isle Royale, eight (15%) of fifty-four wolf-killed adult moose whose bone marrow was checked by either Shelton or me had marrow that was either fully depleted of fat or nearly so. Those eight animals very probably would have died soon whether or not wolves had attacked them, so it can be assumed that their weakened state did predispose them to predation.

A similar conclusion seems logical in the case of wolf-killed moose that are heavily infested with cysts of the hydatid tapeworm (*Echinococcus granulosus*). These cysts occur in the lungs, where they may become quite large. Probably their main effect on a moose is in interfering with its breathing, for large numbers of cysts may replace a great percentage of lung tissue. Perhaps this would cause little harm to an animal not forced to exert itself, but to an individual that must run from wolves or stop and fend them off, the condition could have dire consequences.

In Ontario, a fresh, wolf-killed moose was found, and its lungs taken to a laboratory for examination. Peterson (1955: 176) described one of the lungs as follows: "It was found to be so completely filled with hydatid cysts of tapeworms that it seemed incredible that it could have functioned sufficiently to keep the animal alive during normal activity, much less allow it to ward off an attack by timber wolves. Well over 50 percent of the volume of the lung was occupied by large cysts up to one inch in diameter."

On Isle Royale, I examined one wolf-killed moose that harbored fifty-seven golf-ball-sized cysts in his lungs, and another that was infected with thirty-five of about the same size. Shelton found a moose with at least fifty such cysts and another with at least twenty. These were the only four wolf-killed adult moose that were found intact enough to be examined for cysts. In contrast to these, four adult Isle Royale moose that died from factors other than wolf predation harbored the following numbers of cysts: zero, zero, four, and ten (Mech, 1966a; Shelton, 1966).

Although both samples are small, the striking differences in infection rates between the moose killed by wolves and those killed by nonselective factors strongly implicate the tapeworm in predisposing Isle Royale moose to wolf predation.

An observation by Lois Crisler (1956: 345), who also studied the selection of prey by wolves, adds further evidence that hydatid tapeworms may be important in wolf-prey relations: "On September 29, 1954, two two-year-old caribou cows came through together. When surprised by a wolf, one ran lightly away. The other ran but remarkably slowly. Five wolf puppies that we were raising lumbered after it, single file. It turned and faced them and sank on one knee, then lay down. Hesitatingly the small wolves surrounded it. It got up and ran. Then, untouched, it faced and voluntarily lay down again. Cris examined it later. Its lungs were partly deflated and contained eight abscesses, some as big as ping-pong balls, half buried in the tissue and full of watery fluid. They seemed to be tapeworm cysts."

In her studies of wolf-caribou relationships on the arctic tundra, Crisler also found wolf kills with severely injured or diseased hoofs. She summarized her results as follows: "At least half of the kills that we observed involved crippled or sick caribou, whose incidence is in the neighborhood of 1.8 per cent among stragglers and even lower among the main herds. Presumably, therefore, predation was highly selective for unhealthy individuals" (Crisler, 1956: 346).

Banfield also noticed caribou in poor health during his studies in the Northwest Territories. Some had broken limbs, others had flesh wounds, and still others had bacterial infections. He concluded the following: "From a study of wolf hunting techniques and the caribou reaction to pursuit it may be concluded that single animals, sleeping individuals, inexperienced calves, and wounded, sick, and aged animals would be most likely to succumb to the stalking and flushing type of pursuit" (Banfield, 1954: 50).

During an investigation of bison in Wood Buffalo National Park, Fuller came to the same general conclusion because the only three middle-aged bison that he found killed by wolves were greatly weakened in various ways. One had been wounded by a bullet, another suffered from advanced tuberculosis, and the third had broken a leg. All the other wolf kills he examined were either calves or very old animals.

It was shown in previous sections that wolves kill mainly the youngest and oldest animals, probably because weak and inferior individuals are the only ones that the predators *can* kill under the usual conditions. The above evidence that many of the middle-aged animals killed by wolves were injured, diseased, or parasitized further supports this concept; apparently these individuals succumbed because they too were easier and safer to capture.

Because most of the above figures were based merely on the examination of the bones or partly eaten carcasses of wolf kills, it is remarkable that such high rates of maladies were found. Such a situation strongly suggests that, if large numbers of intact carcasses could be examined, almost every animal killed by wolves could be classified as young, old, or otherwise inferior.

A contrary claim. In direct conflict with all the evidence and conclusions presented in this chapter is the following excerpt from *The Wolves of North America* (Young, 1944: 268): "An opinion held by many present-day game conservationists is that one of the outstanding roles which predators play in the complex predator-game relationship is the removal by killing for food, of weakened individuals of the prey species. Predators are assumed, therefore, through a process of selection, to improve the agility and vitality of the herds of deer or other big game. It is assumed that a wolf, for instance, seeks out as its prey the puniest and weakest of the species because of the ease by which it may be attacked and killed. However, the hundreds of observations made and citations left us by other observers, do not in any way bear out the foregoing contentions. In the heyday of the North American wolf it was common knowledge that these animals invariably killed some of the healthiest, choicest, and fattest steers in the herd. These ranged in age from long yearlings up to four-year-olds. Nor is there any evidence that when wolves entered a herd of cattle they purposely sought out the weakest as their prey."

This passage from one of the most lengthy works ever written about the wolf requires further discussion. In the first place, the credibility and value of the "hundreds of observations made and citations left us by other observers," referred to above, have already been questioned in previous chapters.

A second problem is that wolf predation on domestic animals cannot be equated with predation on natural wild prey. In terms of alertness and defense and escape ability, there can be no comparison between these groups of animals. It seems safe to claim that in these very critical respects all domestic animals are inferior to all but the most debilitated of the wolf's natural prey. Indeed, the very fact that domestic animals were so widely preyed upon is further evidence that the wolf kills primarily the weaker individuals.

The Mechanics of Selection

Although wolf predation generally selects out the young, old, sick, weak, injured, and diseased members of prey populations, one must be very careful to avoid the conclusion that wolves perform such services deliberately, intentionally, or purposely.

It is absurd to think that a wild wolf would turn down any available prey, especially a large, fat, prime individual. As is true with most predators, the wolf is an opportunist. Whatever meat

FIGURE 51. A white wolf of the artic feeds on the remains of a dead musk-ox on Ellesmere Island, in the Northwest Territories of Canada. (*D. F. Parmelee*)

is available the animal will eat, including refuse, carrion (Fig. 51), bait, and fresh prey. There is no reason to believe that the wolf would purposely refuse to eat prime, healthy animals and choose only the inferior ones.

However, there is good reason to believe that the wolf has no choice in the matter. The predator takes whatever it can catch. If the wolf could capture prime, healthy prey, it certainly would. But most of the time it cannot. It happens that all the prey species of the wolf are well equipped with superb detection, defense, and escape systems. As long as these systems are in good working order, a prey animal is usually safe from wolf attack. When they become defective, however, the individual is doomed if wolves frequent its range. The same is also true for an animal in which these systems have not yet fully developed—unless it is protected adequately by another animal in which they are operating normally.

Thus selection for young, old, and otherwise inferior individuals can be thought of as a very mechanical process. Prey animals, in great multitudes, eat, reproduce, and constantly strive to maintain their lives by resisting predation. At the same time, predators, in much fewer numbers, constantly strive to support their own lives by overcoming the prey.

The pressure of predation is thus continually exerting a force on the resistance of the prey. Whenever the resistance is not strong enough to withstand the pressure, a kill is made and the less resistant animal is removed from the prey population. Selection has then occurred, but it is automatic and has nothing to do with any intent of the predator, except the animal's natural tendency to kill whatever prey it can.

CHAPTER IX / EFFECTS OF WOLF PREDATION

The interactions among members of the living community are so complex that a change at any point in the system can cause profound effects throughout the community. Obviously any animal that preys on others will bring about changes. Since the wolf is the dominant nonhuman predator on large animals in the Northern Hemisphere, it could be expected to exert especially strong influences. Some ideas about the nature of the wolf's effects can even be deduced.

Measuring the extent of the influences and proving that they were caused by the wolf is much more difficult. For example, one chain of events that might result from wolf predation on a moose follows: (1) where the moose falls, its blood, hair, bones, and stomach contents slowly disintegrate and add their minerals and humus to the soil, (2) as a result, the general area of the kill becomes more fertile and eventually supports a lush stand of small herbs and shrubs, (3) a litter of snowshoe hares pays frequent visits to the area to feed on the nutritious plants, (4) the presence of the hares draws foxes and other predators, and incidentally these remove many of the mice that live nearby, (5) a weasel that used to hunt these mice then shifts its activities to another area, and in doing so falls prey to an owl.

The above example could go on and on forever. The "chain" is endless and is interlinked with many others that have resulted from other effects of the same act of predation and from other unrelated events. Similar sequences of effects would result from the wolf's use of certain trails, its deposition of feces, and from various other activities. Although the study of the indirect effects of wolf predation would be fascinating, it is far too complex a subject to attempt to analyze in detail here.

At the present about all that can be discussed are certain occurrences, or changes in the living community, that are thought to be direct results of wolf predation. These effects fall into four groups: (1) the culling of inferior prey, (2) the control or partial control of prey populations, (3) the stimulation of productivity in herds of prey, and (4) the feeding of scavenging animals.

The "Sanitation Effect"

The culling of biologically inferior individuals from a population has been called the "sanitation effect" of predation. In Chapter VIII it was shown that wolf predation generally is selective, resulting in the removal of young, old, and otherwise inferior animals from prey populations.

The benefits that come from the culling out of certain segments of a herd are not well defined for the most part. The main exception to this generalization is in the case of diseased animals being removed from the herd. It is easy to see how the continued culling of individuals with contagious diseases could help prevent the diseases from spreading through the entire population.

A good example of this effect was provided by Fuller (1966: 36) in his study of bison in Wood Buffalo National Park: "An adult male was autopsied on July 6, 1951. That animal had been seen alive the previous day when it appeared too weak to rise to its feet as a vehicle passed nearby. It had probably been dead less than 24 hours when examined, but most of the abdominal viscera had been removed by wolves. The autopsy showed retropharyngeal glands with tubercular lesions larger than oranges, lung lesions, and 'grapes' on the pleura, sufficient evidence on which to base a diagnosis of advanced generalized tuberculosis. That animal must have been a menace to any that came in contact with it. The wolves had actually performed a service in herd sanitation when they ended its career."

No doubt similar "services" are carried out every day throughout the wolf's range, for the diseases of hoofed animals are numerous. Internal and external parasites also plague the prey of the wolf, so in some cases wolf predation might help reduce their numbers by culling out the individuals carrying them. On the other hand, certain parasites such as the hydatid tapeworm discussed in the previous chapter are actually spread by the wolf when that animal eats prey infected with the larval stages. The larvae become adults in the wolf, and their eggs are expelled with the wolf's feces; when prey swallow vegetation or water contaminated with these eggs, the animals may contract the parasite and complete the cycle.

Other effects of differential predation on big game are less obvious. Wounded, injured, crippled, or old animals may be of little harm to the herd, so the only effect their removal might have is to relieve whatever misery they might experience.

It could be argued, however, that old, diseased, or injured animals are of little detriment to a herd as individuals but that as a group they form an inefficient part of the population. Perhaps such animals are less effective reproducers. Fuller found that only one-third of the aged bison in Wood Buffalo Park bred, compared to 100% of the younger adults. If this holds true for other species and for sick and injured animals, this class would be contributing little to the herd, yet would be using just as much, if not more, food, space, and cover as the effective reproducers. Their presence in the herd, therefore, might be of some disadvantage to the truly prime individuals, and their removal might have some long-range benefits.

The role of the wolf in the development and maintenance of various physical and behavioral traits in its prey species is also open to speculation. According to the principles of natural selection, species evolve as a result of environmental forces that tend to eliminate most quickly the individuals least adapted to living in a given environment. In the long run, this selective process allows the best adapted individuals to live longer and thus produce greater numbers of offspring with their more favorable traits.

Any environmental forces that affect the survival of a living thing would influence the development of the species to which it belongs. Because the wolf and its ancestors have long exerted such a direct effect on the survival of great numbers of prey, there can be no doubt that wolf predation has helped modify several prey species. Probably those traits most closely related to detection of danger, to defense, and to escape would be most affected.

It is obvious that if a genetic strain of caribou were to arise that has superior leg musculature, for instance, individuals with this trait would tend to survive longer and produce more offspring (assuming that such musculature had no disadvantages). No doubt the same is true for a strain that possesses superior senses. One would expect then that in most species of the wolf's prey increased alertness and running speed would be a direct result of millions of years of wolf predation. The defense formation of musk-oxen, the size and strength of bison and moose, the fleetness of deer, and the nimbleness and agility of mountain sheep probably developed in this way. In an informative discussion of the wolf's effect on the natural selection of Dall sheep, Murie (1944: 127) stated the additional possibility that "as an evolutionary force the wolf may function most effectively by causing the sheep to dwell in a rocky habitat."

An interesting contrast that might show the effects of the wolf on the defensive traits of its prey species is the comparison between the ease with which domestic animals are killed and the difficulty with which wild creatures are captured (Chapters VIII and X). It is reasonable to suggest that the difference results from the lack of continued predation pressure on domestic species, pressure that has ensured the persistence of traits such as alertness and fleetness in wild animals.

In addition to helping maintain the protective properties of the prey species, wolf predation probably would also help eliminate any tendencies toward congenital abnormalities or proneness to diseases and accidents. For example, any individual with shortened or missing limbs or incomplete heart valves would fall easy prey to a wolf pack. Any animal with low resistance to diseases or parasites, or any ill-co-ordinated creature would quickly be weeded out of the population.

Predation would exert its strongest selective effect in removing immature members of a herd. Any inferior animals killed before they breed would, of course, fail completely to pass their traits on to others. In this respect it is significant that such high percentages of prey killed by wolves are immature (Chapter VIII). Evidently a fairly thorough "screening" takes place during the prey animal's first year, because once an individual lives through that period its chances of dying from predation are very low until it grows old. Thus those prey that do survive their first year stand a much greater chance of passing their traits on to offspring and of furthering the process of the "survival of the fittest."

Control of Prey Populations

The field of interest known as "predator-prey relations" involves the study of the interactions between a great range of diverse predatory animals and their even more diverse prey. Some students of the subject believe that the principles that apply to the relations between one species of predator and its prey will apply to the relations between all species of predators and their prey.

This view may hold true for some extremely general principles. However, the simple, unqualified question of whether or not predators control the numbers of their prey cannot, in my opinion, be covered by any broad generality. Rather, because of the extreme diversity of predators and prey, the question can only logically be asked of a given species of predator preying on a given species of prey under certain specified conditions.

Whether or not robins control earthworm populations has little relation to the question of whether or not wolves control deer numbers. (Indeed, whether or not wolves control deer numbers may have little relation to the question of the influence of wolves on caribou herds.) Because of this, I have made no attempt to discuss any other predator-prey relations than those involving the wolf.

The subject of population control itself is extremely complex and can only be treated superficially here, except as it applies to the wolf. The question of whether or not a specific mortality factor is controlling a population is especially confusing. At first glance it would seem that any factor causing death to even a single animal would be helping to control the population. However, when one finds that upon removing a known mortality factor no increase in population results, the plot thickens. Such a situation can arise because of the effects of a phenomenon known as "compensation" (Errington, 1946).

Compensation of mortality factors can be defined as the process in which one or more mortality factors increase in effect as the effect of another decreases. Complete compensation would take place when, for example, one of two mortality factors on a population was removed and the other then accounted for the same amount of mortality as both together did before. If the remaining factor accounted for more mortality than it did before the removal of the other, but less than the total of the two, this would be partial compensation.

In most, if not all, natural populations there are several mortality factors, and each usually is at least partly compensatory. For example, in a deer herd that has been greatly reduced by disease, few deer will die from other factors. But, if the disease is wiped out and the herd increases, more deer will be killed by such factors as hunting pressure and starvation. As Paul Errington (1967: 229) explained compensation, "The death of one individual may mean little more than improving the chances for living of another one."

A second element confusing the problem is the fact that some mortality factors are relatively light, such as accidents, whereas others are very important, such as hunting. A factor like disease may be of little consequence in a certain year or herd, yet in another herd or at some other time it may almost wipe out a population.

Still another problem that adds confusion is the fact that different mortality factors may become important at various population levels. For instance, starvation does not often kill many deer until the herd has built up to an unusually high level. This is frequently true with disease also.

In trying to discover how much effect any mortality factor has in controlling a population, one must consider all these problems. In addition, when trying to generalize about the role of wolf predation in population control, there are at least three other factors to be considered: (1) the extreme differences in individual and population characteristics of the various species of wolf prey, (2) the variation in prey-predator ratios with different prey species and with the same species in different areas, and (3) the possible difference between the amount of food wolves must consume in order to survive and what they might consume if prey were more easily obtained.

Regarding the first factor, it is obvious that wolf predation might produce different effects on different populations that vary in such important aspects as density and reproductive potential. For example, to control a herd of deer, which may reach a density of thirty or more per square mile, many more animals would have to be killed than would be necessary to control a herd of moose, which may occur in a density of less than one moose per square mile. In addition, members of some species such as deer may bear young when only one year old and eventually may produce twins or triplets. A much higher mortality rate would be required to control such animals than to control bison, for instance, which may not breed until three or four years old and which then produce only one calf per year.

Another factor that would influence the degree of control among various species of the wolf's prey is size. This is because wolves would have to kill fewer large animals to obtain their food requirements than they would smaller ones. For example, on the average it would take four or five deer to supply as much food as one bison. This size factor, however, is at least partly compensated for by the fact that larger animals generally occur in lower densities.

The second major consideration that must be made in trying to generalize about the effects of wolf predation on population control is the relative prey-predator ratios in various populations. Reported prey-predator ratios have varied from roughly thirty moose per wolf on Isle Royale to three or four hundred head of big game (mule deer, elk, moose, caribou, mountain sheep, and mountain goats) per wolf in Jasper Park, Alberta. Further, the weight of the prey must also be considered. A ratio of thirty moose per wolf, for instance, may be similar in weight to a ratio of 150 deer per wolf.

The prey-predator ratio could even be important in influencing the effect of wolf predation on different populations of the same species of prey. Thus wolves might exert a much stronger control when their density is high and the prey density is low than in situations where the wolf density is low and the prey density is high.

The third factor to consider in examining the wolf's role in the control of any population is the possible latitude in the amount of food consumed by the wolf. As discussed in Chapter VI, the apparent food consumption rate for wolves in the wild may be more than twice the rate required for even very active wolves in captivity. It appears from this that wolves in the wild may eat more food than actually necessary when it is available; when prey is more difficult to obtain, they may be able to survive on much less food than usual. This is just speculation, but the possibility must be considered.

All the above factors are discussed to show how difficult it is to tell whether or not wolves control their prey populations. Familiarity with these factors should also prevent the error of generalizing about this subject on the basis of information from a single population. In other words, if wolves were shown to be controlling caribou on a certain part of the tundra, this would not necessarily mean that they control the deer population in Michigan.

In philosophizing about the controlling effect of wolves on their prey, one is also faced with the fact that under primitive conditions there probably was no single factor that was consistently so important in big-game mortality as wolf predation was. Because of this, the wolf would be the prime suspect in a search for the controlling factor on big-game herds. However, several studies to be discussed below have indicated that wolf predation is not controlling all big-game herds. In fact, big game in numerous areas, with or without wolves, appears to be limited mainly by a lack of food at present.

For several biological reasons, starvation seems to be a very unnatural type of control on any population, and recently Pimlott has outlined a theory to explain the existing situation. In an article discussing the subject of wolf control on big-game herds, he wrote the following (Pimlott, 1967b: 275): "The question of whether or not wolves constitute an effective limiting factor on ungulates, and particularly on deer, moose, and caribou, is one that has only been partially answered. In considering the population dynamics of some big-game species, deer and moose in particular, the question arises, as to why intrinsic mechanisms of population control have not evolved to prevent them from increasing beyond the sustaining level of their food supply. It seems reasonable to postulate that it may be because they have had very efficient predators, and the forces of selection have kept them busy evolving ways and means not of limiting their own numbers but of keeping abreast of mortality factors.

"Contemporary biologists often have a distorted viewpoint about the interrelationships of ungulates and their predators. We live in an age when there is a great imbalance in the environments inhabited by many of the ungulates. In the case of deer and moose the environmental changes, or disturbances, have been favorable and populations are probably higher than they have ever been. Under such circumstances it is not much wonder that we have been inclined to argue that predators do not act as important limiting factors on deer and moose populations. I doubt, however, that it was a very common condition prior to intensive human impact on the environment. In other words, I consider that adaptations between many of the ungulates, particularly those of the forest, and their predators probably evolved in relatively stable environments that could not support prey populations of high density."

If Pimlott's theory is correct, as I believe it is, wolf predation could very well have been the main limiting factor on most, if not all, big game before man so greatly disturbed the habitat. Much of the information about big-game population control, then, might apply not to truly natural situations, but only to artificially high populations. This fact must be kept in mind in the following discussions.

Because of all the complications mentioned above, it is difficult to learn in any particular situation whether wolf predation is merely a contributing cause of mortality or whether it is the primary limiting factor. Two methods have been used by researchers for making this distinction. One is to compare a population being preyed upon by wolves to a similar one that is not. The other method is to compute the percentage of the herd killed by wolves per year and compare this figure with the annual reproduction of the herd. The latter method, unless used along with the first, does not consider the possibility that if wolf numbers were reduced other factors might compensate for predation and bring about the same number of deaths as formerly caused by wolves. Nevertheless, both methods furnish insight into the effect of wolf predation on prey populations.

Cases of control. Situations in which wolves are truly controlling a big-game herd can be defined as those in which removal of the wolves would result in a substantial population increase. In other words, they are cases in which other mortality factors cannot compensate fully for wolf predation.

This is thought to have been the situation in Mount McKinley Park, Alaska, when Murie conducted his study of wolf-Dall sheep relations from 1939 to 1941. During a period before this, there were few or no wolves in the area, and the sheep herd had increased to a point of overpopulation (about 1928). Widespread mortality then took place during the following winters. Eventually wolf numbers grew, however, and during Murie's study, the sheep population remained relatively stable.

In drawing his conclusion that the wolves were controlling the sheep herd, Murie (1944: 141) wrote the following: "The fact that sheep increased rapidly in the absence of wolves and have not increased during their presence strongly indicates that the wolves have been the factor preventing the sheep from increasing. I am fully aware how frequently 'obvious conclusions' are wrong, especially in prey-predator relationships. However, I found no other factor which seemed sufficiently operative to hold the sheep numbers in check. It seems, therefore, that the wolves are the controlling influence."

The prey-predator ratio in this situation was twenty-five to thirty-seven sheep (average weight about 200 pounds) per wolf, or 5000 to 7400 pounds of prey per wolf. A complicating factor is that these same wolves also preyed upon caribou. Nevertheless, the fact that the prey-predator ratio is so low compared to those from most other areas tends to make up for the fact that the wolves were also taking other kinds of prey.

The second area in which wolves were found to be controlling the numbers of their prey is Isle Royale National Park in Lake Superior (Mech, 1966a). There the prey-predator ratio is about thirty moose (averaging about 800 pounds each) per wolf, or approximately 24,000 pounds of moose per wolf. The 210-square-mile island supports at least 600 moose in late winter. The annual calf crop is calculated at approximately 225 animals, but only about eighty-five of these survive their first year and are added to the herd of adults. The wolf population, which has averaged about twenty-three animals each winter from 1959 through 1966 (Chapter II), kills a calculated 140 calves and eighty-three adults per year. Comparison of these figures shows that the annual production of the moose herd and the annual kill by wolves are about the same and that therefore the wolves are taking enough moose to control the herd.

(Since publication of the above figures for the Isle Royale moose herd, Jordan *et al.,* in a 1967 article on the Isle Royale wolves mentioned incidentally that Jordan had estimated the moose population at 800 to 1000 animals. However, no documentation was given for these figures, nor was the type of sampling and censusing procedure described. Because of this and because moose censuses are usually thought to give gross estimates only, there is as yet little reason to believe that the size of the Isle Royale moose herd has changed between the time the two censuses were taken, 1960 and 1966.)

A stronger line of evidence that wolves are controlling the Isle Royale moose comes from the history of the herd. Moose have lived on the island for most of this century, but wolves did not arrive there until about 1949. Before that time, the moose herd increased to an estimated 1000 to 3000 animals in the early 1930s (Murie, 1934), decreased drastically through disease and starvation a few years later (Hickie, 1936), then built up and suffered starvation again in the late 1940s (Krefting, 1951). However, since the wolves arrived, moose numbers have been lower than they were previously, the herd has remained relatively stable, and the browse has begun to recover.

In Algonquin Provincial Park, Ontario, it also appears that wolves are controlling their prey population, in this case deer. Pimlott, using wolf food-consumption figures modified from the Isle Royale studies, calculated that it would require a deer density of about ten per square mile with an annual productivity of 37% to support a wolf population of one per ten square miles, which is the estimated wolf density in the park. If this is true, it also means that with these population densities wolves would be controlling the deer herd. According to Pimlott (1967b: 274), "The data on the deer population in Algonquin Park suggest a density of 10 to 15 per square mile, or a ratio of wolf to deer of between 1:100 and 1:150. The deer are primary prey of the wolves and predation may have been important in preventing major irruptions such as those that have occurred in many deer ranges where wolves are absent. . . ."

The prey-predator ratios mentioned by Pimlott would convert to about 15,000 to 22,500 pounds of deer per wolf, assuming average adult deer weights to be about 150 pounds.

In another wolf-deer study, it was concluded that the combination of wolf predation and human hunting was controlling the deer population in certain sections of Minnesota, with wolves accounting for about two-thirds of the control. The prey-predator ratio in this area was about 153 deer (approximately 23,000 pounds) per wolf, as calculated from figures by Stenlund (1955). It is interesting that this ratio is somewhat higher than that estimated by Pimlott to be the highest in which wolves alone could exert control.

Other areas in which wolves are thought to be limiting their prey are certain of the islands in southeast Alaska. There the wolves' main prey is the black-tailed deer. Klein and Olson (1960), without giving documentation, stated that on wolf-free islands in that area overpopulation of deer was evident, whereas on wolf-inhabited islands winter mortality of deer was light and winter ranges were in better condition. In addition, when thirty-square-mile Coronation Island was stocked with four wolves, the deer population dropped over a period of four years (Merriam, 1964). Of course this latter situation was highly unnatural in that just the original stocking of wolves was at a higher density than has ever been reported for natural populations (Table 7).

Wherever wolves are controlling the numbers of their prey, they do so primarily by removing the young from the herd. Murie considered that the loss of lamb and yearling sheep to wolves was the most important factor in the control of the Dall sheep population in Mount McKinley Park. On Isle Royale, an estimated 62% or more of the moose killed by wolves throughout the year were calves, and in Algonquin Park, Pimlott considered that fawns composed about 55% of the deer killed per year. It is only logical that mortality of young would have the most influence in population control by wolves because (1) this age class is almost always by far the largest in the population and thus could cause a great increase in any herd if not trimmed down, and (2) with young animals, many more individuals would have to be killed to fulfill the wolf's food requirements because of the great size difference between young and adults.

A second generalization that can be made from the above studies is that the highest prey-predator ratio in which control was thought to have occurred was the 24,000 pounds of living prey per wolf found on Isle Royale. Of course, if wolves were to eat only a small part of each prey animal and therefore were to kill many more individuals than they actually required, they could control populations with much larger prey-predator ratios. However, the very fact that wolves do not seem to limit populations with higher ratios, as discussed below, suggests that they probably do not often kill more than they eat.

Cases of noncontrol. In the Rocky Mountains of Canada, from 1943 to 1946, Jasper National Park supported a wolf population of about one wolf per ten square miles of winter range. Three other parks in the same general region contained almost no wolves.

A study by Cowan (1947: 147) of big game in both areas revealed that "there is no discernible significant difference in the survival of young, or in the sex ratios within the two groups." Cowan concluded that wolves were not controlling the big-game herds. The prey-predator ratio in these parks was three to four hundred head of big game (bighorn sheep, elk, moose, deer, mountain goat, and caribou) per wolf. Assuming an average weight of all these species to be about three hundred pounds, the prey-predator ratio would be 90,000 to 120,000 pounds of prey per wolf.

During a study of deer populations in a wolf-inhabited area and a wolf-free area of Wisconsin, the same conclusion was reached. D. Q. Thompson (1952: 438) wrote the following: "The similarity in deer population behavior on the Oneida wolf range and the wolf-free range agrees with the inference drawn from range conditions within the wolf area; namely, that the timber wolves at present densities did not prevent an overpopulation of deer from developing in the past two decades. Browse tallies and deer-yard inspections in the wolf range in Iron County reveal very similar conditions." The wolf density was about one animal per thirty-five square miles, and over a six-year period the density of deer increased from about ten to thirty per square mile on both wolf-inhabited and wolf-free areas. At just the lower deer density, the prey-predator ratio was about 350 deer (or 52,500 pounds) per wolf.

A third study from which the conclusion was drawn that wolves were not controlling the numbers of their prey was the caribou investigation in the Northwest Territories of Canada. Banfield (1954: 51) stated that in this region "the annual loss from wolf predation is probably not greater than 5 per cent of the total population, even during periods of wolf abundance." If this is true, wolves cannot be controlling the population because the annual reproduction of caribou is much greater than 5%. The wolf population in this area is estimated at about 8000 animals (Kelsall, 1957), and the caribou herd at 670,000 (Banfield, 1954). This would be a prey-predator ratio of eighty-four caribou (or about 25,000 pounds) per wolf, by far the lowest ratio reported in a situation where wolves are *not* thought to be controlling their prey.

However, it is possible that the estimated number of wolves in this area is too high. Evidence that this might be the case comes from the wolf-control figures reported by Kelsall (1968). Control of the wolf population appeared to have been brought about after some 2000 wolves per year were taken. It was shown in Chapter II that over 50% of a winter population of wolves must be killed each year to effect control of the population. This would suggest that the number of wolves in the Northwest Territories when control was being applied was closer to 4000 than to 8000. If this is so, then the prey-predator ratio would be about 50,000 pounds of caribou per wolf.

Summarizing the results of the above studies, one finds that definite control by wolves is reported at prey-predator ratios of 7400 pounds; 15,000 to 22,500 pounds; and 24,000 pounds of prey per wolf; that about two-thirds control by wolves is reported at an estimated prey-predator ratio of approximately 23,000 pounds per wolf, and that little or no controlling influence is reported at ratios of 25,000 to 50,000; 52,500; and 90,000 to 120,000 pounds of prey per wolf.

Although most of these figures are rough, the tentative conclusion seems justified that wolf predation is the major controlling mortality factor where prey-predator ratios are 24,000 pounds of prey per wolf or less, but that at higher ratios wolf predation cannot keep up with annual reproduction; it then becomes only one of several other contributing mortality factors and cannot be considered a primary controlling influence.

Stimulation of Productivity in Prey

Big-game herds that have an adequate food supply and that include a minimum of old, sick, and debilitated individuals would be expected to reproduce the most vigorously. Unfortunately, few situations exist in which production figures for a big-game population that is heavily cropped by wolves can be compared with those from a similar population without wolf predation. The only place where such a comparison has been made so far is Isle Royale. Because the moose herd inhabited the island for decades before wolves became established, calf production before and after the advent of the wolf can be compared. The only figure for which enough data are available is the twinning rate, but this statistic is probably the most sensitive indicator of productivity in a moose herd. It is derived by taking the number of cows seen with twins as a percentage of the total number of cows seen with singles or twins.

Before wolves arrived on Isle Royale, about 1949, very few twin calves were observed. In 1929 and 1930, Murie (1934) saw only three cows with twins (6%) out of fifty-three cows that he observed with young. However, in 1959, after wolves had cropped the moose herd for ten years, I found a twinning rate of about 38%, and in 1960 approximately 15%. Shelton reported a twinning rate of 38% for the combined summers of 1961, 1962, and 1963 on that island. This rate is much higher than any of those recorded for other moose populations anywhere in North America (Pimlott, 1959).

Although there is no proof that the increased twinning rate of the Isle Royale moose herd is a direct result of wolf predation, no other possible cause has been found. The only known difference between the two eras in the history of the moose herd is wolf predation and the favorable changes it has brought to the herd. Thus it is logical to relate the wolf to the increase in the moose twinning rate.

Probably the high productivity of the Isle Royale moose herd is a direct result of the increased availability of food and/or space caused by the limiting influence of wolf predation. Level of nutrition is known to affect the ovulation rate in deer (Cheatum and Severinghaus, 1950), and it is also believed to influence the twinning rate in moose (Pimlott, 1959). Other authorities have shown that, within limits, the ovulation rate in animals of various other species also increases with the amount of space available to each individual.

Another pathway through which wolf predation might affect the productivity of a herd is by reducing the numbers of the less productive members of a population. In Wood Buffalo Park, Fuller showed that only one-third of the aged bison cows reproduced, whereas 100% of the younger adults bore young. If lowered productivity with old age holds true for other big game, then the wolf's removal of older animals would result in a more efficient production of young in these species also.

Supplying Food for Scavengers

A fourth direct effect of wolf predation is the providing of numerous scavengers with food. Whenever wolves leave a large carcass, either temporarily to go off and rest or permanently upon abandoning the kill, a wealth of food becomes available to smaller birds and mammals. Even a bone well chewed by a wolf can yield much nourishment for such an animal as a chickadee or a Canada jay.

Many scavengers depend a great deal on predators to provide their food, at least at certain times of the year. Some of these animals, such as crows, ravens, jays, and red squirrels, are poorly adapted for killing other animals themselves. Thus it becomes more efficient for them to spend most of their time gleaning bits and pieces of leftovers from the abandoned kills of predators. Other species, such as foxes, coyotes, bobcats, fishers, and eagles, are only part-time scavengers. Most of the time they prey on other animals themselves, but they do rely on scavenging to hold them over while their own prey is scarce or unavailable.

In many regions, including Isle Royale and Minnesota, it is common for ravens to follow wolf packs, wait for them to make a kill, and then feed on it as soon as the wolves leave. During winter a flock of ravens on Isle Royale seems completely dependent on wolves for their food. In Minnesota, most fresh kills are usually covered with two or three dozen ravens unless the wolves are still feeding, and often a bald eagle joins them. Once I saw several ravens, an eagle, and a wolf all sharing a freshly killed deer. Another time, on Isle Royale, I watched four foxes feeding together on the remains of a wolf-killed moose.

It is true that even where no wolves are present carcasses of big game would still be available to scavengers. However, without wolves the causes of mortality on big game are often catastrophic factors such as starvation or disease. These may provide vast amounts of food for scavengers during short periods. But for an area to support numbers of scavenging beasts there must be food available all year round, not just during a month or two of the year. Because wolf predation provides a relatively stable quantity of food throughout the year, it probably allows an area to support higher numbers of scavengers than other mortality factors would.

CHAPTER X / RELATIONS WITH
NONPREY SPECIES

As wolves wander throughout their range, they occasionally come into contact with animals other than their prey, primarily with scavengers and other predators. The wolf's reactions to these creatures vary from outright attack upon them, through tolerance, to avoidance and escape, depending mostly on the species but also somewhat on the circumstances.

The Bear

Bears, both the North American black and the brown (including the grizzly) are large, formidable animals. Blacks may weigh up to 600 pounds, and browns up to 1300. Long sharp claws, guided by powerful front shoulders, are the bears' main weapons, although the creatures can also tear an animal apart with their massive teeth. Within the wolf's present range, the black bear occurs in the Great Lakes states of North America and throughout much of Canada. The brown inhabits Alaska, western Canada, and the wilder regions of northern Eurasia.

The wolf's reaction to bears depends mainly on the behavior of the bears. If a bear decides to take over a wolf kill, the wolves will try to resist, but usually they fail to drive the beast away. One case has been observed, however, of both a large grizzly and a large wolf feeding only inches apart on a caribou carcass in Alaska (Lent, 1964).

Similar tolerance between wolves and grizzlies has been seen by Murie at a garbage dump in Alaska. One evening when two wolves were feeding there, a female grizzly and three yearlings approached them. One wolf moved off to the side, but the other continued feeding while carefully watching the bears. Then suddenly one of the yearlings charged from about twenty-five feet away, but the wolf easily avoided the animal. As the wolves continued feeding among the grizzlies, the yearlings rushed them several more times, and each time the wolves outmaneuvered them. Once one of the wolves walked between two bears that were only twenty to twenty-five feet apart, keeping its eyes on them constantly.

Evidently a yearling grizzly and a wolf are fairly evenly matched. Murie watched the same individuals that were involved in the dump episode meet on another occasion. One of the wolves chased one of the yearling bears, but then the bear turned and chased the wolf. Both repeated this several times.

Probably the most serious encounters between bears and wolves take place around wolf dens. Murie (1944: 205) described two such incidents: "A female [bear] with three lusty yearlings approached the den from down wind. They lifted their muzzles as they sniffed the enticing smell of meat, and advanced expectantly. They were not noticed until they were almost at the den, but then the four adult wolves that were at home dashed out at them, attacking from all sides. The darkest yearling seemed to enjoy the fight, for he would dash at the wolves with great vigor, and was sometimes off by himself, waging a lone battle. (On later occasions I noticed that this bear was particularly aggressive when attacked by wolves.) The four bears remained at the den for about an hour, feeding on meat scraps and uncovering meat the wolves had buried. During all this time, the bears were under attack. When the pillaging was complete the bears moved up the slope.

"The following morning I was at the wolf den a little before 8 o'clock. The female grizzly and the three yearlings were on a snowbank about half a mile above the den. The yearlings were inclined to wander down to the den when the bears started for the river bar, but the female held a course down a ravine to one side. On the bar the bears fed on roots, gradually moving out of view behind a hump of the ridge I was on.

"At 10 o'clock the black male wolf returned to the den, carrying food in his jaws. He was met by four adults and there was much friendly tail wagging. While the wolves were still bunched, a dark object loomed up in the east. It was a grizzly and it appeared to be following a trail, probably the trail of the female grizzly with the yearlings, for they had come along that way the day before. The bear was in a hurry, occasionally breaking into a short gallop. It is possible that this was a male interested in the female with the yearlings. As it came down wind from the den it threw up its muzzle and sniffed the air, no doubt smelling both meat and wolves. It continued to gallop forward. The five wolves did not see the grizzly until it was a little more than 100 yards away. Then they galloped toward it, the black male far in the lead. When the bear saw the approaching wolves, it turned and ran back over its trail, with the black wolf close at its heels.

"The bear retreated a few jumps at a time but had to turn to protect its rear from the wolves which tried to dash in and nip it. When all the wolves caught up with the bear they surrounded it. As it dashed at one wolf another would drive in from behind, and then the bear would turn quickly to catch this aggressor. But the wolves were the quicker and quite easily avoided its rushes. Sometimes the lunge at a wolf was a feint and in the sudden turn following the feint the bear would almost catch a wolf rushing in at his rear. In lunging at a wolf both paws reached forward in what appeared to be an attempt to grasp it. There was no quick slapping at a wolf with its powerful arms. The target was perhaps too distant for such tactics. After about 10 minutes the two female wolves withdrew toward the den and shortly thereafter the wolf identified as Grandpa moved off.

"The black male and the black-mantled male worried the bear for a few minutes and then the latter lay down about 75 yards away. A few minutes later the black father also departed. Left alone, the bear resumed his travels in a direction which would take him a little to one side of the den, but not for long. The black-mantled male quickly attacked and the other four wolves approached at a gallop. After another 5 minutes of worrying the bear, the wolves moved back toward the den, the black male again being the last to leave. The bear turned and slowly retraced his steps, disappearing in a swale a half mile or more away. It did not seem that the wolves actually bit the bear. The bear did not touch any of the wolves, although once the black-mantled male escaped from the bear's outstretched arms only by strenuous efforts. On this occasion, at least, the wolves had surely discouraged the bear with their spirited attack."

What might happen to a wolf if a bear connects with it was discovered by Joslin (1966) in Ontario. He found the fresh carcass of a female wolf near her den of pups in Ontario. Eleven of the wolf's ribs were broken, as were the tips of two of her neck vertebrae. Black-bear hair in the den entrance showed what kind of animal had probably caused the wolf's violent death.

Another time an encounter between wolves and a black bear was seen by Ontario biologists who were watching an area occupied by a wolf pack. The bear crossed the pack's territory, sometimes chasing the wolves and sometimes being chased by them, but neither the bear nor the wolves were injured (Rutter and Pimlott, 1968).

No doubt wolves sometimes kill bears, but it is likely that such bears would be young, old, or otherwise weakened animals. A few instances of wolves eating bear carcasses have been reported (Pulliainen, 1965), although the only published account that I have come across of a successful wolf attack on a bear was based on hearsay from a trapper.

According to Pulliainen and other authors from Europe and Asia cited by him, bears and wolves do not often co-occupy the same regions in Eurasia. Furthermore, as wolves increased in a certain section of Finland, bears disappeared over vast areas. Pulliainen believed that this was because wolves preyed on the bears. However, there may be other explanations for the distribution data, for in North America both wolves and bears inhabit the same range over large areas.

The Wolverine

The wolverine is one of the largest members of the weasel family, adults weighing up to sixty pounds. Within the present range of the wolf, the animal occurs throughout most of Alaska, northern and western Canada, and northern Eurasia. Wolverines are very aggressive fighters, and they possess most of the traits of weasels, but in giant-sized versions. They feed on prey that they catch themselves and on the remains of animals killed by other predators.

It is this latter trait that sometimes gets the wolverine into trouble with wolves. B. L. Burkholder (1962) once found tracks in the snow showing where a pack of wolves had killed a female wolverine that was feeding on a caribou carcass. The pack of eight had been approaching the carcass when three broke from the group and fanned out toward the wolverine about a hundred yards away. The wolverine had run to a ten-foot-high willow bush and evidently had tried to climb it, for limbs were broken from the bush to a height of seven feet. The carcass of the wolverine lay below the bush, eviscerated but completely uneaten. There was no sign of any injury to the wolves.

Murie (1963) also saw signs of wolf-wolverine encounters on three occasions, but in each case the wolverine, pursued by a single wolf, had escaped. In two of the incidents the wolverines had climbed spruces, and the animal in the third case escaped after the wolf had chased it for about 350 yards and then lost interest.

Wolverines often kill prey of the same species that the wolf depends on, so the two animals can be considered direct competitors. In Finland, wolverines take about the same number of reindeer as wolves do, according to Pulliainen. However, as is the situation between bears and wolves in that country, wolverines occupy primarily the regions where there are few or no wolves. In fact, Pulliainen stated that when wolves move into a new area the wolverines move out. This situation does not appear to exist in North America.

The Coyote

The coyote is the wolf's closest wild relative and is often called the "brush wolf." In general, it resembles the wolf but is one-third to one-half the size of that animal. The coyote feeds mostly on rabbits, hares, rodents, and other small mammals and birds, but it sometimes kills deer and other large animals—usually young or weakened individuals. The species is generally distributed throughout much of North America, including most of the range of the wolf on that continent.

What little is known about the relations between the coyote and the wolf suggests that they are not friendly. One winter two game wardens from Minnesota found a male coyote killed by three wolves (Stenlund, 1955). The animal had run from the woods onto a frozen lake and was killed immediately by the wolves, which had been traveling on the lake. A native of British Columbia also reported discovering the remains of a coyote killed and eaten by wolves, and he believed that wolves tend to drive coyotes out of various areas (Munro, 1947).

Whether or not the presence of wolves in an area does tend to prevent numbers of coyotes from building up there is still unknown. In Minnesota, much fewer coyotes were bountied per county from the major wolf range than from a large region just south of this range (Stenlund, 1955). In Algonquin Park, Ontario, where there is a high density of wolves, no coyotes were ever seen during five years of intensive study (Pimlott and Joslin, 1968). However, many factors other than the presence or absence of wolves could account for this difference.

It is also interesting to note that originally coyotes did not inhabit the eastern United States and Canada (Young, 1951), being absent from the entire range of the eastern race of wolf, *Canis lupus lycaon*. However, from about 1927 to the present— some thirty to fifty years since this wolf was exterminated from most of its range—the coyote has been populating the East (Young, 1951; Pringle, 1960). Since this range extension took place while substantial changes were also wrought in the vegetation of the region, it may or may not be directly related to the elimination of the wolf.

On Isle Royale, in Lake Superior, however, the history of the coyote and wolf populations makes one more suspicious about the role of the wolf in coyote declines. Coyotes had been present on Isle Royale ever since the early 1900s, but by 1957, about eight years after the arrival of wolves on the island, very few remained (Cole, 1957). Since that time no sign of coyotes has been found on the 210-square-mile island, even though extensive wildlife observations have continued there since 1958. It seems significant that the apparent extinction of the coyote on Isle Royale took place so few years after the wolf became established there.

There is, however, a very important possible exception to the claim that wolves and coyotes are generally unfriendly to each other. If the red wolf of the southeastern United States is actually a hybrid between wolf and coyote, as is now suspected by some researchers (Chapter I), there must certainly have been some friendly association between the two species.

It is not hard to believe that such association could take place under certain unusual circumstances. Wolves have been known to make social attachments to human beings and to dogs. Perhaps abandoned wolf pups, or pack outcasts, or lone survivors of destroyed packs on the edges of the wolf's range might at some time have formed emotional attachments to coyotes. In such situations, the interbreeding of the two kinds of animals could have resulted.

The Fox

The fox is a member of the same family as wolves and coyotes, the Canidae. It is much smaller than either of these creatures, however, usually weighing eight to twelve pounds. Various similar species of foxes inhabit most of the present range of the wolf, and the animals feed on small birds, rodents, rabbits, hares, berries, carrion, and other miscellany.

Information on the general nature of wolf-fox relations is conflicting. In Mount McKinley Park, Alaska, Murie found that red foxes seemed to have no fear of wolves, and on Isle Royale, I noted incidents that gave the same indications. However, twice I saw foxes run frantically from an approaching wolf pack, and one winter I watched wolves kill one.

In the last instance, I had been following a pack of fifteen wolves by aircraft across a part of Isle Royale. About 5:05 P.M. the large pack was heading through a spruce swamp about a mile southwest of Halloran Lake when suddenly the lead animal sprang toward a running fox 125 yards away. As the wolf passed a moose carcass, from which the animal had run, a second fox scurried off. Within about fifteen yards the wolf caught the fox and shook it violently. It then carried the limp carcass under some trees. Half an hour later I found that the wolf had ripped out the intestines of the fox and abandoned the animal, at least temporarily. The next day the carcass was gone; it may have been eaten or just carried back under the trees.

On another occasion I saw where a pack of five or six wolves in northern Minnesota had killed a male red fox and left it without eating any of it (Mech and Frenzel, unpubl.). The wolves had suddenly veered about ninety degrees, crossed about three-quarters of a mile of ice directly toward the fox, chased it a few yards, and killed it. The animal had been bitten around the base of the skull, in the rib cage, and in the abdomen.

However, these incidents contrast markedly with an observation made on Isle Royale at the same moose carcass where I had watched the wolves kill the fox. During the day after that incident occurred, another fox lay curled up and apparently fast asleep about a hundred feet from the carcass and the feeding wolves. On another occasion I watched a fox venture to within a hundred feet of a lone wolf feeding on a moose carcass. Murie saw a fox follow a wolf, and reported an observation by others in which a fox approached a wolf to within a few feet when the wolf was raiding the fox's food cache around its den.

About the only explanation for these conflicting reports about wolf-fox relations is that the nature of the relationship varies according to circumstances. Perhaps wolves are not antagonistic to foxes when the wolves are intent on eating, unless the foxes are feeding on something that the wolves want. Wolves do eat foxes at times, as both Murie and Pulliainen have found, but foxes compose an insignificant part of the wolf's total food supply.

In certain respects each of these animals sometimes benefits the other. Wolves often use remodeled fox dens in which to bear their young, and foxes may raise their litters in abandoned wolf dens. Wolves will rob the food caches of foxes, and foxes will rob those of the wolf (Murie, 1944). Probably the fox benefits more from its relations with the wolf than does the wolf, however. This is because the wolf provides a great deal of food for the fox in the form of abandoned kills, and in this way may help promote a higher fox population.

The Raven

One of the few birds that regularly maintain a close relationship with the wolf is the raven. This large black member of the crow family occurs throughout most of the wolf's present range and is primarily a scavenger. As mentioned in the previous chapter, flocks of ravens routinely follow wolf packs from kill to kill and dine on the leavings of the packs.

When following wolves, ravens fly ahead of them, land in trees, await the passing of the wolves, and then repeat the process. When the wolves attack prey, the birds sometimes swirl around them excitedly. Once I saw a raven sitting in a tree cawing as wolves harassed a wounded moose. Sometimes the scavengers even join wolves in eating the bloody snow around such a moose.

Besides following wolves directly, ravens often track them. Probably the birds have to resort to tracking because they usually stay at a carcass after the wolves leave and because they do not travel at night, although wolves do. When tracking a wolf pack, ravens fly directly over the trail. They are often rewarded by the discovery of fresh wolf droppings, which they pick apart and feast upon before continuing on.

Another aspect of wolf-raven relations can be seen in the "playful" behavior indulged in by both animals. The following account includes the full range of such behavior that I noticed on Isle Royale (Mech, 1966a: 159): "As the pack traveled across a harbor, a few wolves lingered to rest, and four or five accompanying ravens began to pester them. The birds would dive at a wolf's head or tail, and the wolf would duck and then leap at them. Sometimes the ravens chased the wolves, flying just above their heads, and once, a raven waddled to a resting wolf, pecked its tail, and jumped aside as the wolf snapped at it. When the wolf retaliated by stalking the raven, the bird allowed it within a foot before arising. Then it landed a few feet beyond the wolf and repeated the prank."

Lois Crisler (1958: 283) observed similar activity between her free-ranging wolf pups and a raven and described it as follows: "He let the pups trot to within six feet of him, then rose and settled a few feet away to await them again. He played this raven tag for ten minutes at a time. If the wolves ever tired of it, he sat squawking till they came over to him again."

Despite the close distances involved in the interactions between ravens and wolves, it appears that wolves only rarely capture the birds. Several times I have seen wolves try unsuccessfully, and of thousands of wolf scats that have been examined from several areas, not one has been reported to contain raven remains. Only Pimlott (1968) seems to have any evidence that wolves occasionally do catch ravens.

It appears that the wolf and the raven have reached an adjustment in their relations such that each creature is rewarded in some way by the presence of the other and that each is fully aware of the other's capabilities. Both species are extremely social, so they must possess the psychological mechanism necessary for forming social attachments. Perhaps in some way individuals of each species have included members of the other in their social group and have formed bonds with them, much as wolves raised with humans are able to form social bonds with them.

The Lynx

Lynxes are medium-sized cats that generally weigh up to about thirty-five pounds and that prey mostly on hares, rabbits, rodents, and small birds. They occur throughout much of the wolf's present range in Europe and North America but in very spotty populations.

The only information available on wolf-lynx relations is that given by Pulliainen's study in Finland. According to an authority cited by Pulliainen, the wolf is the most important natural enemy of the lynx. Pulliainen's study itself showed that when lynxes immigrated into Finland in the late 1950s, they did so where the wolf density was the lowest. In addition, statistics on the numbers of wolves and lynxes taken in Finland from 1870 to 1890 show that as wolves decreased in numbers lynxes increased. Pulliainen interpreted this to mean that wolves kept the lynx density low, and that once most of the wolves were removed, the lynx population was able to increase greatly.

No comparable figures are available for North America, but it would be interesting to test this apparent relationship on that continent too.

The Human Being

The human being is by far the most important nonprey species that has ever come into contact with the wolf. Men of various cultures have long been distributed throughout most of the wolf's past and present range. However, because man's density and type of economy have varied so much according to both time and place, the nature of his relationship with the wolf has also varied a great deal. In addition, modern man possesses a wide range of attitudes toward the wolf, and different attitudes cause different types of interactions.

In any discussion of man-wolf relations, the following types of interactions must be recognized: (1) the possible predation by the wolf upon man, (2) the alleged adoption of human infants by wolves, (3) the adoption of wolves by humans, (4) competition by the wolf for man's livestock, (5) the possible competition by the wolf for wild animals that man regards as game, (6) persecution of the wolf by man, and (7) protection of the wolf by man.

Predation upon man. Although only a tiny minority of the human race has ever had any direct experience with the wolf, most people in the more advanced societies of the Northern Hemisphere have a definite attitude toward it, because the wolf has long been featured in folklore and fairy tales such as "Little Red Riding Hood," "The Three Little Pigs," and "Peter and the Wolf."

Furthermore, certain slang expressions in the English language refer to various supposed characteristics of the wolf. A human "wolf," for instance, is a man who "preys" on innocent females.

In most of these fanciful references to the wolf, the animal is viewed as an outright villain, or at least as a creature possessing evil tendencies. Modern day cartoons and comic strips help maintain this attitude among the public. Unfortunately this is the only way the bulk of humanity learns about the wolf, so there is no choice for most people but to view the wolf as evil incarnate.

With such ill-feelings toward the wolf clouding human thought for centuries, it is no wonder that many people harbor mistaken ideas about the animal. One general belief among human beings is that wolves are dangerous to man. No doubt such a notion is fostered by folklore and fairy tales, but there is also enough mention of the possibility in the serious literature to prevent a complete dismissal of this charge as "fanciful."

In Eurasia, the wolf is considered by some authorities to be truly dangerous, whereas in North America most serious writers believe that the animal is not. Because Young has thoroughly reviewed the writings available on this subject up to the early 1940s, only a few examples will be cited here, along with references to the most significant literature published since then.

In the older literature from Europe and Asia, figures were sometimes given on the number of people killed by wolves during certain periods. For instance, in his monograph on the Canidae, Mivart (1890: 5) claimed that "in 1875 one hundred and sixty-one persons fell victims to wolves in Russia. . . ."

The most recent report that I have found of a wolf attack on human beings was dated January 14, 1968. In an article entitled "Blizzards, Severe Cold Plague Europe" in the Minneapolis *Tribune* of that date, the following appeared: "Wolves killed and ate two villagers in the province of Bolu, northwest of Ankara, Turkey, which is now under six feet of snow, the governor reported."

On the other hand, Ognev (1931: 152), writing of Russian wolves, stated the following: "Cases of attacks on men are much rarer than is believed. Dinnik reports that he knows of no authentic case of a (nonrabid) wolf attacking a man in the Caucasas." More recently, Novikov (1956: 51) wrote that ". . . rabid wolves attack even men, although wolves normally avoid humans, and there are less authentic cases of attack on man than is supposed." These references tend to temper the more outlandish claims, although both still imply that there have indeed been a few verified instances of unprovoked wolf predation on man.

Probably the most reliable report that wolves may be harmful to humans in Eurasia is a statement attributed to Erkki Pulliainen, an authority on the wolf in Finland. According to Scott (1967: 378), "Dr. Pulliainen (1966) assures me that authentic cases of wolves attacking and killing people have occurred in Finland and Russia within recent years."

In contrast to these reports is a claim by Bertil Haglund, gamekeeping superintendent for the Swedish Crown Forests, who has studied wolves for many years. In his recent book *Wolf and Wolverine,* he stated that he could not find a single authenticated case of a wolf attacking a human in Europe in the past 150 years (Anonymous, 1967b).

This agrees with information furnished by Robert L. Rausch (1967), who wrote me the following: "A leading mammalogist in the Soviet Union . . . told me that an effort had been made by one of his associates to document some of the reported attacks by wolves. It was impossible to do so, and it was concluded that, with the exception of possible killing of small children wandering alone into remote areas, reports of such attacks had no basis in fact. Such stories probably are based upon reports of attacks by rabid wolves, with the usual exaggeration as they are passed on, eventually becoming established as folk-lore. People like to believe that wolves are dangerous."

Rutter and Pimlott (1968), after reviewing reports of wolf attacks on man in Eurasia, also accepted the conclusion that most of the attacks probably were by rabid wolves. These authors added, however, that there are also indications that wolf-dog hybrids may have been involved in some attacks.

In North America, no scientifically acceptable evidence is available to support the claim that healthy wild wolves are dangerous to man. In fact, I could find only one documented report in a scientific journal of a wolf attack on a human being (Peterson, 1947). In that case, a wolf grabbed a man riding about ten mph on a railroad "speeder" in Canada in 1942. After knocking both man and vehicle from the tracks, the wolf continued its attack for about twenty-five minutes, while the man defended himself with an ax. Even when three other men armed with a pick and other implements intervened, the wolf kept attacking until it was killed. Rutter and Pimlott suggested, on the basis of the wolf's abnormal persistence and lack of fear, that the animal probably was rabid, which certainly seems like a reasonable supposition.

In addition to this account, there are all kinds of "trappers' tales" and other hearsay reports on the subject. However, whenever an attempt has been made to verify such a story, it has failed. The following two passages from Young strongly demonstrate this: "It may be said in comment that in the 25 years that the Fish and Wildlife Service has aided in cooperative wolf control, no incidents have come to the notice of the Service or of any of its personnel indicating unprovoked attack upon man" (Young, 1944: 130), and "During the past 25 years the press has from time to time carried accounts of wolf attacks on humans particularly in the north country. These and similar tales that have been reported direct to the Fish and Wildlife Service, although investigated, have never been substantiated" (Young, 1944: 149).

Lee Smits (1963: 46), of Detroit, Michigan, who also has tried to track down numerous reports of wolf attacks on human beings, concluded that "no wolf, except a wolf with rabies, has ever been known to make a deliberate attack on a human being in North America." Of course, the attacks of rabid wolves must no more be taken as evidence that wolves in general prey on man than the attacks of rabid dogs can be considered proof that dogs prey on people.

Even stronger evidence that healthy North American wolves are harmlesss to humans can be found in the many well-documented accounts of various researchers who have worked in wolf country. Several incidents of wolf-human encounters described in previous chapters are examples. For instance, Murie stole a wolf pup from a den while the parent wolves just barked and whined, and Parmelee also made off with a pup in another area and was followed by its dam all the way back to camp but was never threatened. Joslin lured two wolves to within twelve feet by howling, and they remained near him for twenty minutes without attacking. R. L. Rausch wrote me that "in earlier years, before wolves were so much persecuted in Alaska, I several times had wolves come rather close to determine what kind of animal I was, but they were of course quite harmless."

In my own experiences with wolves I have never come close to danger. Several times on Isle Royale I (and successive workers) have even chased large packs away from prey that they had just killed.

During the first such incident I learned how some of the stories of "close calls" with wolves might have originated. I had just watched from an aircraft as a pack of sixteen killed a nine-month-old moose calf in a small cedar swamp, and had directed the pilot to land me as close to the scene as possible. From a nearby lake I snowshoed in toward the kill, while the pilot circled above. A half hour later I arrived in the immediate vicinity of the carcass. According to the pilot, most of the wolves ran off when I was within 150 yards. Two others, which continued feeding, quickly left when I got to within seventy-five feet of them.

I then spent the next forty-five minutes examining and photographing the carcass while the wolves rested on a ridge some 250 yards away and out of my view, with the plane circling over them. As I was inspecting some of the internal organs of the moose, however, the aircraft suddenly changed course. It began approaching in a series of low dives, and I quickly realized that the wolves were returning.

I looked up from the carcass into the surrounding brush just in time to see two large wolves bounding toward me over the blow-down some twenty-five yards away. I immediately drew my revolver, preparing to fire above them. But I never needed to. At my very first movement, the wolves halted abruptly, turned, and fled back to the pack. Evidently the smell of the fresh carcass had overcome my own odor, and the wolves had not realized that I was still there. When suddenly reminded, they departed quickly.

D. H. Pimlott (1967a: 38), of Ontario, wrote the following about wolf-human relations: "Perhaps even more powerful testimony is that, in spite of one of the highest wolf populations in the world in that area, thousands of children canoe and camp in the wilderness section of Algonquin Park each year and there are no reports of any one of them having been attacked or even threatened by wolves."

In summary, there is no basis for the belief that healthy, wild wolves in North America are of any danger to human beings. On the contrary they are extremely shy of man and usually try to avoid him as much as possible. It appears that wolves in Eurasia, however, may on rare occasions be harmful to humans, although even there the danger from this species seems to have been greatly exaggerated.

Adoption of infants by wolves. One of the most bizarre types of wolf-human relations ever proposed was the alleged adoption of infants by wolves. Of course, this was the motif in the legend of Romulus and Remus, the two "wolf-children" who supposedly founded Rome and in Rudyard Kipling's famous story "Mowgli." However, as late as 1956, at least one textbook in sociology (Sutherland *et al.*, 1956) also taught that there were known cases of wolf adoption of children.

Throughout the world there have long been many newspaper accounts of children having been raised by various animals including wolves (Zingg, 1940). Thus uncritical individuals could point to any number of these as evidence for the notion of adoption of humans by animals. However, the story that gained the most acceptance was that of "Amala" and "Kamala"—the "wolf-children" of Midnapore, India. This tale was publicized by two serious books appearing in the early 1940s, which even included pictures of the girls.

The first work, *Wolf Child and Human Child* (Gesell, 1940), was written by a distinguished child psychologist from Yale University, A. M. Gesell. It was based on the diary of the Reverend J. A. L. Singh, who supposedly had discovered and cared for the children. The second work, *Wolf-Children and Feral Man* (Singh and Zingg, 1942), contained a general survey of the topic of feral man and included the actual Singh diary. The diary recorded in detail not only the progress made by Amala and Kamala while under the care of Reverend Singh, but also *the reverend's observation of them with wolves before capture, and their actual capture in the wolf den with the wolves, by the minister himself!*

There can be no doubt that Amala and Kamala did exist and that they acted more like nonhuman animals than like human beings. However, the crucial point in this case is the children's alleged association and capture with wolves. The scientific value of the entire story depends on this allegation, for there are other possible explanations for the children's weird behavior (Mandelbaum, 1943; Bettelheim, 1959). Thus in 1951, sociologist W. F. Ogburn (1959) and anthropologist N. K. Bose decided to check the evidence for the claim that the children were raised by wolves.

After extensive searching and questioning of natives in the Midnapore area, these workers were unable to find Godamuri, the village that was supposed to have been closest to where the children were said to have been captured. They did, however, locate several witnesses who claimed that the children had been *brought* to the good Reverend Singh. Other people claimed that the reverend was unscrupulous, untrustworthy, and a liar.

Therefore, without more evidence than the deceased reverend's diary, the tale of the wolves' adoption of Amala and Kamala must be rejected. Furthermore, since this case was the best documented of all the wolf-children stories, the entire notion must also be recognized as no more than an imaginative bit of fancy.

Chapter IV includes a discussion of many aspects of wolf family life that would prevent the survival of any infants that a wolf pack might adopt, if a wolf pack ever did try such an unusual stunt. J. P. Scott also discussed the notion of wolf-children and rejected it.

Adoption of wolves for pets by humans. Although there is no acceptable evidence that wolves have ever adopted human beings, many humans have been known to adopt wolves. This is no doubt the way in which the dog became domesticated from the wolf (Chapter I). Anyone who has had the experience of raising a wolf from puppyhood can readily see how easily the process could have started.

There are records of wolf pups taming well after having been taken from their parents at various ages, including shortly after birth, just before the eyes open, just after the eyes open, at approximately twenty-eight days of age, and even at some five to six weeks of age.

However, generally it appears that the chances of taming wolf pups obtained after the transition period (twelve to twenty-one days of age—Chapter IV) are not as good as when the pups are taken before. Young (1944: 174) stated that of many hand-reared wolves he has known of, "those caught at three to four weeks of age proved unmanageable in youth or untrustworthy on maturity."

Of course, wolf pups require a great deal of handling and affection to remain "socialized" to the human being (Woolpy and

Ginsburg, 1967). Under natural conditions, the pups would daily receive hours of affection and attention from adult pack members (Chapter IV), and the human being must replace this.

If adequate handling and care are given to a hand-reared wolf pup, the animal can become gentle, affectionate, and friendly. During a wolf's first few months, however, when the animal develops rapidly, its capabilities sometimes increase faster than its inhibitions. Thus the pup may growl or snap when a person first interferes with some new activity, but eventually it begins to accept the discipline.

Our tame female Lightning, whom we obtained from a zoo at the age of ten days, was raised for eleven months by and with our four children, aged four to eight years old. She was very friendly to the entire family, plus various adults, dogs, and neighborhood children whom she knew, and she constantly besieged us with quantities of wolf "kisses." She sometimes growled at a person when he tried to take a bone or something she liked out of her mouth, but even the children were still able to take objects away. On rare occasions when Lightning objected too strongly, I intervened, and she sometimes got angry and snapped tokenly at my hand. However, the snapping was always inhibited, and her sharp teeth never broke my skin.

These observations are similar to those of Murie, who raised a female wolf and who also knew of two other pet wolves; Lois Crisler, who reared a pair of wolves in the Alaskan wilderness one year and a litter of five the next; Hellmuth (1964), who kept a pet female wolf in his family for at least four years; and Fentress (1967), who raised a male. In each of these cases, the wolves were tame, gentle, and affectionate to their keepers, submissive to dogs whom they knew, and inclined to avoid fights.

Of course, in most places where wolves are raised as pets, they are restrained in some manner. I know of no one who has allowed a tame wolf to run loose in civilization. There is always the risk that someone would shoot the animal or mistreat it in such a way that it might attack in self-defense.

However, in some instances, pet wolves that have escaped on occasions have behaved at least as well as free-running dogs. Our pet was loose a few times in a suburb of Minneapolis, and each time she stayed in the neighborhood to cavort with the numerous dogs. At one time she was "in love" with the local stud, Sam, a shaggy spaniel who remained aloof and didn't seem to quite understand her puppy gestures of affection. Whenever we discovered Lightning missing, we merely rushed to Sam's house and retrieved her. The wolf once spent much of the night asleep just outside Sam's house.

Fentress' wolf Lupey escaped twice, once when he was about nine months old, and once when almost three years old. The first incident occurred in a Washington, D.C., suburb and ended when a young girl, whom the wolf had not known, held him until he could be returned to his home. The second time, Lupey escaped from his kennel in Rochester, New York, and was missing for two days. "When located he was in a neighborhood approximately six miles away playing with local dogs and near several children. According to reports a large chow tried to fight him, but the wolf repeatedly turned his side toward the dog, sometimes pressing his hip against it" (Fentress, 1967: 348).

Naturally much variation can be expected in the degree of tameness that can be achieved in different wolves. This is not only because each wolf has a different personality (Chapter I), but also because the manner in which each person raises a wolf differs markedly. Thus some apparently tame wolves have been known to bite people just as some dogs do. Murie's wolf, for instance, when in her first heat period, apparently tried to attack her keeper. "The caretaker was taking the wolf back to her kennel for the evening when she turned on him. The man claims that he had to climb on the kennel fence in order to get away from the animal which had torn one sleeve of his shirt" (Murie, 1944: 49). In another instance, a wolf that had been raised in an enclosure escaped and bit a child (Miller, 1967).

It must be remembered that wolf pups begin to become wary of strange individuals at the age of three months and that in the wild they probably fear all strangers after the age of five months. Thus tame wolves cannot always be expected to behave toward everyone like they do toward those people who reared them.

Despite the possible problems involved in raising wolves as pets, it appears that at present an increasing number of people in the United States are attempting to do so. The books *Arctic Wild,* by Lois Crisler, *A Wolf in the Family,* by Jerome Hellmuth, and *The World of the Wolf,* by R. J. Rutter and D. H. Pimlott, are recommended for anyone considering such a project.

The following words from the last-mentioned book bear repeating: "Wolves are wild animals. When they are tamed and kept in captivity they should be handled in very special ways. They should have the advantage of facilities that will permit them to have lives of their own, to be wolves and not dogs. I do not mean that they should not have close relationships with people; but such relationships should be restricted to the few who have a real understanding of the animal that is a wolf" (Rutter and Pimlott, 1968: 170).

To this I might add that there is only one place where there are "facilities that will permit them to have lives of their own, to be wolves and not dogs," and that is their natural environment—the wilderness. The problem in raising wolves is not so much in the taming; it is in the imposing of an artificial environment on an animal that has been "programed" for millions of years to function not in the confines of a cage or on a chain but in the freedom of the forests and the fields.

This was impressed upon me very vividly one night when our wolf Lightning escaped when eleven months old. She roamed the neighborhood for half the night with our dog and a young German shepherd they had picked up somewhere. When she returned home about 1:00 A.M. and I fastened her back to the chain that held her to an artificial life, she was a different animal. She suddenly began to struggle fiercely to escape. She was still tame and gentle with me, but she had finally gotten a taste of what it was like to act as her heritage had dictated, to be wild and free.

As I watched Lightning straining desperately at her chain, pacing, whining, and jumping frantically, I suddenly realized how very wrong it is to try to tame a wolf.

Destruction of livestock. Wherever and whenever wolves and domesticated creatures have inhabited the same general area, the domestic animals have been subject to attack. This is understandable when one remembers what the natural role of the wolf is. The animal is inclined to try to attack any large hoofed animal it comes to. Since most wild prey possess adequate defense and escape mechanisms, the result is that failure is frequent but that certain scarce vulnerable individuals are thus finally discovered. However, domestic livestock are all vulnerable. Once they are found, the wolf may just follow its natural tendency and kill them.

Throughout the settlement of the United States, man invaded

wolf country and brought livestock with him. Conflict with the wolf was an inevitable result. Even in Alaska, reindeer were introduced, and they made easy prey for the wolf. Abundant testimony to the thousands of livestock killed and the millions of dollars of damage caused by this particular man-wolf interaction in North America is contained in the works of Young (1944; 1946).

At present this conflict has subsided in the United States because the wolf has been exterminated from all important agricultural regions; the present range of the animal includes only a few remote wilderness areas. In Canada, the conflict continues somewhat but is much less severe because only a small portion of Canada is devoted to agriculture.

However, in Eastern Europe and Asia, wolves still destroy numbers of livestock, particularly in the northern regions, where reindeer are their major prey (Pulliainen, 1965; Makridin, 1962).

Predation on game herds. In the United States and Canada, where the sport of hunting is open to the public, many people believe that the wolf competes significantly with man for the quarry that both seek. It certainly is true that most of the wolf's primary prey species are also highly valued by man for their sporting and trophy qualities. However, the point that is not so clear is whether or not the wolf actually is an important competitor of man for these species.

At first glance it seems obvious that every game animal a wolf kills is one less that man can shoot. But a more careful analysis of the question shows that the relationship is not this simple. The late Paul L. Errington wrote in his book *Of Predation and Life* (1967: 235) that "I regard the outstanding source of error in appraisals of predator-prey relationships as confusion of the *fact* of predation with *effect* of predation."

The problem is much like that which arose in Chapter IX in considering whether or not the wolf is a primary limiting factor on prey populations. In that problem the basic question asked was: "Would the prey population increase if wolf predation were reduced or eliminated?" It is apparent that in cases where the answer to this question is "no" it would also be true that more animals would *not* be made available to the human hunter. Where the reply is "yes," more animals would be available.

For example, it is probable that if hunting had been allowed on

Isle Royale it would have been better during the years of moose overpopulation than it would be now that wolves have controlled the herd.

However, another factor must also be considered. Although any individual hunter's chances of encountering a game animal would be greater where wolves had been controlling a herd but were then removed, the total hunting kill may not be much greater. This is because most areas occupied by wolves are remote and relatively inaccessible. Generally few hunters venture into these areas, and those who do usually spend enough time there to ensure a high rate of success anyway. Unless such an area were made much more accessible so that hunters could harvest most of the surplus that the wolves had been taking, it would not be accurate to state that wolves actually had been competing with hunters to any significant degree.

Of course, in much of the wolf range today predation is not the primary limiting factor on the game population, as discussed in Chapter IX. In such areas the wolf cannot be regarded as a competitor of man.

In this respect, D. L. Allen's (1962: 267) discussion of a 1937 report by E. C. Cross of Ontario is of interest: "He pointed out that in the face of a fairly stable wolf population and increasing numbers of brush wolves, the white-tailed deer had spread northward some 300 miles. 'Not only have these deer penetrated this wolf infested territory, but they have established themselves there, increased in numbers and have continued to spread out in the very teeth of the wolf pack. . . . Failure to control or reduce the wolf population of Ontario at the present time is not a matter of any importance. It is a serious matter, though, that for many years a very large proportion of all expenditure which should have been directed towards bettering game conditions has been wasted in this useless harrying of the wolf.'"

Because of the complexities involved in considering whether or not the wolf competes with the hunter in any given area, controversies over the question often arise. One of the most important of these debates rages continually in the state of Minnesota, where the only substantial wolf population in the contiguous forty-eight states exists. Because many hunters feel that the wolf *must* be competing with them for deer, they have pushed hard for the continuance of a bounty on the wolf (Chapters XI and XII).

Unfortunately, not enough information is known about wolf-deer population dynamics in that state to determine whether or not the wolves are actually limiting the deer herd. In 1955, Stenlund did estimate that wolves accounted for about two-thirds of the annual mortality of the deer in the wolf range, and hunters caused about another third. However, it has not yet been learned whether wolf predation is merely compensating for other mortality factors that would take over if wolves were eliminated or whether it is a primary limitation on the herd.

However, some insight into the question of competition between wolf and man for deer in Minnesota can be gained from the hunter-success rates (the percentages of successful deer hunters) in counties within the major wolf range. Presumably if wolves were seriously competing with the deer hunter, the counties in which wolves occur would have relatively poor hunter-success rates. But such is not the case in Minnesota. The five major wolf counties had an average success rate of 51% from 1963 through 1967, compared to the state-wide average of 41% (Table 24). In other words, the counties with wolves provided far better deer hunting than the average county.

Of course, it could be argued that without wolves the deer hunting might have been even better in these counties, and no one knows whether or not this is true. However, the six relatively wolf-free counties immediately adjoining the major wolf range provide no greater hunter success than do the wolf-inhabited counties (Table 24). Although the wolf-free region is not completely similar to the wolf-inhabited area in degree of wildness, in habitat type, and in topography, these counties do provide the best comparison possible. On the basis of these figures, it does not seem reasonable to consider the wolf a serious competitor of the deer hunter in Minnesota under present conditions.

Because of all the above considerations, it appears that in most of the wolf range of North America the wolf does not compete significantly with the human hunter, despite strong claims to the contrary from certain vocal segments of the public.

In fact, there is a strong possibility that in some areas just the reverse is true. The human big-game hunter could be causing an adverse effect on wolf numbers by preventing herds of wolf prey from increasing. Where deer, for example, are heavily hunted by human beings, their numbers may be so closely cropped that most

TABLE 24. Success rates of deer hunters[1] in various regions of Minnesota.

Year	State-Wide Average	Counties[1] Adjoining Major Wolf Range (Unweighted Average)	Unweighted Average	Counties in Major Wolf Range				
				Lake	Cook	St. Louis	Lake-of-the-Woods	Koochiching
1963[2]	.44	.49	.56	.56	.52	.57	.55	.58
1964[3]	.44	.48	.49	.52	.45	.44	.48	.55
1965[4]	.44	.49	.52	.50	.44	.51	.54	.60
1966[5]	.40	.50	.52	.55	.56	.50	.42	.55
1967[6]	.35	.41	.47	.47	.43	.47	.48	.48
Unweighted Average	.41	.47	.51	.52	.48	.50	.49	.55

[1] Roseau, Marshall, Beltrami, Itasca, Aitkin, Carlton.
[2] Fashingbauer, 1964.
[3] Idstrom and Kinsey, 1965.
[4] Idstrom et al., 1966.
[5] Idstrom et al., 1967.
[6] Karns and Petraborg, 1968.

of the surplus animals may be taken and the rest of the herd may stay in excellent health. Such a herd would contain especially high proportions of young animals. Under these conditions, wolves probably would find it very difficult to locate individuals old, sick, weak, or unwary enough to catch. Thus it would not be surprising to find that extensive areas that are heavily hunted by deer hunters support low numbers of wolves.

Persecution of the wolf. Because of some of the above man-wolf relations, human beings in many areas have engaged in another type of interaction with the wolf, that of vindictive destruction. Hunting, trapping, poisoning, den digging, and several other methods have been, and in many areas still are, used to help eliminate the wolf. During the settlement of the United States, there was no choice but to exterminate the species from large areas so that livestock could be raised to support the growing human populations. As recently as 1965, the state of Minnesota paid a bounty to anyone who killed a wolf, and Alaska, Ontario, Quebec, and the Northwest Territories still do. Other Canadian provinces have replaced their bounty program with a poisoning campaign.

In Eastern Europe and Russia, a great war is being waged at present to eradicate wolves—in hopes of saving thousands of head of livestock each year.

These matters will be discussed in more detail in the next two chapters.

Protection of the wolf. In other areas, man has assumed a protective relationship with the wolf. These are areas where livestock interests are nonexistent and the creature's primary prey are wild. In most cases, these areas also happen to be closed to the hunting of big game by humans, a factor that tends to reduce objections by the public to the protection of the wolf. Examples of these areas are Isle Royale National Park, Michigan; Mount McKinley National Park, Alaska; and Algonquin Provincial Park, Ontario.

This type of relationship between man and wolf is relatively new and represents a significant change in the thinking of part of the human race. No doubt it results from the combination of a decrease in conflict between man and wolf in many areas and the general increase in man's esthetic desire to preserve interesting species and natural phenomena. This subject will be expanded in Chapter XII.

CHAPTER XI / FACTORS HARMFUL
TO THE WOLF

Every living thing is faced with elements and conditions that make its life more difficult and that in certain combinations may overcome it. The wolf is no exception. This animal must put up with adverse factors ranging from parasitism by tapeworms to persecution by man. Some of these factors are immediately fatal, but others merely exert an extra drag on the wolf's life. This latter type of adversity, of course, may gradually make an individual so inefficient that it eventually succumbs.

In terms of limitation or control of wolf numbers, some factors that are harmful to individuals, such as accidents, are totally insignificant because they affect so few members of the population. On the other hand, a factor such as stress may do little harm to individual wolves but nevertheless could help control a population by affecting breeding success. Of course, in areas where man has interfered with the natural course of events, which includes much of the wolf's present range, control of wolf numbers may be brought about directly by human actions. All these factors will be discussed below.

Parasitism

Parasitism, the phenomenon in which one living thing (the parasite) gains its nourishment directly from another (the host) without killing it, is an example of a factor that may merely put a drag on an animal's life. Some individuals infected with parasites live for years, but in cases where other harmful factors are also involved, the parasites may suddenly take over and cause more damage.

Wolves harbor both internal and external parasites, although they have many more species of the former. The internal parasites, or endoparasites, that have been found in the wolf are of the three most common groups, the flukes, the tapeworms, and the roundworms. The external parasites, or ectoparasites, include lice, fleas, mites, ticks, tongue worms, and various flies.

Flukes. Flukes, or trematodes, are usually small, unsegmented flatworms, many of which occur as adults in mammals. Most flukes attach themselves to the host by means of suckers. The types most often recorded from the wolf and other canine animals are found in the intestine. At least nine species have been reported in the wolf (Table 25).

TABLE 25. Flukes (Trematoda) of wolves.

Parasite	Location in Wolf	Intermediate Hosts	Geographic Location
Alaria americana Hall and Wigdor, 1918	Intestine[1]	Snail to frog to mouse[1]	Ontario[2]; Alberta[10]
A. alata (Goeze, 1782)	Intestine, stomach[5]	Snail to frog to mouse[1]	Europe and/or Asia[5]; U.S.S.R.[9]
A. arisaemoides Augustine and Uribe, 1927	Intestine[1]	Snail to frog[10]	Alberta[10]
A. canis LaRue and Fallis, 1934	Intestine[1]	Snail to frog to mouse[1]	Ontario[3]; Alaska[4]
Heterophyes heterophyes Siebold, 1853[6,7]	Intestine[1]	Snail to fish[1]	—
H. persica (Braun, 1901)	Intestine[5]	Snail to fish[1]	Europe and/or Asia[5]
Metorchis conjunctus (Cobbold, 1860)	Liver[10]	Snail to fish[1]	Alberta[10]
Paragonimus westermanii Kerbert, 1878	Lungs[5]	Snail to crayfish, crab[1]	Korea[5]
Pseudamphistomum sp.	Gall bladder[8]	Fish[8]	Europe and/or Asia[5]

[1] Noble and Noble, 1961.
[2] Law and Kennedy, 1932.
[3] Pearson, 1956.
[4] R. L. Rausch and Williamson, 1959.
[5] Stiles and Baker, 1934.
[6] Cameron, 1927.
[7] Nicoll, 1927.
[8] Yamaguti, 1958.
[9] Morozov, 1951.
[10] Holmes and Podesta, 1968.

The life cycles of these parasites involve two or three kinds of intermediate hosts. The first intermediate host is always a snail, but later developmental stages of the parasite occur in fishes, frogs, and rodents. When a wolf eats such animals containing the infective larvae, the larvae develop to the adult stage and begin reproducing. Eggs passed in the excreta of the wolf hatch if the environment where they land is favorable, freeing larvae infective to snails, and the life cycle is completed.

Nothing is known about the effect of flukes on the health of the wolf, but two (*Heterophyes heterophyes* and *Paragonimus westermanii*) may cause serious disease in man.

Tapeworms. Tapeworms, or cestodes, are flatworms having ribbonlike bodies made up of segments. Tapeworms of some species are very small, whereas others may be several feet long. The adults live in the intestines of various vertebrates, including the wolf, where they attach by suckers and/or hooks arranged on a headlike structure called a "scolex." The worms are bathed in the digesting food of the host from which they absorb nutrients through their body walls.

Tapeworms are highly adapted for reproduction. The end segments, containing hundreds to thousands of eggs, usually are expelled from the host in its feces. The breaking down of these segments allows dispersal of the eggs, some of which may then be eaten by a suitable intermediate host. In the case of the tapeworms infecting wolves, the intermediate host is usually an animal of a species regularly preyed upon by wolves. The larval tapeworms develop to the infective stage in the intermediate host, and when animals containing such larvae are eaten by a wolf, the adult stage develops in the wolf's gut. Because of the asexual reproduction that occurs in some of these larval tapeworms, many adults may develop from a single egg.

At least twenty-one species of tapeworms have been recorded from the wolf (Table 26). Rates of infection vary with the species of tapeworm and the geographic locality, depending upon several ecological factors.

One species, the hydatid tapeworm (*Echinococcus granulosus*), deserves special mention because it can infect man. G. K. Sweatman (1952) showed that the adult is found mainly in the wolf, and that although the larvae may infect several types of hoofed mammals, the moose is the most important host for the larvae in North America. It is this intermediate stage of the hydatid tapeworm that may infect human beings, usually encysting in the liver or lungs. These larvae develop from eggs dispersed by wolves, coyotes, or dogs that have eaten the lungs or liver

TABLE 26. Tapeworm (Cestoda) parasites of wolves.

Parasite	Intermediate Host	Geographic Location	Rates of Infection
Diphyllobothrium latum Linnaeus, 1758	Fishes	Western Great Lakes[1]; Ontario[2]	—
Dipylidium caninum Linnaeus, 1758	Fleas	U.S.S.R.[3]	—
Echinococcus granulosus Batsch, 1786	Moose, deer, caribou, elk	Minnesota[4]; Ontario[2]; Alberta[5]; Europe and/or Asia[6]	20–63%
E. multilocularis Leuckart, 1856	Rodents	U.S.S.R.[7]	—
Joyeuxiella pasqualei (Diamare, 1893)	Lice, fleas	Europe and/or Asia[6]	—
Mesocestoides lineatus (Goeze, 1782)	Rodents	Europe and/or Asia[6]; U.S.S.R.[3]	—
Spirometra erinacei-europaei (Rudolphi, 1819)	—	Europe and/or Asia[6]	—
S. janickii Furmaga, 1953	—	Poland[8]	—
Taenia crassiceps (Zeder, 1800)	Small rodents	Ontario[9]; Europe and/or Asia[6]; U.S.S.R.[7]	2%
T. hydatigena Pallas, 1776	Moose, caribou, deer	Minnesota[10]; British Columbia and Alberta[5]; Europe and/or Asia[6]; U.S.S.R.[3]	8–100%
T. krabbei Moniez, 1879	Moose, caribou	U.S.S.R.[3]; Alaska[11]; Alberta[14]	20–61%
T. laticollis Rudolphi, 1819	—	Ontario[9]	2%
T. macrocystis (Diesing, 1850)	Asian squirrels, rabbits, hares	U.S.S.R.[7]	—
T. (Multiceps) multiceps Leske, 1780	Snowshoe hares	Minnesota[10]; U.S.S.R.[12]; Europe and/or Asia[6]; Alberta[14]	6–29%
T. omissa Lühe, 1910	Deer	Alberta[14]	1%
T. (Multiceps) packii (Christenson, 1929)	—	U.S.S.R.[7]	—
T. pisiformis Bloch, 1780	Rabbits, hares	Ontario[13]; Minnesota[10]; U.S.S.R.[12]; Alberta[14]	13–28%
T. polyacantha Leuckart, 1856	Rodents	U.S.S.R.[7]	—
T. (Multiceps) serialis Gervais, 1847	Asian rabbits, hares	U.S.S.R.[7]	—
T. (Multiceps) skriabini (Popov, 1937)	Sheep, goats	U.S.S.R.[7]	—
T. taeniaeformis Batsch, 1786	Rodents	Alberta[14]	—

[1] Young, 1944.
[2] DeVos and Allin, 1949.
[3] Morozov, 1951.
[4] Riley, 1933.
[5] Cowan, 1947.
[6] Stiles and Baker, 1934.
[7] Abuladze, 1964.
[8] Furmaga, 1953.
[9] Freeman *et al.*, 1961.
[10] Erickson, 1944.
[11] R. L. Rausch and Williamson, 1959.
[12] Bondareva, 1955.
[13] Law and Kennedy, 1932.
[14] Holmes and Podesta, 1968.

of infected big-game animals. Most infections in human beings are thought to result from association with infected dogs.

Little is known about the effect of adult tapeworms of most species in animals other than man. A. B. Erickson (1944) found that wolves in Minnesota harbored so many *Taenia hydatigena* that their intestines seemed to be partly blocked by them. L. P. E. Choquette (1956) reported that three of eight dogs experimentally infected with *Echinococcus granulosus* suffered loss of weight, severe diarrhea, and weakness after about a month, dying soon after appearance of these signs. Whether or not wolves are similarly affected is unknown.

Roundworms. The most diverse group of worms parasitizing the wolf are the roundworms, or nematodes. These are round in cross-section and are unsegmented. They vary greatly in size, location in the host, and in type of life cycle. Some are less than an inch long, whereas others may reach forty inches in length. Many live in the small intestine, but some inhabit the heart, kidney, or stomach. The life cycles of a few roundworms are simple, with infection of a new host resulting from the incidental swallowing of eggs passed directly from the body of another host. However, other species require a complex passage of larval stages through one or more intermediate hosts, such as fishes, fleas, or mosquitoes.

At least twenty-four species of nematodes have been recorded from wolves (Table 27), although some seem to occur rarely in this host, and others are known only from captive animals. The heartworm, *Dirofilaria immitis,* and the giant kidney worm, *Dioctophyma renale,* may cause severe damage to the organs inhabited and may lead to the death of the host. Heavy infections of *Toxascaris leonina* or *Toxocara canis* may have the same adverse effects on wolf pups as are seen in young dogs. Hookworms, *Uncinaria stenocephala,* when present in large numbers, also are harmful. The effects of other species have not been defined, but probably some of them are also damaging to the host.

Thorny-headed worms. The acanthocephala, or thorny-headed worms, are uncommon parasites of wolves, at least in North America. These worms superficially resemble roundworms, but they have a spiny "proboscis" at their front end, which they

TABLE 27. Roundworm (Nematoda) parasites of wolves.

Parasite	Location in Wolf	Geographic Location	Rate of Infection
Ancylostoma braziliense de Faria, 1910	Intestine	Asia[1]	—
A. caninum Ercolani, 1859	Intestine	Asia[1]; U.S.S.R.[2]	—
Capillaria aerophila (Creplin, 1839)	Lungs	U.S.S.R.[13]; Alberta[14]	1%
C. plica (Rudolphi, 1819)	Urinary bladder	Germany; Ireland[1]; U.S.S.R.[13]	—
Crenosoma vulpis (Dujardin, 1845)	Lungs	Europe[1]; U.S.S.R.[13]	—
Dioctophyma renale (Goeze, 1782)	Kidney, body cavity[3]	Minnesota[3]; Europe and/or Asia[1] (Zool. Gardens)[4]	6%
Dirofilaria immitis (Leidy, 1856)	Heart	Europe and/or Asia[1]	—
Eucoleus aerophilus Creplin, 1839	Lungs	Minnesota[3]	6%
Filaroides osleri (Cobbold, 1879)	Trachea	Persia[1]	—
Physaloptera papilloradiata von Linstow, 1899	Pectoral cavity	?[12]	—
P. rara Hall and Wigdor, 1918	Stomach	U.S.S.R.[2]	—
Rictularia affinis Jaegerskioeld, 1904	Intestine	U.S.S.R.[2]	—
R. cahirensis Jaegerskioeld, 1904	Intestine	U.S.S.R.[2]	—
R. lupi Panin and Lavrov, 1962	Intestine	Germany[1]; U.S.S.R.[5]	—
Spirocerca lupi (Rudolphi, 1809)	Stomach, duodenum	U.S.S.R.[2]	—
Strepropharagus sp.	—	—	—
Toxascaris leonina (von Linstow, 1902)	Intestine	U.S.S.R.[5]; Alaska[6]; Northwest Territories[7]; Alberta[14]	6-84%
Toxocara canis (Werner, 1782)	Intestine	U.S.S.R.[5]; Asia[1]; W. Canada[8]	2–20%
T. mystax (Zeder, 1800)	Intestine	Europe and/or Asia[1]	—
Trichinella spiralis (Owen, 1835)	Intestine and skeletal muscles	Alaska[9]	33%
Trichuris vulpis (Frolich, 1789)	Cecum	Europe and/or Asia[1]	—
Uncinaria catholica Onelli, 1905	Intestine	?[10]	—
U. criniformis (Goeze, 1782)	Intestine	(Museum)[1]	—
U. stenocephala (Railliet, 1884)	Intestine	Minnesota[3]; U.S.S.R.[11]; Alaska[6]; Alberta[14]	4–28%

[1] Stiles and Baker, 1934.
[2] Panin and Lavrov, 1962.
[3] Erickson, 1944.
[4] Hartley, 1938.
[5] Morozov, 1951.
[6] R. L. Rausch and Williamson, 1959.
[7] Fuller and Novakowski, 1955.
[8] Cowan, 1947.
[9] R. L. Rausch et al., 1956.
[10] Yamaguti, 1961.
[11] Rodonoaia, 1956.
[12] Morgan, 1941.
[13] Shaldybin, 1957.
[14] Holmes and Podesta, 1968.

insert deeply into the intestinal wall of the host. The effects of infection by thorny-headed worms are probably limited to local inflammation of the intestinal wall, unless large numbers of worms are present. The following three species have been reported from wolves in the Soviet Union: *Oncicola skrjabini* Morozov, 1951, *Macracantho-rhynchus catulinus* Kostylev, 1927, and *Moniliformis moniliformis* (Bremser, 1811; Panin and Lavrov, 1962).

External parasites. Several species of external parasites have been found on the wolf, among them two kinds of lice, one kind of flea, seven species of ticks, a tongue worm, and a mange mite (Table 28). This last parasite probably is the most important, for it causes mange, a condition in which the wolf loses most if not all of its fur.

Cowan (1947) reported on several mangy wolves found in the Rocky Mountain National Parks of Canada. One was almost half denuded and weighed only thirty-seven pounds; it was also infected with internal parasites and showed evidence of other pathological conditions as well. Thus it could not be determined whether the mange was a cause or effect of the animal's poor condition.

The external parasites mentioned above are those that actually live on their hosts. There are many others that merely visit their hosts, feed, and then leave. It is difficult to tell just which of these species parasitize the wolf, but mosquitoes, deer flies, horseflies, black flies, and other biting insects probably are included.

TABLE 28. External parasites of wolves.

Parasite	Common Name	Authority
Amblyomma americanum (Linnaeus, 1758)[1]	Tick	Bishopp and Trembley, 1945
A. maculatum Koch, 1844[1]	Tick	Bishopp and Trembley, 1945
Dermacentor variabilis (Say, 1821)[1]	Tick	Bishopp and Trembley, 1945
Haemaphysalis bispinosa Neumann, 1897[2]	Tick	Stiles and Baker, 1934
Ixodes hexagonus Leach, 1815[2]	Tick	Stiles and Baker, 1934
I. kingi Bishopp, 1911	Tick	Bishopp and Trembley, 1945
I. ricinus (Linnaeus, 1758)[1]	Tick	Bishopp and Trembley, 1945
Linguatula serrata Frolich, 1789[2]	Tongue worm	Stiles and Baker, 1934
Pulex irritans Linnaeus, 1758[3]	Flea	Stiles and Baker, 1934; Trembley and Bishopp, 1940
Sarcoptes scabei De Geer, 1778[2]	Mange mite	Stiles and Baker, 1934
Trichodectes canis De Geer, 1778[2]	Louse	Stiles and Baker, 1934

[1] Known for North America only.
[2] Known for Europe and/or Asia only.
[3] Known for both.

A wolf pup that I reared was continually bitten on the tips of his ears by insects resembling houseflies, probably stable flies (*Stomoxys* sp.). The pup was very weak from distemper and did not bother to wiggle his ears, so the flies fed at their leisure and began concentrating on small areas, which they made raw. This can be considered a case of secondary parasitism because, if the wolf had been well enough, he would have been able to keep the flies away, as did his more healthy littermate.

Diseases and Physical Disorders

Wolves are subject to a great number of diseases and disorders (Table 29), but the prevalence of these conditions in wild populations is unknown. Intact carcasses of wild animals are rarely found, especially those of wilderness species like the wolf. Thus there has been little chance to learn about the incidence of various

TABLE 29. Pathological conditions reported for the wolf.

Condition	Authority
Adenocarcinoma sarcomatodes of the thyroid	Fox, 1926
Adenomatous polyp of uterus	Fox, 1926
Arthritis	Cross, 1940
Bladder stone and chronic nephritis	Hamerton, 1945
Canine distemper	Goss, 1948
Carcinoma of liver	Lucas, 1923
Carcinoma of neck	Plimmer, 1915
Carcinoma of thyroid	Lucas, 1923
Carcinoma of tonsil	Scott, 1928
Chronic diffuse nephritis	Fox, 1926
Chronic interstitial nephritis	Hamerton, 1932
Chronic parenchymatous nephritis	Hamerton, 1931
Cretinism	Fox, 1923
Duodenal ulcer	Fox, 1927
Encephalitis	Young, 1944
Exopthalmic goiter	Fox, 1923
Glanders	Blair, 1919
Haemorrhagic cystitis	Plimmer, 1916
Hyperplasia of thyroid	Fox, 1923
Jaundice	Fox, 1927
Listeriosis	Rutter and Pimlott, 1968
Multicentric hypernephroma	Fox, 1926
Myocardial and arterial degeneration	Hamerton, 1936
Pancreatitis	Fox, 1923
Rabies	Young, 1944
Rickets	Blair, 1908
Salmonella infection	Fox, 1941
Salmon poisoning*	Young, 1944
Senile degeneration of kidney, liver, and heart	Hamerton, 1945
Tumor of lung, adrenal, kidney, thyroid, cerebellum	Fox, 1926
Viruslike disease of respiratory tract	Fox, 1941

disorders and to appraise their effect on individual wolves or populations.

Most of the knowledge about diseases and disorders of wolves has come from autopsies performed on animals that died in captivity (Fox, 1923). Many of the afflictions found in these animals, such as cancer, chronic inflammation of the kidneys, and degeneration of the heart and arteries, appear when an individual is very old. They may rarely occur in wild wolves because most of these animals die before ever reaching old age (Chapter II).

The most important disease known to affect wild wolves is rabies. Also known as madness and hydrophobia, rabies has been recorded from wolves for centuries (Young, 1944). It is caused by a virus that affects the brain and results in general listlessness, followed usually be excessive salivation (a condition also common to other diseases), and a tendency to wander and bite at both animals and inanimate objects. When a rabid wolf wounds another animal, the virus is transferred from the wolf's saliva into the wound of the victim, which may be another wolf or one of any number of other animals, including dogs, foxes, and human beings.

A rabid wolf in the Northwest Territories of Canada once chased a farmer into his house and then fastened his teeth into the door in an attempt to open it (Adlam, 1953). The next morning the farmer ventured out and found the wolf asleep in a haystack. When awakened, the animal repeated its performance of the previous night but was eventually killed. Laboratory tests showed that it was rabid. It is easy to see how such incidents could foster the belief that all wolves are dangerous.

Usually when an epidemic of rabies occurs in wolf country, foxes, dogs, and wolves are involved, although foxes seem to be most subject to the disease, perhaps because of their greater numbers and density.

Whether or not rabies is important as a control on wolf populations at certain times is still open to debate. In 1949, Cowan suggested that rabies might limit the numbers of foxes and possibly even of wolves. However, R. L. Rausch (1958: 255), who confirmed the existence of rabies in thirty-three foxes and two wolves in Alaska from 1949 through 1957, concluded the following: "Knowledge is insufficient at the present time to allow the conclusion that rabies is important in the control of populations of canine animals in high boreal regions. Such sometimes may be the case, but additional investigation is needed."

Another viral disease affecting the wolf's nervous system is distemper. It is especially prevalent among young animals and is often fatal. Individuals infected with distemper become listless and fail to eat. Unless their resistance overcomes the infection, they eventually become extremely emaciated and die. Often death is a direct result of pneumonia and other secondary bacterial infections. Individuals with milder infections or more resistance may overcome the disease but are often left with yellowed "distemper teeth" or with various minor nervous disorders such as muscle twitches, poor eyesight, or impaired hearing.

Because distemper is so dangerous to domestic dogs and may wipe out entire teams in certain areas, it has been thought that the disease might also have drastic effects on wolf populations. However, I know of no reliable report of the occurrence of distemper in wild wolves, and R. L. Rausch (1958) stated that the existence of the disease in wild canids of Alaska has not been confirmed.

L. J. Goss (1948), without providing details, did report that wolves are susceptible to canine distemper. In addition, one of my wolf pups died of the disease at the age of about fourteen weeks. This animal had been injected with a series of three shots of dead distemper virus in an attempt to bring about immunity to the disease. One of the veterinarians that treated the wolf, Dr. J. F. Anderson, of the University of Minnesota, told me that he had examined a wild wolf from Ontario whose teeth showed definite signs that the animal had overcome an infection of distemper. R. L. Rausch (1967) wrote me that two captive, unvaccinated wolves of his died of distemper, and added that wolves are protected by a single injection of attenuated, live-virus vaccine. No doubt the disease does affect wild wolves, but its incidence and significance in wild populations are still unknown.

Another disease that affects wild wolves is arthritis. E. C. Cross (1940) examined two wolves from Ontario that were afflicted by this condition. In one case so much bone had been deposited in the right elbow joint of an animal that movement of the joint was judged to have been difficult and painful. The left knee joint on the same creature was similarly affected and was in even worse condition. The arthritis in this wolf was thought to have resulted basically from the animal's old age.

A second wolf examined by Cross appeared to have escaped from a steel trap many years before after having been caught by its left hind foot. This injury is believed to have brought on the arthritic condition that affected not only that foot but also the right hind foot and a long section of the backbone, probably making movement both difficult and painful. Jordan *et al.* (1967) also reported arthritis in the backbone and knees of a wolf found dead on Isle Royale.

No doubt there are many other diseases and physical disorders that affect wolves in the wild, but most of them have not yet been studied. The pathological conditions that have been reported for wolves in captivity show what a wide range of possibilities exists (Table 29).

Injuries

All animals risk being injured accidentally during their normal activities. The wolf travels widely and charges headlong through thick swamps, tangled blowdown, and other treacherous cover in pursuit of prey. Thus one might expect that it would be even more prone to accidents than are most animals. In addition, the wolf certainly places itself in a hazardous position anytime it tries to kill its prey, since the prey is usually large and powerful.

Of course, it would be very difficult to learn how many wolves are killed by prey or accidents, for so few carcasses are ever found under circumstances allowing an interpretation of the cause of death. There can be no doubt, however, that wolves are sometimes injured by their intended prey. The Isle Royale studies showed that a pack of fifteen or sixteen wolves actually "tested" an average of about four moose per day during winter. Projected year round, this would be almost 1500 moose encounters per year. It seems reasonable that sooner or later some wolf would make a misjudgment and get badly kicked by a powerful hoof.

I have seen both an adult moose and a nine-month-old calf each pound wolves into the snow with their front hoofs. But evidently the snow cushioned the blows, for the wolves appeared from the air to be uninjured after a few minutes. Nevertheless, it certainly is possible that they had suffered such injury as broken ribs or damaged internal organs without showing immediate ill effects. Either of such injuries could cause a gradual weakening of the animal and make it more subject to other harmful conditions.

What happens when snow does not cushion the blows from a moose can be seen from the observations of both R. R. Mac-Farlane (1905) and J. F. Stanwell-Fletcher. MacFarlane found a live adult wolf with a hind leg shattered by a kick from a bull moose in the Canadian Northwest Territories. In British Columbia, Stanwell-Fletcher (1942: 138) came upon a similar scene. He discovered a large male wolf, barely alive, with broken ribs and legs. "Surrounded by moose tracks, blood patches and moose hair, the wolf had been crippled in a great battle."

Both of the arthritic wolves from Ontario that Cross examined had had previous injuries. The old individual had broken a rib, and the animal that at one time had escaped from a trap had suffered two broken ribs on one side and one on the other, plus a broken left leg, and later a fractured pelvis.

Further indications that wolves often sustain injuries, presumably from accidents or prey, come from the examination of skulls and bones of specimens. Young mentioned museum specimens showing healed skull injuries, which he believed came from large prey. More recently R. A. Rausch, who examined 4000 left front leg bones and 1250 skulls and skeletons of Alaskan wolves, found many healed or healing fractures. He stated (Rausch, 1967a: 258): "Compression fractures of the skull, involving the nasal and the frontal bones suggested heavy blows with a blunt object, presumably the hoof of a moose. Blows sufficient to cause compression fractures of the skull probably kill if delivered a few centimeters higher on the skull. Because of the probability of direct mortality, there is no way of determining the relative frequency with which wolves are killed or succumb to injuries inflicted while gathering food."

One can imagine that the individuals most apt to be struck by prey would be pups on their first hunting expeditions. Inexperienced at contending with large animals and unaware of the abilities of their prey, these pups would stand a higher chance of being injured. Those that learned quickly to avoid the rushes of their intended victims would survive and become adept hunters. The slower or more inept animals might quickly be weeded out.

Malnutrition

Of all the factors that could bring harm to the wolf, the one that most often comes to mind as a natural control on wolf numbers is food supply. Without enough food, any animal must perish, and because the wolf must hunt hard to obtain its prey, it would seem to be more affected by its food supply than are most animals. Unfortunately, however, this is another subject that must be covered more by speculation than by reference to definite knowledge.

One of the main problems in determining whether or not food supply is a major factor in the natural control of wolf populations is that in most areas the numbers of both wolves and their prey have been affected so strongly by man's activities (Chapter IX).

A second problem is lack of information about wolf populations. Not enough figures are available on wolf densities, annual survival and mortality rates, and age ratios (Chapter II).

A third problem is that the effects of an inadequate food supply might never show themselves directly on a wolf population. That is, if wolves were not getting enough food, they probably would not perish from starvation itself; rather they might become weakened and more subject to diseases, parasites, and other stress factors. Domestic dogs are considered less resistant to stress in general when their body weight falls to less than 15% below normal (Fuller and DuBuis, 1962). Possibly starving wolves would even risk attempts to kill prey that they normally would avoid, such as healthy moose, and would be killed in the process.

One way that malnutrition could act directly might be in affecting pup survival. If the adult wolves did not get enough to eat, they might fail to feed the pups. Or what little food was brought to the den might be devoured by only the strongest, most aggressive pups; the others then would slowly lose weight and die. One carcass of a wolf pup that might have starved was found by Jordan on Isle Royale. The animal definitely was emaciated, but it must be pointed out that such a condition can also result from distemper and probably from any of several other diseases.

It does not seem likely, however, that malnutrition during the pup-rearing period is generally an important factor in limiting wolf numbers. There are two reasons for this statement. First, in Algonquin Park, Ontario, where there was a calculated summer pup mortality of 57% (Chapter II), some wolf packs were known to be raising full litters throughout the summer (Joslin, 1966). If there was enough food available for entire litters to survive, it hardly seems likely that other packs would encounter a food shortage in the same area.

The second reason that malnutrition does not seem likely to be important during summer is that this is the period when the wolf's prey also bear their young, and there would appear to be an abundant food supply for wolves in most areas. Just by scavenging on the large numbers of young big-game animals that usually perish during their first few months (even in wolf-free areas—Cowan, 1947), wolves could obtain a substantial food supply. In addition, beavers and other smaller animals plus a certain number of adult big-game animals would also be obtainable.

Nevertheless, one must contend with the statement by Jordan *et al.* (1967: 251) that on Isle Royale "survival of pups, and more generally, growth of the population is limited by food available to the family group during the rearing season." These authors found a rough correlation between years of high moose twinning rates and years of successful wolf reproduction. However, they compared years in which twinning rates were 15% to 25% with years in which they were 38% to 48%. These figures, derived from Mech (1966a) and Shelton (1966) for five of the seven years under consideration, were based on small sample sizes and therefore had wide and overlapping confidence limits. Thus it is possible that the apparent differences in twinning rates resulted more from the small samples than from real differences in the actual rates. Because of this, the data must be considered useful only as a basis for an hypothesis and not as evidence for a relationship between pup survival and food supply.

The Isle Royale studies do suggest another manner in which malnutrition could affect wolf numbers. This is through the continued attrition of lone wolves and social subordinates, which appear to be "outcasts" of the larger packs. These animals usually scavenge on the leavings of the packs and thus obtain a much poorer food supply; their chances of survival no doubt are much less than those of wolves within a pack. Any mortality resulting from such a process as this, however, is actually caused by a combination of food shortage, social factors, and whatever directly causes the death, such as disease or parasitism.

Of course, if there were no other factors controlling a wolf population, ultimately it would be limited by a shortage of food. Pimlott (1967b) has calculated that with wolves occurring at their maximum known density for a large area (one per ten square miles) they would require an average density of ten deer (or their equivalent) per square mile producing a total of 3.7 offspring per year to provide the wolves with their food requirements. If his assumptions, including 7.2 to 8.4 pounds of food required per wolf per day, are correct, a deer density less than this would limit wolf numbers in the area. If wolves could actually survive on half this food, however (Chapter VI), they might not be limited by food supply until the density was less than five deer per square mile.

It should be pointed out that if food supply does control wolf numbers in certain areas the real limitation would not be just a relative lack of prey but rather a shortage of *vulnerable* prey. Thus if wolves removed all the vulnerable young, old, and weak individuals from a herd of prey, food would be unavailable to them, and they would be expected to starve or move, even though there would still be numbers of healthy prey remaining.

In view of the wolf's traveling and hunting routine (Chapters V and VII), it seems likely that, rather than starve during a shortage of vulnerable prey, wolves would move to another region. Since the normal travels of any one pack are so extensive, wolves could have knowledge about prey populations over a very large area. The animals might be aware that in certain locations they obtain a greater frequency of reward for their hunting efforts. While they are consistently killing prey in these areas, they might also explore others and thus be continually learning about future sources of vulnerable prey. Then as their hunting efficiency dwindles to a certain minimum level in the former areas, they might gradually shift their activities to the new regions.

This hypothetical view of the wolf's travel routine could explain the animal's habit of traveling so widely after abandoning a kill. For example, on Isle Royale the moose killed by wolves were often concentrated in certain areas during each winter, showing that each of these areas did contain several vulnerable animals. However, whenever wolves killed and ate one of these moose, the pack then left and hunted in other areas. Several days or weeks later the wolves might return and kill another moose in the first area.

Of course, if vulnerable prey is absent from an entire region used by a wolf pack, the pack would then have to move much farther to find food, and it is possible that the wolves would starve in the process. However, before that happened their movements probably would take them into areas used by other wolf packs. This could then bring a whole new factor into play—that of social stress, which will be discussed in the next section.

In summary, it is possible that malnutrition may be an important factor in the life of the wolf, but if it is, it probably does not act directly. With lone wolves and social subordinates, it could lower their general resistance to stress and thus subject them to other harmful factors, which eventually might cause their deaths. In affecting populations, malnutrition might result in extensive wandering of packs, bringing them into too frequent contact with neighboring packs and thus exposing them to too much social stress.

Social Stress

As seen in Chapters II and III, wolf society is highly organized through a system of complex behavioral mechanisms. A rigid social order exists within each pack, and among packs intolerance and a degree of spacing or territoriality seems to be the rule. In other words, a certain amount of tension exists throughout the wolf community, holding each individual and each pack in its place. This tension results from the constant competition among individuals within a pack and among packs within a population.

Such social tension, when it becomes too great, can result in harm to individual wolves and can restrict breeding, as captivity studies show (Rabb *et al.*, 1967). Although no definite conclusions can yet be drawn about the role of social stress in populations of wild wolves, there is increasing speculation that some intrinsic factor could be one of the main regulators of wolf numbers (Mech, 1966a; Pimlott, 1967b). V. C. Wynne-Edwards (1962) has even suggested that populations of most, if not all, animals are regulated basically through social stress.

In Chapter II it was shown that some 76% of the reduction in a potential wolf population under natural control can result from a decreased reproductive potential and a low young-pup survival rate (Table 7). However, in the same area where these figures were obtained, entire litters of pups are known to have been raised successfully throughout the period of high pup mortality (Joslin, 1966). This suggests that, whatever the mortality factor is, it might act mainly in destroying whole litters of pups rather than a few pups from each litter. If that is the case, then a physiological or psychological upset such as might cause still-births, abandonment of young, or poor viability of newborn pups would be highly suspect.

Several pathways certainly exist within the framework of wolf social relations through which such intrinsic population control could take place. These pathways have properties that would enable mechanisms to begin operating when wolf numbers reach a certain maximum density, even when there is an adequate supply of vulnerable prey. However, they would also allow stress to act as a control at less than maximum densities in areas or times of food shortages.

Stress as a possible primary cause of population control. Where and when wolf numbers have stabilized despite an abundant supply of food and without interference by man, population control might be mediated by social stress both within and between packs. As any wolf population increases, there must be changes either in the total number of wolves per pack or the total number of packs per area, or in both. R. A. Rausch has shown that in Alaska the average pack is larger where wolf densities are higher. On Isle Royale, the site of one of the highest wolf densities known, one pack reached the very unusual size of fifteen to twenty-two members.

The more wolves there are in a pack, however, the greater the social complications would become during the courtship and breeding process (Chapter IV). Competition for preferred mates, such as the leader, or alpha male, would increase. The disruption of mating acts caused by wolves not involved in those acts would also become more frequent. In addition, there probably would be more subordinate nonbreeding members. It seems significant that in the Brookfield Zoo's experimental wolf pack no animal less than three years old ever conceived young except for the original parents of the pack, which mated when two years old (Rabb *et al.*, 1967).

For all these reasons, when a pack increases to a certain size, the chances of successful matings may drop to a point where reproduction is greatly curtailed. In the Brookfield pack, 1296 courtship actions were seen during four breeding seasons, but only thirty-one (2.4%) ended in complete copulations.

Although a decrease in successful matings in large packs could result entirely from such behavioral complications, there could also be strong physiological involvement. The possible pathways through which this involvement could take place are many; probably the hormonal system, and the adrenal gland in particular, plays a major role (Selye, 1950; Christian, 1959).

If social competition within packs grew extreme enough that actual fighting occurred, another factor could become important. In serious battles, it is likely that males, being larger and stronger, would survive in greater numbers than females. This would be especially true among pups. A preponderance of males, as often found in wolf populations, would decrease the total number of potential breeding animals and could account for a certain degree of population control (Chapter II).

In addition to the increased social stress occurring within a large pack, greater pack size probably would also increase the amount of tension between packs. This is because a larger pack would need more food than a smaller one and thus would have to travel more often and more widely to locate vulnerable prey. In doing so, it is more apt to encounter other packs or their signs and to leave more signs of its own presence in the region. The few meetings that have been witnessed between wolf packs and aliens show that much social tension, and even bodily harm, may attend such meetings (Chapter III).

When wolf populations become more dense, not only do packs become larger, but the total number of packs or social units in the area might also increase. Such an increase could result from the greater chance that subordinate members will drop out of the packs and become lone wolves or form small, nonbreeding groups. Secondly, even the natural process of breeding-pack formation (Chapter II) might be increased, since potentially there would be more possible pairs in larger packs. Either way, the result would be a higher number of social units in the wolf population.

With more packs in a given area, the amount of stress occurring between social units would increase. Every new pack or lone wolf would greatly increase the frequency of chance meetings of social units. At the same time, the amount of exclusive territory available to each unit would decrease. Thus the more packs and lone wolves there are in an area, the more fighting, chasing, enmity, and general tension there would be in the population. Lone wolves and members of smaller packs might be wounded or killed with greater frequency.

It is even conceivable that some wolf packs, harassed by larger or more aggressive groups, would fail to reproduce. On Isle Royale from 1959 to 1966 there was one dominant pack of fifteen to twenty-two wolves, one or two packs of two or three individuals, and some lone wolves (Mech, 1966a; Jordan *et al.,* 1967). Until 1965 only the large pack showed any sign of breeding activity. During 1965, a new group of five animals was seen, and because the large pack had decreased since the previous winter, the new pack was thought to have split from the large one. Breeding activity occurred in the new pack in 1965, but apparently no pups survived to 1966.

Failure of subordinate packs to breed might result from the same process that prevents subordinate individuals within a pack from breeding. It appears that low-ranking wolves that are harassed by dominant ones become so conditioned that even a glance by a dominant animal will cause them to cringe (Schenkel, 1947). They seem to lose all social initiative and live in a continual state of stress. Thus a pack that is attacked whenever it is discovered by a larger one might also become similarly stressed and lose its urge to breed.

It must be emphasized that direct encounters between social units might not even be necessary to bring about and maintain stress in subordinate groups. This is because there is so much indirect communication among wolf packs (Chapter III). Once a lone wolf or pack has learned its status by direct contact with various other social units, it might then be reminded of its standing every time it hears or smells other groups.

As discussed in Chapter III, howling can be heard over an area of about fifty square miles, so it could easily serve to advertise the immediate presence, and perhaps the size, of various packs in an area. It is noteworthy that upon hearing a howl a pack will usually howl in return and that captive wolves that I have seen seemed very excited and highly motivated when replying. Some important psychological effect appeared to be taking place.

Three peculiarities of wolf howling would be explained by the concept that one of its main functions is in informing surrounding wolves of the location and size of each pack. The first is that for fifteen to thirty minutes after a pack has howled it usually will not call again. The function of this silent period could be to allow each pack to gain an impression of where each neighboring group is. If wolves were to repeat their howling right away, the air might be filled with the simultaneous calls of several packs, and none could determine the location or size of the others.

The two other characteristics of wolf howling that could be explained by this idea are (1) the great variation in howls of different wolves (Chapter III), and (2) the tendency for wolves to enter a pack chorus on different notes and to avoid unison howling (Crisler, 1958). Both traits would enable other wolves to gain at least a relative idea about the number of wolves in the chorus. If all the wolves in a pack howled on the same note, this information would be much harder to determine.

The wolf's other main method of indirect communication, the scent-post system, could also provide information on the number and size of social units. Wolves urinate frequently on various stumps, rocks, and other conspicuous objects as they travel about their range (Chapter III). Often each wolf, or at least each high-ranking male, will squirt his urine on the scent post as he passes. I have also seen where apparently only single members of a pack have urinated on posts along the pack's trail. Such scent posts were only about a hundred yards apart, so probably different members of the pack had marked at different places.

In any case, as long as alien wolves could distinguish individual animals by scent, they could gain some knowledge about the size of each pack. In addition, they could also learn the approximate area traveled by each pack and the frequency with which each pack uses various areas.

There can be no doubt that scent posts have at least some meaning to wolves outside the pack that made them and that they can contribute to an outsider's social stress. The following observation by Jordan *et al.* (1967: 244) illustrates this well: "A single wolf was observed moving west on Lake Desor. It encountered a north-south set of tracks made by the large pack [fifteen] less than 10 hours before. After sniffing these, the animal went to the edge of a small island where the pack had evidently left a scent post. There it sniffed and cowered submissively. It alternated this behavior with short forays out into the open, apparently to scan the lake. After a series of movements suggesting disturbed indecisiveness, the animal resumed its previous course. It crossed the pack's trail at a right angle. While still on the lake, it reacted nervously to three ravens which were swooping low. This was unusual, the wolves being completely accustomed to the close presence of ravens. We then brought the plane down to within 150 feet, and the wolf ran—looking behind as though expecting pursuit from something on the ground. Evidently the noise of the plane added to the animal's uneasy state."

Thus it appears that mechanisms do exist that could directly and indirectly keep each wolf and each pack aware of the number of other social units in and immediately around its range. When the density gets too high in an area, the lone wolves and subordinate packs might become so stressed that they fail to reproduce. Within the more dominant packs, social complications could grow so severe during periods of high density that breeding success would decline to a low point. Through these mechanisms a wolf population could become self-limiting when it grew too dense, whether or not food was in adequate supply.

There is evidence that wolf populations tend to level off at a density of not more than about one wolf per ten square miles. This is the highest density reported from large areas, and it has been found in Jasper Park, Alberta, during winter, on Isle Royale, Michigan, and in Algonquin Park, Ontario (Table 9). In the last two locations, the density has stayed the same for several years despite complete protection from man and despite a food supply that appears to have been adequate (Chapter II).

A density of a least one wolf per three square miles has existed on Coronation Island, Alaska (Merriam, 1964). However, this is a rather special case in that the island is small (thirty square miles in area), the wolves were stocked there, and only a few years have elapsed since the release of the animals. The fact that the initial release of four wolves immediately created an artificially high density (one per 7.5 square miles) further confuses the matter. However, it will be most interesting to watch the outcome of the experiment after a few more years.

Social stress and food supply. In areas where there is not enough vulnerable prey to enable wolves to reach the density of one per ten square miles, social stress could still react with the food factor in helping to limit the population. It was pointed out in the section on malnutrition that, as vulnerable prey grew scarcer, wolf packs would have to travel farther and more often. This would expose them to more indirect signs of neighboring packs, such as scent posts, and would increase their chances of meeting up with one of these packs. Either way, social stress might increase to the point where the smaller or more subordinate packs might fail to breed. Perhaps the dominant packs would even take over the kills made by the smaller packs. If so, the subordinate packs would gradually succumb to a combination of malnutrition, stress, parasitism, and disease.

Even within each pack, social stress would increase as food supplies became scarce because there would be more and more occasions for conflicts. With food scarce, competition would become keener whenever prey was killed. The result would be that the most subordinate members would have to fight severely for their food or accept their status and go hungry. Either alternative could eventually cause a decrease in the population. In addition, the increased psychological stress might also tend to limit the breeding success even of the dominant animals.

In all the above ways, then, "feedback" could take place between food supply and the amount of social stress in the wolf population. Such feedback would allow the natural regulation of wolf numbers in most areas to be accomplished by a combination of food and stress factors. It will take a great deal more research on both captive and wild populations before the accuracy of these speculations is known, however.

Persecution and Exploitation by Man

All the above elements that are detrimental to the wolf are natural ones, and the wolf has evolved along with them and survived in spite of them. Although they may be harmful to individual animals, none of these factors has ever eliminated the species from any extensive regions. None of them has ever threatened to wipe the wolf off the face of the earth. Only the devices of man have been able to do this.

The wolf's predation on livestock was discussed in Chapter X. Suffice it to say here that throughout the settled areas of the world the wolf competed directly with man. It was impossible for the two species to live in high densities in the same areas. Thus man devised a great many methods to deal with the wolf and at present continues to employ his most advanced technology to help eliminate the animal from areas where he believes it to be destructive to his interests.

The topic of wolf control will not be treated in detail here because Young (1944) devoted much of his writings to the subject. He discussed the following devices and methods for capturing the wolf: traps, pits, corrals, deadfalls, the ice box trap, the edge trap, piercers, fishhooks, snares, set guns, steel traps, ring hunts, drives, hamstringing and lassoing, the use of dogs, stalking, den hunting, professional hunting, bountying, and poisoning. To these methods can now be added the technique of hunting wolves from airplanes and helicopters. It should be evident that the wolf was, and in some places still is, a problem and that man has sought a great variety of solutions.

The methods most used for destroying and controlling wolves today are steel trapping, snaring, aerial hunting, and poisoning. These are used mainly by government personnel and private citizens motivated by the payment of bounties from either public or private sources. All these techniques are extremely effective on the wolf when applied intensively both because the wolf travels in packs and because the animals occur in such low densities. When a person wipes out one pack, he may be destroying the entire population of wolves in an area of from fifty to five thousand square miles. Therefore, if public opinion so dictated, man could now exterminate the wolf from the entire earth within a few years using these techniques.

Steel trapping. Steel traps are devices that when triggered cause a set of strong metal jaws to spring around an animal's foot and hold it firmly. The standard size used for wolves is the No. 4½, which has two long springs and a 6¾-inch jaw spread. It is buried lightly near natural or artificial scent posts, around carcasses of large animals, on wolf trails, or in front of small baited holes known as "dirt holes." Wolf urine and/or powerful-smelling scent is often used near the trap. The scent is concocted from one of any number of carefully guarded formulas usually including muskrat glands, beaver castor glands, wolf urine, a touch of skunk musk, oil of rotten fish, and a dash of some kind of tainted brains.

Wolves are generally considered by trappers to be extremely wary and difficult to catch. This is no doubt true where wolves have long been subject to intensive trapping and have seen their packmates caught or have had their own toes pinched lightly. A long list of notorious wolves such as Three Toes, Peg Leg, the Phantom Wolf, and many others earned reputations during the settlement of the United States as possessing almost supernatural qualities allowing them to outwit even the best trappers.

Young (1944: 275) discussed these crafty individuals as follows: "Entire communities sought the renegades by every means, such as the use of dogs, traps, poison baits, or set guns, despite which these wolves often carried on for many years. As these predators were only gaining their subsistence in the manner nature had taught them, they commanded a certain measure of admiration and respect, even from the stockmen who suffered most from their depredations. To that they seemed entitled because of the mental and physical qualities that enabled them to hold their own for so long a period against such overwhelming odds. To terminate their depredations necessitated all of the ability of the most experienced hunters—men thoroughly familiar with more than average wolf psychology and habits. Even they required, at times, many months of hard work to succeed."

However, where wolves have not been trapped recently, they are not considered hard to catch. In Ontario, biologists who trapped the animals to outfit with radio-collars attained a success rate of one capture per fifty trap nights (Kolenosky and Johnston, 1967).

Steel traps have been used on wolves for decades and are still utilized today by individual trappers both in North America and in Eurasia. They are especially effective in autumn, when ground conditions are good for setting them. However, they have the disadvantages of being expensive and heavy, the latter trait making it difficult for trappers in wilderness areas to set large numbers of them. Further, in winter it is hard to keep steel traps operating properly, although the Eskimos in the Brooks Range of Alaska do manage to use them successfully all winter in wind-swept locations (R. L. Rausch, 1967).

Snaring. The disadvantages of the steel trap can be completely overcome by the use of snares. These are made of wire or cable set in a sliding loop and hung along wolf trails or in other areas where one expects a wolf to travel. The wolf accidentally sticks its neck through the snare and chokes itself. Snares are inexpensive, light, simple to set, and easy to keep operating even in cold and snowy weather. During winter, a trapper using a snowmobile can string many hundreds of snares throughout the wolf's range.

Because wolf trails often coincide with local deer trails, however, many deer are also captured in wolf snares.* Trappers usually justify these accidental catches by claiming that for every wolf they kill they actually save a great number of deer. Nevertheless, snaring, although highly effective, is meeting with more and more adverse public opinion, and in Minnesota it has even been outlawed.

Aerial hunting. One of the newer techniques of killing large numbers of wolves involves the use of either fixed-wing aircraft or helicopters. This method is usually limited to periods when snow covers the ground, for it depends a great deal on an aerial hunter's ability to track wolves over long distances. However, because of the efficiency of this technique, large numbers of wolves can be wiped out of a region in just a few weeks of winter hunting.

An aircraft traveling eighty to 120 miles per hour can cover so much territory that on a sunny afternoon it is not unusual for an aerial hunter to come across the tracks of several wolf packs. In wooded areas, the packs usually follow frozen lakes, rivers, and streams, and the wolves are often caught out on these open areas sunning themselves. The usual tactic used by the pilot when wolves are found is to make low passes, herding the animals away from shore. They may then be shot with buckshot at close range either from the air or from the taxiing aircraft. Sometimes individual wolves are chased and harassed until exhausted, making an easier mark for the shooter. Entire packs may be killed off in this way.　·

Aerial hunting was used in Minnesota's northern wilderness areas in the late 1940s, and one hunter killed thirty-eight wolves during his first winter. However, some wolves managed to escape, and these animals quickly learned to avoid open areas when they heard aircraft. According to Stenlund (1955: 34), "In two instances wolves were actually seen to turn and run for the shore before observers heard the plane in the distance. They reappeared and continued their travels on the ice after the plane had passed."

On open tundra areas, aerial hunting is especially deadly to wolves because there is little cover to which the animals can escape. In the Soviet Union, thousands of wolves are destroyed each year by aerial hunting, which is carried out year round in some areas both with airplanes and helicopters (Makridin, 1962). The intent of wolf hunters in that country is to eradicate the wolves from all regions, and this is given official sanction and support from the government (Chapter XII). In fact, contests are even held to encourage each hunter to kill as many wolves as possible (Plotnikov, 1964).

Only a few years ago persecution was also the primary purpose of many aerial wolf hunters in Alaska, but this campaign has now been partly converted into a quest for sport. In 1963, the legislature recognized the wolf as a game animal. It has imposed restrictions on aerial hunting throughout the arctic region of the state, allowing only two wolves per year to be taken from each aircraft (R. A. Rausch, 1964). To many hunters, shooting wolves from an airplane is the ultimate in sport (Fig. 52). To other people, however, the activity is the lowest form of recreation imaginable.

FIGURE 52. Wolf hunting from an aircraft is a favorite sport of some people; others consider it the lowest form of recreation imaginable. (*U. S. Department of the Interior, Fish and Wildlife Service*)

FIGURE 53. In many areas of the world, wolves are still considered vermin and are poisoned in large numbers. Here a poisoned deer carcass, and a number of wolves killed with it, are shown with a lynx also poisoned in the process. (*National Film Board of Canada*)

Poisoning. The use of poison is no doubt the most effective and efficient method of controlling or exterminating wolves (Fig. 53). Past efforts at poisoning have been hampered by inadequate means of distributing poison baits, but this problem has now been over-come by the use of airplanes, helicopters, and snowmobiles. The poisons that have been used most are strychnine, cyanide, fluorine-acetate of barium, and sodium fluoroacetate (compound 1080).

The methods for using poison are the same for all types of com-pounds except cyanide, which is fired from a small gun implanted in the ground. The "getter," as the device is known, is triggered when the wolf chews on the baited end sticking up from the ground, and it blasts the poison into the wolf's mouth. All the other poisons are placed in carcasses or chunks of bait. The latter can then be dropped onto frozen lakes from aircraft.

Even before modern methods of distributing poison were avail-able, the basic technique was very efficient. In the 1800s, the use of strychnine was common over large areas of North America. Young (1944: 335) wrote the following about this era: "Destruc-tion by this strychnine poisoning campaign that covered an em-pire hardly has been exceeded in North America, unless by the slaughter of the passenger pigeon, the buffalo, and the antelope. There was a sort of unwritten law of the range that no cowman would knowingly pass by a carcass of any kind without inserting in it a goodly dose of strychnine sulphate, in the hope of eventually killing one more wolf."

The efficiency of poisoning as a wolf-control technique was demonstrated during a study in Wood Buffalo National Park in the winter of 1951–52. During two periods totalling ten weeks, ap-proximately 70% of the wolf population in the poisoned area was eradicated (Fuller and Novakowski, 1955).

At present, poisoning is still the main method of government wolf control throughout most of Canada; both strychnine and sodium fluoroacetate are used. The stated policy of the government in these programs is generally to bring about control rather than extermination (Pimlott, 1967a).

On the other hand, in Eastern Europe and the U.S.S.R. the goal is eradication, and at least in Russia poison is playing an important role in this program. In 1963, approximately 25% of the 5045 adult wolves killed in that country were taken by fluorine-acetate of barium, according to Plotnikov.

Government programs. All the above methods of wolf control have been used by the governments of the United States, Canada, and the Soviet Union, or their political subdivisions. Generally, hunters, trappers, and poisoners are hired by a government agency and may be on the payroll year round or merely temporarily. At present the governments of most of the Canadian provinces employ professional wolf-control personnel. In the U.S.S.R. wolf eradication is the duty of many professionals, plus approximately eleven thousand amateur hunters aided and encouraged by the government (Plotnikov, 1964). Official programs of wolf control in Alaska are now confined to the domestic reindeer ranges (R. A. Rausch, 1964).

Bounties. Money or other valuable tender, such as livestock, paid for the killing of animals is known as a bounty. Bounties have been paid on wolves for at least 2700 years, and in the United States they were begun as early as 1630, in Massachusetts (Young, 1944). The payment of bounties has provided much of the motivation for private citizens to use the methods described above for killing wolves. Bounties are usually paid by federal, state, or local governments, but they have also been offered by various special-interest groups such as livestock organizations. Up to $150 per wolf killed has been paid, and during the settlement of the United States, many professional "wolfers" lived off wolf bounties.

In general the bounty system is an ineffective and inefficient method of reducing, controlling, or eliminating a species, and millions of dollars have been wasted through bounty payments (Allen, 1962). However, when payments are high, capture techniques efficient, and the density of the species to be bountied low, bounties may be effective. One of the very few animals to which these conditions sometimes apply is the wolf. In certain areas, particularly on the edges of the wolf's range or where the range is limited, the bounty could be a significant factor in reducing a wolf population.

The bounty system merits special consideration in a discussion of factors harmful to the wolf because it alone possesses self-perpetuating properties aside from any influence it might have on wolf numbers. Thus whether or not wolves need to be controlled in a certain area, the bounty system tends to persist once it has been begun. Whether or not bounties are even controlling wolves, they continue to be paid.

The reason that bounties tend to perpetuate themselves is that they can become a strong political tool. Through the bounty system, any citizen can obtain money from the government by killing an animal on which the bounty is paid. The killing can even be accidental such as in the case of the fourteen wolves hit by cars and submitted for bounty during one year in Ontario (DeVos, 1949). Or it can occur in conjunction with such sports as hunting and trapping. This means that any sportsman operating in wolf range has at least a chance of collecting a "prize" from the government. Such a program has wide appeal.

If a legislator can couple such an appeal with a claim that wolves are destructive to human beings, livestock, and game populations, he has an attractive vote-producing gimmick. This is especially useful to legislators representing people on the fringes of wilderness areas because of two main reasons. First, some of these people are more in need of supplementary income, which the bounty can provide; second, there are relatively few spectacular and important issues that can project the representative from such an area into the headlines.

Thus if the legislator can turn the bounty battle into a feud between the "outstaters" and the urbanites (who usually are much less in favor of bounties), he suddenly becomes the Defender of His People. A dash of behind-the-scenes vote swapping with urban legislators can squeeze the bounty program through the legislature and complete the recipe for keeping the outstate representative in office. All this is aside from whether or not the bounty is necessary or useful.

In a similar way, the bounty issue has also been beneficial to other publicity-seeking individuals. Durward L. Allen expressed it this way in his book *Our Wildlife Legacy* (1962: 276): "Unfortunately the bounty is well adapted to the needs of the poorly informed, politically minded administrator or the table-pounding fireball in a sportsman's club. It is likely to be used, and once it is entrenched, the profits enlist loyal supporters."

However, despite the powerful political advantages of the bounty system, its shortcomings as a tool of wildlife management have gradually become apparent to the public. Sportsmen, who often foot the entire bill for bounties, have seen through the system and have begun to object. At present, states, provinces, and other governmental divisions that still maintain a bounty system are generally regarded as backward. Only Alaska, Ontario, Quebec, and the Northwest Territories still pay bounties on wolves, although certain elements in Minnesota are attempting to restore the system in that state.

CHAPTER XII / FUTURE OF THE WOLF

The wolf is a strong, sensitive, intelligent animal with complex social behavior and lasting family ties. It has a tendency to travel long distances and to seek out vulnerable big-game animals that it can kill and eat with enough safety and efficiency to maintain its species. All the while, the wolf is subject to any number of stresses from its environment, and must constantly contend with forces tending to suppress its numbers. With minor variations in this mode of living, the wolf has survived and evolved for millions of years in a variety of habitats throughout most of the Northern Hemisphere.

But a new force has now suddenly arisen on the earth, a force that could quickly snuff out the unique flame of life that is the wolf's. This is the expansive force of the human population, with its aggressive tendency to occupy all of the planet in high densities and to overcome or destroy anything that might stand in its way. At present it is not evident whether this force will continue relentlessly or whether reason will prevail in time to check it and to prevent the destruction of all areas that still remain unpopulated.

Whenever "modern" man has populated new regions in the Northern Hemisphere, one of his first actions has been to wipe out the wolf. In place of the real animal, man has substituted myths, tales, and legends. These might help him rationalize his actions, but they also symbolize the artificiality of his own life as opposed to the naturalness of the original life in the area. Thus the persistence of the wolf in certain regions today is a sensitive indicator of the naturalness of those areas.

Many people now believe that it is time to halt the destruction of the remaining natural wilderness. They feel it is healthy for humanity to preserve certain sections of the earth just as they evolved. To those of us who share this view, the continued existence of the wolf in the future will be a measure of man's rationality.

Aside from the fact that the wolf is part of the dwindling wilderness which should be preserved for future generations, the animal itself has certain other values that also argue strongly for sparing the species. Nevertheless, the present status of the wolf throughout the world certainly is not encouraging, and its future does not look bright. Fortunately there is still time left to rescue the species from its plight. Whether or not this is done depends on man's knowledge of the ecology and behavior of the wolf, his continued research into the ways of the wolf, and his learning to think of the wolf not as a competitor but as a fellow creature with which the earth must be shared.

Value of the Wolf

To some people the mere existence of any species has a certain value because it is an example of one more interesting way in which life can be organized. The wolf, of course, must be of more interest to people than are most living things, for it is referred to often in everyday expressions, in stories, legends, articles, and laws.

However, the wolf is far more than a mere biological curiosity. It is a significant part of the natural community, and in at least some areas is a crucial part of the community. It is also an important subject for the study of various principles of ecology, psychology, and sociology. In addition, the wolf is of considerable esthetic value to sportsmen, nature lovers, and wilderness enthusiasts.

The wolf and the biological community. Biological communities that last for long periods generally reach relatively stable states in which various elements of each community become adjusted to each other. If they did not, the community would continue to change until such adjustments did take place. Regulating mechanisms even develop within them that tend to maintain the stability when the elements of the community fluctuate in numbers or degree of influence. The stability of biological communities usually allows each species in the system to live efficiently and in relative harmony and equilibrium with the others even though all constantly compete for energy from the same basic sources.

Any sudden drastic change or removal of an element of the community will disrupt these adjustments. The greater the change and the more significant the element that changes, the more disruption there will be in the entire system. Expected results of substantial changes would include: (1) a sudden takeover of a few species to the detriment of several others, (2) decreased efficiency and vigor of some species, (3) greater fluctuations in the numbers of various species, and (4) a decrease in the general stability of the community.

The wolf is an important element in the biological community of which it is a part, and as such it is adjusted to the other members of the system, and they to it. The basic elements of the community in which the wolf is most important can be classified very grossly as (1) vegetation, (2) large plant eaters, and (3) the wolf. Under natural conditions, these three elements tend to remain in relative stability and equilibrium. In Isle Royale National Park, the wolf functions as a control on the numbers and quality of moose, which feed on the vegetation. As a result the wolves, the moose, and the vegetation thrive in apparent stability (Mech, 1966a). It seems significant that Isle Royale supports a higher density of both wolves and moose than does any other large area for which figures are available.

The present situation on Isle Royale contrasts dramatically to that of earlier years when the wolf was not present in the island community (Chapter IX). It also differs markedly from the situation in other U.S. national parks such as Yellowstone in Wyoming. There wolves were exterminated long ago. Now great herds of elk ravage the vegetation, starve periodically, and cause bitter public controversy over the manner in which man should substitute for the wolf as a mortality factor.

Another area in which the ecological differences can be seen between biological communities that include and exclude the wolf is southeast Alaska. Klein and Olson (1960: 87) compared wolf-free areas there with areas containing wolves, and although they cautioned that other factors might be involved, they wrote the following: "The characteristics which as a general rule are unique to deer populations and ranges in those areas where wolves are absent are: stable or slowly increasing populations in excess of the winter range capacity, heavy winter mortality, and severely deteriorated winter ranges. In contrast, the typical characteristics of ranges to the southeast supporting both deer and wolves are: rapidly increasing deer populations, light winter mortality from starvation, and winter ranges in fair to good condition. The wolf-populated ranges, as a general rule, during the period of the study supported a greater annual hunter harvest of deer per unit of area under comparable hunting pressure."

As seen in Chapter IX, there are areas where wolves apparently are not controlling herds of big game at present. However, this lack of controlling ability may well be the result of upsets in the biological community caused by man's cutting and burning of the vegetation.

In addition to controlling or helping to control numbers of large plant-eaters, the wolf also tends to cull out prey animals that are the least healthy and vigorous and those that are the most poorly adapted for survival (Chapters VIII and IX). By doing this, it helps ensure the stability of the community far into the future.

The significant contributions of the wolf to the stability of natural communities cited above are of sufficient value that on these grounds alone man should spare the wolf from extinction wherever the animal does not seriously conflict with livestock interests.

The wolf and scientific research. Another value of the wolf is as a subject for research. Just as the white rat has aided in the study of psychology, the wolf has become important in investigations of the ecology of natural communities and especially of the principles of predation and big-game population dynamics. Results of this research helps man understand the mechanics of the interactions between animals and their environment, an understanding that is gaining in significance as man becomes increasingly concerned about his own environment.

Scientists are also finding the wolf of considerable interest to studies of sociology and behavior. Research on the animal's ability to form emotional attachments, on its social order, and on its complex patterns of expression and communication contribute to the general understanding of individual and social behavior. Advances in these fields of study cannot help but be of value to man.

Recent increased scientific interest in the wolf culminated in the sponsoring of a "Wolf Symposium" in August 1966 by the Animal Behavior Society, the Ecological Society of America, and the American Society of Zoologists. An entire day was devoted to the presentation of reports on wolf research by scientists from England, Canada, Finland, Switzerland, and the United States, and these reports were published in the May 1967 issue of *American Zoologist*.

Sporting and aesthetic values of the wolf. Ever since the woodsman slew the wolf that gobbled up Little Red Riding Hood's grandmother, men have considered the slaughter of a wolf to be an indication of prowess and masculinity. Even today, many a hunter would rather bag a wolf than a deer, and some people pay high prices to hire an airplane and pilot for a wolf-hunting expedition. The state of Alaska has even begun imposing regulations on the taking of wolves in certain areas. In addition, *Outdoor Life,* a national sporting magazine, has suggested classifying the wolf as a game animal throughout North America, thereby helping to protect the species from overexploitation (Bauer, 1968).

Trophies from a successful wolf hunt can be the mounted head of the wolf (with all forty-two teeth bared menacingly) or a wolfskin rug. The latter is extremely beautiful, and many people pay a hundred dollars or more to purchase one.

Even more beautiful than a wolfskin rug is the general appearance of a live wolf in its winter coat. Acquaintances of mine who had little or no experience with wild animals were continually amazed at the beauty of my pet female, Lightning, lying majestically on the snow in our backyard. There can be no doubt that, if these same people could see a wild wolf on a snow-covered lake surrounded by spruces and birches, they would be even more impressed by its beauty.

Although the beauty of the wolf is one reason that people may want to catch a glimpse of the animal in its natural surroundings, there are several other reasons. Because the wolf is such a rare animal, is so shy and sensitive to disturbance by man, and leads such a dynamic and dramatic life, many people consider the sight of one to be the highlight of their outdoor experiences. They often choose the location for a camping trip on the basis of whether or not there is a possibility of seeing a wolf.

Unfortunately the sight of a wolf in the wild is rare indeed, and only a small percentage of the people who would like to see the animal ever do so. However, the next best outdoor experience for these people is hearing wolves howl, and this is much more possible.

Wolf howling can usually be heard for a mile or more, and many hunters and campers have listened to it. Even people with little outdoor experience appreciate hearing the wild chorus.

Thanks to studies by Pimlott in Ontario, it has been found feasible in certain areas to stimulate wolves into howling. The method is to broadcast recordings of wolves howling or merely to imitate the howling by voice. If wolves are nearby, they often will reply. This technique has been exploited for the public with great success in Algonquin Provincial Park, Ontario. There park naturalists lead convoys of up to a hundred cars and six hundred people at a time down a lonely road into wolf country for an evening "wolf howl."

Pimlott (1967a: 42) wrote the following about such an event: "When finally wolves are located and the pack begins to howl, excitement is high and shivers run rampant up and down the spines of the listeners. . . . Almost inevitably the silence that follows the end of the howling of the pack is suddenly broken by an intense babble of the voices of people all talking together, excitedly sharing the thrill of a superb wilderness experience. Almost inevitably too, disinterest fades and people begin to understand why man should always be prepared to share his environment with creatures of nature."

Such a personal interest in the wolf is a relatively new phenomenon, and it is growing rapidly. Besides the wolf-howling program at Algonquin Park, several other factors have promoted this interest among the general public. Lois Crisler's excellent book *Arctic Wild,* describing her adventures in raising a couple of litters of free-ranging wolves on the tundra, was published in 1958. Adolph Murie's *A Naturalist in Alaska,* recounting in detail his experiences with wild wolves, appeared in 1963. That same year an article in *National Geographic* (Allen and Mech, 1963) featuring the Isle Royale wolf studies also reached numbers of people. Jerome Hellmuth's *A Wolf in the Family* was published in 1964, and it related the true story of a tame wolf raised by a family in Seattle. *The World of the Wolf,* by R. J. Rutter and D. H. Pimlott, released in 1968, provided a factual popular account of the wolf's life history and included numerous beautiful photos of the animal.

One other book on the wolf that has been widely read was Farley Mowat's *Never Cry Wolf,* published in 1963. Even reading clubs and discussion groups, including individuals who have no particular interest in animals or the outdoors, have used the book in their programs. Indeed, the wolf that the reading public seems to know best at present is that portrayed by Mowat.

Never Cry Wolf differs, however, from the works mentioned previously. Whereas the other books and articles were based strictly on facts and the experiences of the authors, Mowat's seems to be basically fiction founded somewhat on fact. It appears to have been compounded of his own limited adventures with wild wolves plus a generous quantity of unacknowledged experiences of other authors; a certain amount of imagination and embellishment probably completed the formula for the book.

Although *Never Cry Wolf* does present a somewhat different view of the wolf than that seen by the scientist, it has served to stir the public from its apathy regarding the plight of the wolf. In this respect it offsets the effects of the classic "Little Red Riding Hood."

If the reviews by Banfield (1964) in *The Canadian Field Naturalist* and Pimlott (1966) in the *Journal of Wildlife Management* are consulted before one reads *Never Cry Wolf,* a more realistic view of the wolf will result. The only substantial harm caused by the book comes when these reviews go unread and the work becomes accepted by other writers as fact and is cited as documentation for theories on natural phenomena, as was done in Robert Ardrey's *Territorial Imperative* (1966).

In addition to the popular literature recently published about the wolf, the sudden increase in scientific publications about the animal has also stimulated public interest in the species. Newspapers, popular magazines, and television have all recently presented features on the present status of the wolf in North America.

The net result of all the sympathetic publicity is that an increasing number of people have come to appreciate the wolf as a symbol of the wilderness; an unwitting agent of nature's complex processes; a beautiful beast, shy and strong, wild and free. To these people the wolf is of considerable aesthetic value, and if it had no other worth at all, they would fight to preserve it on these grounds alone. They even feel that their right to enjoy the wolf should deserve as much consideration as the big-game hunter's right to enjoy his sport.

Present Status of the Wolf

At present the wolf's status in the world is highly uncertain. In a few locations the animal is protected from all human interference, but in most regions it is persecuted vindictively and unmercifully.

Most of the areas where the wolf is completely protected today are national parks. In the United States this protection is incidental to the general protectionist policy for all wildlife in the parks. However, only two national parks, Isle Royale and Mount McKinley, are known to harbor resident wolf populations, although Glacier (Martinka, 1967) and Yellowstone (Cole, 1968) may still support a few animals.

In Canada, the wolf has been protected in Algonquin Provincial Park since 1959. In Alaska, it was also legally protected in Game Management Unit 13 and part of 14, a total of twenty thousand square miles (R. A. Rausch, 1967a). However, because of the size of the protected area, enforcement was difficult, and a heavy illegal kill resulted. In 1967, a regulated annual kill of three hundred wolves was being allowed there.

The state of Wisconsin placed the wolf under legal protection in 1957, but it was already too late, for the species is now considered extinct there (Keener, 1967). A few individuals may occasionally wander back and forth from Michigan's Upper Peninsula, where an estimated twelve to twenty wolves are thought to remain (Steuwer, 1968); these animals were given legal protection in Michigan in 1965.

The only substantial population of wolves in the contiguous forty-eight states occurs in Minnesota, and there the future legal status of the animal is especially uncertain. Until 1965 a thirty-five-dollar bounty was maintained on the species, and from 1952 to 1965, an annual take of 122 to 252 animals was reported, an average of 188 per year (Anonymous, 1967a). Such a consistent annual kill did not seem to decrease the population.

In 1965 the Minnesota legislature again passed a bounty bill, but Governor Karl F. Rolvaag vetoed the appropriations for it. During 1967 a bounty bill reached Governor Harold LeVander's desk. However, due to a technicality the bill had to be recalled and amended; it then repassed the House, but in the Senate it lost by a tie vote. A concerted attempt to reintroduce the bill, involving considerable bargaining, failed.

During the 1969 legislative session, a bill providing an outright bounty was soundly defeated in both houses, but a modified bounty was restored. Its main thrust is against coyotes, which sometimes prey on sheep in the northwestern part of the state, but it also includes provisions against wolves. A clause that may be the most significant in the act (H. F. 2286) follows:

"The [conservation] commissioner shall specify the county or other defined area in which the predator control activities are to be conducted, the objectives to be achieved, payments to be made, and he shall approve the methods to be used. All of the controllers shall cease their activities when the objective is achieved or when so directed by the commissioner."

This act differs considerably from an outright bounty in that the bounty is paid indiscriminately for long durations and over a large area, whereas the new act allows the Conservation Department to designate (1) specific areas where predator control may be necessary, (2) the methods to be used, (3) the payments to be made (within the limits of twenty-five to sixty dollars per wolf), (4) the individual agents who can collect the bounty, and (5) the duration of the control program. Although such a plan does not seem as desirable as one involving salaried control agents hired for specific predator problems, it is far better than an outright bounty.

At this writing (1969) the wolf is neither protected nor persecuted in Minnesota. Some wolves are still taken by trappers and deer hunters, but without a price on their heads throughout large areas of their range the Minnesota wolves probably will not be in serious danger. No one knows how many wolves remain in the state. Estimates are sometimes given, but after conducting field work involving many hours of winter flying in northern Minnesota, I do not believe that enough data have yet accumulated to allow an accurate estimate. At this time all one can say is that there are still many packs of wolves throughout the north-central and northeastern part of the state, in much the same areas as reported by Stenlund in 1955.

In Mexico, where wolves are also considered in danger of extinction, they are legally protected in all states except Sonora and Chihuahau, but their numbers are still decreasing (Chapter I).

Except for the areas discussed above, the wolf is either extinct or subject to intensive persecution throughout the rest of the world (Chapters X and XI). Bounties of fifty dollars per wolf are paid in Alaska, thirty-five dollars in Quebec, forty dollars in the Northwest Territories, and twenty-five dollars in Ontario. In the spring of 1967 a great deal of unsuccessful political pressure was brought to bear on the Ontario legislature to double the bounty payments and to conduct poisoning campaigns against the wolf. Both strychnine and sodium fluoroacetate (1080) are still used for wolf control throughout much of Canada.

The Canadian control campaign was explained by Pimlott (1961) and by Kelsall (1968). The primary goal of the governement in attempting wolf control is to help prevent a continuing decrease in the numbers of Canada's caribou. Great herds of these animals in northern Canada have been seriously reduced by human hunting in recent years.

Man is considered to be the major predator on the endangered caribou herds, and wolves are thought to take only about 5% of the population (Banfield, 1954). Nevertheless, government authorities believe that wolf control might in some way help stop the caribou decline. So from 1954 through 1958, approximately two thousand wolves were killed each year in the Northwest Territories alone (Kelsall, 1968). By 1960, the kill had dropped to less than a thousand, and control programs were reduced.

In Eastern Europe and in the Soviet Union, a "Great War on Wolves" is currently being fought. In 1963, 17,600 men were employed on the wolf-extermination program in Russia alone, and each year courses and seminars are held to teach the most effective methods of destroying wolves (Plotnikov, 1964). Poisoning, trapping, den destruction, and aerial hunting are the main methods used.

The effectiveness of the antiwolf campaign in the U.S.S.R. can be seen in the annual kill figures reported by Plotnikov. Since 1946, when approximately 42,600 wolves were destroyed, the kill has declined steadily until in 1963 only 8800 animals were taken. This era in Russian history corresponds with the period of about 1915 to 1935 in the history of the United States, when the federal government wiped out the wolf from most of the country (Young, 1944).

The status of the red wolf of the southeastern United States is most precarious. Only in a few restricted areas of Texas and Louisiana are these creatures known to survive, no doubt in dangerously low numbers (Chapter I). They are still being trapped and hunted indiscriminately (Pimlott and Joslin, 1968).

Future Outlook for the Wolf

It is possible that in Europe and Asia certain reservations might be set aside in which numbers of wolves may be allowed to live under protection or limited harvest. No sign of such a program is yet evident, but hopefully the more farsighted people, including scientists interested in the wolf for study, will soon begin to urge a new policy for the species.

In Canada, it appears that this type of progress is taking place at present. Pimlott (1967a: 40) wrote the following: "There is some evidence of changing attitudes. In large remote areas wolf control programs have now become more moderate and the stated policy of most governments in Canada is to exercise control where it is needed but not to exterminate wolves. In addition, support for wolf preservation appears to be developing quite rapidly." If this trend continues, it is possible that wolves may remain a valuable part of the Canadian wilderness for decades to come.

The future outlook for the wolf in most of the United States is serious. In Alaska it does appear that with continual effort the animal can be saved for many years, at least in certain areas. The few wolves found in Michigan's Isle Royale National Park and possibly in Montana's Glacier National Park might also be preserved. In the rest of the United States the wolf is either extinct or in possible danger of becoming so. The last dozen or so wolves remaining on the Michigan mainland probably will disappear soon, just as Wisconsin's did. This leaves northern Minnesota as the only area in which a significant population of wolves might be spared.

Recognizing this grave situation, the U. S. Department of the Interior has listed the wolf as an "endangered species" in the forty-eight contiguous states. Such a classification helps focus attention on the serious plight of the wolf and should stimulate the granting of funds to carry out research aimed at saving the species. One of the first objectives of this research should be an accurate inventory of the wolves present in both Michigan and Minnesota and the extent of their range and movements. The second step should include an assessment of the effects of the wolf on domestic and game animals in those areas. Based on the results of these studies, recommendations should then be made about the proper method of managing and maintaining the wolf population.

Future comprehensive studies of the wolves in northern Minnesota will have a good base from which to begin. Milt Stenlund conducted studies of the wolf in the Superior National Forest from 1946 through 1953 and published the results in 1955. Since 1966 L. D. Frenzel, Jr. and I have been engaged in wolf studies in the same area, under the auspices of Macalester College, and are greatly impressed with the potential for continued productive investigations (Frenzel and Mech, 1967; Mech and Frenzel, 1969).

The Endangered Species Preservation Act of 1966 provides for research on endangered animals, and in addition it allows for their legal protection on all federal lands. This is especially pertinent in the case of the wolf, for in Minnesota almost half of the major wolf range lies in the Superior National Forest. If necessary, the U. S. Government could prohibit the taking of wolves in that entire area.

However, because of local political sentiment, it would be better for the wolf, for the federal government, and for the state government for protection of the wolf to come from the state level rather than the federal. In this respect the recent actions of the Minnesota State Legislature are not entirely discouraging. The proposed bounty bill in 1967 contained a prohibition against the payment of bounties on any animals taken in the "No-cut Zone" of the Boundary Waters Canoe Area (about 600,000 acres) within the Superior National Forest. In 1969, the defeated bounty bill contained a provision to protect the wolf in the northeastern one-fifth of its Minnesota range.

It is true that these provisions would have been very difficult to enforce. Nevertheless, the gesture on the part of the bills' sponsors was significant. In part, the special prohibitions no doubt were motivated by an effort to make the bill acceptable to more legislators. However, from watching the actions on the bills both in committees and on the floor and from talking with the bills' supporters, I am convinced that even some of the advocates of the bounty recognized the value of preserving the wolf.

For the next several years attempts to restore an outright bounty on the wolf can be expected in Minnesota. The usual unfounded arguments about wolves being dangerous and harming deer hunting (Chapter X) can also be anticipated. No doubt some bounty proponents will even continue to drag in the carcasses of frozen wolves during each legislative session, pose with them on the steps of the state capitol building, and exhibit the teeth of these "vicious predators" during committee hearings.

However, as an increasing number of years go by during which wolves are not bountied, more and more people will see that the predators have not wiped out the deer herd or even hurt deer hunting. Gradually the many values of the wolf discussed above will become apparent to more Minnesotans. Hopefully then an increasing number of individuals and organizations will follow the lead of the Minnesota Izaak Walton League, the Minnesota Conservation Federation, the Natural History Society, the Minnesota Wildlife Society, the Sierra Club, and the United Northern Sportsmen's Clubs in opposing a wolf bounty.

It should be pointed out here that bounties usually do not cause a permanent reduction in the numbers of most species. Rather they seem merely to substitute for natural mortality. Certainly the fact that a consistent number of wolves were being bountied each year in Minnesota showed that the breeding population was not being seriously cut into. In other words, hunters and trappers were only substituting for nature.

However, because wolves occur in such low densities, travel in packs, and have a relatively low reproductive rate, bounties could effectively reduce or eliminate them under certain circumstances. A high price on the wolf's head, a return to the practice of snaring, and the increased use of snowmobiles to help trappers penetrate the wilderness would all contribute to the success of a wolf bounty.

Therefore, if an outright bounty is restored on wolves in Minnesota, the federal government should keep close watch on the results. If there is any sign that the breeding population of wolves is being reduced, steps should be taken to protect the animals, even if this means prohibiting the taking of wolves on all federal land in the state. This can be justified in the same way that the preservation of other interesting natural phenomena, such as Grand Canyon, is justified. In a sense both Grand Canyon and the wolves of the Superior National Forest belong to all the people of the country rather than to just the citizens living near them.

One can easily envision the day when numbers of people from various parts of the country may wish to see wild wolves or hear them howl. It is evident that Pimlott (1967a: 43) foresaw this day when he wrote the following: "In North America a vast array of people are seeking opportunities to study nature in new, less traditional ways. This is evidenced by nature tours across the country and around the world. Similarly, areas like Algonquin Park and the Superior National Forest could attract thousands of people who wish to travel in a wilderness where there are wolves, with the objective of hearing and even seeing them. Once trapping and hunting is discontinued wolves adapt to the presence of people. It would not take long for people offering guiding service or conducting tours to determine the most favorable locations for wolf listening, and as the word spread interest would increase rapidly. If wolf listening became popular as a nature experience, the image of the wolf would undergo a rapid transformation. Before long the U. S. National Park Service would be encouraged to re-introduce wolves into Yellowstone National Park and in Canada they would be re-introduced to Banff and Jasper National Parks."

Fortunately there are many places throughout the world where wolves could still be live-trapped for restocking in other areas. This is not true for the peculiar creature of Louisiana and Texas known as the red wolf, however. Whether the animal is truly a separate species or is a fertile hybrid between wolf and coyote (Chapter I), the fact remains that it lives in only one tiny part of the world.

Although the red wolf has now also been added to the list of endangered species, it is not legally protected and is even still being trapped, according to Pimlott and Joslin. These authors have suggested that immediate steps be taken to capture some of the remaining red wolves and breed them in captivity. Meanwhile, other programs can be started to preserve or re-establish the species in certain parts of its native habitat. This plan seems to be the only hope for the red wolf at present.

A Plea for the Wolf

In 1944, Stanley Young concluded his section of *The Wolves of North America* (1944: 385) with the statement that "there still remain, even in the United States, some areas of considerable size in which we feel that both the red and gray species, in their respective habitats, may be allowed to continue their existence with little molestation." Since that time those remaining areas have shrunk considerably, and so has the wolf population.

At present, wolves in the United States, excluding Alaska, are confined to wilderness areas where there is little conflict with livestock interest. Therefore there appears to be no valid reason that these interesting animals cannot be allowed to continue living their lives in these areas much as they have for millions of years. The same is true for certain primitive areas of Alaska, Canada, Europe, and Asia. Whether or not wolves *are* permitted to survive in these areas depends completely on the attitudes of the public.

Unfortunately there still exists in certain segments of human society an attitude that any animal (except man) that kills another is a murderer. To these people, the wolf is a most undesirable creature. "They're all dirty killers," is the way one Minnesota state representative expressed this attitude.

Once blinded emotionally by such hate, the antiwolf people fail to see that the wolf has no choice about the way it lives; that it cannot thrive on grass or twigs any more than man can. To them the wolf pack is a cowardly assemblage of wanton slayers, the animal's howl a bloodcurdling condemnation of all the innocent big game in the country.

These people cannot be changed. If the wolf is to survive, the wolf haters must be outnumbered. They must be outshouted, outfinanced, and outvoted. Their narrow and biased attitude must be outweighed by an attitude based on an understanding of natural processes. Finally their hate must be outdone by a love for the whole of nature, for the unspoiled wilderness, and for the wolf as a beautiful, interesting, and integral part of both.

It is my fervent hope that the preceding pages will contribute to the growth of this feeling.

APPENDIX A / SUBSPECIES OF
WOLVES

The problem of classifying various species of animals into geographic subspecies is much greater than the problem of distinguishing species. This is because most species differ markedly from each other in several important respects, and generally they do not interbreed. However, subspecies do interbreed. Thus there is often a complete blending of differences in the traits considered significant in telling subspecies apart.

Another difficulty is that large numbers of specimens of both sexes and of various ages from the same general area must be studied to really separate subspecies. However, in many cases, subspecies have been described from only a few specimens.

Even the criteria used in drawing subspecific distinctions are more or less arbitrary. With wolves, pelage and skeletal characters have been relied on almost exclusively, even though these may not be of any integral importance. Until recently, moreover, these characters have been compared singly rather than as a part of a group. However, as Pierre Jolicoeur (1959: 285) has demonstrated, "groups of organisms may be entirely distinct with respect to several characters jointly and yet overlap with respect to every one of the same characters separately."

Because of these problems, authorities often disagree on wolf classification, as pointed out in Chapter I. No doubt as the study of classification, or taxonomy, progresses, improvements in methods will be made. Jolicoeur has already paved the way by applying the technique of multivariate statistical analysis to measurements of five hundred wolf skulls from Alaska and northwestern Canada. This consideration of groups of characters has led him to conclude that probably far too many subspecific designations are now in use.

In the future, not only will more refined statistical techniques be used in taxonomy, but probably differences in chromosomal structure and composition, in blood plasma proteins, and in behavior will become significant factors in classifying wolves. Until that time, however, authorities will continue to disagree, and the total number of subspecies of wolves recognized will continue to vary according to the authority.

In listing and discussing the following subspecies of wolves, I have relied on the latest and most comprehensive references: R. I. Pocock's "The Races of *Canis lupus*" (1935); E. A. Goldman's *Classification of Wolves* (1944); J. R. Ellerman and T. C. S. Morrison-Scott's *Checklist of Palaearctic and Indian Mammals* (1951); G. A. Novikov's *Carnivorous Mammals of the Fauna of the U.S.S.R.* (1956); and E. R. Hall and

K. R. Kelson's *The Mammals of North America* (1959). The full synonymy of the subspecies can be found in those works, and the geographic distribution of each subspecies can be seen in Figs. 7 and 8.

Subspecies of Wolves in North America

1. *Canis lupus alces* Goldman, 1941. Kennai Peninsula wolf. This Alaskan subspecies is know only from skulls, but these skulls indicate that it is one of the largest North American wolves. Goldman (1944) believed that its large size may be an adaptation resulting from the animal's dependence on the very large moose of the Kennai. In order to complete the description of *C. l. alces* and determine the validity of the subspecies, it is imperative that a collection of skins and skulls be made from the Kennai Peninsula and studied.

2. *C. l. arctos* Pocock, 1935. Melville Island wolf. *C. l. arctos* is known to occur only on the arctic islands from Melville Island to Ellesmere Island. Pocock described it on the basis of two skulls, and Goldman examined one skull and one skin. On the basis of these specimens, the animal is said to be white and of medium size.

3. *C. l. baileyi* Nelson and Goldman, 1929. Mexican wolf. This is the smallest North American wolf and the most southern in geographic distribution. It inhabits the Sierra Madre and surrounding region of western Mexico and originally extended northward into the southeastern United States. It is generally dark and grizzly in color.

4. *C. l. beothucus* G. M. Allen and Barbour, 1937. Newfoundland wolf. The Newfoundland wolf, now extinct, was almost pure white and of medium size. Only four skulls and one skin are all that are known to be left to represent this animal (Goldman, 1944).

5. *C. l. bernardi* Anderson, 1943. Banks Island tundra wolf. This subspecies is known only from Banks Island in the Northwest Territories but may also occur on Victoria Island. It is described as a large rangy wolf, mostly white but with black-tipped hairs along the mid-length of the back.

6. *C. l. columbianus* Goldman, 1941. British Columbia wolf. *C. l. columbianus* occurs throughout most of British Columbia. It is a large wolf, variable in color but generally dark and grizzled; it sometimes occurs in a black color phase.

7. *C. l. crassodon* Hall, 1932. Vancouver Island wolf. This is a medium-sized, grayish-black wolf from Vancouver Island.

8. *C. l. fuscus* Richardson, 1839. Cascade Mountains wolf. The Cascade Mountains wolf, a medium-large animal, was once known as the "brown wolf" because of its basically cinnamon or buffy color. If it still survives today, its range would be restricted to southwestern British Columbia.

9. *C. l. hudsonicus* Goldman, 1941. Hudson Bay wolf. According to Goldman (1944: 428), this is "a light-colored subspecies of medium size; winter pelage nearly white. . . ." It is a "tundra wolf" inhabiting the area west and north of Hudson Bay but apparently migrating south with caribou herds into the described range for *C. l. griseoalbus* Baird, 1858, a "timber wolf" (Kelsall, 1968).

10. *C. l. griseoalbus* Baird, 1858. Goldman (1944: 395) did not recognize this subspecies, stating the following: "[Baird] seems to have entertained a somewhat composite concept of a widely ranging race varying in color

from 'pure white to grizzled gray.' No type was mentioned, and the name does not appear to be valid or clearly assignable to the synonymy of any particular race." However, Hall and Kelson considered this subspecies valid, citing a later paper by Baird and mentioning a type specimen from Cumberland House, Saskatchewan. They depict its range as being primarily in central Manitoba and northern Saskatchewan.

11. *C. l. irremotus* Goldman, 1937. Northern Rocky Mountain wolf. This is a medium-large, light-buff-colored animal that once occurred in the northern Rocky Mountains including southern Alberta. In the United States it is thought to be extinct, although recent reports of a few wolves in Glacier Park, Montana, might be of animals of this subspecies.

12. *C. l. labradorius* Goldman, 1937. Labrador wolf. Varying in color from dark gray to almost white, this medium-sized wolf occurs throughout northern Quebec and Labrador.

13. *C. l. ligoni* Goldman, 1937. Alexander Archipelago wolf. *C. l. ligoni* is smaller, darker, and shorter-haired than the other subspecies from northwestern North America; a black phase is common. The animal inhabits southeastern Alaska, including the Alexander Archipelago.

14. *C. l. lycaon* Schreber, 1775. Eastern wolf. This wolf originally had the most extensive range of all North American subspecies, extending throughout eastern North America from Hudson Bay southward to Florida and westward into Minnesota and eastern Manitoba. It still remains in Ontario, Quebec, northern Minnesota, and northern Michigan. The usual color of the animal is grizzly gray, but in northern Minnesota I have seen one wolf pack containing three black-phase individuals and two grays, and another composed of one black wolf, one creamy-white animal, and three grays. The Eastern wolf is one of the smallest subspecies, and if, as has been suggested (Chapter I), the so-called "red wolf" is really a hybrid between the wolf and the coyote, it would be this subspecies (*C. l. lycaon*) of wolf that is involved.

15. *C. l. mackenzii* Anderson, 1943. Mackenzie tundra wolf. Although *C. l. mackenzii* is a medium-sized animal, it is smaller than most of the wolves of the subspecies adjacent to it. Its color ranges from black to white, but buff or white individuals are most common. The range of this wolf is along the arctic coast in the Northwest Territories eastward from the Mackenzie River and south to Great Bear Lake.

16. *C. l. manningi* Anderson, 1943. Baffin Island tundra wolf. This is the smallest arctic wolf, and is generally white or lighter-colored. It occurs on Baffin Island and probably the nearby surrounding islands.

17. *C. l. mogollonensis* Goldman, 1937. Mogollon Mountain wolf. No doubt this wolf is now extinct; it formerly occurred in central Arizona and New Mexico. Members of the subspecies were small and usually dark, although some were almost white.

18. *C. l. monstrabilis* Goldman, 1937. Texas gray wolf. Formerly inhabiting western Texas and northeastern Mexico, this subspecies is now thought to be extinct. Its members were usually small and dark, but some were lighter colored and nearly white.

19. *C. l. nubilus* Say, 1823. Great Plains wolf; buffalo wolf; loafer. This is another extinct subspecies. It once extended throughout the Great Plains from southern Manitoba and Saskatchewan southward to northern Texas. Members were medium-sized and variable in color. Generally they were light, but there was also a black color phase.

20. *C. l. occidentalis* Richardson, 1829. Mackenzie Valley wolf. This subspecies ranges from the upper Mackenzie River Valley southward into central Alberta. It represents some of the largest wolves in North America. The color of these animals varies considerably, as the following description of fifty-nine individuals trapped in Wood Buffalo National Park (and presumably ascribable to this subspecies) shows: "In colour, the animals varied from black . . . to nearly white. The two which were lightest in colour were cream-coloured dorsally, and almost pure white ventrally. Thirty-four were classed as grey, although these had varying amounts of black, particularly on the dorsum. Two others were predominantly light brown or buff in colour, rather than grey. Twenty-one were black, which usually became silvery grey on the flanks and under parts" (Fuller and Novakowski, 1955: 3).

21. *C. l. orion* Pocock, 1935. Greenland wolf. The correct status of this proposed subspecies from Greenland is uncertain. Pocock described it on the basis of a skull and skin of unknown sex, and Goldman examined only two specimens. There is question about whether or not this subspecies is the same as *C. l. arctos*, which inhabits the islands west of Greenland. The three specimens reported on were white or whitish-gray.

22. *C. l. pambasileus* Elliot, 1905. Interior Alaskan wolf. Wolves of this subspecies are among the largest in North America. Their color is usually dark, and there is a high frequency of the black color phase in the group. The subspecies is distributed throughout interior Alaska, except the tundra region of the arctic coast.

23. *C. l. tundarum* Miller, 1912. Alaska tundra wolf. This is a large wolf with long, light-colored pelage. It is closely related to *C. l. pambasileus* but is paler and grayer. Its range is the tundra region of Alaska's arctic coast.

24. *C. l. youngi* Goldman, 1937. Southern Rocky Mountain wolf. Although this wolf once occurred in the Rocky Mountain region of Nevada, Utah, and Colorado, it is now extinct. It was a medium-large animal of light buff color.

Subspecies of Wolves in Eurasia

25. *Canis lupus albus* Kerr, 1792. Tundra wolf, Turukhan wolf. The tundra wolf is said to occur throughout the Eurasian tundra and forest-tundra region from Finland (Pulliainen, 1967) eastward to the Kamchatka Peninsula. It is a large, long-furred, light-colored animal much like *C. l. tundarum*, its North American counterpart (Ognev, 1931). Ellerman and Morrison-Scott (1951) considered that *C. l. dybowskii* Domaniewski, 1926, of Kamchatka also belongs to this subspecies.

26. *C. l. arabs* Pocock, 1934. This wolf is small and has a short, thin, buff-colored coat. It is said to occur in southern Arabia.

27. *C. l. campestris* Dwigubski, 1804. Steppe wolf. The steppe wolf is a small animal inhabiting the deserts and steppes of Central Asia. It has a short, coarse coat, dull gray with an ochre tint. Synonyms for this subspecies include *C. l. desertorum* Bogdanov, 1882 and *C. l. cubanensis* Ognev, 1923.

28. *C. l. hattai* Kishida, 1931. This subspecies once inhabited Hokkaido, Japan. The form *C. l. rex* Pocock, 1935, considered by Ellerman and Morrison-Scott to be a synonym for *C. l. hattai*, was reported surviving in Sakhalin and perhaps in the Kurile Islands in 1945 (Harper, 1945). It is said

to be a much larger wolf than the other Japanese animal, *C. l. hodophilax* Temminck, 1839.

29. *C. l. hodophilax* Temminck, 1839. (Also known as *C. l. hodophylax* and *C. l. hodopylax.*) Now extinct, *C. l. hodophilax* once occurred in Hondo (Honshu), Japan. It was described as smaller than *C. l. lupus* Linnaeus, 1758, and of shorter legs, with its coat short and smooth.

30. *C. l. laniger* Hodgson, 1847. Tibetan wolf. Also recognized as *C. l. chanco* Gray, 1863, by Ellerman and Morrison-Scott, this is a medium-sized animal with long, lightly colored fur. It inhabits the mainland of China, Manchuria, Mongolia, Tibet, and southwestern Russia.

31. *C. l. lupus* Linnaeus, 1758. Common wolf. This is the wolf that once occurred throughout Europe and the entire forest zone of Russia. It is a medium-sized animal with relatively short, coarse, dark fur. Ellerman and Morrison-Scott considered the following proposed European subspecies as distinct from *C. l. lupus: C. l. deitanus* Cabrera, 1907; *C. l. italicus* Altobello, 1921; *C. l. kurjak* Bolkay, 1925; *C. l. signatus* Cabrera, 1907. However, Pocock provided good arguments for lumping these with *C. l. lupus,* although he did consider *C. l. altaicus* Noack, 1911, distinct, whereas Ellerman and Morrison-Scott did not.

32. *C. l. pallipes* Sykes, 1831. The range of this subspecies is said to be from India westward through Iraq. The animal is described as slightly smaller than *C. l. laniger,* with a much shorter and thinner winter coat.

APPENDIX B / MANNER OF
CALCULATING
THE APPARENT SURVIVAL RATES
GIVEN IN TABLE 6

I. *"Natural Control" Column*
  A. 6% survival of pups from birth to age of 5 to 10 months.
    1. Figures from Kelsall (1968) show that pups composed 13% of a previously unexploited population sampled in winter. The sex ratio was 55 males: 45 females.
    2. Thus adults[1] made up 87% of the sample.
    3. Assume that this age ratio remains constant until the new pups are born.
    4. Assume a stable population.
    5. Assume that 100% of the adult females breed and bear an average of 6 pups each. (See B-5 below.)
    6. .45×87 gives 39 breeding females per 100 wolves.
    7. 39×6 gives 234 pups produced per 100 wolves.
    8. Thus, of each 334 wolves in the population (100+234), there are 234 pups, or 70% pups, or 70 pups for each 30 wolves aged 1 year old and older.
    9. If this ratio remained constant until the next winter, one would expect 203 pups for each 87 adults; i.e., 30 adults to 70 pups is the same ratio as 87 adults to 203 pups.
    10. However, the actual ratio found was 87 adults to 13 pups.
    11. Thus for each 87 adults, only 13 of the 203 pups survived.
    12. 13/203 gives a 6% survival rate.
  B. 13% survival of pups from birth to age of 5 to 10 months.
    1. Figures from Kelsall (1968) show that pups composed 13% of a previously unexploited population sampled in winter. The sex ratio was 55 males: 45 females.
    2. Thus adults made up 87% of the sample.
    3. Assume that this age ratio remains constant until the new pups are born.
    4. Assume a stable population.
    5. Assume only 59% of the adult females breed and bear an average of 5 pups each (Pimlott *et al.,* 1969).

[1] Throughout Appendix B, "adults" are considered animals at least 1 year old.

6. .59×39 females (see No. 6 above) gives 23 breeding females per 100 wolves.
7. 23×5 gives 115 pups produced per 100 wolves.
8. Thus of each 215 wolves in the population (100+115), there are 115, or 53%, pups, or 53 pups for each 47 adults.
9. If this ratio remained constant until the next winter, one would expect 98 pups for each 87 adults, i.e., 47 adults to 53 pups is the same ratio as 87 adults to 98 pups.
10. However, the actual ratio found was 87 adults to 13 pups.
11. Thus for each 87 adults, only 13 of the 98 pups survived.
12. 13/98 gives a 13% survival rate.

C. 10% survival of pups from birth to age of 5 to 10 months.
1. Figures from Fuller and Novakowski (1955) show that pups composed 20% of a previously unexploited population sampled in winter. The sex ratio was even.
2. This leaves 80% adults.
3. Assume that this age ratio remains constant until the new pups are born.
4. Assume a stable population.
5. Assume that 100% of the adult females breed and bear an average of 6 pups each.
6. Breeding females equal 40.
7. 40×6 gives 240 pups.
8. Thus of each 340 wolves in the population (100+240), there are 240, or 71%, pups, or 71 pups for each 29 adults.
9. If this ratio remained constant until the next winter, one would expect 196 pups for each 80 adults, i.e., 29 adults to 71 pups is the same ratio as 80 adults to 196 pups.
10. However, the actual ratio found was 80 adults to 20 pups.
11. Thus for each 80 adults, only 20 of the 196 pups survived.
12. 20/196 gives a 10% survival rate.

D. 20% survival rate of pups from birth to age of 5 to 10 months.
1. Figures from Fuller and Novakowski (1955) show that pups composed 20% of a previously unexploited population sampled in winter. The sex ratio was even.
2. This leaves 80% adults.
3. Assume that this age ratio remains constant until the new pups are born.
4. Assume a stable population.
5. Assume only 59% of adults breed and bear an average of 5 young per litter.
6. 40×.59 gives 24 breeding females.
7. 24×5 gives 120 pups.
8. Thus of each 220 wolves in the population (100+120), there are 120, or 55%, pups, or 55 pups for each 45 adults.
9. If this ratio remained constant until the next winter, one would expect 98 pups for each 80 adults, i.e., 45 adults to 55 pups is the same ratio as 80 adults to 98 pups.
10. However, the actual ratio found was 80 adults to 20 pups.
11. Thus for each 80 adults, only 20 of the 98 pups survived.
12. 20/98 gives a 20% survival rate.

E. 43% survival of pups from birth to age of 5 to 10 months.
1. Figures from Pimlott *et al.* (1969) show that in 1964 and 1965 pups composed 31% of the population.
2. This leaves 69% adult wolves.
3. Assume that this age ratio remains constant until the new pups are born.
4. Assume a stable population.
5. Assume only 59% of the adult females breed and bear an average of 5 pups each (Pimlott *et al.*, 1969).
6. Assume even sex ratio.
7. Females equal 35.
8. .59×35 gives 21 breeding females.
9. 21×5 gives 105 pups.
10. Thus of each 205 wolves in the population (100+105), there are 105, or 51%, pups, or 51 pups for each 49 adults.
11. If this ratio remained constant until the next winter, one would expect 72 pups for each 69 adults, i.e., 49 adults to 51 pups is the same ratio as 69 adults to 72 pups.
12. However, the actual ratio found was 69 adults to 31 pups.
13. Thus for each 69 adults, only 31 of the 72 pups survived.
14. 31/72 gives a 43% survival rate.
F. 55% survival of yearlings from 5 to 10 months of age to 17 to 22 months of age.
1. Figures from Pimlott *et al.* (1969) show that in 1964 and 1965, after wolves were protected for 6 years, pups composed 31% of the population, and yearlings 17%.
2. Assume a stable population.
3. Thus the percentage of pups would have been the same for previous year.
4. But of every 31 pups, only 17 survived to become yearlings.
5. 17/31 gives a 55% survival rate.
G. 78% survival of wolves from age of 17 to 22 months to age of about 34 months.
1. Figures from Pimlott *et al.* (1969) show that in 1964 and 1965 yearlings composed 17% of the population, and adults 52%.
2. Assume a stable population.
3. Assume that once wolves survive their second winter and become mature each has an equal chance of being killed, i.e., mortality rate is about the same for all adults.
4. Assume that the maximum life span of wolves in the wild is 8 to 10 years.
5. By trial and error find a constant mortality rate that when applied to a cohort of 17 wolves entering adulthood will leave enough surviving to the age of 10 years to total 52.
6. Try a mortality rate of 22%.
7. (See Fig. 54.)
8. Because an annual 22% mortality rate applied to 17 wolves in the 2-year-old age class gives a total number of survivors approximating the 52% adults actually found in the population, the annual survival rate of the adult wolves in this population can be considered approximately 78%.

Age	Population	Mortality	Survivors
22 mos.	17.0	3.7	13.3
3 years	13.3	2.9	10.4
4 years	10.4	2.3	8.1
5 years	8.1	1.8	6.3
6 years	6.3	1.4	4.9
7 years	4.9	1.1	3.8
8 years	3.8	0.8	3.0
9 years	3.0	0.7	2.3
10 years	2.3	2.3	0.0
Total	52.1 wolves over 2 years old		

II. *"Human Exploitation" Column*
   A. 28% survival of pups from birth to the age of 5 to 10 months.
      1. Figures from Pimlott *et al.* (1969) show that pups composed 35% of an exploited population.
      2. Assume that this age ratio remains constant until the new pups are born.
      3. Assume a stable population.
      4. Assume that the sex ratio is even, that 100% of the adult females breed, and that they bear an average of 6 pups each.
      5. 33 breeding females×6 gives 198 pups produced.
      6. Thus of each 298 wolves in the population (100+198), there are 198, or 66%, pups, or 66 pups for each 34 adults.
      7. If this ratio remained constant until the next winter, one would expect 126 pups for each 65 adults, i.e., 65 adults to 126 pups is the same ratio as 34 adults to 66 pups.
      8. However, the actual ratio found was 65 adults to 35 pups.
      9. Thus for each 65 adults, only 35 of the 126 pups survived.
      10. 35/126 gives a 28% survival rate.
   B. 56% survival of pups from birth to age of 5 to 10 months.
      1. Figures from Pimlott *et al.* (1969) show that pups composed 35% of an exploited population.
      2. Assume that this age ratio remains constant until the new pups are born.
      3. Assume a stable population.
      4. Assume that the sex ratio is even, that 59% of the adult females breed, and that the average litter size is 5.
      5. 33×.59 gives 19 breeding females.
      6. 19×5 gives 95 pups.
      7. Thus of each 195 wolves in the population (100+95), there are 95, or 49%, pups, or 49 pups for each 51 adults.
      8. If this ratio remained constant until the next winter, one would expect 62 pups for each 65 adults, i.e., 65 adults to 62 pups is the same ratio as 51 adults to 49 pups.
      9. However, the actual ratio found was 65 adults to 35 pups.
      10. Thus for each 65 adults, only 35 of the 62 pups survived.
      11. 35/62 gives a 56% survival rate.

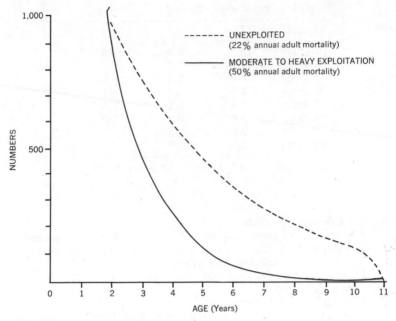

FIGURE 54. Age structure of exploited and unexploited adult wolf populations.

C. 45% survival of pups from birth to age of 5 to 10 months.
1. A sample of 593 *female* wolves from Alaska was composed of 41% pups and 59% adults (R. A. Rausch, 1967a).
2. Assume that this age ratio remains constant until the new pups are born.
3. Assume a stable population.
4. 89% of the adults breed and bear 6 young per litter (R. A. Rausch, 1967a).
5. .89×59 gives 52 breeders.
6. 52×3 female pups per litter gives 156 female pups produced.
7. Thus of each 256 female wolves in the population (100+156), there are 156, or 61%, female pups, or 61 female pups for each 39 adult females.
8. If this ratio remained constant until the next winter, one would expect 92 pups for each 59 adults, i.e., 59 adults to 92 pups is the same ratio as 39 adults to 61 pups.
9. However, the actual ratio found was 59 adults to 41 pups.
10. Thus for each 59 adults, only 41 of the 92 pups survived.
11. 41/92 gives a survival rate of 45%.
D. 52% survival of pups from birth to age of 5 to 10 months.
1. Figures from Table 4 of R. A. Rausch (1967a) show that pups compose 44% of an exploited population, so adults make up 56%.
2. Assume that this age ratio remains constant until the new pups are born.

3. Assume a stable population.
4. The sex ratio is even, so adult females equal 28%.
5. 89% of the females breed (R. A. Rausch, 1967a), so .89× 28 gives 25 breeding females per 100 wolves.
6. At 6 pups per litter, 6×25 gives 150 pups produced.
7. Thus of each 250 wolves in the population (100+150), there are 150, or 60%, pups, or 60 pups for each 40 adults.
8. If this ratio remained constant until the next winter, one would expect 82 pups for each 56 adults, i.e., 56 adults to 82 pups is the same ratio as 40 adults to 60 pups.
9. However, the actual ratio found was 56 adults to 44 pups.
10. Thus for each 56 adults, only 44 of the 82 pups survived.
11. 44/82 gives a survival rate of 52%.

E. 88% survival rate of pups from birth to age of 5 to 10 months.
1. Figures from Fuller (1954) show that after human exploitation pups composed 55% of the population.
2. Assume that this age ratio remains constant until the new pups are born.
3. Assume a stable population.
4. Assume that the sex ratio is even, that all 23 adult females breed, and that the average litter size is 6.
5. 23×6 gives 138 pups produced.
6. Thus of each 238 wolves in the population (100+138), there are 138, or 58%, pups, or 58 pups for each 42 adults.
7. If this ratio remained constant until the next winter, one would expect 62 pups for each 45 adults, i.e., 45 adults to 62 pups is the same ratio as 42 adults to 58 pups.
8. However, the actual ratio found was 45 adults to 55 pups.
9. Thus for each 45 adults, only 55 of the 62 pups survived.
10. 55/62 gives a survival rate of 88%.

F. 69% survival of wolves from 5 to 10 months of age to 22 months of age.
1. Figures from R. A. Rausch (1967a) show that in a sample of 353 female wolves there were 246 pups:170 yearlings (22 months of age):177 adults.
2. Assume an even sex ratio.
3. Assume a stable population.
4. Thus the percentage of pups was the same for the previous year as for this.
5. But only 170 yearlings survived from the 246 pups.
6. 170/246 gives 69% survival rate.

G. 100% survival of wolves from 5 to 10 months of age to 22 months of age.
1. Figures from Pimlott *et al.* (1969) show that in a sample of 48 wolves there were 17 pups:19 yearlings:12 adults.
2. Assume a stable population.
3. Thus the percentage of pups was the same for the previous year as for this.
4. 19/17 gives 100% plus survival rate. (The excess may be due to a small sample size or to an extra-large year class.)

H. 36% survival of wolves from age of 17 to 22 months to age of 34 months.

    1. Figures from Pimlott *et al.* (1969) show that under human exploitation yearlings composed 40% of the population, and adults 25%.

    2. Assumptions and methods the same as in I.G., p. 356.

    3. A constant mortality rate of 64% per year applied to 40% yearlings will give 25% adults.

    4. This annual survival rate for adults is 36%.

I. 50% survival of wolves from age 22 months to age of 34 months.

    1. Figures from R. A. Rausch (1967a) show a ratio of 170 yearlings:177 adults.

    2. Assumptions and methods the same as in I.G., p. 356.

    3. A constant mortality rate of 50% per year applied to 170 yearlings will give 177 adults.

    4. Thus annual survival rate for adults is 50%. (See Fig. 54.)

APPENDIX C / SCIENTIFIC NAMES OF ORGANISMS REFERRED TO IN TEXT

Below are listed the scientific names of the plants and animals referred to in the text, except for the parasites whose latin names are given in the tables of Chapter XI. The organisms are listed alphabetically within each of the four major categories: invertebrates, birds, mammals, and trees.

INVERTEBRATES

Earthworms	Lumbricidae
Fleas	Siphonaptera
Flies	Diptera
black flies	*Simulium*
deer flies	*Chrysops*
horseflies	*Tabanus*
stable flies	*Stomoxys*
Flukes	Trematoda
Grasshoppers	Orthoptera
Lice	Anoplura
Mites	*Sarcoptes*
Mosquitoes	Culicidae
Roundworms	Nematoda
Tapeworms	Cestoda
Thorny-headed worms	Acanthocephala
Ticks	Ixodidae
Tongue worms	Pentastomidae

BIRDS

Chickadee	*Parus atricapillus*
Chicken, domestic	*Gallus domesticus*
Crow	*Corvus brachyrhyncos*
Ducks	Anatidae
Eagle, bald	*Haliaeetus leucocephalus*
Hawks	Accipitriidae
Jays	Corvidae
Owls	Strigiformes
Passenger pigeon	*Ectopistes migratorius*
Ptarmigan	*Lagopus*
Raven	*Corvus corax*
Robin	*Turdus migratorius*

MAMMALS

Antelope	*Antilocarpa americana*
Bears	Ursidae
black bear	*Euarctos americanus*
grizzly bear	*Ursus arctos*
Beaver	*Castor canadensis*
Bison	*Bison bison*
Bobcat	*Lynx rufus*
Buffalo	*Bison bison*
Caribou	*Rangifer tarandus*
Cat, domestic	*Felis catus*
Cattle	*Bos taurus*
Cow	*Bos taurus*
Coyote	*Canis latrans*
Deer	*Odocoileus*
black-tailed deer	*Odocoileus hemionus*
mule deer	*Odocoileus hemionus*
Sitka black-tailed deer	*Odocoileus hemionus*
white-tailed deer	*Odocoileus virginianus*
Dhole	*Cuon alpinus*
Dingo	*Canis dingo*
Dog	*Canis familiaris*
African hunting dog	*Lycaon pictus*
bush dog	*Speothos venaticus*
domestic dog	*Canis familiaris*
raccoon dog	*Nyctereutes procyonoides*
small-eared dog	*Atelocynus microtis*
Elk	*Cervus canadensis*
Fisher	*Martes pennanti*
Fox	*Vulpes fulva*
arctic fox	*Alopex lagopus*
crab-eating fox	*Cerdocyon thous*
European red fox	*Vulpes vulpes*
gray fox	*Urocyon cinereoargenteus*
kit fox	*Vulpes velox*
red fox	*Vulpes fulva*
South American fox	*Dusicyon culpaeus*
Goat, mountain	*Oreamnos americanus*
Hare, arctic	*Lepus arcticus*
snowshoe	*Lepus americanus*
Horse	*Equus cabalus*
Human being	*Homo sapiens*
Jackal, black-backed	*Canis mesomelas*
golden	*Canis aureus*
side-striped	*Canis adustus*
Lion	*Panthera leo*
African lion	*Panthera leo*
Lynx	*Lynx canadensis*
Mice	Cricetidae
Mink	*Mustela vison*
Moose	*Alces alces*
Musk-ox	*Ovibus moschatus*

Muskrat	*Ondatra zibethicus*
Pig	*Sus scrofa*
Rabbits	Leporidae
Reindeer	*Rangifer tarandus*
Seal, harbor	*Phoca vitulina*
Squirrels	Sciuridae
red squirrel	*Tamiasciurus hudsonicus*
Sheep, bighorn	*Ovis canadensis*
Dall	*Ovis dalli*
domestic	*Ovis aries*
Swine	*Sus scrofa*
Tiger	*Panthera tiger*
Weasels	*Mustela*
Wisent	*Bison bonasus*
Wolf, common or gray	*Canis lupus*
maned	*Chrysocyon brachyurus*
red	*Canis rufus*
Wolverine	*Gulo gulo*

TREES

Balsam	*Abies balsamea*
Cottonwoods	*Populus*
Hazelnut, beaked	*Corylus cornuta*
Maple, sugar	*Acer saccharum*
Pine, jack	*Pinus banksiana*
Spruces	*Picea*
black spruce	*Picea mariana*
Willows	*Salix*

BIBLIOGRAPHY

Abuladze, K. I. 1964. Osnovy Tsestodologii, Vol. IV. Teniaty—lentochnye gel'minty zhivotnykh i cheloveka i vyzyvaemye imi zabolevaniia. Nauka, Moscow. 530 pp. (Cited from R. L. Rausch, 1967.)

Adlam, G. H. 1953. Observations on rabies. Can. J. Comp. Med. and Vet. Sci. 17: 418–21.

Adolph, E. F. 1943. Physiological regulations. Cattell. Lancaster, Penn. 502 pp. (Cited from Fuller and DuBuis, 1962.)

Allen, D. L. 1962. Our wildlife legacy (Rev. Ed.). Funk and Wagnalls Co., Inc., New York. 422 pp.

Allen, D. L., and L. D. Mech. 1963. Wolves versus moose on Isle Royale. Nat. Geog. 123(2): 200–19.

Andreev, A. A. 1925. The resonance theory of Helmholz in the light of new observations upon the function of the peripheral and of the acoustic analyzer in the dog. Pavlov Jubilee Volume. Leningrad. 339–63. (Cited from Fuller and DuBuis, 1962.)

Anonymous. 1967a. Some facts on the bounty. Minn. Dept. of Cons., Div. Game and Fish. 6 pp. (mimeo.).

Anonymous. 1967b. The virtuous wolf. Defenders of Wildlife News 42(1): 50.

Ardrey, R. 1966. The territorial imperative. Atheneum. New York. 390 pp.

Atwell, G. 1963. An aerial census of wolves in the Nelchina wolf study area. Proc. Alaska Sci. Conf. 14: 79–83.

Atwell, G. 1964. Wolf predation on moose calf. J. Mammal. 45: 313–14.

Audubon, J. J., and J. Bachman. 1967. The quadrupeds of North America. Hammond, Inc. Maplewood, N.J. 307 pp.

Aulerich, R. J. 1966. The wolf. Nat. Parks Mag. 40(230): 10–13.

Bailey, V. 1926. A biological survey of North Dakota. U. S. Dept. Agric., Biol. Surv. N. Am. Fauna 49. 416 pp.

Banfield, A. W. F. 1951. Populations and movements of the Saskatchewan timber wolf (Canis lupus knightii) in Prince Albert National Park, Saskatchewan, 1947 to 1951. Can Wildl. Serv., Wildl. Mgmt. Bull. Ser. 1, No. 4. 24 pp.

Banfield, A. W. F. 1953. The range of individual timber wolves (Canis lupus). J. Mammal. 34: 389–90.

Banfield, A. W. F. 1954. Preliminary investigation of the barren ground caribou. Part II. Life history, ecology, and utilization. Can. Wildl. Serv., Wildl. Mgmt. Bull. Ser. 1, No. 10B. 112 pp.

Banfield, A. W. F. 1964. Review of F. Mowat's Never Cry Wolf. Can. Field Nat. 78: 52–54.

Bauer, E. A. 1968. I say make wolves big game! Outdoor Life 141(1): 27–29, 76–81.

Bettelheim, B. 1959. Feral children and autistic children. Am. J. Sociol. 64: 455–67.

Bishopp, F. C., and Helen L. Trembley. 1945. Distribution and hosts of certain North American ticks. J. Parasit. 31: 1–54.

Blair, W. R. 1908. Report of the veterinary pathologist. 13th Ann. Rept. N. Y. Zool. Soc.: 137–42.

Blair, W. R. 1919. Report of the veterinarian. 24th Ann. Rept. N. Y. Zool. Soc.: 82–87.

Bohlken, H. 1961. Haustiere und Zoologische Systematik. Zeitschrift Tierzuchtung Züchtungs-Biol. 76(1): 107–13. (Cited from Biol. Abstr. 42: 1584) (No. 20057).

Bondareva, V. I. 1955. Rol' domashnikh i dikikh plotoiadnykh v epidemiologii i epizootologii larval'nykh tsestodozov. Part 2. Fauna tsestod volkov. Trudy Inst. Zool., Akad. Nauk Kazakh. SSR 3: 101–4. (Cited from R. L. Rausch, 1967.)

Brown, C. E. 1936. Rearing wild animals in captivity, and gestation periods. J. Mammal. 17: 10–13.

Burkholder, B. L. 1959. Movements and behavior of a wolf pack in Alaska. J. Wildl. Mgmt. 23: 1–11.

Burkholder, B. L. 1962. Observations concerning wolverine. J. Mammal. 43: 263–64.

Cahalane, V. H. 1964. A preliminary study of distribution and numbers of cougar, grizzly and wolf in North America. N. Y. Zool. Soc. 12 pp.

Cameron, T. W. M. 1927. The helminth parasites of animals and human disease. Proc. R. Soc. Med. (Sect. of Comp. Med.) 20: 15–24.

Cheatum, E. L. 1949. Bone marrow as an index of malnutrition in deer. N. Y. State Conservationist 3(5): 19–22.

Cheatum, E. L., and C. W. Severinghaus. 1950. Variations in fertility of the white-tailed deer related to range conditions. Trans. N. Am. Wildl. Conf. 15: 170–89.

Choquette, L. P. E. 1956. Observations on experimental infection of dogs with *Echinococcus.* Can. J. Zool. 34: 190–92.

Christian, J. J. 1959. The roles of endocrine and behavioral factors in the growth of mammal populations. *In* A. Gorbman (ed.), Comparative endocrinology. John Wiley and Sons, Inc., New York. 71–97.

Chung, Ka Bun, University of Hong Kong. 1967. Personal correspondence to the author.

Clarke, C. H. D. 1940. A biological investigation of the Thelon Game Sanctuary. Nat. Mus. Can. Bull. 96. Biol. Ser. No. 25.

Cole, G. F., Yellowstone National Park. 1968. Personal correspondence to the author.

Cole, J. E. 1956. 1956 winter wildlife study, Isle Royale National Park. U. S. Nat. Park Serv. Rept., Isle Royale Nat. Park files. 56 pp. (typewritten).

Cole, J. E. 1957. Isle Royale wildlife investigations, winter of 1956–57. U. S. Nat. Park Serv. Rept., Isle Royale Nat. Park files. 42 pp. (typewritten).

Cottam, C., and C. S. Williams. 1943. Speed of some wild mammals. J. Mammal. 24: 262–63.

Cowan, I. M. 1947. The timber wolf in the Rocky Mountain national parks of Canada. Can. J. Res. 25: 139–74.

Cowan, I. M. 1949. Rabies as a possible population control of arctic Canidae. J. Mammal. 30: 396–98.

Criddle, S. 1947. Timber wolf den and pups. Can. Field Nat. 61: 115.

Crisler, Lois. 1956. Observations of wolves hunting caribou. J. Mammal. 37: 337–46.

Crisler, Lois. 1958. Arctic wild. Harper and Bros., New York. 301 pp.

Cross, E. C. 1940. Arthritis among wolves. Can. Field Nat. 54: 2–4.

DeVos, A. 1949. Timber wolves (*Canis lupus lycaon*) killed by cars on Ontario highways. J. Mammal. 30: 197.

DeVos, A. 1950. Timber wolf movements on Sibley Peninsula, Ontario. J. Mammal. 31: 169–75.

DeVos, A., and A. E. Allin. 1949. Some notes on moose parasites. J. Mammal. 30: 430–31.

Dixon, J. S. 1916. The timber wolf in California. Calif. Fish and Game. 2: 125–29.

Dixon, J. S. 1934. Mother wolf carries food twelve miles to her young. J. Mammal. 15: 158.

Ellerman, J. R., and T. C. S. Morrison-Scott. 1951. Checklist of Palaearctic and Indian mammals. British Museum (Nat. Hist.), London. 810 pp.

Erickson, A. B. 1944. Helminths of Minnesota Canidae in relation to food habits, and a host list and key to the species reported from North America. Am. Midl. Nat. 32: 358–72.

Errington, P. L. 1946. Predation and vertebrate populations. Quart. Rev. Biol. 21: 144–77, 221–45.

Errington, P. L. 1967. Of predation and life. Iowa State University Press, Ames. 277 pp.

Fashingbauer, B. A. 1964. Deer harvest and other mortality data, 1963. Minn. Dept. Cons. P. R. Quarterly Progress Rept. 24(2): 5–13 (mimeo.).

Fentress, J. 1967. Observations on the behavioral development of a hand-reared male timber wolf. Amer. Zool. 7: 339–51.

Fischel, W. 1956. Haushunde. Handbuch d. Zoologie 8: 1–16. (Cited from Schenkel, 1967.)

Fletcher, J. A., St. Paul, Minn. 1967. Personal conversation with the author.

Fox, H. 1923. Disease in captive wild mammals and birds. Lippincott. Philadelphia. 665 pp.

Fox, H. 1926. Rept. Lab. Comp. Path., Philadelphia.

Fox, H. 1927. Rept. Lab. Comp. Path., Philadelphia.

Fox, H. 1941. Report of the Penrose Res. Lab. Zool. Soc. of Phil.

Freeman, R. S., A. Adorjan, and D. H. Pimlott. 1961. Cestodes of wolves, coyotes, and coyote-dog hybrids in Ontario. Can. J. Zool. 39: 527–32.

Frenzel, Jr., L. D., and L. D. Mech. 1967. Wolf-deer relations in northeastern Minnesota. The Naturalist, spring: 8–9.

Fuller, J. L., and E. M. DuBuis. 1962. The behavior of dogs. 415–52. *In* E. Hafez (ed.). The behavior of domestic animals. Bailliere, Tindall & Cox. London. 619 pp.

Fuller, W. A. 1954. Wolf control operations, Southern Mackenzie District, 1954–1955. Can. Wildl. Serv. Rept., October 1955 (typewritten).

Fuller, W. A. 1966. The biology and management of the bison of Wood Buffalo National Park. Can. Wildl. Serv., Wildl. Mgmt. Bull. Ser. 1, No. 16, 52 pp.

Fuller, W. A., and N. S. Novakowski. 1955. Wolf control operations, Wood Buffalo National Park, 1951–1952. Can. Wildl. Serv., Wildl. Mgmt. Bull. Ser. 1, No. 11.

Furmaga, S. 1953. *Spirometra janicki* sp. n. (Diphyllobothriidae). Acta Parasit. Polon. 1(2): 29–59. (Cited from Yamaguti, 1959.)

Garceau, P. 1960. Reproduction, growth, and mortality of wolves in southeastern Alaska. Alaska Dept. of Fish and Game. Federal Aid, Alaska, W-6-R-1, Work Plan K, Job No. 2. 18 pp. (mimeo.).

Garceau, P. 1961. Wolf predation studies on black-tailed deer. Alaska Dept. of Fish and Game. Federal Aid, Alaska, W-6-R-2, Work Plan K, Job No. 1. 13 pp. (mimeo.).

Garceau, P. 1963. Wolf predation on Sitka black-tailed deer. Alaska Dept. of Fish and Game. Federal Aid, Alaska, W-6-R-3, Work Plan K, Job No. 3. 16 pp. (mimeo.).

Gesell, A. 1940. Wolf child and human child. Harper and Bros. New York and London. 107 pp.

Ginsburg, B. E. 1965. Coaction of genetical and nongenetical factors influencing sexual behavior, pp. 53–75. In F. Beach (ed.), Sex and behavior, John Wiley and Sons, New York, 592 pp.

Goldman, E. A. 1937. The wolves of North America. J. Mammal. 18: 37–45.

Goldman, E. A. 1944. The wolves of North America, Part II. Classification of wolves. The Amer. Wildl. Instit. Washington, D.C. 389–636.

Golley, F. B., G. A. Petrides, E. L. Rauber, and J. H. Jenkins. 1965. Food intake and assimilation by bobcats under laboratory conditions. J. Wildl. Mgmt. 29: 442–47.

Goss, L. J. 1948. Species susceptibility to the virus of Carre and feline enteritis. Am. J. Vet. Res. 9: 65–68.

Hagar, J. A., Marshfield Hills, Mass. 1968. Personal correspondence to the author.

Hakala, D. R. 1953. Moose browse and wildlife study at Isle Royale, February 17 to March 16, 1953. U. S. Nat. Park Serv. Rept., Isle Royale Nat. Park files (typewritten).

Hakala, D. R. 1954. Wolf on Isle Royale! Nat. Mag. 47(1): 35–37.

Hall, E. R., and K. R. Kelson. 1959. The mammals of North America, Vol. II. The Ronald Press, New York. 547–1083.

Hamerton, A. E. 1931. Report on the deaths occurring in the society's gardens during 1930. Proc. Zool. Soc. Lon. 1931: 527.

Hamerton, A. E. 1932. Report on the deaths occurring in the society's gardens during 1931. Proc. Zool. Soc. Lon. 1932: 613.

Hamerton, A. E. 1936. Report on the deaths occurring in the society's gardens during 1935. Proc. Zool. Soc. Lon. 1936: 659.

Hamerton, A. E. 1945. Report on deaths occurring in the society's gardens during 1944. Proc. Zool. Soc. Lon. 115: 371.

Harper, F. 1945. Extinct and vanishing mammals of the Old World. Spec. Publ. Amer. Comm. Int. Wildl. Prot. No. 12. (Cited from Ellerman and Morrison-Scott, 1951.)

Harrop, A. E. 1955. Some observations on canine semen. Vet. Rec. 67: 494–98.

Hartley, J. 1938. Pathology of *Dirofilaria* infestation. Report of a case with chronic arteritis. Zoologica. New York. 23: 235–46.

Hellmuth, J. 1964. A wolf in the family. The New American Library, New York. 127 pp.

Hickie, P. F. 1936. Isle Royale moose studies. Proc. N. Am. Wildl. Conf. 1: 396–98.

Hildebrand, M. 1952. The integument in Canidae. J. Mammal. 33: 419–28.

Holmes, J. C., and R. Podesta. 1968. The helminths of wolves and coyotes from the forested regions of Alberta. Can. J. Zool. 46: 1193–1204.

Idstrom, J. M., and C. Kinsey. 1965. Deer harvest and other mortality data, 1964. Minn. Dept. Cons. P. R. Quarterly Progress Rept. 25(2): 85–93 (mimeo.).

Idstrom, J. M., C. Kinsey, and W. Petraborg. 1966. Deer harvest and other mortality data, 1965. Minn. Dept. Cons. P. R. Quarterly Progress Rept. 26(1): 1–13 (mimeo.).

Idstrom, J. M., C. Kinsey, and W. Petraborg. 1967. Deer harvest and other mortality data, 1966. Minn. Dept. Cons. P. R. Quarterly Progress Rept. 27(3): 127–41 (mimeo.).

Iljin, N. A. 1941. Wolf-dog genetics. J. Genetics 42: 359–414.

Imaizumi, Yoshinori, and Yoshikazu Hasegawa, National Science Museum, Japan. 1967. Personal correspondence to the author.

Ingles, L. G. 1963. Status of the wolf in California. J. Mammal. 44: 109.

Johnson, C. E. 1921. A note of the habits of the timber wolf. J. Mammal. 2: 11–15.

Jolicoeur, P. 1959. Multivariate geographical variation in the wolf *Canis lupus* L. Evol. 13: 283–99.

Jordan, P. A., P. C. Shelton, and D. L. Allen. 1967. Numbers, turnover, and social structure of the Isle Royale wolf population. Amer. Zool. 7: 233–52.

Joslin, P. W. B. 1966. Summer activities of two timber wolf (*Canis lupus*) packs in Algonquin Park. Unpubl. M.S. thesis. University of Toronto. 99 pp.

Joslin, P. W. B. 1967. Movements and home sites of timber wolves in Algonquin Park. Amer. Zool. 7: 279–88.

Karns, P., and W. Petraborg. 1968. Deer harvest and other mortality data, 1967. Minn. Dept. Cons. P. R. Quarterly Progress Rept. 28, in press.

Keener, J. M., Wisconsin Conservation Department. 1967. Personal correspondence to the author.

Kelly, M. W. 1954. Observations afield on Alaskan wolves. Proc. Alaska Sci. Conf. 5: 35.

Kelsall, J. P. 1957. Continued barren-ground caribou studies. Can. Wildl. Serv., Wildl. Mgmt. Bull. Ser. 1, No. 12, 148 pp.

Kelsall, J. P. 1960. Co-operative studies of barren-ground caribou 1957–58. Can. Wildl. Serv., Wildl. Mgmt. Bull. Ser. 1, No. 15.

Kelsall, J. P. 1968. The migratory barren ground caribou of Canada. Can. Wildl. Serv., Queen's Printer, Ottawa, 340 pp.

Klatt, K. 1913. Über den Einfluss der Gesamtgrösse auf das Schadelbild nebst Bemerkungen über die Vorgeschichte der Haustiere. Arch. Entw. Mech. Org. 36. (Cited from Iljin, 1941.)

Kleiman, Devra. 1966. Scent marking in the Canidae. Symp. Zool. Soc. London. 18: 167–77.

Kleiman, Devra. 1967. Some aspects of social behavior in the Canidae. Amer. Zool. 7: 365–72.

Klein, D. R., and S. T. Olson. 1960. Natural mortality patterns of deer in southeast Alaska. J. Wildl. Mgmt. 24: 80–88.

Knezevic, M., and R. Knezevic. 1956. Vuk zivot, stetnost i tamanjenje. Sarajevo. 205 pp. (Cited from Pulliainen, 1965.)

Kolenosky, G. B., and D. H. Johnston. 1967. Radio-tracking timber wolves in Ontario. Amer. Zool. 7: 289–303.

Kozlov, V. 1964. The wolf. Hunting and Hunting Economy 9: 18–20. (Translation by A. Adorjan.) (Cited from Joslin, 1966.)

Krefting, L. W. 1951. What is the future of the Isle Royale moose herd? Trans. N. Am. Wildl. Conf. 16: 461–70.

Kuyt, E. 1962. Movements of young wolves in the Northwest Territories of Canada. J. Mammal. 43: 270–71.

Law, R. G., and A. H. Kennedy. 1932. Parasites of fur-bearing animals. Dept. of Game and Fisheries, Ontario. Bull. 4.

Lawrence, Barbara. 1967. Early domestic dogs. Sonderdruck aus Zeitschrift f. Saugetierkunde Bd. 32, H. 1, S. 44–59.

Lawrence, Barbara, and W. H. Bossert. 1967. Multiple character analysis of *Canis lupus, latrans,* and *familiaris,* with a discussion of the relationships of *Canis niger.* Amer. Zool. 7: 223–32.

Lent, P. C. 1964. Tolerance between grizzlies and wolves. J. Mammal. 45: 304–5.

Leyhausen, P., and R. Wolff. 1959. Das Revier einer Hauskatze. Zeitschrift f. Tierpsych. 16: 666–70. (Cited from Schaller, 1967.)

Ligon, J. S. 1917. Sexes and breeding notes. Rept. to U. S. Biol. Surv. Aug. 22. (cited from Goldman, 1944.)

Ligon, J. S. 1926. When wolves forsake their ways. Nat. Mag. 7: 156–59.

Lorenz, K. Z. 1952. King Solomon's ring. Methuen & Co., Ltd., London. 202 pp. (Translated by Marjorie Kerr Wilson.)

Lorenz, K. Z. 1955. Man meets dog. Methuen & Co., Ltd., London. 198 pp.

Lorenz, K. Z. 1963. Das sogenannte Bose. Eine Naturgeschichte der Aggression. Borotha, Wien. (Cited from Schenkel, 1967.)

Lucas, N. S. 1923. Report on the deaths occurring in the society's gardens during 1922. Proc. Zool. Soc. Lon. 1923: 125.

MacFarlane, R. R. 1905. Notes on mammals collected and observed in the northern Mackenzie River district, Northwest Territories of Canada. Proc. U. S. Nat. Mus. 28: 673–764.

Makridin, V. P. 1959. Material' po biologii volka v tundrah nenetskogo natsional'nogo okruga. Zool. Zhur. 39: 1719–28. (Cited from Pulliainen, 1965.)

Makridin, V. P. 1962. The wolf in the Yamal north. Zool. Zhur. 41(9): 1413–17. (Translation by Peter Lent.)

Mandelbaum, D. G. 1943. Wolf-child histories from India. J. Soc. Psychol. 17: 25–44.

Martinka, C. J., U. S. National Park Service. 1967. Personal correspondence to the author.

Martins, T., and J. R. Valle. 1948. Hormonal regulation of the micturition behavior of the dog. J. Comp. Physiol. Psychol. 41: 301–11.

Matthew, W. D. 1930. The phylogeny of dogs. J. Mammal. 11: 117–38.

Mayer, Jean. 1953. Caloric requirements and obesity in dogs. Gaines Veterinary Symposium. New York.

McCarley, H. 1962. The taxonomic status of wild *Canis (Canidae)* in the south central United States. S. W. Naturalist 7(3–4): 227–35.

McCay, C. M. 1943. Nutrition of the dog. Comstock Publ. Co., Inc., Ithaca, N.Y. 140 pp.

McCullough, D. R. 1967. The probable affinities of a wolf captured near Woodlake, Calif. Calif. Fish and Game. 53: 146–53.

Mech, L. D. 1966a. The wolves of Isle Royale. U. S. Nat. Park Serv. Fauna Ser. No. 7. 210 pp.

Mech, L. D. 1966b. Hunting behavior of timber wolves in Minnesota. J. Mammal. 47: 347–48.

Mech, L. D. 1967. Telemetry as a technique in the study of predation. J. Wildl. Mgmt. 31: 492–96.

Mech, L. D., and L. D. Frenzel, Jr. 1969. Continuing timber wolf studies. Naturalist 20(1): 30–35.

Mech, L. D., and L. D. Frenzel, Jr. Unpublished. Studies of wolves in Minnesota.

Mech, L. D., J. R. Tester, and D. W. Warner. 1966. Fall daytime resting habits of raccoons as determined by telemetry. J. Mammal. 47: 450–66.

Merriam, H. R. 1964. The wolves of Coronation Island. Proc. Alaska Sci. Conf. 15: 27–32.

Miller, G. S. 1919. Review of Einar Lönnberg's "Remarks on some South American Canidae." J. Mammal. 1: 149–50.

Miller, J. L. 1967. A natural habitat for wolves. Defenders of Wildlife News 42(1): 57–59, 75.

Mivart, St. G. J. 1890. Dogs, jackals, wolves, and foxes: a monograph of the Canidae. R. H. Porter. London. 216 pp.

Morgan, B. B. 1941. A summary of the Physalopterinae (Nematoda) of North America. Proc. Helminth. Soc. Wash. 8: 28–30.

Morozov, F. N. 1951. Gel'minty volkov Mordovskogo Gosudarstvennogo Zapovednika. Trudy Gel'mint. Lab. 5: 146–50. (Cited from R. L. Rausch, 1967.)

Moulton, D. G., E. H. Ashton, and J. T. Eayrs. 1960. Studies in olfactory acuity. 4. Relative detectability of n-aliphatic acids by the dog. Anim. Behav. 8: 117–28.

Mowat, F. 1963. Never cry wolf. Dell Publishing Co., Inc., N.Y. 175 pp.

Munro, J. A. 1947. Observations of birds and mammals in central British Columbia. Occasional Papers Brit. Col. Prov. Mus. 6, 165 pp.

Murie, A. 1934. The moose of Isle Royale. Univ. Mich. Mus. Zool. Misc. Publ. 25. 44 pp.

Murie, A. 1944. The wolves of Mount McKinley. U. S. Nat. Park Serv. Fauna Ser. No. 5. 238 pp.

Murie, A. 1963. A naturalist in Alaska. Doubleday and Co., Inc., New York. 302 pp.

Nasimovich, A. A. 1955. The role of the regime of snow cover in the life of ungulates in the U.S.S.R. Moskva, Akademiya Nauk S.S.R. 403 pp. (Cited from Kelsall, 1968.)

Nicoll, W. 1927. A reference list of the trematode parasites of man and the primates. Parasit. 19: 338–51.

Noble, E. R., and G. A. Noble. 1961. Parasitology. Lea and Febiger, Philadelphia. 767 pp.

Novikov, G. A. 1956. Carnivorous mammals of the fauna of the U.S.S.R. Zool. Instit. Acad. Sci. U.S.S.R. Moscow. 284 pp. (Israel Program for Scientific Translations, Jerusalem. 1962.)

Nowak, R. M. 1967. The red wolf in Louisiana. Defenders of Wildlife News 42(1): 60–70.

Ogburn, W. F., and N. K. Bose. 1959. On the trail of the wolf-children. Genet. Psych. Mon. 60: 117–93.

Ognev, S. I. 1931, Mammals of Eastern Europe and Northern Asia, Vol. II. (Israel Program for Scientific Translations, Jerusalem. 1962.)

Olson, S. F. 1938. Organization and range of the pack. Ecology 19: 168–70.

Panin, V. Ia., and L. I. Lavrov. 1962. K gel'mintofaune volkov Kazakhstana. *In* Parazity dikikh zhivotnykh Kasakhstana. Trudy Inst. Zool., Akad. Nauk Kazakh. S.S.R. 26: 57–62. (Cited from R. L. Rausch, 1967.)

Paradiso, J. L. 1965. Recent records of red wolves from the Gulf Coast of Texas. S. W. Naturalist. 10: 318–19.

Paradiso, J. L. 1968. Notes on recently collected specimens of east Texas canids, with comments on the taxonomy of the red wolf. Amer. Midl. Nat. 80: 529–34.

Parmelee, D. F. 1964. Myth of the wolf. The Beaver, spring: 4–9.

Passmore, R. C., R. L. Peterson, and A. T. Cringan. 1955. A study of mandibular tooth wear as an index to age of moose. App. A. 223–46. In R. L. Peterson, North American moose, Univ. of Toronto Press, Toronto. 280 pp.

Pearson, J. C. 1956. Studies on the life cycles and morphology of the larval stages of *Alaria arisaemoides* Augustine and Uribo, 1927, and *Alaria canis* LaRue and Fallis, 1936 (Trematoda: Diplostomidae). Can. J. Zool. 34: 295–387.

Peterson, R. L. 1947. A record of a timber wolf attacking a man. J. Mammal. 28: 294–95.

Peterson, R. L. 1955. North American moose. Univ. of Toronto Press, Toronto. 280 pp.

Pimlott, D. H. 1959. Reproduction and productivity of Newfoundland moose. J. Wildl. Mgmt. 23: 381–401.

Pimlott, D. H. 1960. The use of tape-recorded wolf howls to locate timber wolves. 22nd Midwest Wildl. Conf. 15 pp. (mimeo.).

Pimlott, D. H. 1961. Wolf control in Canada. Can. Audubon Mag. Nov.–Dec.: 145–52.

Pimlott, D. H. 1966. Review of F. Mowat's *Never Cry Wolf.* J. Wildl. Mgmt. 30: 236–37.

Pimlott, D. H. 1967a. Wolves and men in North America. Defenders of Wildlife News 42(1): 36–53.

Pimlott, D. H. 1967b. Wolf predation and ungulate populations. Amer. Zool. 7: 267–78.

Pimlott, D. H., University of Toronto. 1968. Personal correspondence to the author.

Pimlott, D. H., and P. W. Joslin. 1968. The status and distribution of the red wolf. Trans. N. Am. Wildl. Conf. 33: 373–89.

Pimlott, D. H., J. A. Shannon, and G. B. Kolenosky. 1969. The ecology of the timber wolf in Algonquin Park. Ont. Dept. Lands and Forests. 92 pp.

Plimmer, H. G. 1915. Report on the deaths occurring in the society's gardens during 1914. Proc. Zool. Soc. Lon. 1915: 123.

Plimmer, H. G. 1916. Report on the deaths occurring in the society's gardens during 1915. Proc. Zool. Soc. Lon. 1916: 77.

Plotnikov, D. 1964. The dangerous predator will be exterminated. Hunting and Hunting Economy, September: 21–22. (Translation from Russian by A. Adorjan.)

Pocock, R. I. 1935. The races of *Canis lupus*. Proc. Zool. Soc. London, Part 3, Sept.: 647–86.

Pringle, L. P. 1960. Notes on coyotes in southern New England. J. Mammal. 41: 278.

Pruitt, W. O., Jr. 1960. Locomotor speeds of some large northern mammals. J. Mammal. 41: 112.

Pruitt, W. O., Jr. 1965. A flight releaser in wolf-caribou relations. J. Mammal. 46: 350–51.

Pulliainen, E. 1965. Studies of the wolf (*Canis lupus* L.) in Finland. Ann. Zool. Fenn. 2: 215–59.

Pulliainen, E., University of Helsinki. 1967a. Personal correspondence to the author.

Pulliainen, E. 1967b. A contribution to the study of the social behavior of the wolf. Amer. Zool. 7: 313–17.

Rabb, G. B., Chicago Zoological Society. 1968. Personal correspondence to the author.

Rabb, G. B., B. E. Ginsburg, and Susan Andrews. 1962. Comparative studies of *Canid* behavior, IV. Mating behavior in relation to social structure in wolves. Amer. Zool. 2: 440.

Rabb, G. B., J. H. Woolpy, and B. E. Ginsburg. 1967. Social relationships in a group of captive wolves. Amer. Zool. 7: 305–11.

Rausch, R. A. 1961. Present status and possible future management of wolf populations in interior and arctic Alaska. Proc. Alaska Sci. Conf. 12: 28, and mimeo., 6 pp.

Rausch, R. A. 1964. Progress in the management of the Alaskan wolf population. Proc. Alaska Sci. Conf. 15: 43.

Rausch, R. A. 1967a. Some aspects of the population ecology of wolves, Alaska. Amer. Zool. 7: 253–65.

Rausch, R. A., Alaska Dept. of Fish and Game. 1967b. Personal correspondence to the author.

Rausch, R. L. 1958. Some observations on rabies in Alaska, with special reference to wild Canidae. J. Wildl. Mgmt. 22: 246–60.

Rausch, R. L., U. S. Public Health Service, Alaska. 1967. Personal correspondence to the author.

Rausch, R. L., B. B. Babero, R. V. Rausch, and E. L. Schiller. 1956. Studies on the helminth fauna of Alaska. XXVII. The occurrence of larvae of *Trichinella spiralis* in Alaskan mammals. J. Parasit. 42: 259–71.

Rausch, R. L., and F. S. L. Williamson. 1959. Studies on the helminth fauna of Alaska. XXXIV. The parasites of wolves, *Canis lupus* L. J. Parasit. 45: 395–403.

Riley, W. A. 1933. Reservoirs of *Echinococcus* in Minnesota. Minn. Med. 16: 744–45.

Rodonoaia, T. E. 1956. Gel'mintofauna dikikh mlekopitaiushchikh Ladogekh-skogo gosudarstvennogo zapovednika. Trudy Inst. Zool., Akad. Nauk Gruzinsk. S.S.R. 14: 147–87. (Cited from R. L. Rausch and Williamson, 1959.)

Rowan, W. 1950. Winter habits and numbers of timber wolves. J. Mammal. 31: 167–69.

Rutter, R. J., and D. H. Pimlott. 1968. The world of the wolf. J. B. Lippincott Co., Philadelphia. 202 pp.

Schaller, G. B. 1967. The deer and the tiger. Univ. of Chicago Press, Chicago. 370 pp.

Schenkel, R. 1947. Expression studies of wolves. Behaviour. 1: 81–129. (Translation from German by Agnes Klasson.)

Schenkel, R. 1967. Submission: its features and function in the wolf and dog. Amer. Zool. 7: 319–29.

Schenkel, R., Univ. of Basel. 1968. Personal correspondence to the author.

Schönberner, Dagmar. 1965. Observations on the reproductive biology of the wolf. Zeitschrift f. Sauzetierkunde 30(3): 171–78. (Translated from German by S. Van Zyll de Jong.)

Scott, H. H. 1928. Carcinoma of the tonsil in a common wolf (*Canis lupus*). Proc. Zool. Soc. Lon. 1928: 43.

Scott, J. P. 1950. The social behavior of dogs and wolves: an illustration of sociobiological systematics. Ann. N. Y. Acad. Sci. 51: 1009–21.

Scott, J. P. 1967. The evolution of social behavior in dogs and wolves. Amer. Zool. 7: 373–81.

Scott, J. P., and J. L. Fuller. 1965. Genetics and the social behavior of the dog. Univ. of Chicago Press, Chicago. 468 pp.

Selye, H. 1950. The physiology and pathology of exposure to stress. Acta, Inc., Montreal. 822 pp.

Sergeant, D. E., and D. H. Pimlott. 1959. Age determination in moose from sectioned incisor teeth. J. Wildl. Mgmt. 23: 315–21.

Shaldybin, L. S. 1957. Parasitic worms of wolves in the Modrvinian ASSR. Uch. Sap. Gor'kovsk. Gos. Ped. Inst. 19: 65–70. (From Biol. Abstr. 35: 2241: No. 22505.)

Shaw, Tsen Hwang. 1962. Economic animals in China. Science Press. (Cited from Chung, 1967.)

Shelton, P. C. 1966. Ecological studies of beavers, wolves, and moose in Isle Royale National Park, Michigan. Unpubl. Ph.D. thesis. Purdue University, Lafayette, Ind. 308 pp.

Shoemaker, H. W. 1917–19. Extinct Pennsylvania animals. 2 vols. Altoona, Pa. (Cited from Young, 1944.)

Singh, J. A. L., and R. M. Zingg. 1942. Wolf-children and feral man. Harper, New York. 379 pp.

Smits, L. 1963. King of the wild. Mich. Conservation 32(1): 45.

Snow, Carol. 1967. Some observations on the behavioral and morphological development of coyote pups. Amer. Zool. 7: 353–55.

Soper, J. D. 1941. History, range, and home life of the northern bison. Ecol. Monog. 11: 347–412.

Soper, J. D. 1942. Mammals of Wood Buffalo Park, northern Alberta, and District of Mackenzie. J. Mammal. 23: 119–45.

Stanwell-Fletcher, J. F. and Theodora C. 1942. Three years in the wolves' wilderness. Nat. Hist. 49(3): 136–47.

Stebler, A. M. 1944. The status of the wolf in Michigan. J. Mammal. 25: 37–43.

Stenlund, M. H. 1955. A field study of the timber wolf (*Canis lupus*) on the Superior National Forest, Minnesota. Minn. Dept. Cons. Tech. Bull. 4. 55 pp.

Steuwer, F. W., Michigan Conservation Dept. 1968. Personal correspondence to the author.

Stiles, C. W., and Clara E. Baker. 1934. Key-catalogue of parasites reported for carnivora (cats, dogs, bears, etc.). Nat. Inst. of Health, U. S. Treas. Dept., Public Health Serv. Bull. 163: 913–1223.

374 Bibliography

Sutherland, R. L., J. L. Woodward, and M. A. Maxwell. 1956. Introductory sociology. J. B. Lippincott Co., Chicago. 598 pp.

Sweatman, G. K. 1952. Distribution and incidence of *Echinococcus granulosus* in man and other animals with special reference to Canada. Can. J. Pub. Health. 43: 480–86.

Tembrock, G. 1963. Acoustic behavior of mammals. 751–83. In R. Busnel (ed.). Acoustic behavior of animals. El Sevier Publishing Co., London. 933 pp.

Tener, J. S. 1954a. A preliminary study of the musk-oxen of Fosheim Peninsula, Ellesmere Island, N. W. T. Can. Wildl. Serv., Wildl. Mgmt. Bull., Ser. 1, No. 9. 1–34.

Tener, J. S. 1954b. Three observations of predators attacking prey. Can. Field Nat. 68: 181–82.

Tener, J. S. 1960. The present status of the barren-ground caribou. Can. Geog. J. 60(3): 98–105.

Theberge, J. B., and J. B. Falls. 1967. Howling as a means of communication in timber wolves. Amer. Zool. 7: 331–38.

Thompson, D. Q. 1952. Travel, range, and food habits of timber wolves in Wisconsin. J. Mammal. 33: 429–42.

Trembley, Helen L., and F. C. Bishopp. 1940. Distribution and hosts of some fleas of economic importance. J. Econ. Ent. 33: 701–3.

Villa, B. R., Universidad Nacional Autónoma de Mexico. 1968. Personal correspondence to the author.

von Uexküll, J., and E. G. Sarris. 1931. Das Duftfeld des Hundes. Z. Hundeforschung 1: 55–68. (Cited from Scott and Fuller, 1965.)

Walker, E. P., Florence Warnick, K. I. Lange, H. E. Uible, Sybil E. Hamlet, Mary A. Davis, and Patricia F. Wright. 1964. Mammals of the world. Johns Hopkins Press, Baltimore. 1500 pp.

Whitney, L. F. 1947. How to breed dogs. Orange Judd, New York. 418 pp.

Whitney, L. P. 1949. Feeding our dogs. D. Van Nostrand Co., Inc., New York. 243 pp.

Woolpy, J. H. 1968. The social organization of wolves. Nat. Hist. 77(5): 46–55.

Woolpy, J. H., and B. E. Ginsburg. 1967. Wolf socialization: a study of temperament in a wild social species. Amer. Zool. 7: 357–63.

Wright, B. S. 1960. Predation on big game in East Africa. J. Wildl. Mgmt. 24: 1–15.

Wynne-Edwards, V. C. 1962. Animal dispersion in relation to social behaviour. Hafner Publishing Co., New York. 653 pp.

Yamaguti, S. 1958. Systema helminthum, Vol. I. Parts 1 and 2. Interscience Publishers, Inc., New York. 1575 pp.

Yamaguti, S. 1959. Systema helminthum, Vol. II. Interscience Publishers, Inc., New York. 860 pp.

Yamaguti, S. 1961. Systema helminthum, Vol. III. Interscience Publishers, Inc., New York. 1261 pp.

Young, S. P. 1944. The wolves of North America, Part I. Amer. Wildl. Instit. Washington, D.C. 385 pp.

Young, S. P. 1946. The wolf in North American history. Caxton Printers, Ltd., Caldwell, Idaho. 149 pp.

Young, S. P. 1951. The clever coyote, Part I. Stackpole Co., Harrisburg, Pa., and Wildl. Mgmt. Inst., Washington, D.C. 226 pp.

Zingg, R. M. 1940. Feral man and extreme cases of isolation. Amer. J. Psychol. 53: 487–517.

SUBJECT INDEX

AUTHOR INDEX

AUTHOR BIOGRAPHY

L. DAVID MECH has studied wolves intensively and continuously for as long as any biologist in the land. His graduate work with Dr. Durward Allen on the Isle Royale wolf study has become a classic in the penetrating study of a predator-prey relationship. Dr. Mech lives in Minneapolis, where he was recently associated with Macalester College. He is now with the U. S. Bureau of Sport Fisheries and Wildlife.